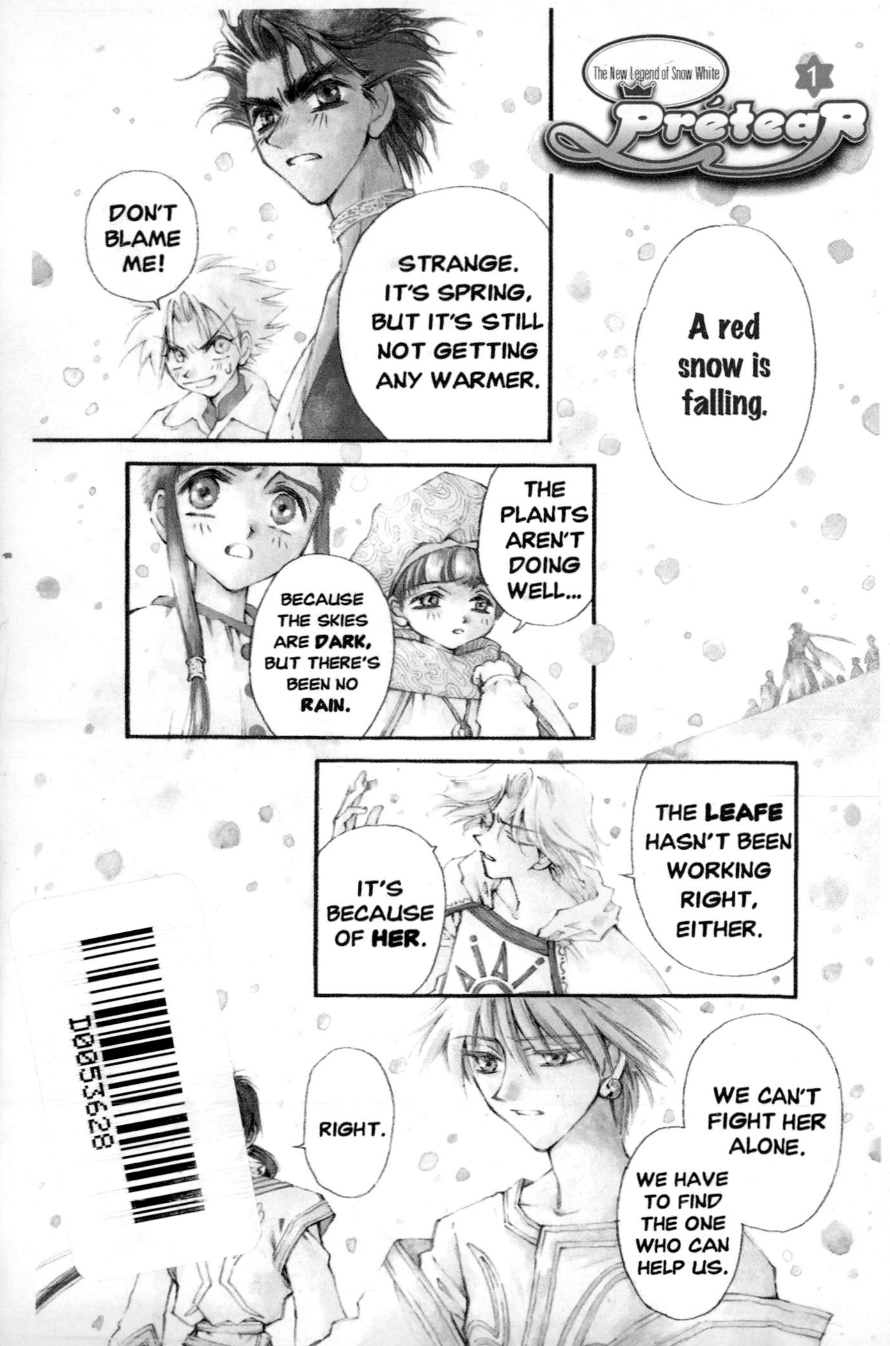
The New Legend of Snow White
Prétear
1
STRANGE. IT'S SPRING, BUT IT'S STILL NOT GETTING ANY WARMER.
DON'T BLAME ME!
A red snow is falling.
THE PLANTS AREN'T DOING WELL...
BECAUSE THE SKIES ARE DARK, BUT THERE'S BEEN NO RAIN.
THE LEAFE HASN'T BEEN WORKING RIGHT, EITHER.
IT'S BECAUSE OF HER.
WE CAN'T FIGHT HER ALONE.
WE HAVE TO FIND THE ONE WHO CAN HELP US.
RIGHT.

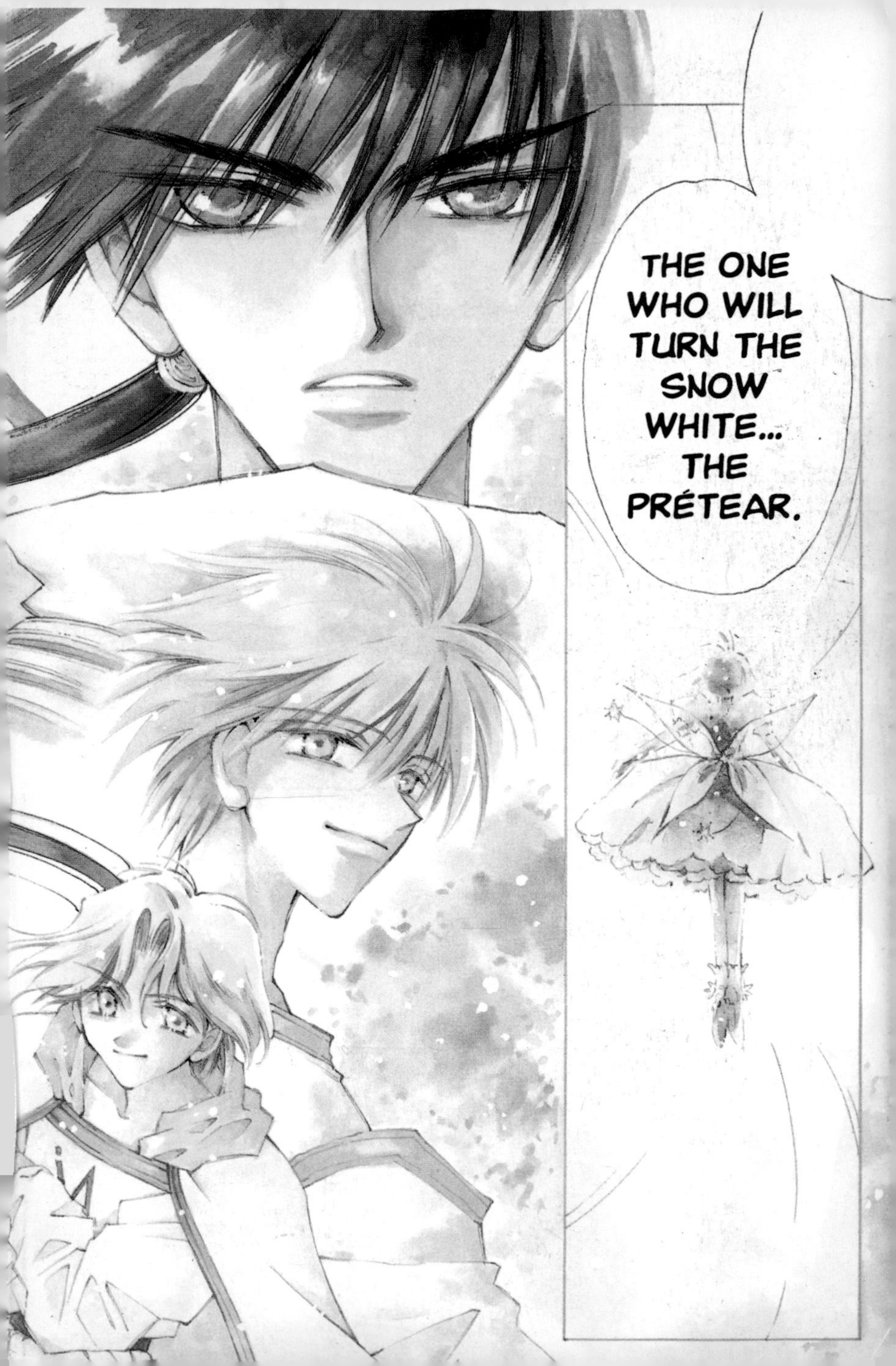
THE ONE WHO WILL TURN THE SNOW WHITE... THE PRÉTEAR.

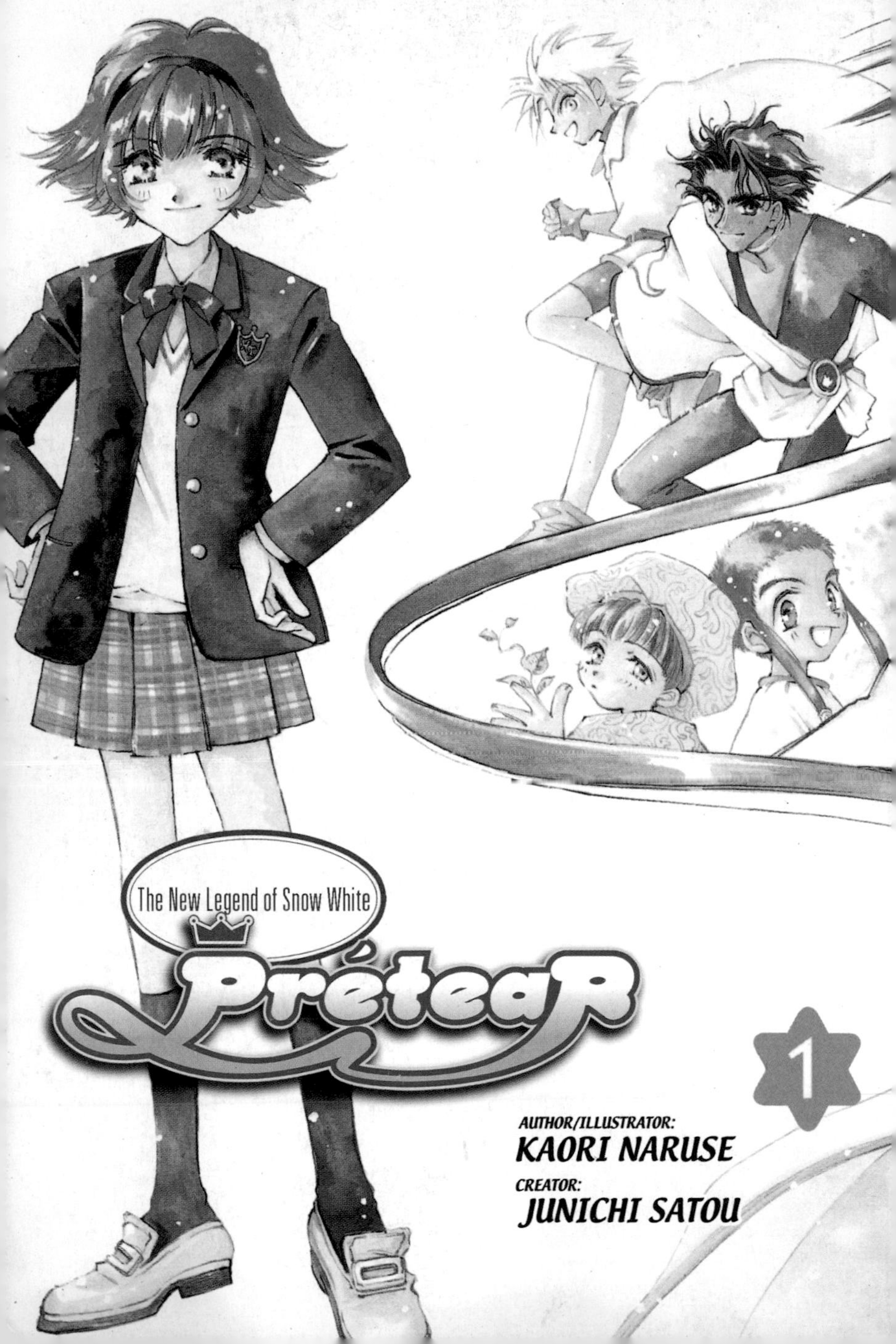

The New Legend of Snow White
Prétear
1
AUTHOR/ILLUSTRATOR:
KAORI NARUSE
CREATOR:
JUNICHI SATOU

| | |
|---|---|
| Chapter 1 | p. 1 |
| Chapter 2 | p. 49 |
| Chapter 3 | p. 81 |
| Chapter 4 | p. 113 |
| Chapter 5 | p. 145 |
| Hang in there, Mr. Tanaka! | p. 176 |

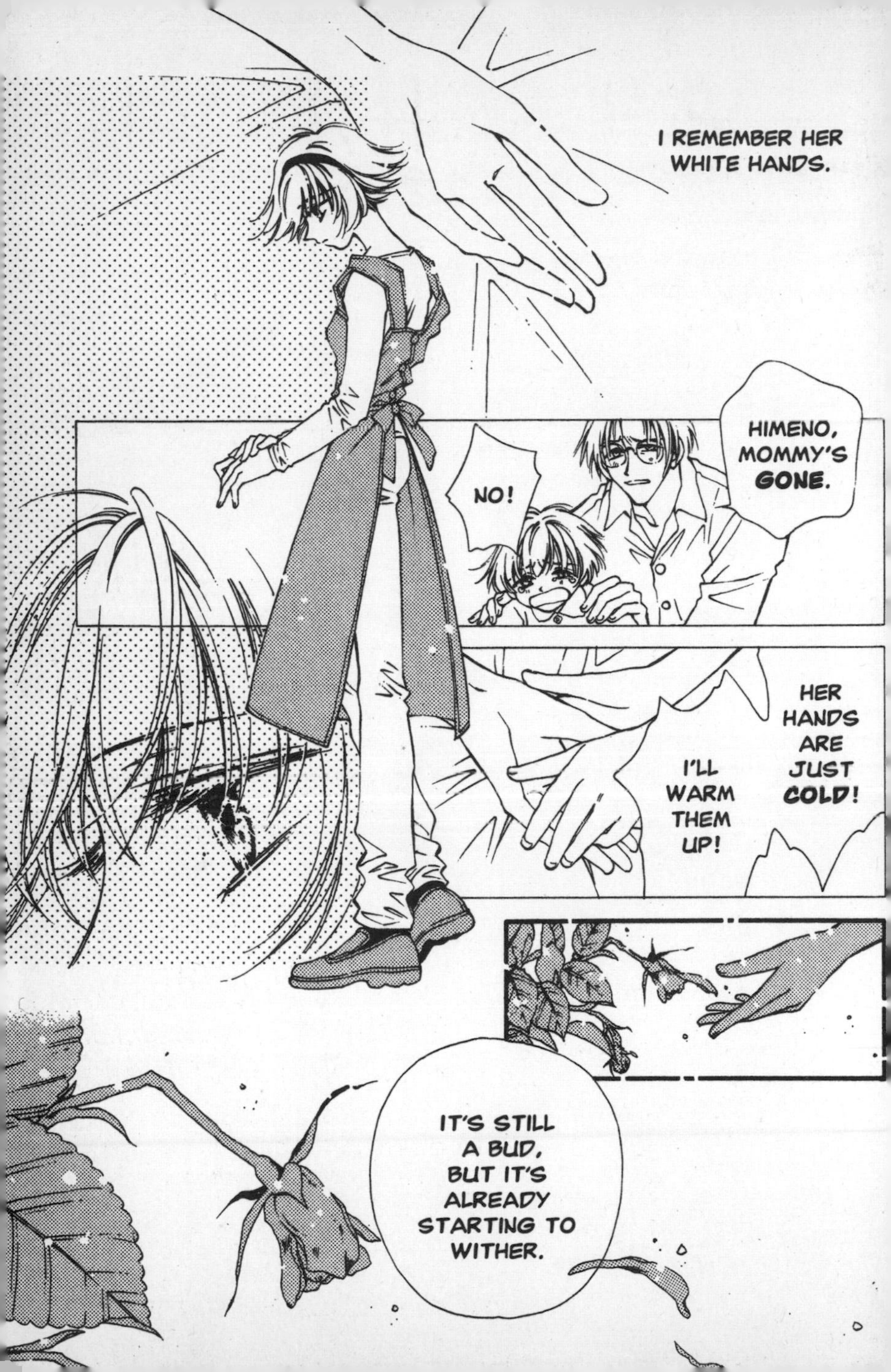
I REMEMBER HER WHITE HANDS.
HIMENO, MOMMY'S GONE.
NO!
HER HANDS ARE JUST COLD!
I'LL WARM THEM UP!
IT'S STILL A BUD, BUT IT'S ALREADY STARTING TO WITHER.

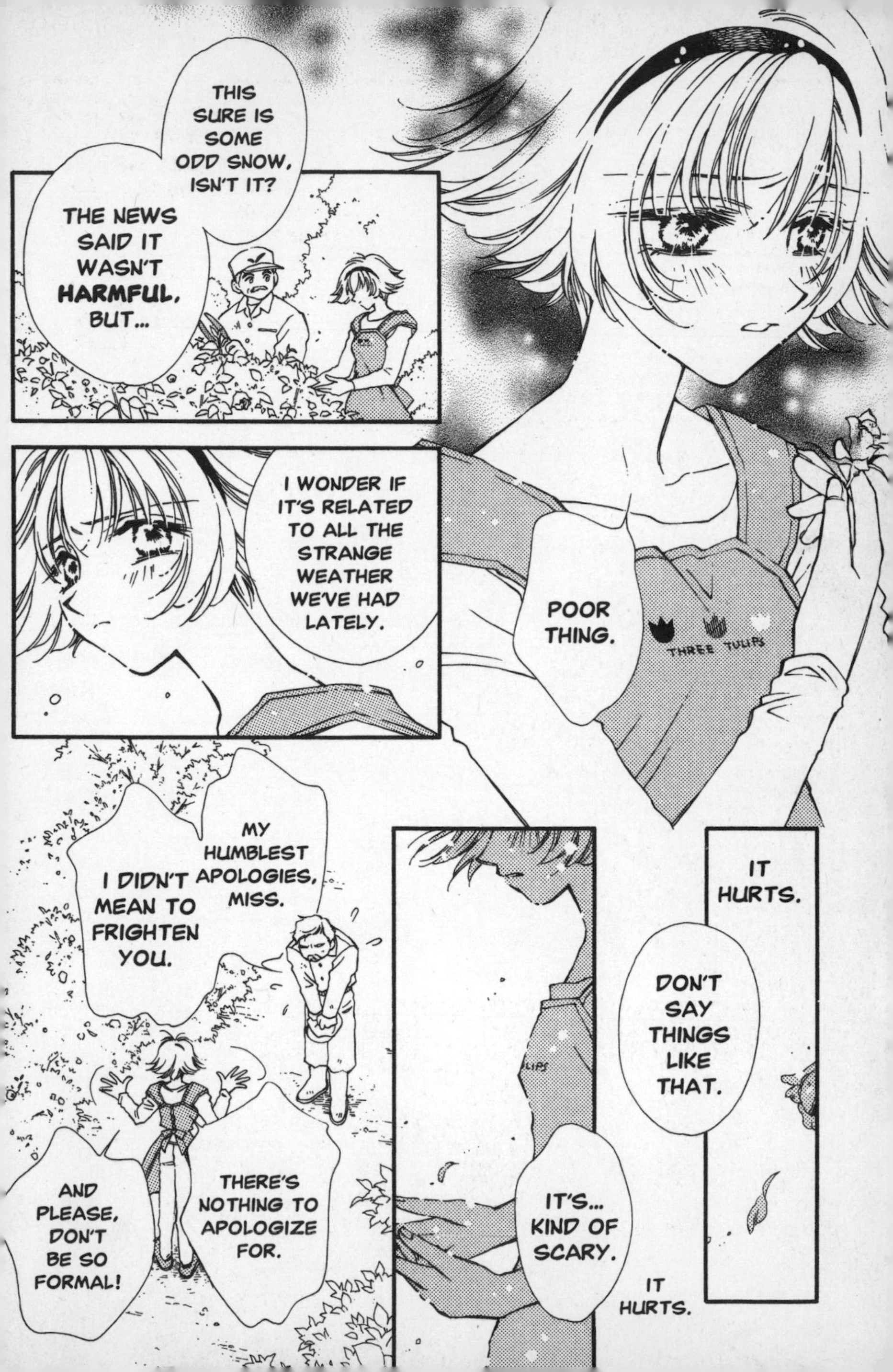
THIS SURE IS SOME ODD SNOW, ISN'T IT?
THE NEWS SAID IT WASN'T HARMFUL, BUT...
I WONDER IF IT'S RELATED TO ALL THE STRANGE WEATHER WE'VE HAD LATELY.
POOR THING.
THREE TULIPS
IT HURTS.
DON'T SAY THINGS LIKE THAT.
IT'S... KIND OF SCARY.
IT HURTS.
MY HUMBLEST APOLOGIES, MISS.
I DIDN'T MEAN TO FRIGHTEN YOU.
THERE'S NOTHING TO APOLOGIZE FOR.
AND PLEASE, DON'T BE SO FORMAL!

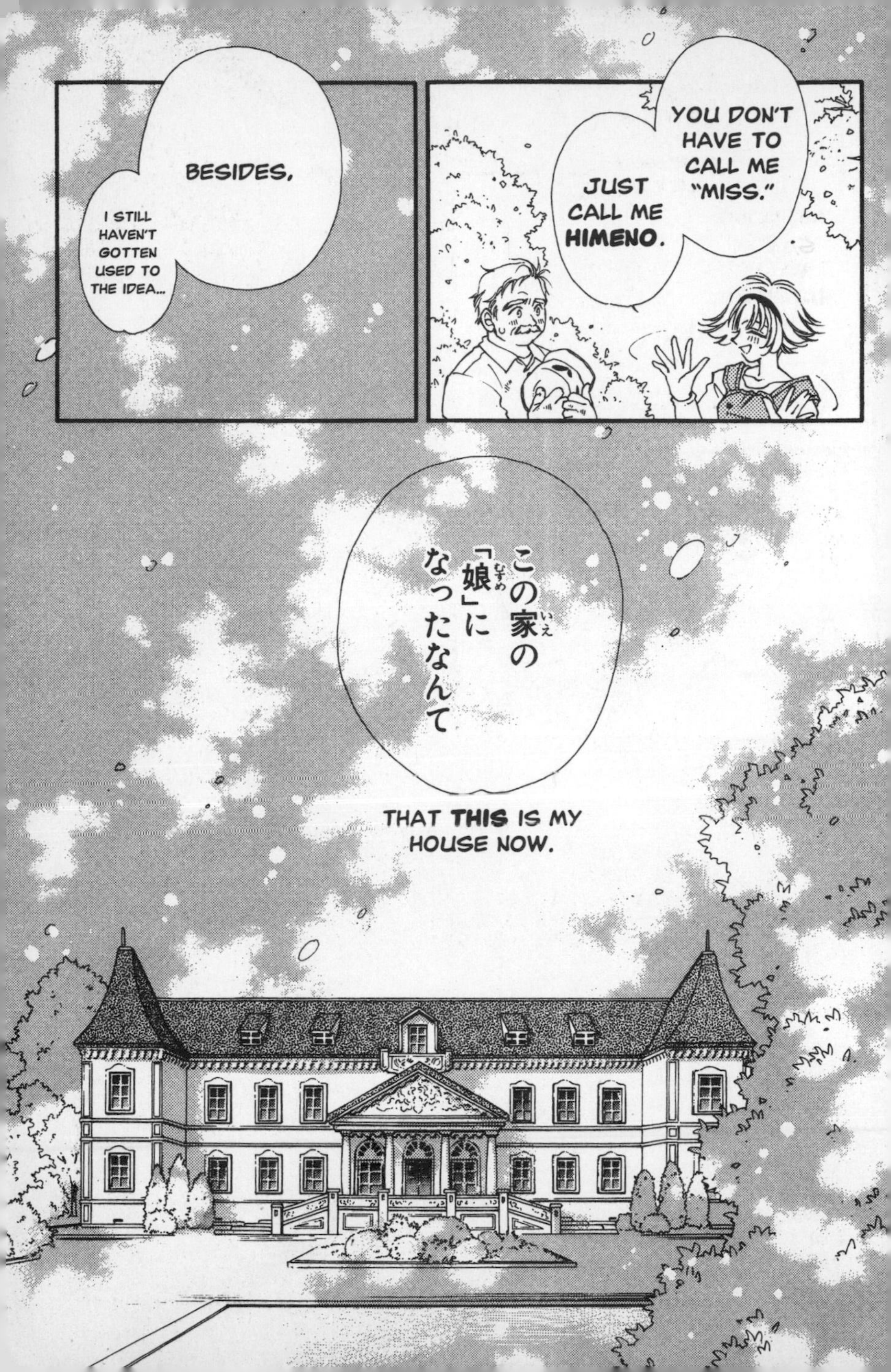
YOU DON'T HAVE TO CALL ME "MISS."
JUST CALL ME HIMENO.
BESIDES,
I STILL HAVEN'T GOTTEN USED TO THE IDEA...
この家の「娘」になったなんて
THAT THIS IS MY HOUSE NOW.

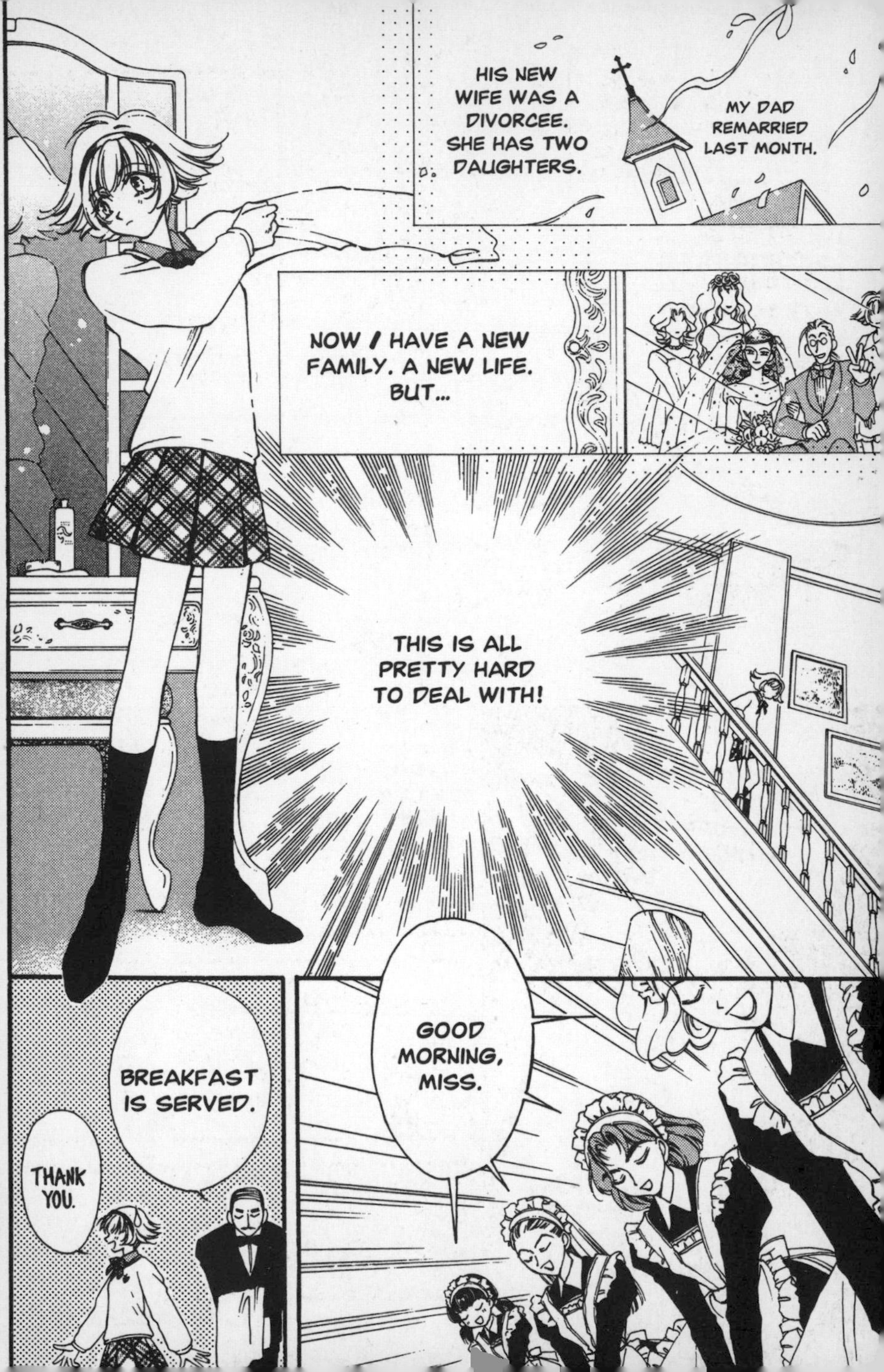
MY DAD REMARRIED LAST MONTH.
HIS NEW WIFE WAS A DIVORCEE. SHE HAS TWO DAUGHTERS.
NOW I HAVE A NEW FAMILY. A NEW LIFE. BUT...
THIS IS ALL PRETTY HARD TO DEAL WITH!
GOOD MORNING, MISS.
BREAKFAST IS SERVED.
THANK YOU.

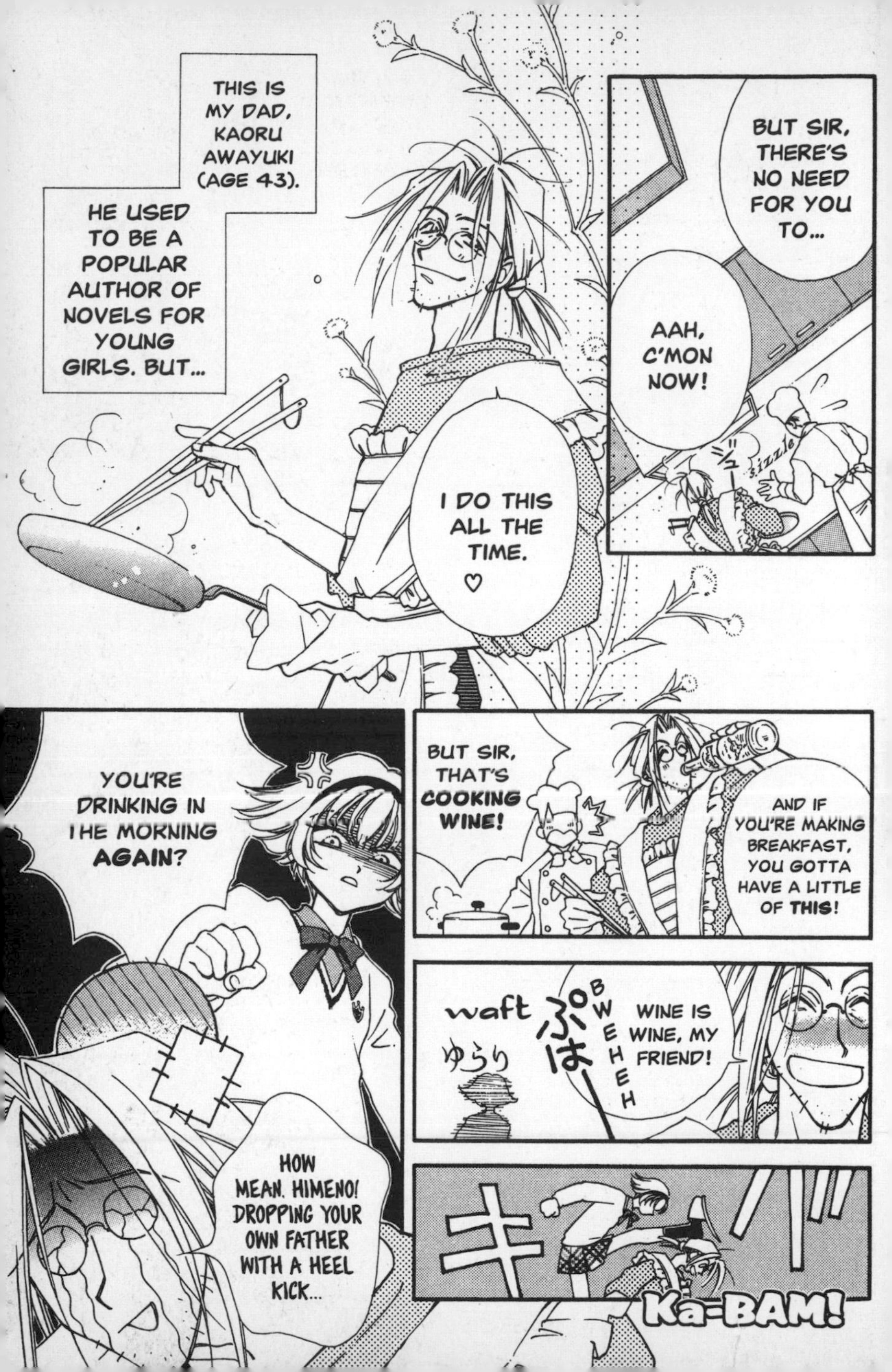
BUT SIR, THERE'S NO NEED FOR YOU TO...
AAH, C'MON NOW!
sizzle
THIS IS MY DAD, KAORU AWAYUKI (AGE 43).
HE USED TO BE A POPULAR AUTHOR OF NOVELS FOR YOUNG GIRLS. BUT...
I DO THIS ALL THE TIME. ♡
AND IF YOU'RE MAKING BREAKFAST, YOU GOTTA HAVE A LITTLE OF THIS!
BUT SIR, THAT'S COOKING WINE!
WINE IS WINE, MY FRIEND!
ぷは
BWEHEH
waft
ゆらり
キ
ド
Ka-BAM!
YOU'RE DRINKING IN THE MORNING AGAIN?
HOW MEAN, HIMENO! DROPPING YOUR OWN FATHER WITH A HEEL KICK...

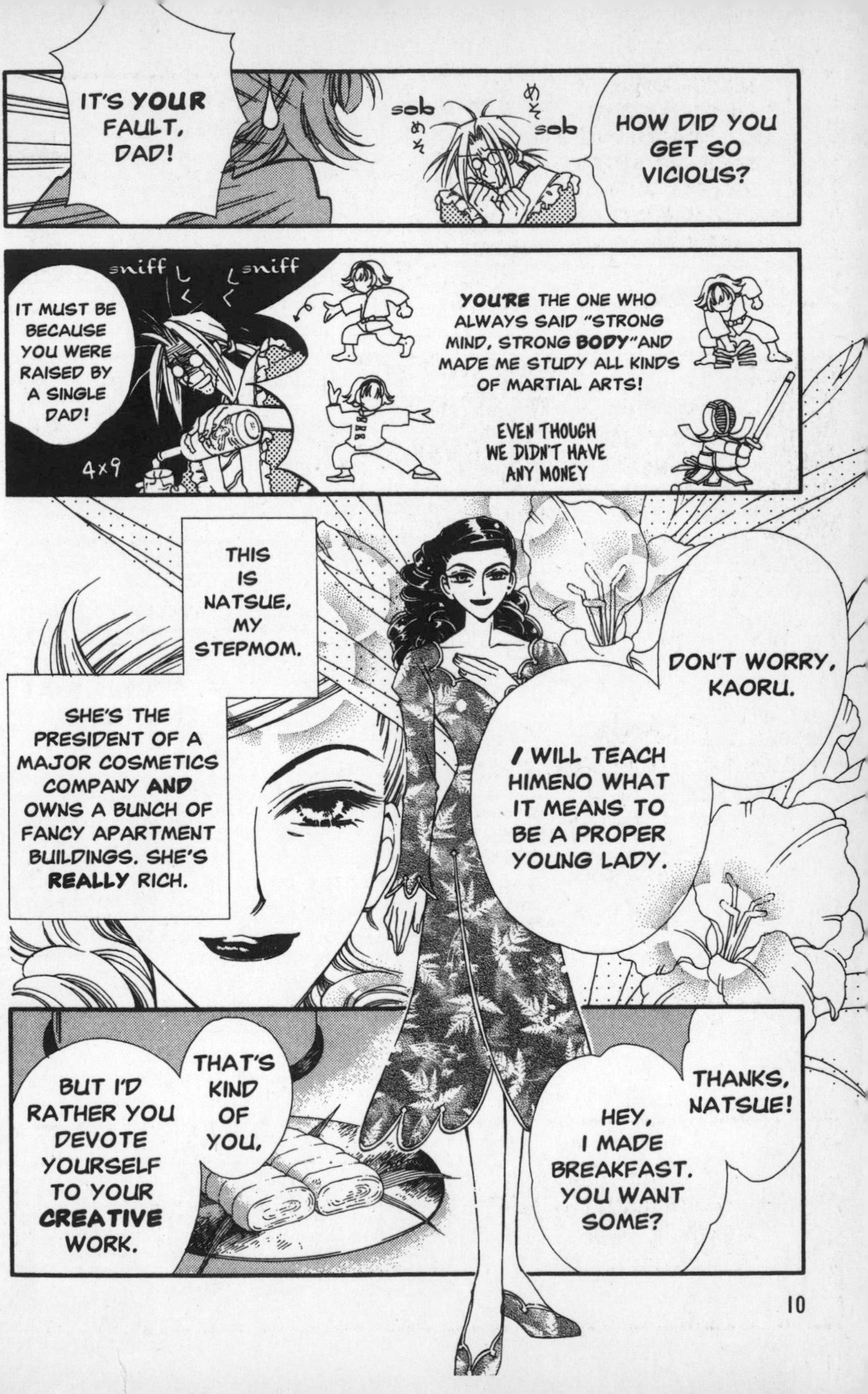
HOW DID YOU GET SO VICIOUS?
sob めそ
sob めそ
IT'S **YOUR** FAULT, DAD!
**YOU'RE** THE ONE WHO ALWAYS SAID "STRONG MIND, STRONG **BODY**" AND MADE ME STUDY ALL KINDS OF MARTIAL ARTS!
EVEN THOUGH WE DIDN'T HAVE ANY MONEY
sniff しく
sniff しく
IT MUST BE BECAUSE YOU WERE RAISED BY A SINGLE DAD!
4×9
THIS IS NATSUE, MY STEPMOM.
SHE'S THE PRESIDENT OF A MAJOR COSMETICS COMPANY **AND** OWNS A BUNCH OF FANCY APARTMENT BUILDINGS. SHE'S **REALLY** RICH.
DON'T WORRY, KAORU.
**I** WILL TEACH HIMENO WHAT IT MEANS TO BE A PROPER YOUNG LADY.
THANKS, NATSUE!
THAT'S KIND OF YOU,
BUT I'D RATHER YOU DEVOTE YOURSELF TO YOUR **CREATIVE** WORK.
HEY, I MADE BREAKFAST. YOU WANT SOME?

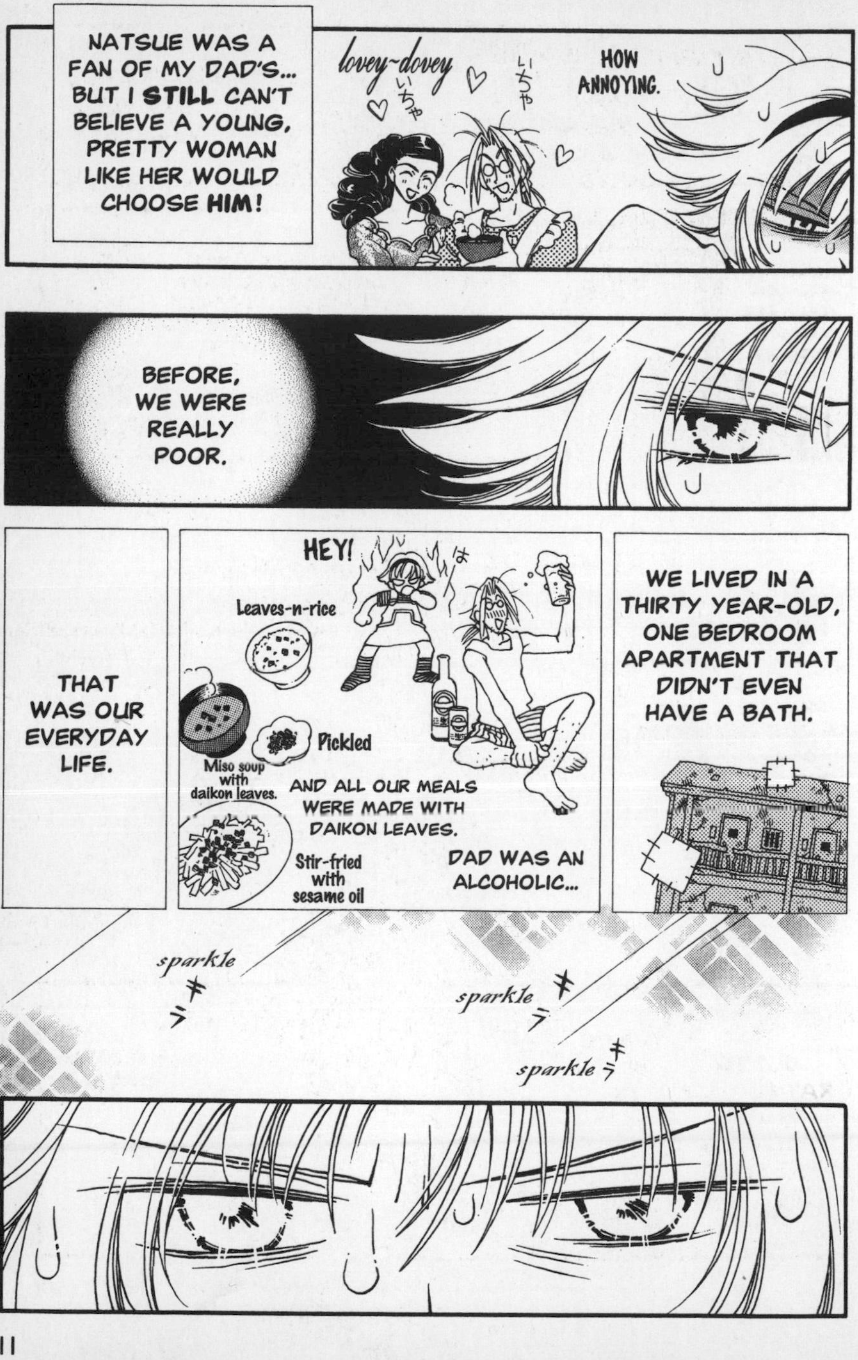
NATSUE WAS A FAN OF MY DAD'S... BUT I STILL CAN'T BELIEVE A YOUNG, PRETTY WOMAN LIKE HER WOULD CHOOSE HIM!
lovey~dovey
いちゃ
いちゃ
HOW ANNOYING.
BEFORE, WE WERE REALLY POOR.
THAT WAS OUR EVERYDAY LIFE.
HEY!
は
Leaves-n-rice
Pickled
Miso soup with daikon leaves.
AND ALL OUR MEALS WERE MADE WITH DAIKON LEAVES.
Stir-fried with sesame oil
DAD WAS AN ALCOHOLIC...
WE LIVED IN A THIRTY YEAR-OLD, ONE BEDROOM APARTMENT THAT DIDN'T EVEN HAVE A BATH.
sparkle
キラ
sparkle
キラ
sparkle
キラ

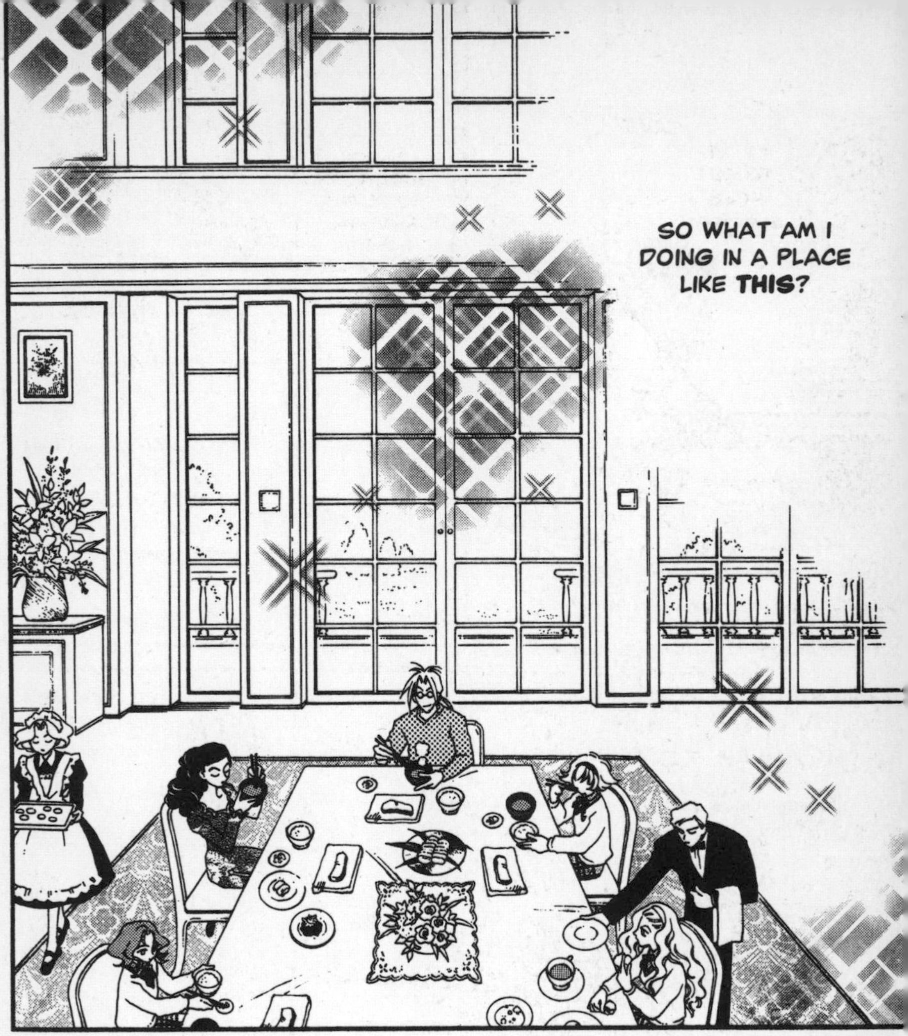
SO WHAT AM I DOING IN A PLACE LIKE THIS?

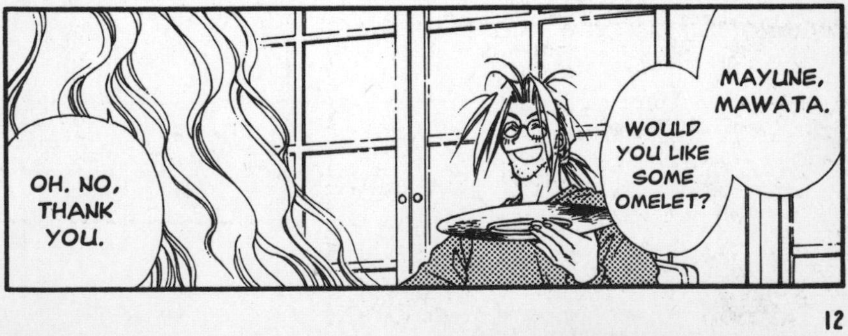
MAYUNE, MAWATA.
WOULD YOU LIKE SOME OMELET?
OH. NO, THANK YOU.

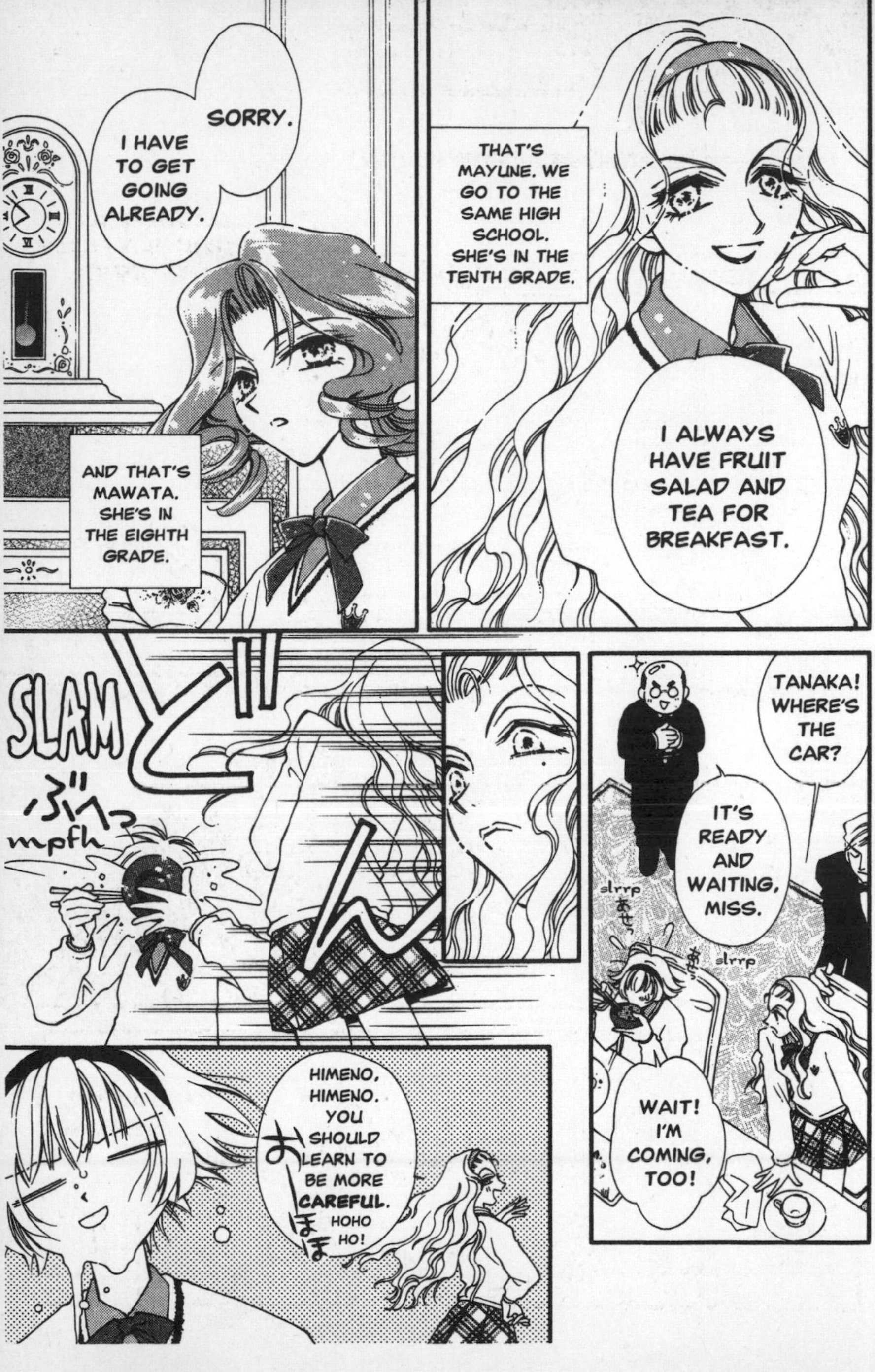

THAT'S MAYUNE. WE GO TO THE SAME HIGH SCHOOL. SHE'S IN THE TENTH GRADE.
I ALWAYS HAVE FRUIT SALAD AND TEA FOR BREAKFAST.
SORRY. I HAVE TO GET GOING ALREADY.
AND THAT'S MAWATA. SHE'S IN THE EIGHTH GRADE.
TANAKA! WHERE'S THE CAR?
IT'S READY AND WAITING, MISS.
slrrp
slrrp
WAIT! I'M COMING, TOO!
SLAM
ぶへっ
mpfh
HIMENO, HIMENO. YOU SHOULD LEARN TO BE MORE CAREFUL.
HOHO HO!

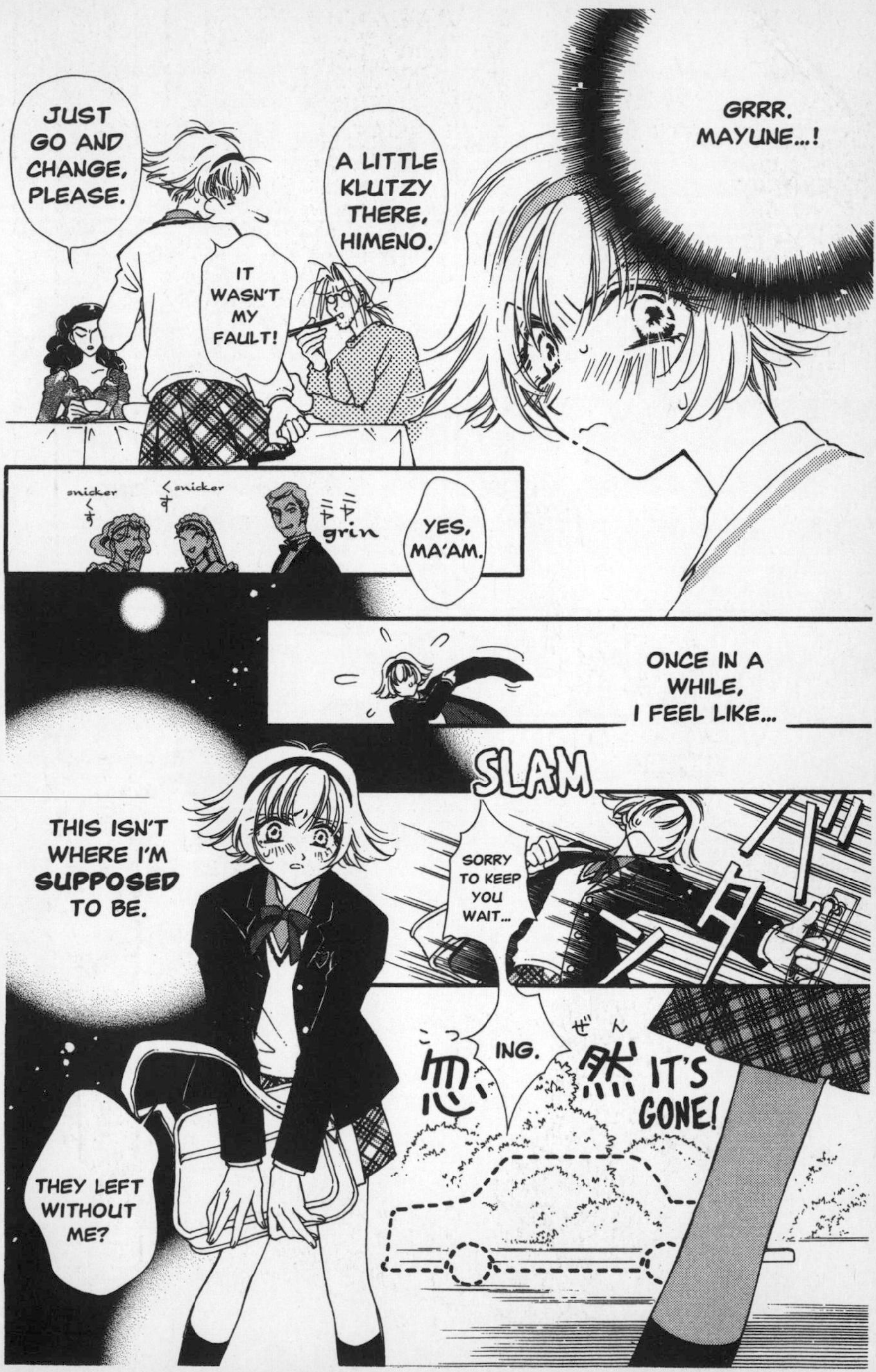

GRRR. MAYUNE...!
A LITTLE KLUTZY THERE, HIMENO.
IT WASN'T MY FAULT!
JUST GO AND CHANGE, PLEASE.
YES, MA'AM.
ニヤ ニヤ grin
くす snicker
くす snicker
ONCE IN A WHILE, I FEEL LIKE...
SLAM
SORRY TO KEEP YOU WAIT...
ING.
こつ 忽 ぜん 然 IT'S GONE!
THIS ISN'T WHERE I'M SUPPOSED TO BE.
THEY LEFT WITHOUT ME?

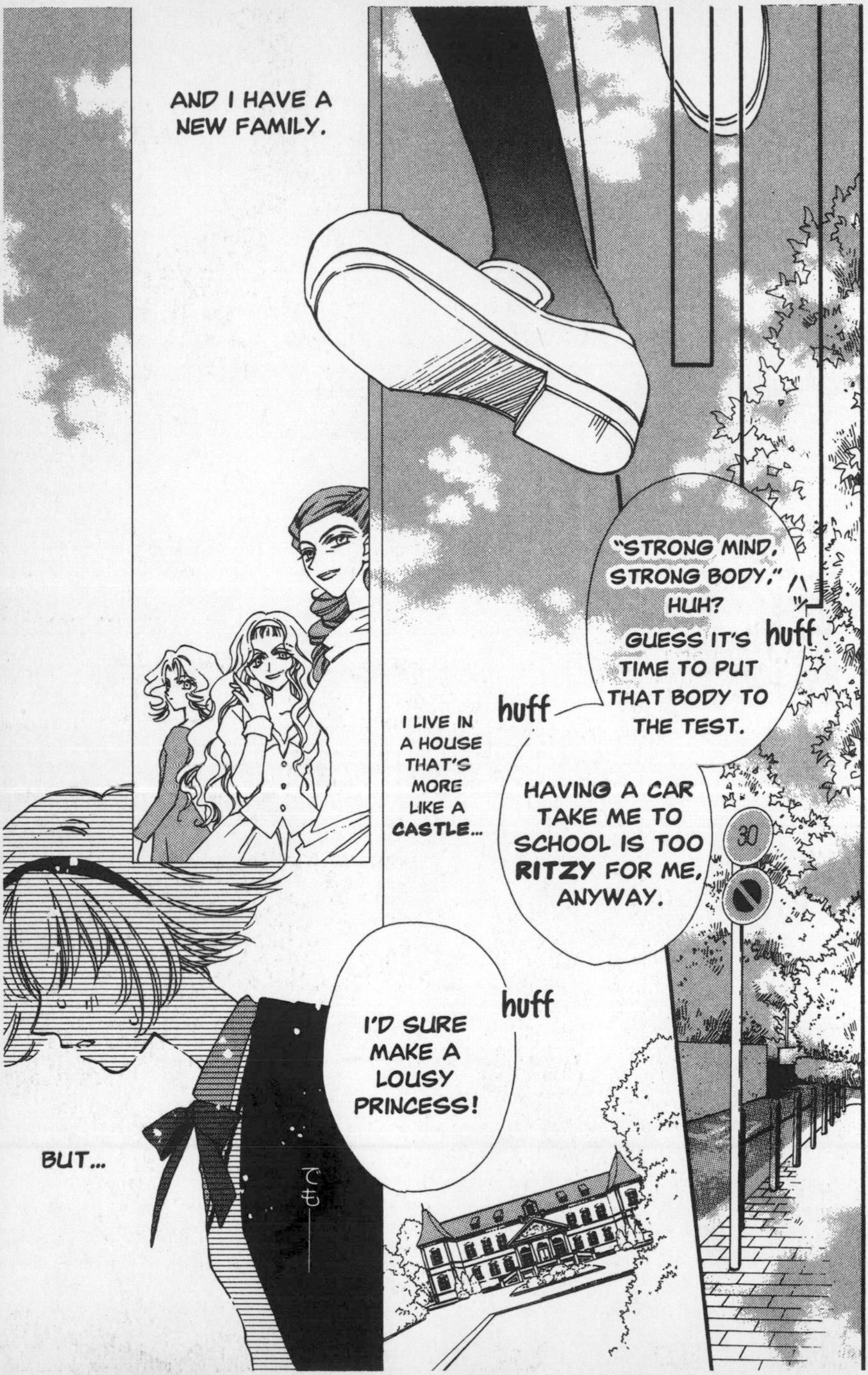
"STRONG MIND, STRONG BODY," HUH? GUESS IT'S TIME TO PUT THAT BODY TO THE TEST.
ハッ
huff
huff
AND I HAVE A NEW FAMILY.
I LIVE IN A HOUSE THAT'S MORE LIKE A CASTLE...
HAVING A CAR TAKE ME TO SCHOOL IS TOO RITZY FOR ME, ANYWAY.
30
huff
I'D SURE MAKE A LOUSY PRINCESS!
BUT...
でも——

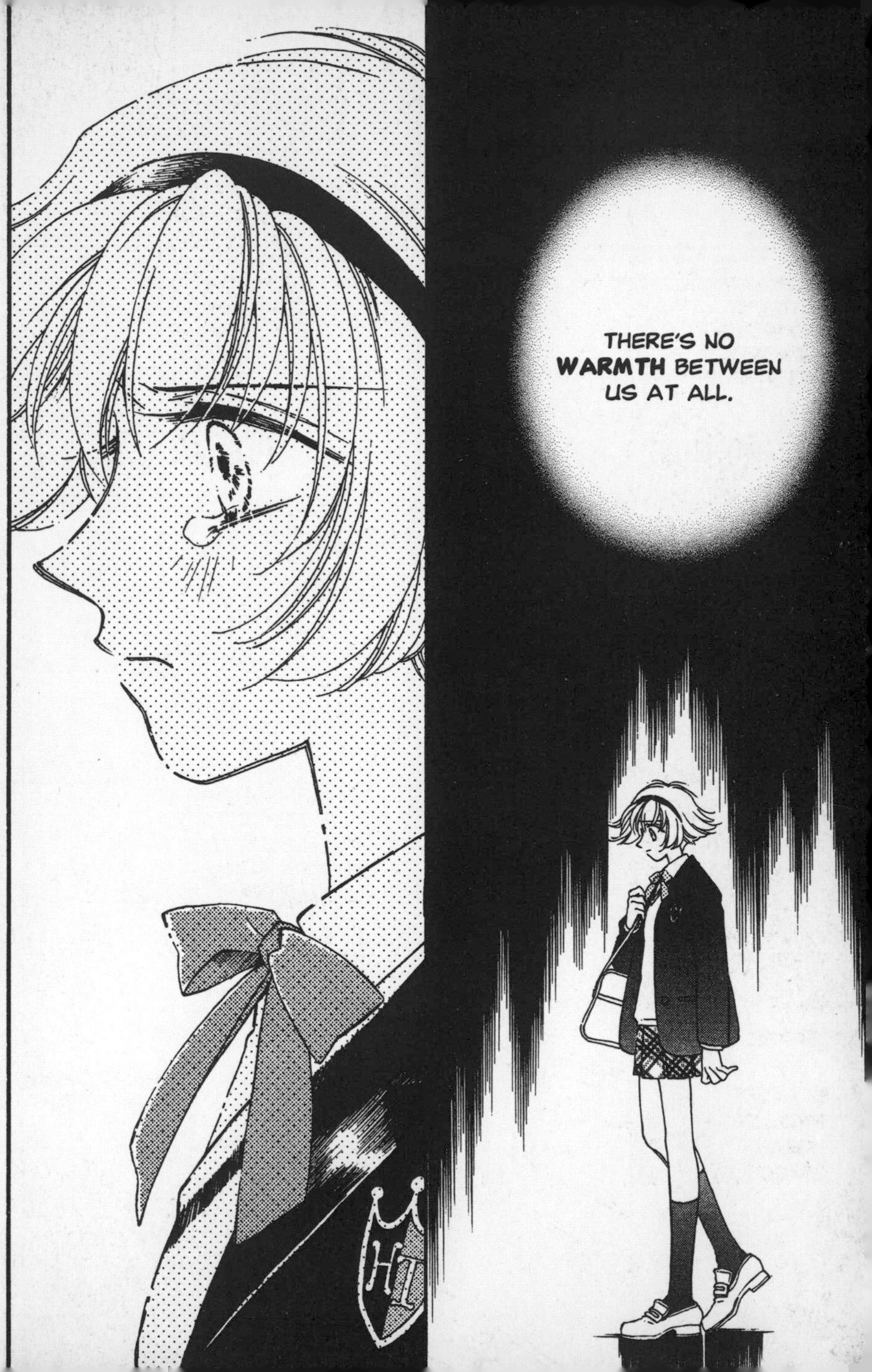
THERE'S NO WARMTH BETWEEN US AT ALL.

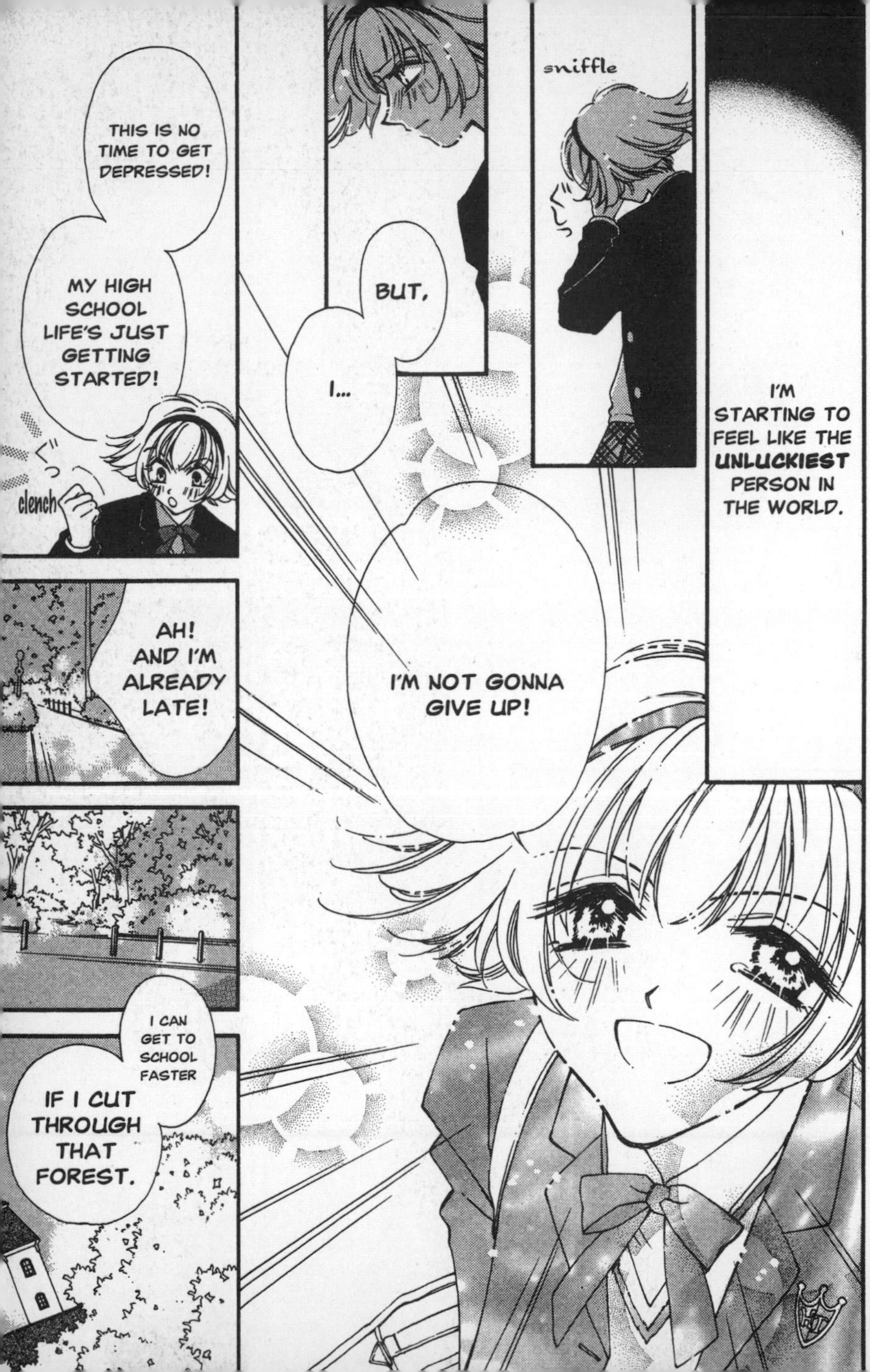
sniffle
I'M STARTING TO FEEL LIKE THE **UNLUCKIEST** PERSON IN THE WORLD.
BUT,
I...
I'M NOT GONNA GIVE UP!
THIS IS NO TIME TO GET DEPRESSED!
MY HIGH SCHOOL LIFE'S JUST GETTING STARTED!
clench
AH! AND I'M ALREADY LATE!
I CAN GET TO SCHOOL FASTER
IF I CUT THROUGH THAT FOREST.

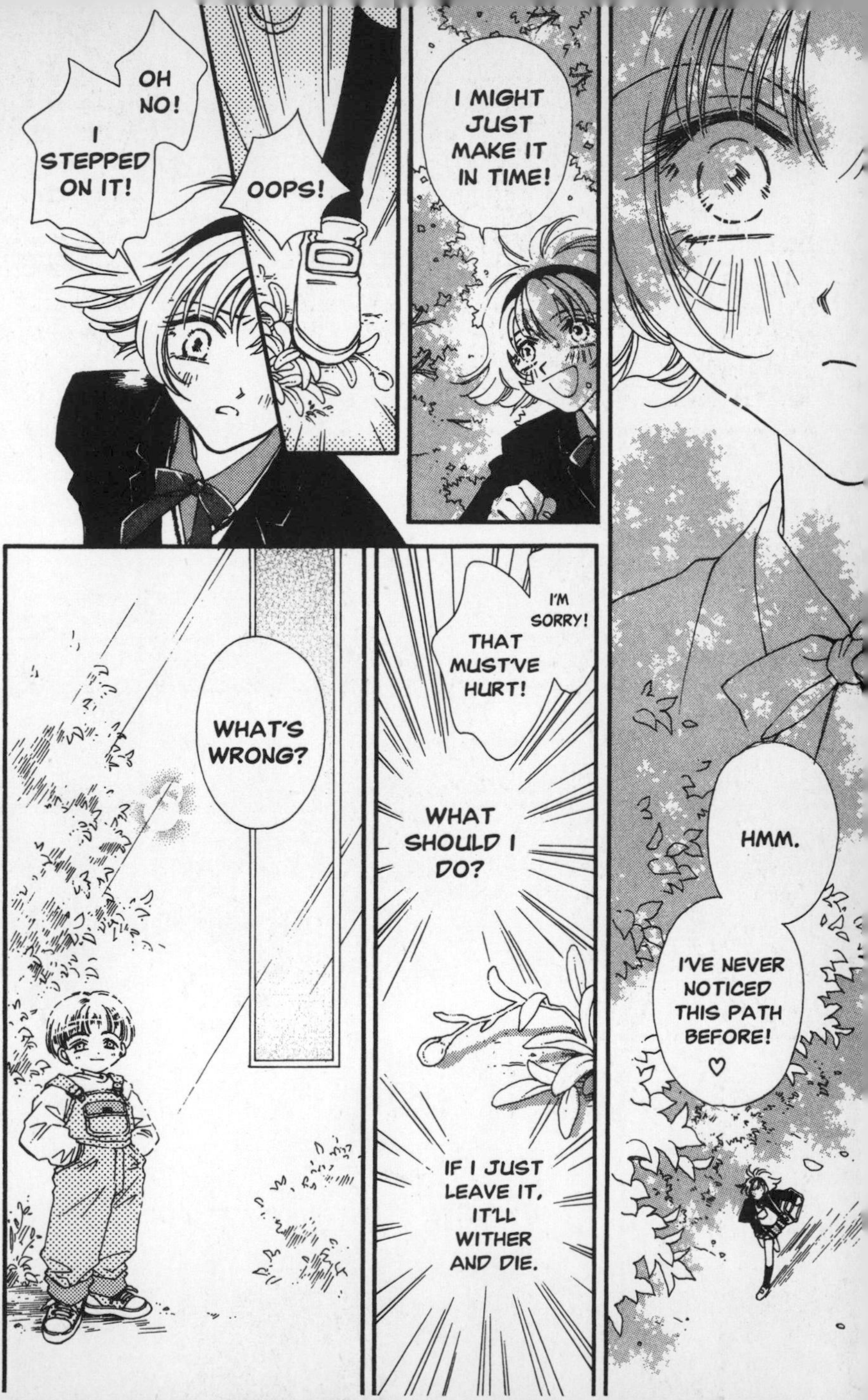
HMM.
I'VE NEVER NOTICED THIS PATH BEFORE! ♡
I MIGHT JUST MAKE IT IN TIME!
OOPS!
OH NO! I STEPPED ON IT!
I'M SORRY! THAT MUST'VE HURT!
WHAT SHOULD I DO?
IF I JUST LEAVE IT, IT'LL WITHER AND DIE.
WHAT'S WRONG?

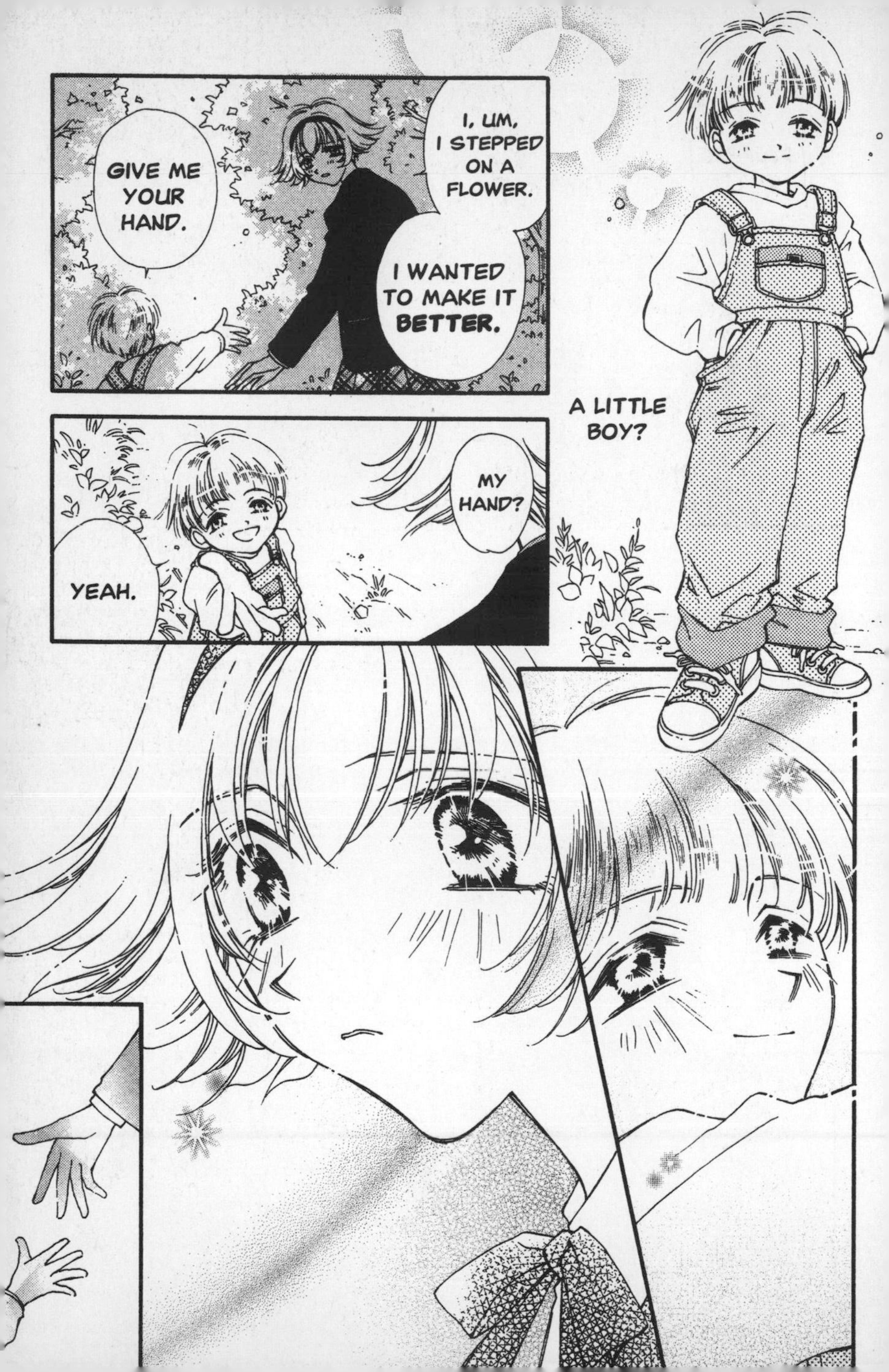
GIVE ME YOUR HAND.
I, UM, I STEPPED ON A FLOWER.
I WANTED TO MAKE IT BETTER.
A LITTLE BOY?
MY HAND?
YEAH.

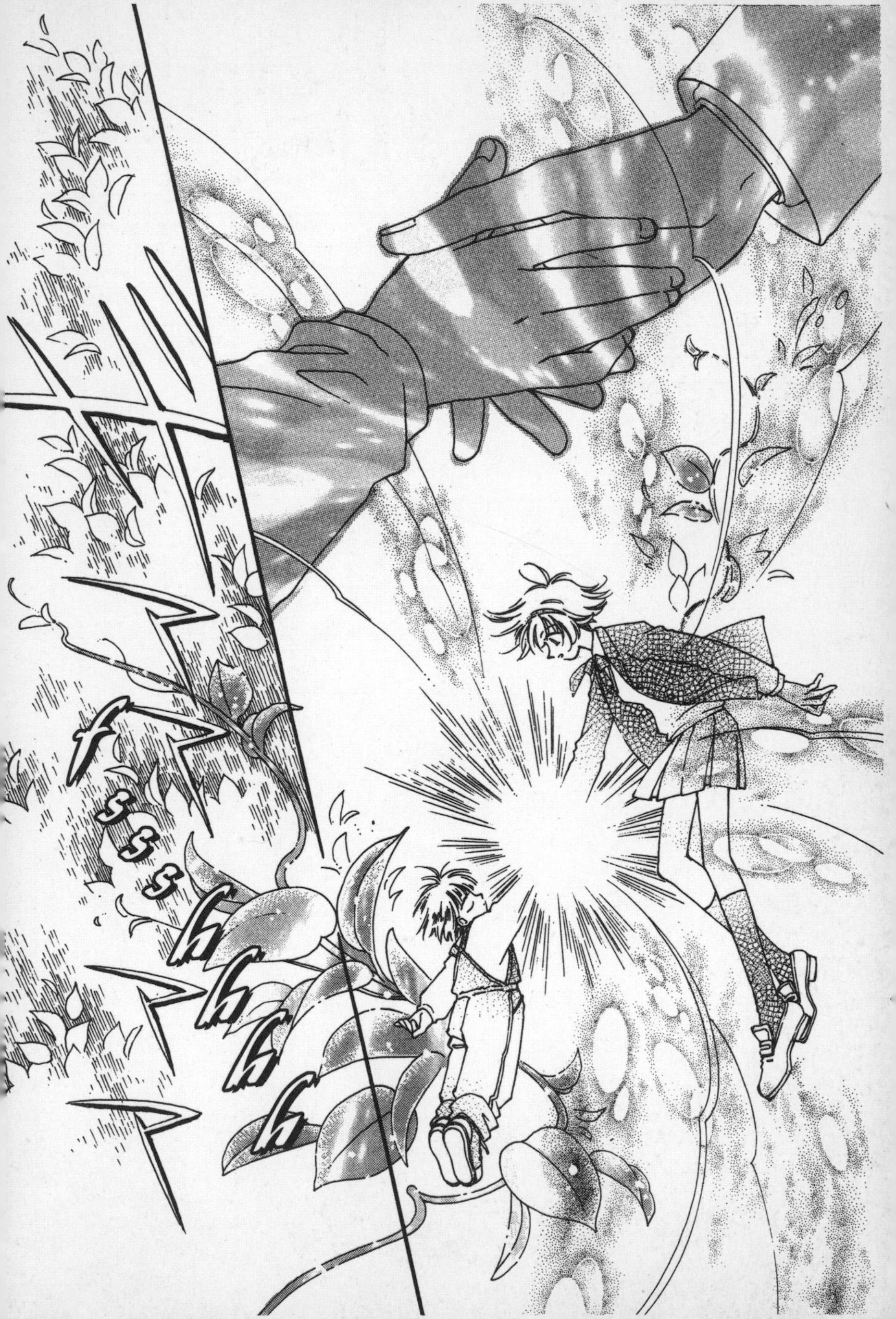
fssshhhh

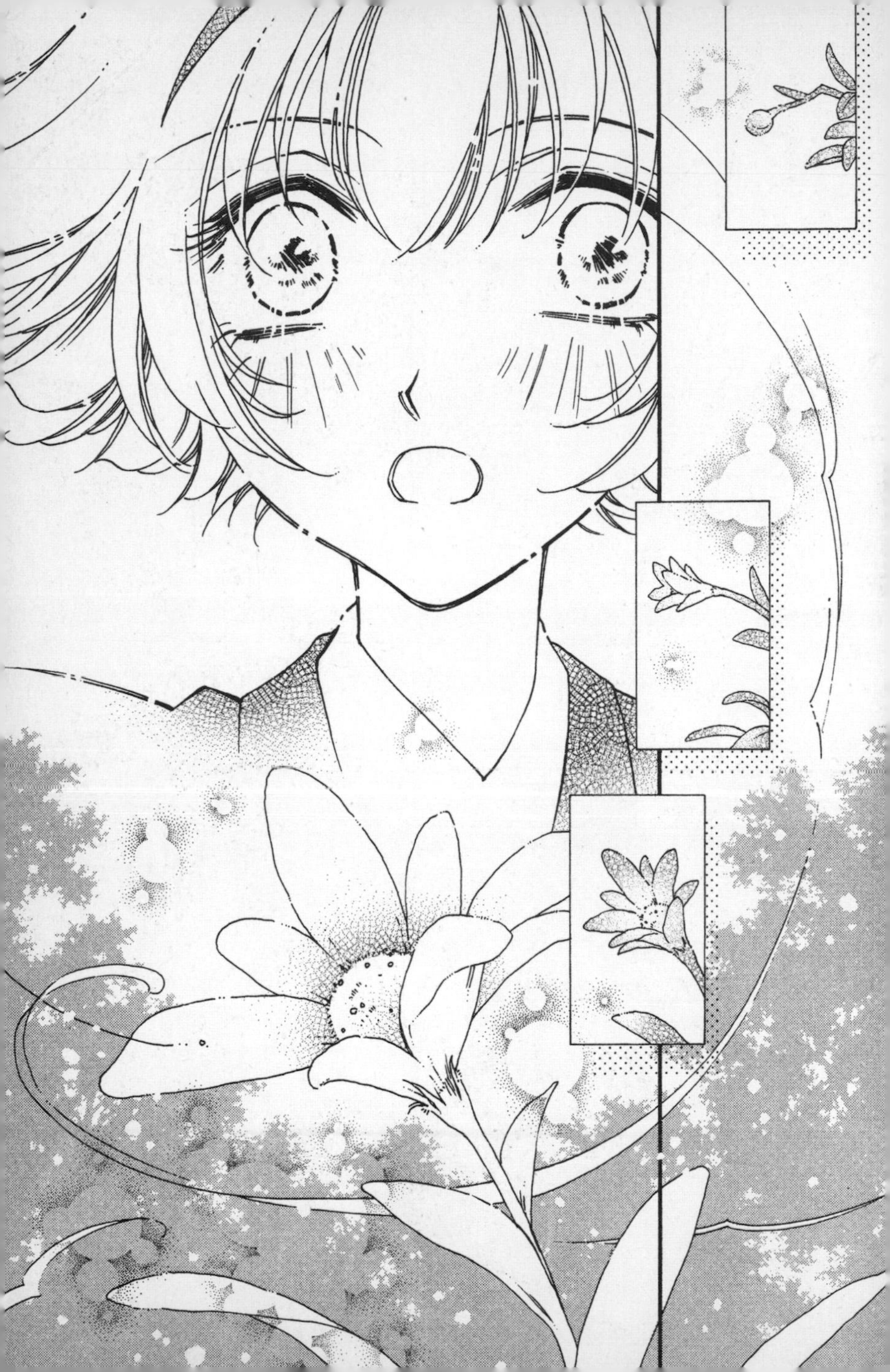

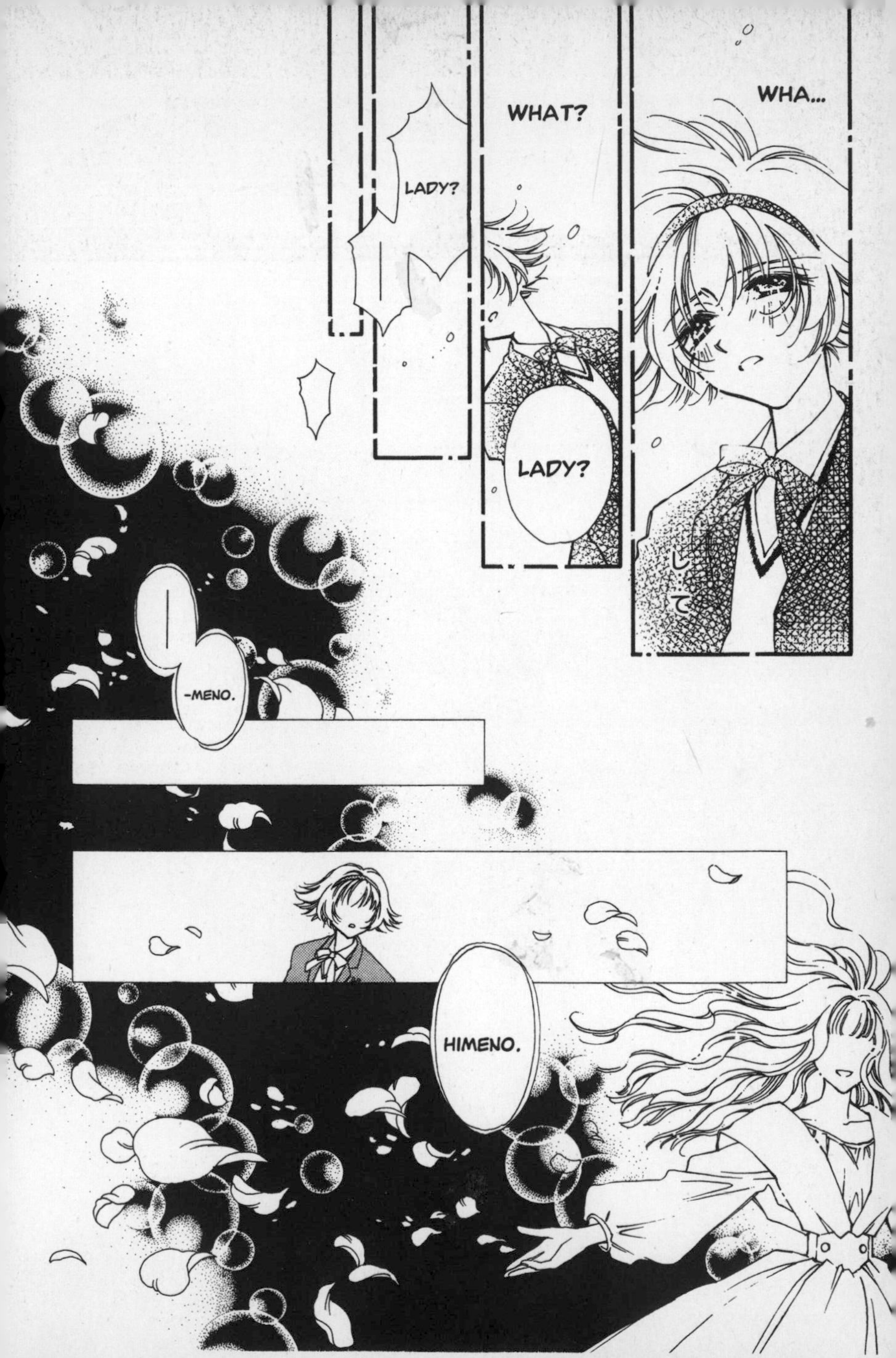
WHA...
して
WHAT?
LADY?
LADY?
-MENO.
HIMENO.

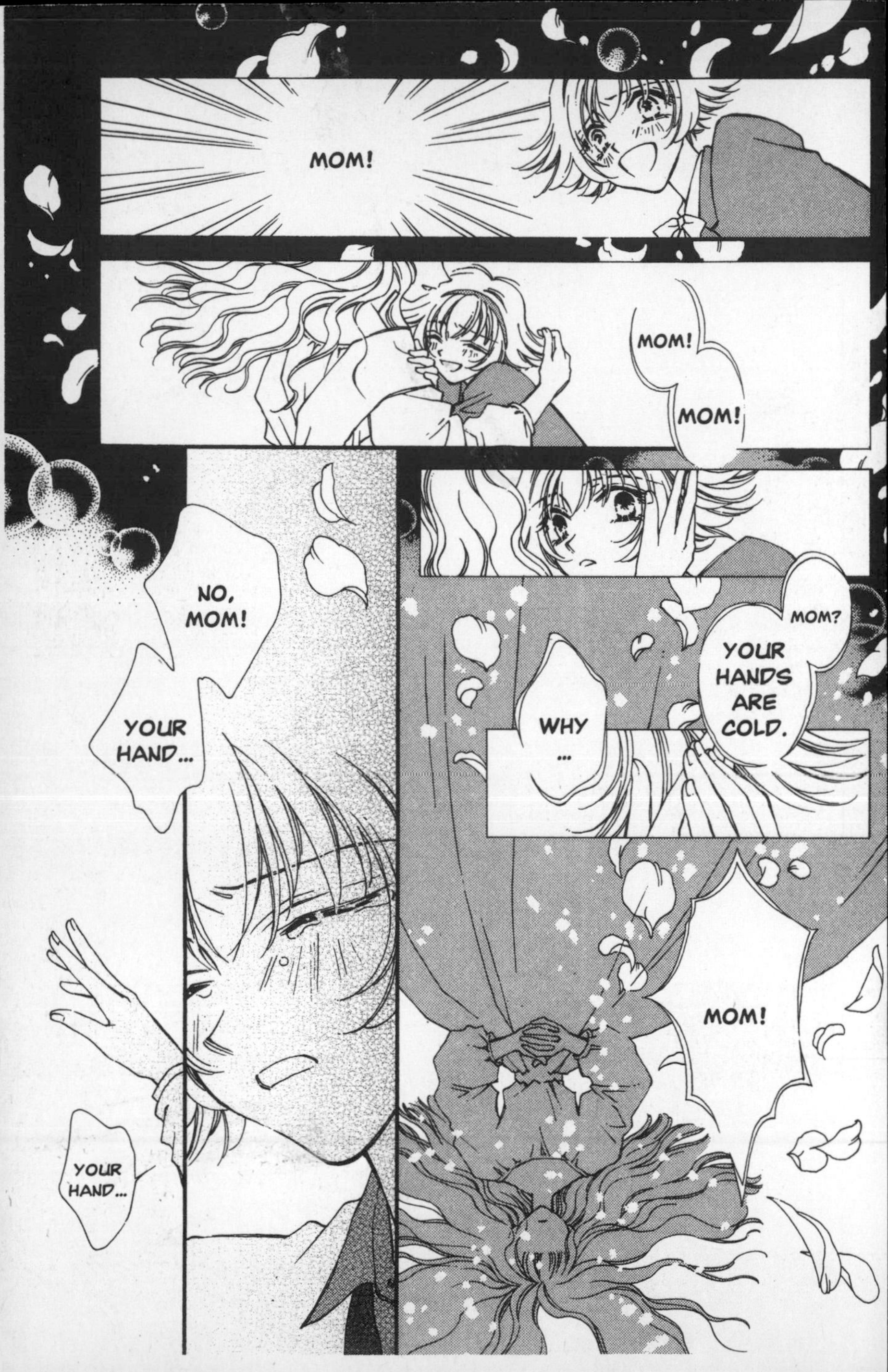
MOM!
MOM!
MOM!
MOM? YOUR HANDS ARE COLD.
WHY ...
MOM!
NO, MOM!
YOUR HAND...
YOUR HAND...

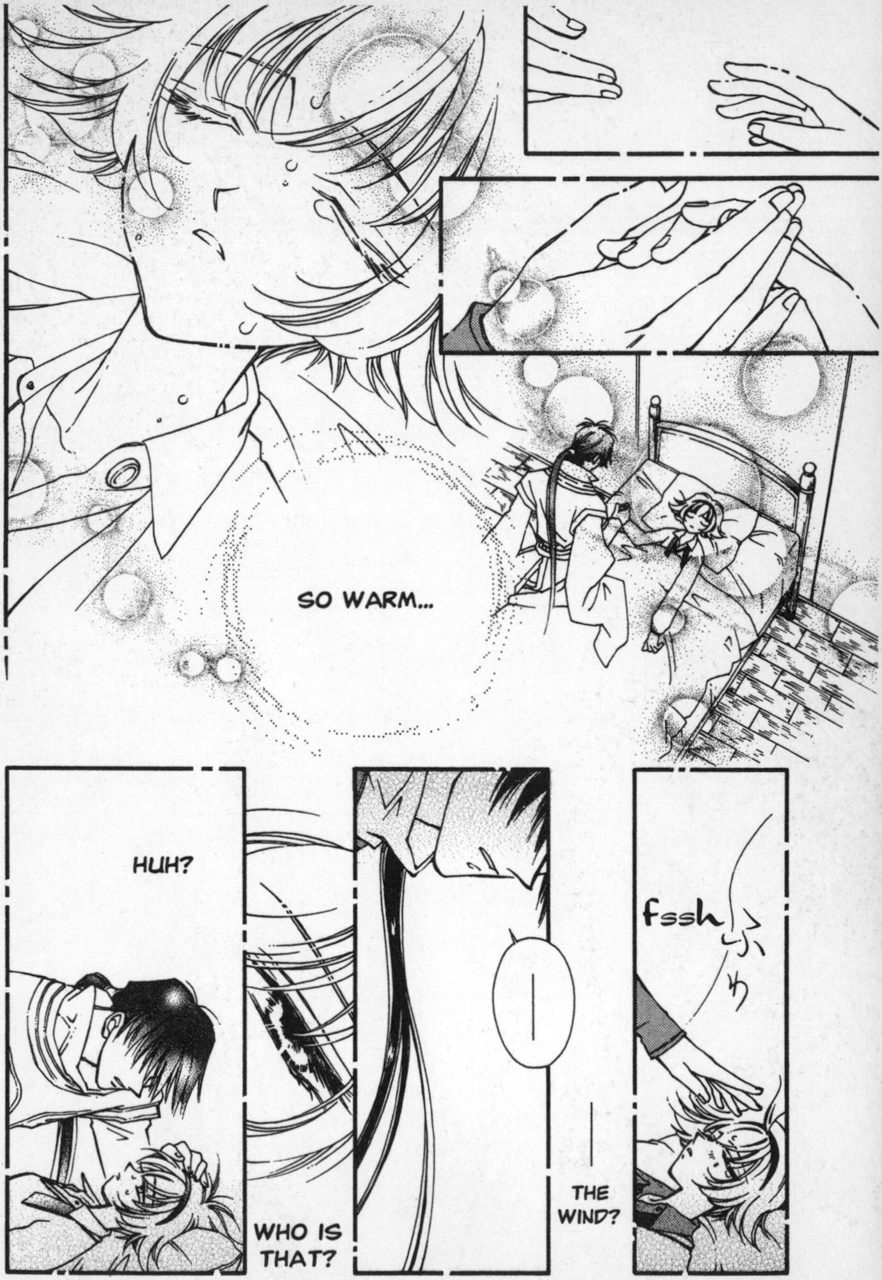
SO WARM...
fssh
ふわ
THE WIND?
WHO IS THAT?
HUH?

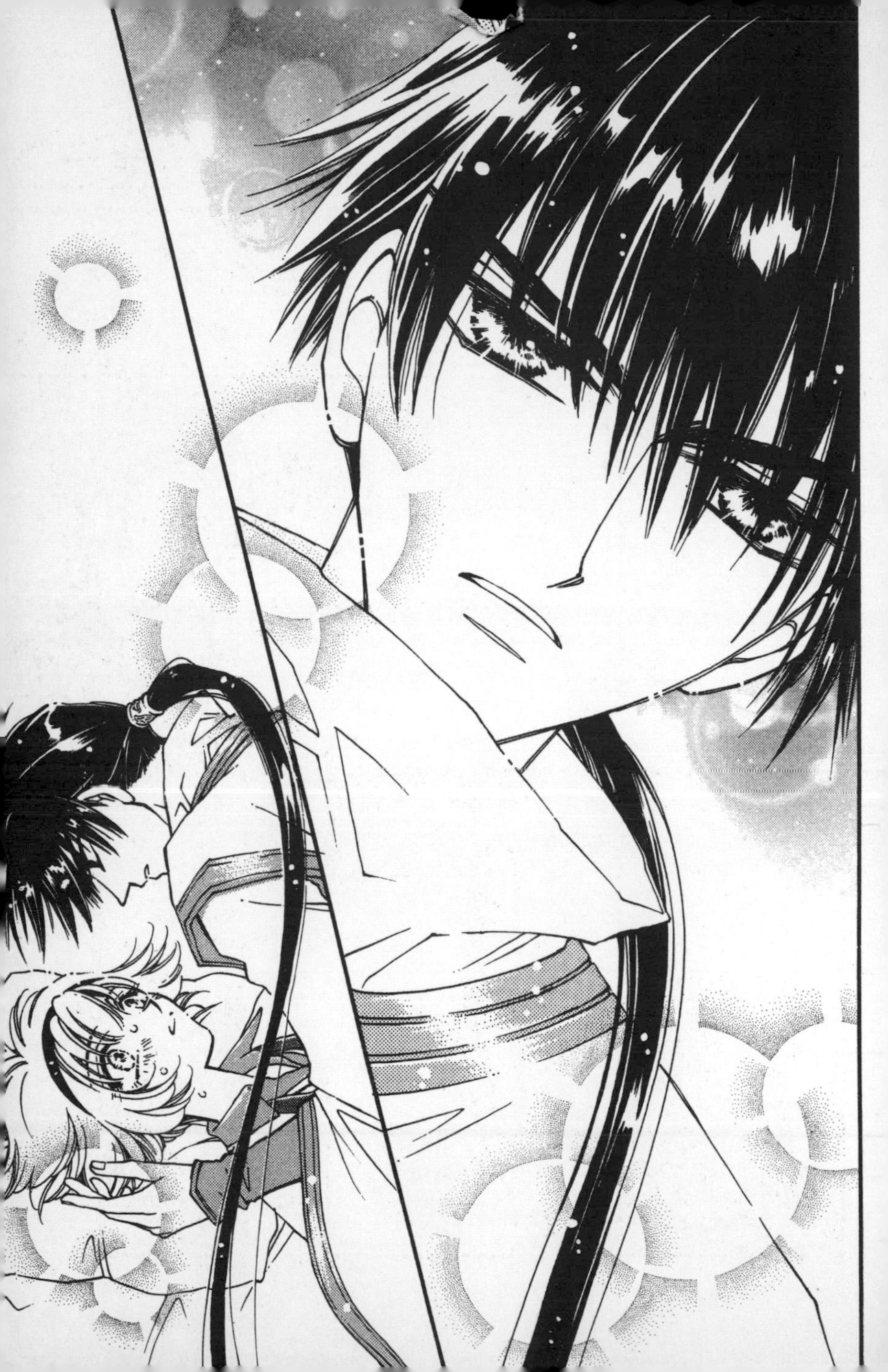

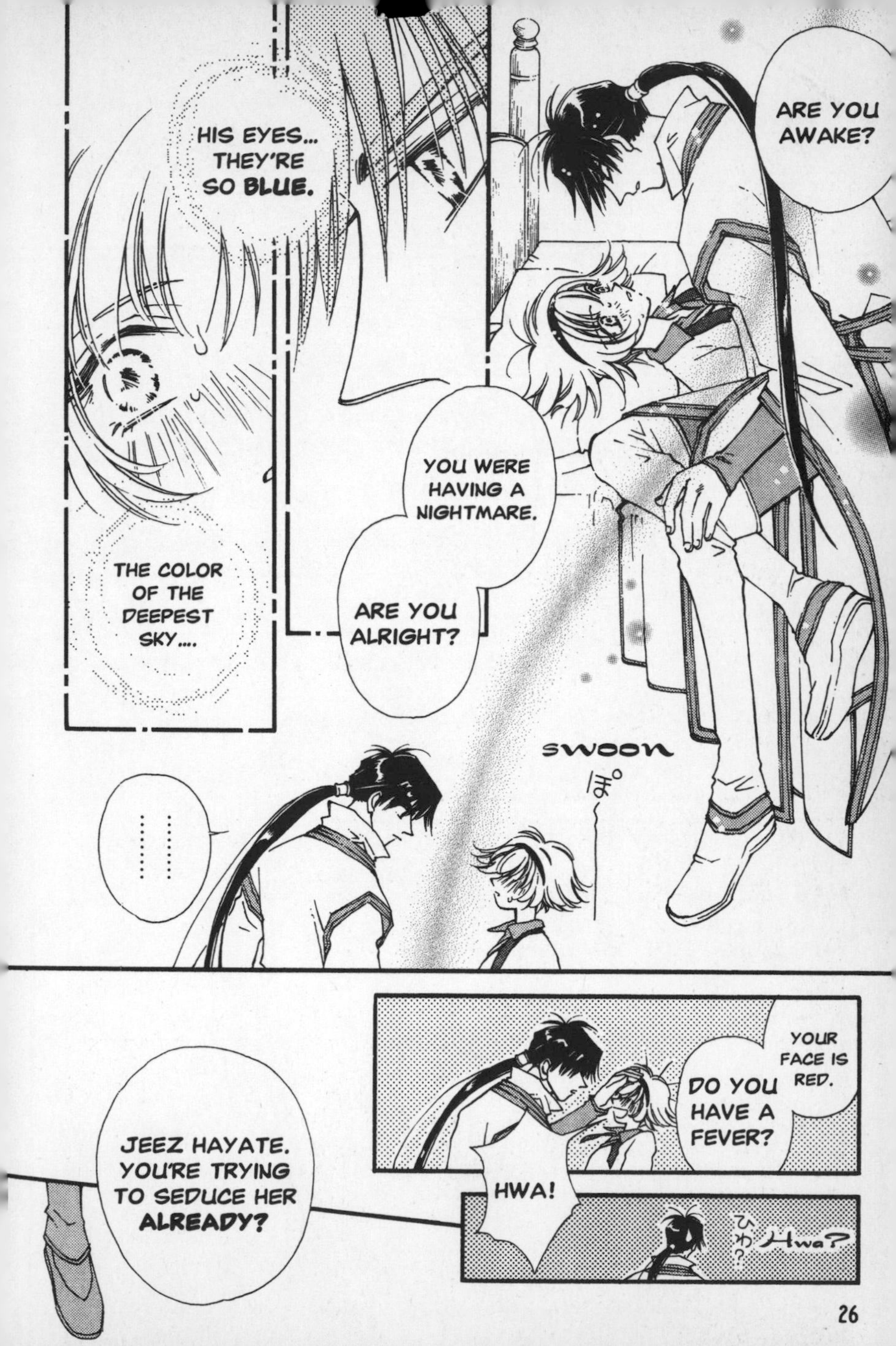
ARE YOU AWAKE?
YOU WERE HAVING A NIGHTMARE.
ARE YOU ALRIGHT?
HIS EYES... THEY'RE SO BLUE.
THE COLOR OF THE DEEPEST SKY....
SWOON
ぽ~
......
YOUR FACE IS RED.
DO YOU HAVE A FEVER?
HWA!
ひわ?
Hwa?
JEEZ HAYATE. YOU'RE TRYING TO SEDUCE HER ALREADY?

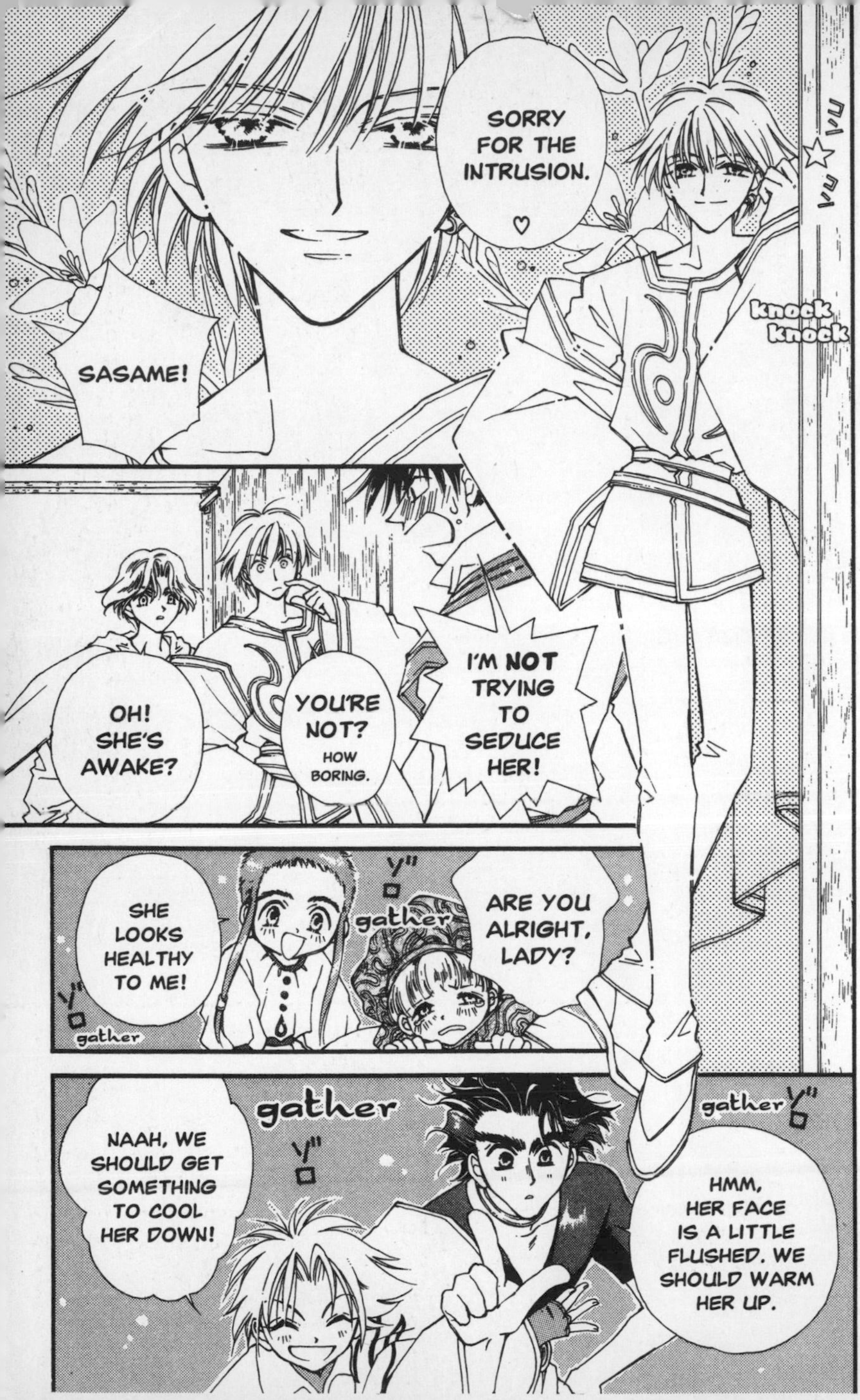
SORRY FOR THE INTRUSION. ♡
knock knock
SASAME!
I'M **NOT** TRYING TO SEDUCE HER!
YOU'RE NOT? HOW BORING.
OH! SHE'S AWAKE?
ARE YOU ALRIGHT, LADY?
gather
SHE LOOKS HEALTHY TO ME!
gather
gather
HMM, HER FACE IS A LITTLE FLUSHED. WE SHOULD WARM HER UP.
gather
NAAH, WE SHOULD GET SOMETHING TO COOL HER DOWN!

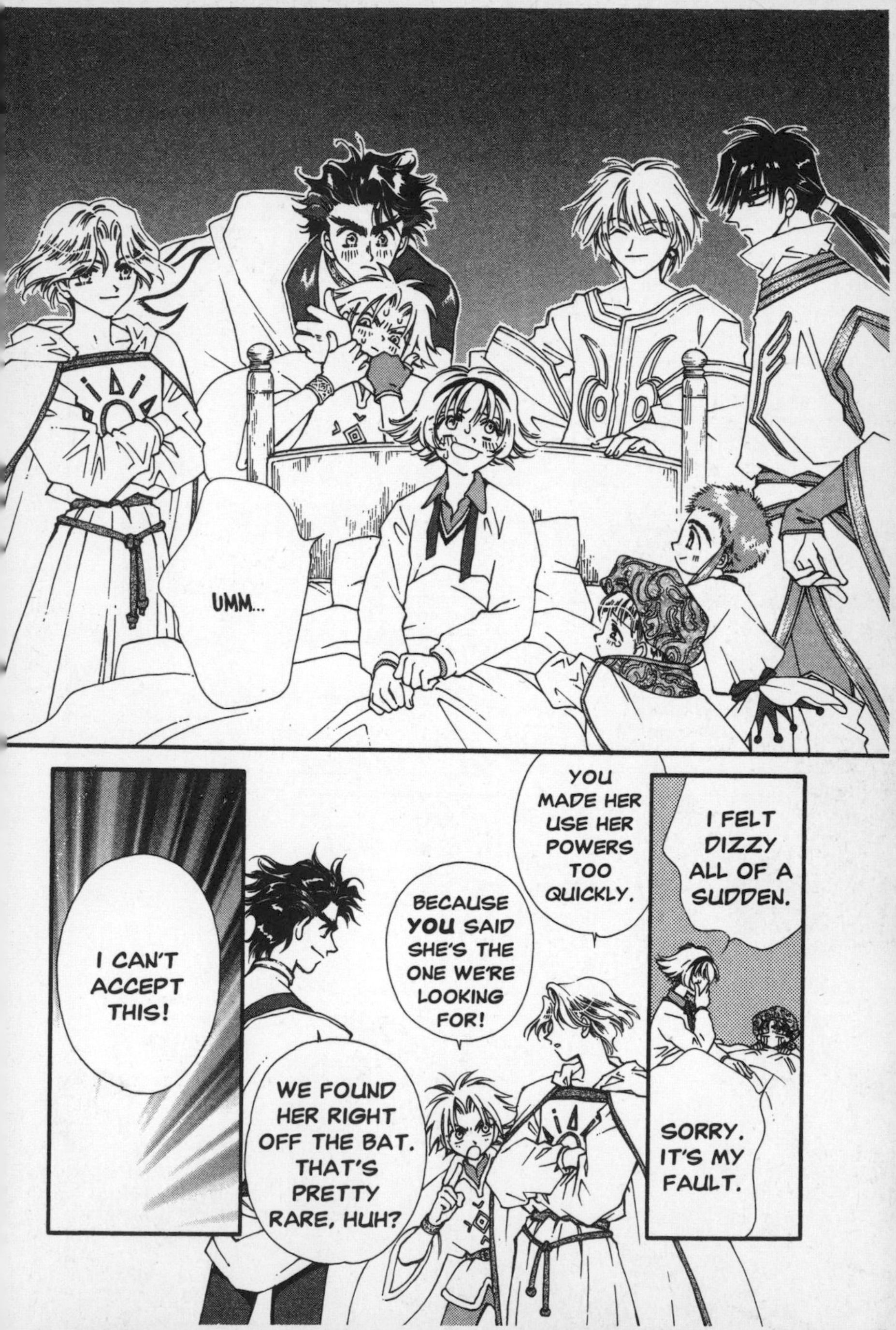
UMM...
I FELT DIZZY ALL OF A SUDDEN.
SORRY. IT'S MY FAULT.
YOU MADE HER USE HER POWERS TOO QUICKLY.
BECAUSE **YOU** SAID SHE'S THE ONE WE'RE LOOKING FOR!
WE FOUND HER RIGHT OFF THE BAT. THAT'S PRETTY RARE, HUH?
I CAN'T ACCEPT THIS!

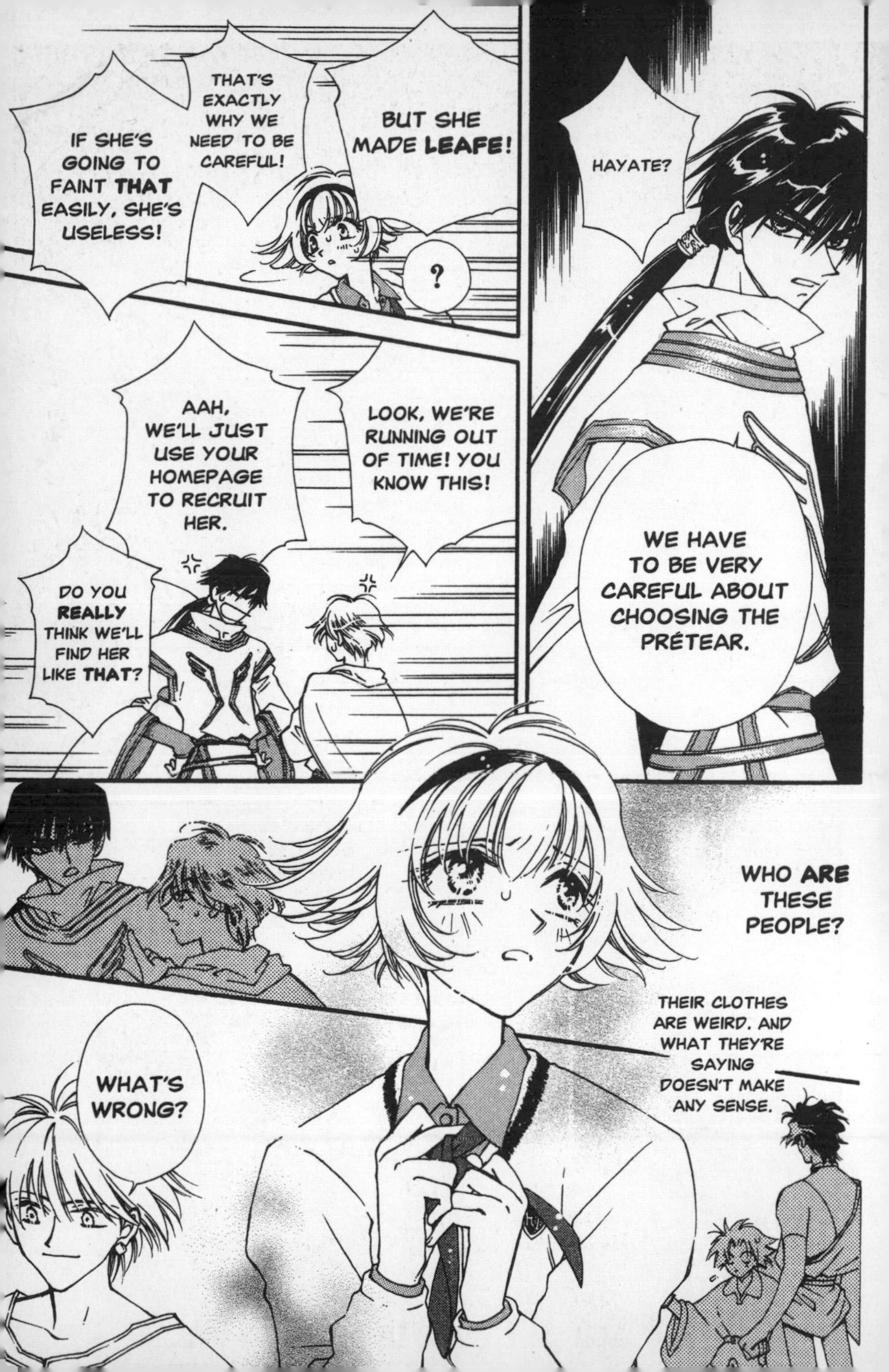
IF SHE'S GOING TO FAINT THAT EASILY, SHE'S USELESS!
THAT'S EXACTLY WHY WE NEED TO BE CAREFUL!
BUT SHE MADE LEAFE!
?
AAH, WE'LL JUST USE YOUR HOMEPAGE TO RECRUIT HER.
LOOK, WE'RE RUNNING OUT OF TIME! YOU KNOW THIS!
DO YOU REALLY THINK WE'LL FIND HER LIKE THAT?
HAYATE?
WE HAVE TO BE VERY CAREFUL ABOUT CHOOSING THE PRÉTEAR.
WHO ARE THESE PEOPLE?
THEIR CLOTHES ARE WEIRD. AND WHAT THEY'RE SAYING DOESN'T MAKE ANY SENSE.
WHAT'S WRONG?

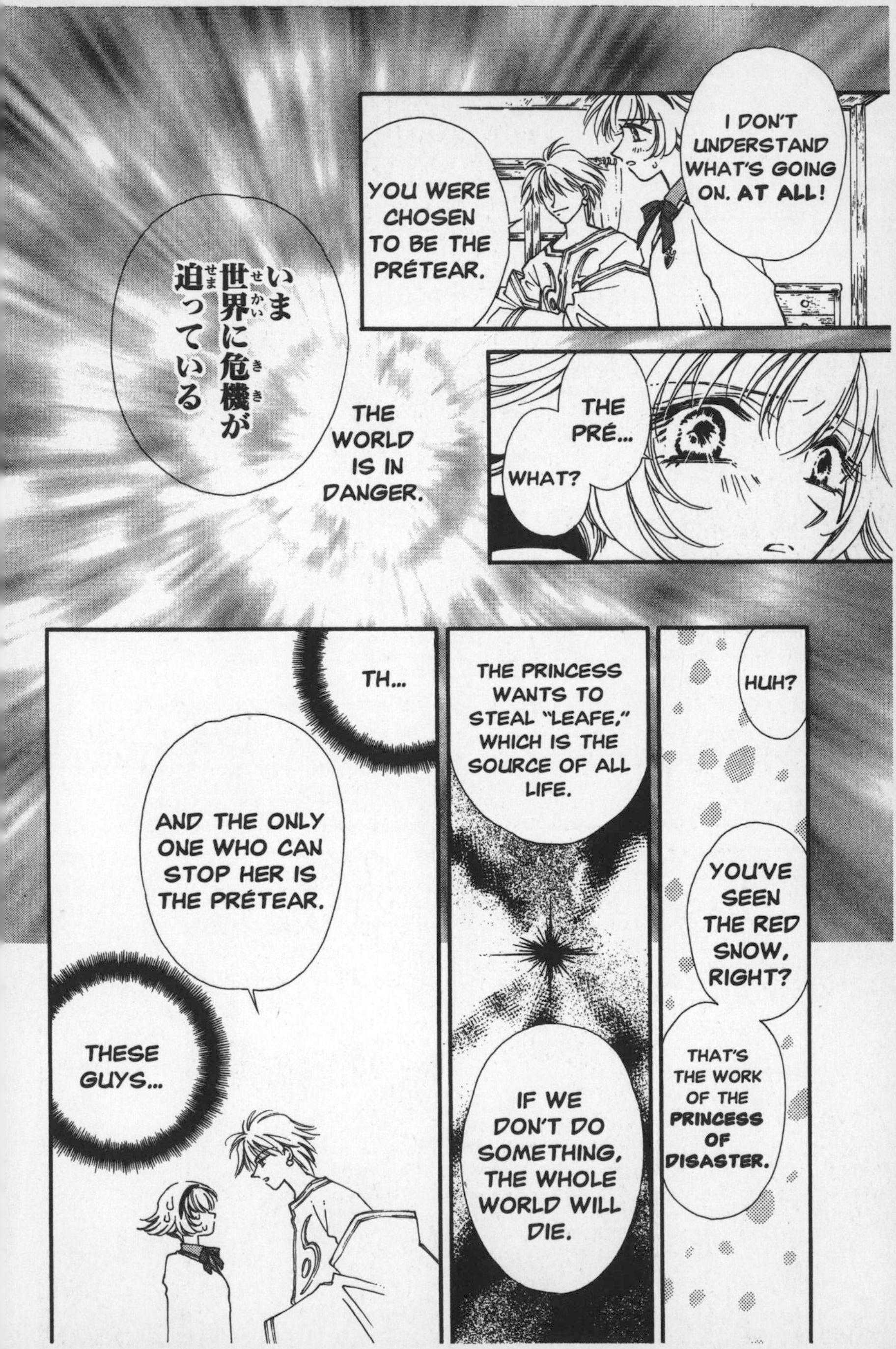
I DON'T UNDERSTAND WHAT'S GOING ON. AT ALL!
YOU WERE CHOSEN TO BE THE PRÉTEAR.
THE PRÉ...
WHAT?
いま世界に危機が迫っている
THE WORLD IS IN DANGER.
HUH?
YOU'VE SEEN THE RED SNOW, RIGHT?
THAT'S THE WORK OF THE PRINCESS OF DISASTER.
THE PRINCESS WANTS TO STEAL "LEAFE," WHICH IS THE SOURCE OF ALL LIFE.
IF WE DON'T DO SOMETHING, THE WHOLE WORLD WILL DIE.
TH...
AND THE ONLY ONE WHO CAN STOP HER IS THE PRÉTEAR.
THESE GUYS...

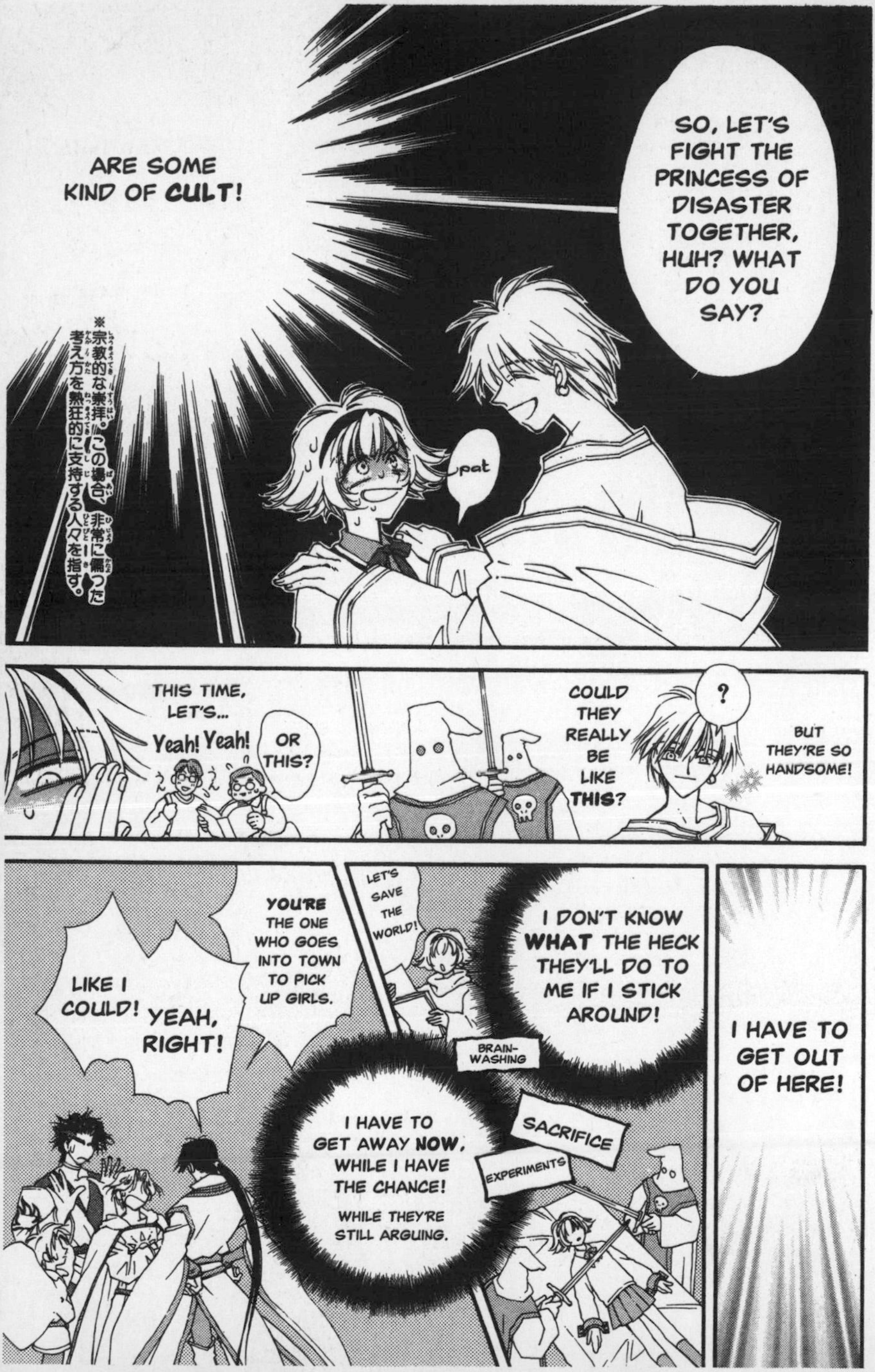
SO, LET'S FIGHT THE PRINCESS OF DISASTER TOGETHER, HUH? WHAT DO YOU SAY?
ARE SOME KIND OF CULT!
※宗教的な崇拝。この場合、非常に偏った考え方を熱狂的に支持する人々を指す。
pat
?
BUT THEY'RE SO HANDSOME!
COULD THEY REALLY BE LIKE THIS?
OR THIS?
Yeah! Yeah!
THIS TIME, LET'S...
I HAVE TO GET OUT OF HERE!
I DON'T KNOW WHAT THE HECK THEY'LL DO TO ME IF I STICK AROUND!
LET'S SAVE THE WORLD!
BRAIN-WASHING
SACRIFICE
EXPERIMENTS
I HAVE TO GET AWAY NOW, WHILE I HAVE THE CHANCE!
WHILE THEY'RE STILL ARGUING.
YOU'RE THE ONE WHO GOES INTO TOWN TO PICK UP GIRLS.
YEAH, RIGHT!
LIKE I COULD!

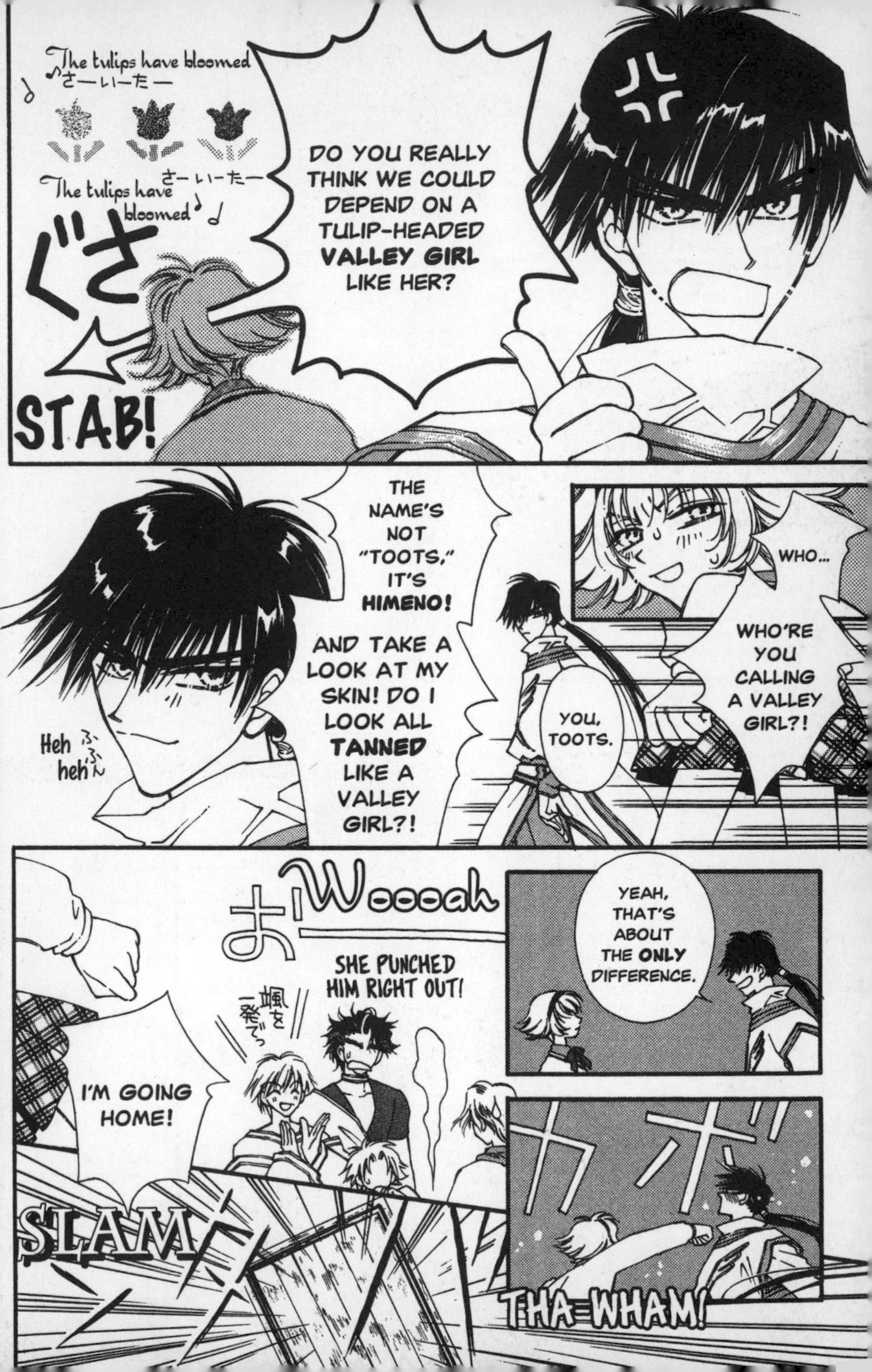

DO YOU REALLY THINK WE COULD DEPEND ON A TULIP-HEADED **VALLEY GIRL** LIKE HER?
The tulips have bloomed さーいーたー
The tulips have bloomed さーいーたー
ぐさ
STAB!
WHO...
WHO'RE YOU CALLING A VALLEY GIRL?!
YOU, TOOTS.
THE NAME'S NOT "TOOTS," IT'S **HIMENO!**
AND TAKE A LOOK AT MY SKIN! DO I LOOK ALL **TANNED** LIKE A VALLEY GIRL?!
Heh heh ふふん
YEAH, THAT'S ABOUT THE **ONLY** DIFFERENCE.
THA-WHAM!
お Woooah
SHE PUNCHED HIM RIGHT OUT!
颯を一発でっ
I'M GOING HOME!
SLAM

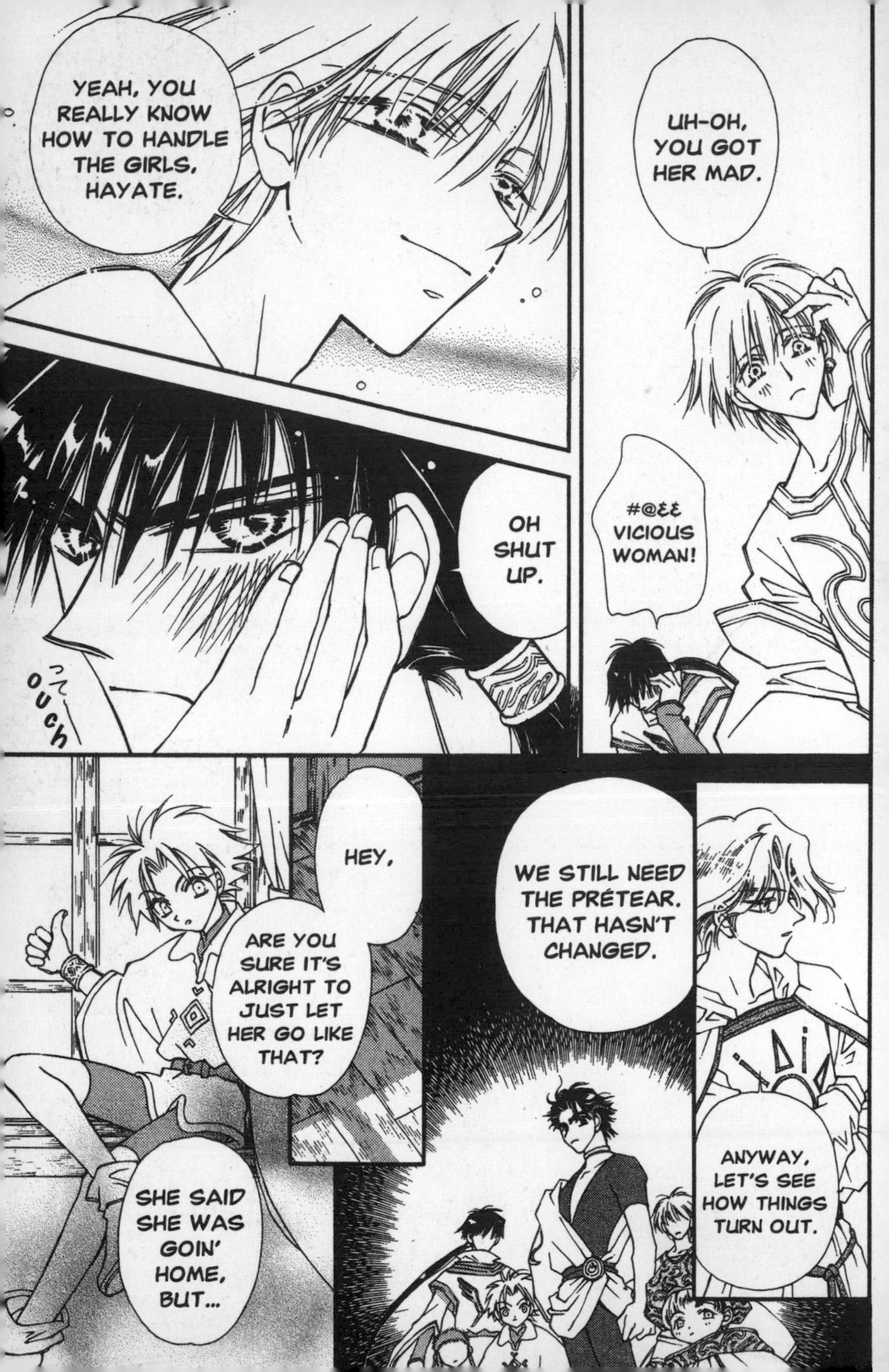
UH-OH, YOU GOT HER MAD.
#@&& VICIOUS WOMAN!
YEAH, YOU REALLY KNOW HOW TO HANDLE THE GIRLS, HAYATE.
OH SHUT UP.
OUCH
HEY,
ARE YOU SURE IT'S ALRIGHT TO JUST LET HER GO LIKE THAT?
SHE SAID SHE WAS GOIN' HOME, BUT...
WE STILL NEED THE PRÉTEAR. THAT HASN'T CHANGED.
ANYWAY, LET'S SEE HOW THINGS TURN OUT.

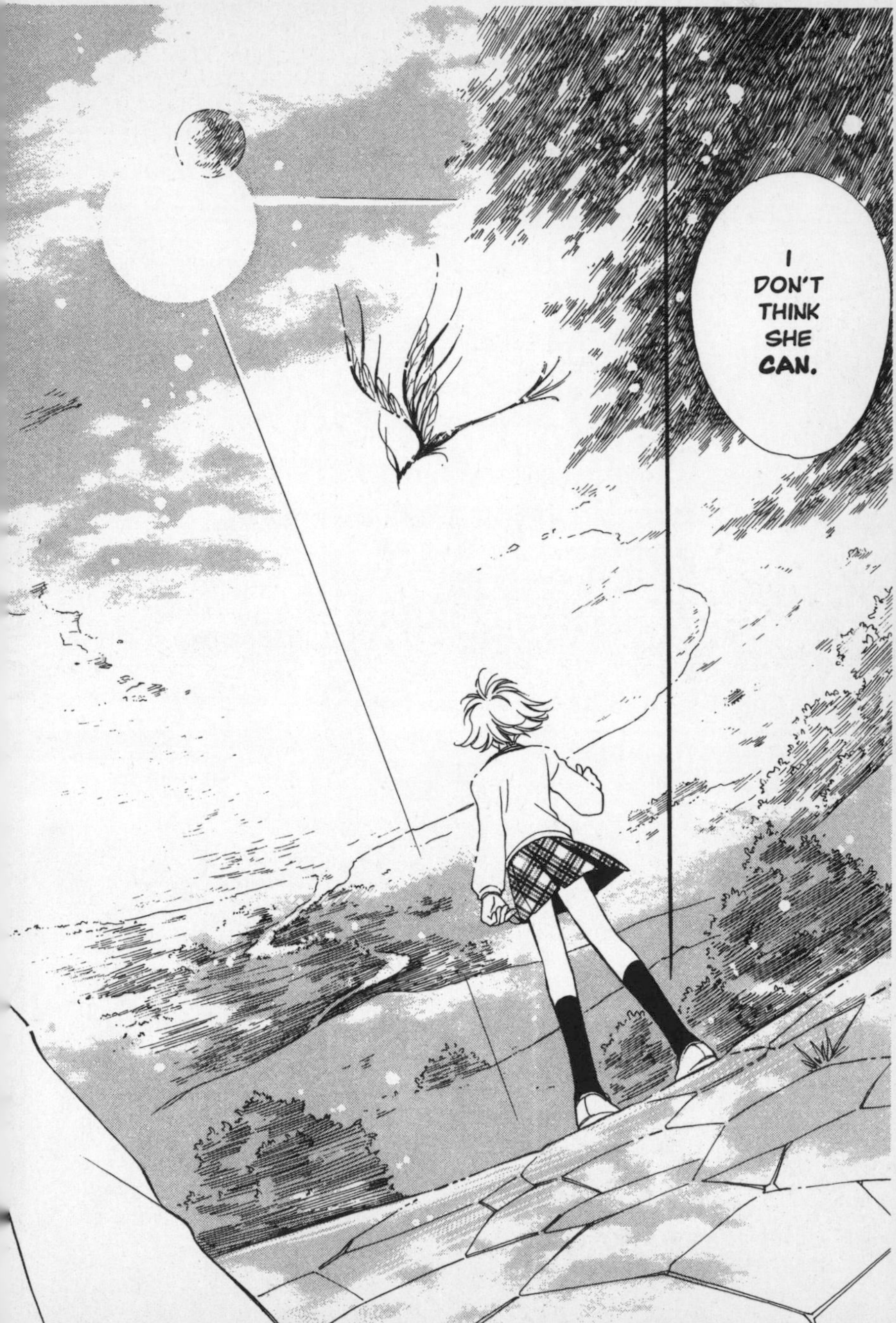
I DON'T THINK SHE CAN.

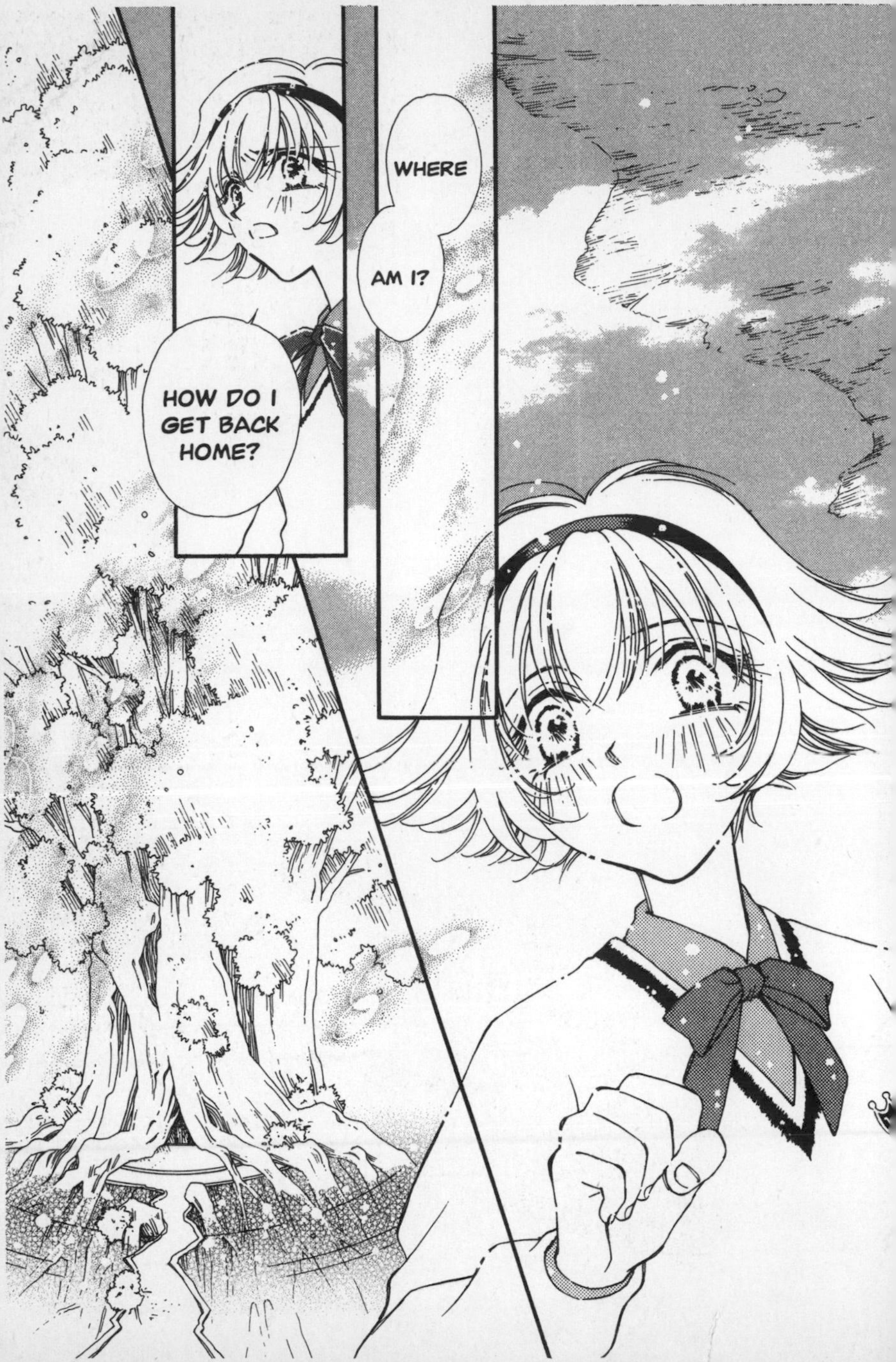
WHERE
AM I?
HOW DO I GET BACK HOME?

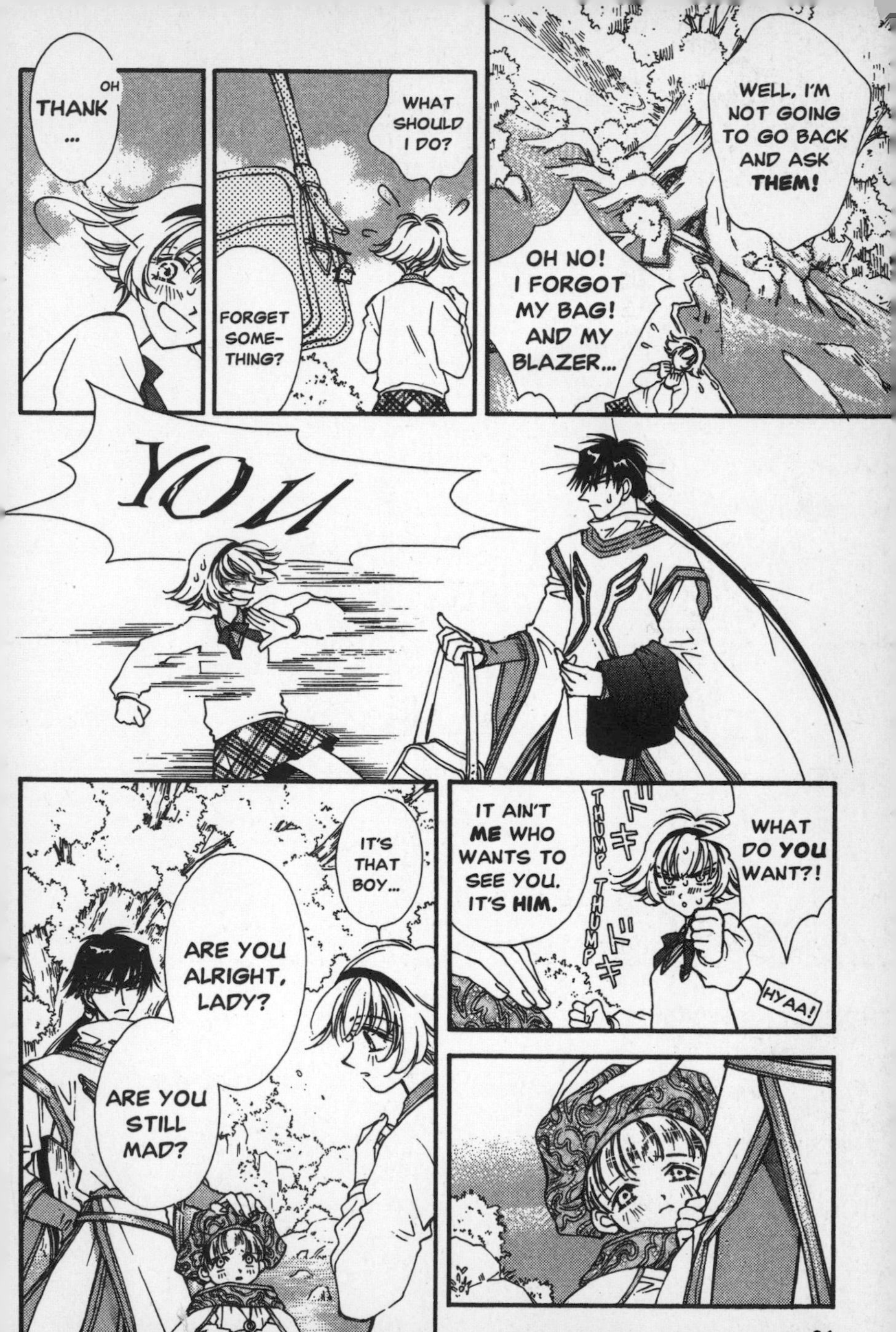
OH NO! I FORGOT MY BAG! AND MY BLAZER...
WELL, I'M NOT GOING TO GO BACK AND ASK THEM!
WHAT SHOULD I DO?
FORGET SOMETHING?
OH THANK ...
YOU
WHAT DO YOU WANT?!
HYAA!
THUMP THUMP
IT AIN'T ME WHO WANTS TO SEE YOU. IT'S HIM.
IT'S THAT BOY...
ARE YOU ALRIGHT, LADY?
ARE YOU STILL MAD?

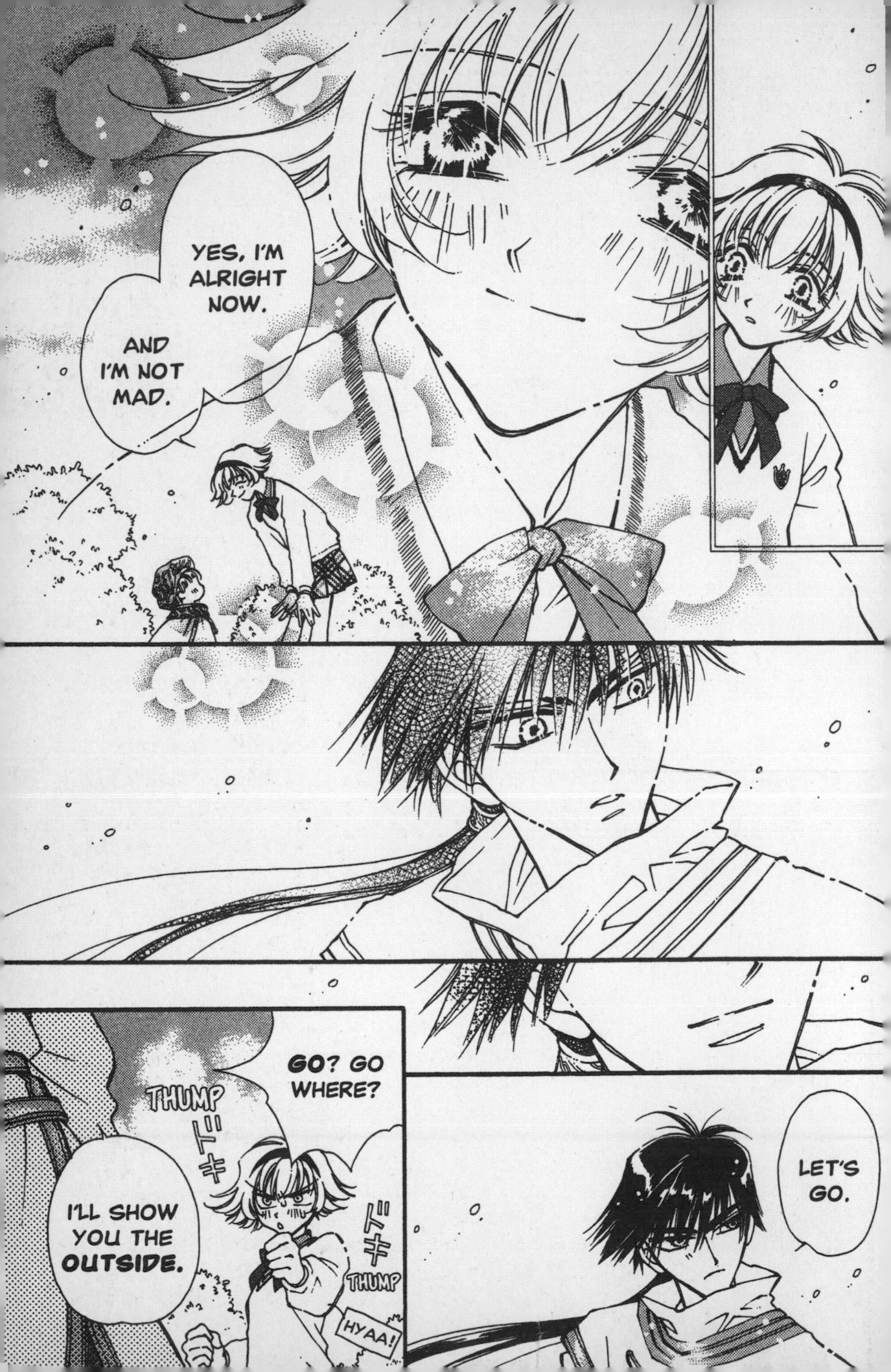
YES, I'M ALRIGHT NOW.
AND I'M NOT MAD.
LET'S GO.
GO? GO WHERE?
THUMP ドキ
I'LL SHOW YOU THE **OUTSIDE.**
ドキ THUMP
HYAA!

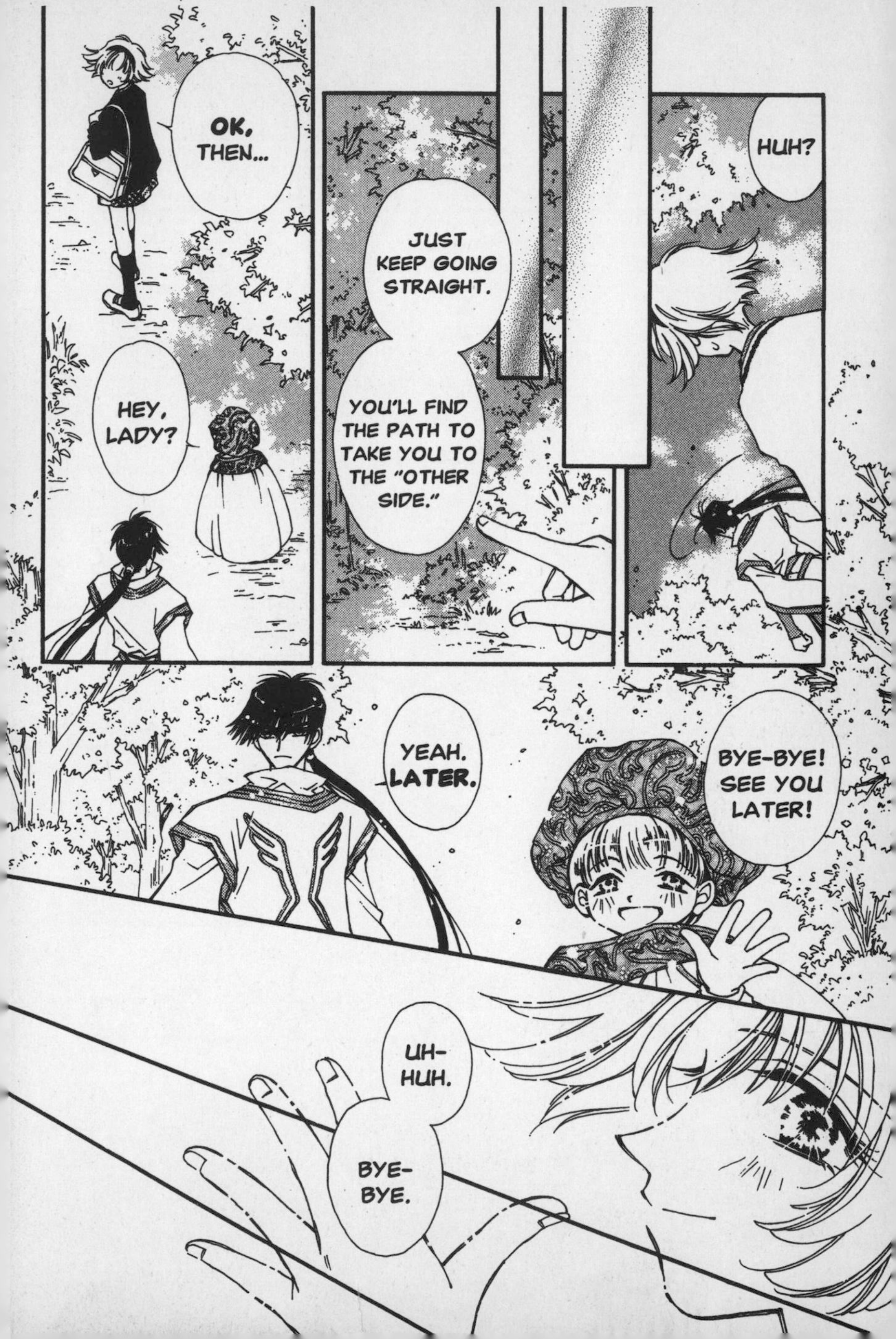
HUH?
JUST KEEP GOING STRAIGHT.
YOU'LL FIND THE PATH TO TAKE YOU TO THE "OTHER SIDE."
OK, THEN...
HEY, LADY?
BYE-BYE! SEE YOU LATER!
YEAH. LATER.
UH-HUH.
BYE-BYE.

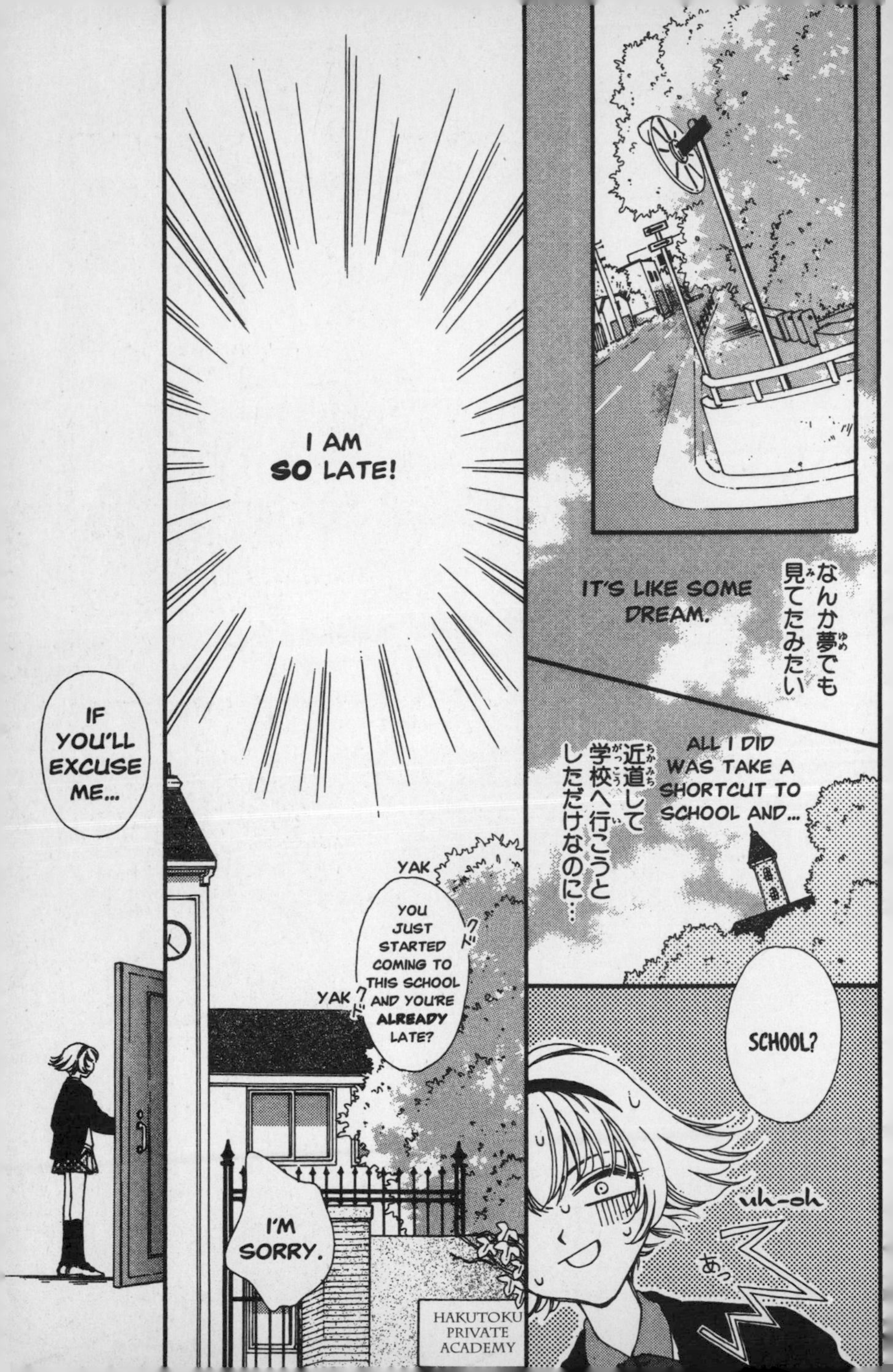
なんか夢でも見てたみたい
IT'S LIKE SOME DREAM.
近道して学校へ行こうとしただけなのに…
ALL I DID WAS TAKE A SHORTCUT TO SCHOOL AND...
SCHOOL?
uh-oh
あっ
I AM SO LATE!
YAK
YOU JUST STARTED COMING TO THIS SCHOOL AND YOU'RE ALREADY LATE?
YAK
I'M SORRY.
HAKUTOKU PRIVATE ACADEMY
IF YOU'LL EXCUSE ME...

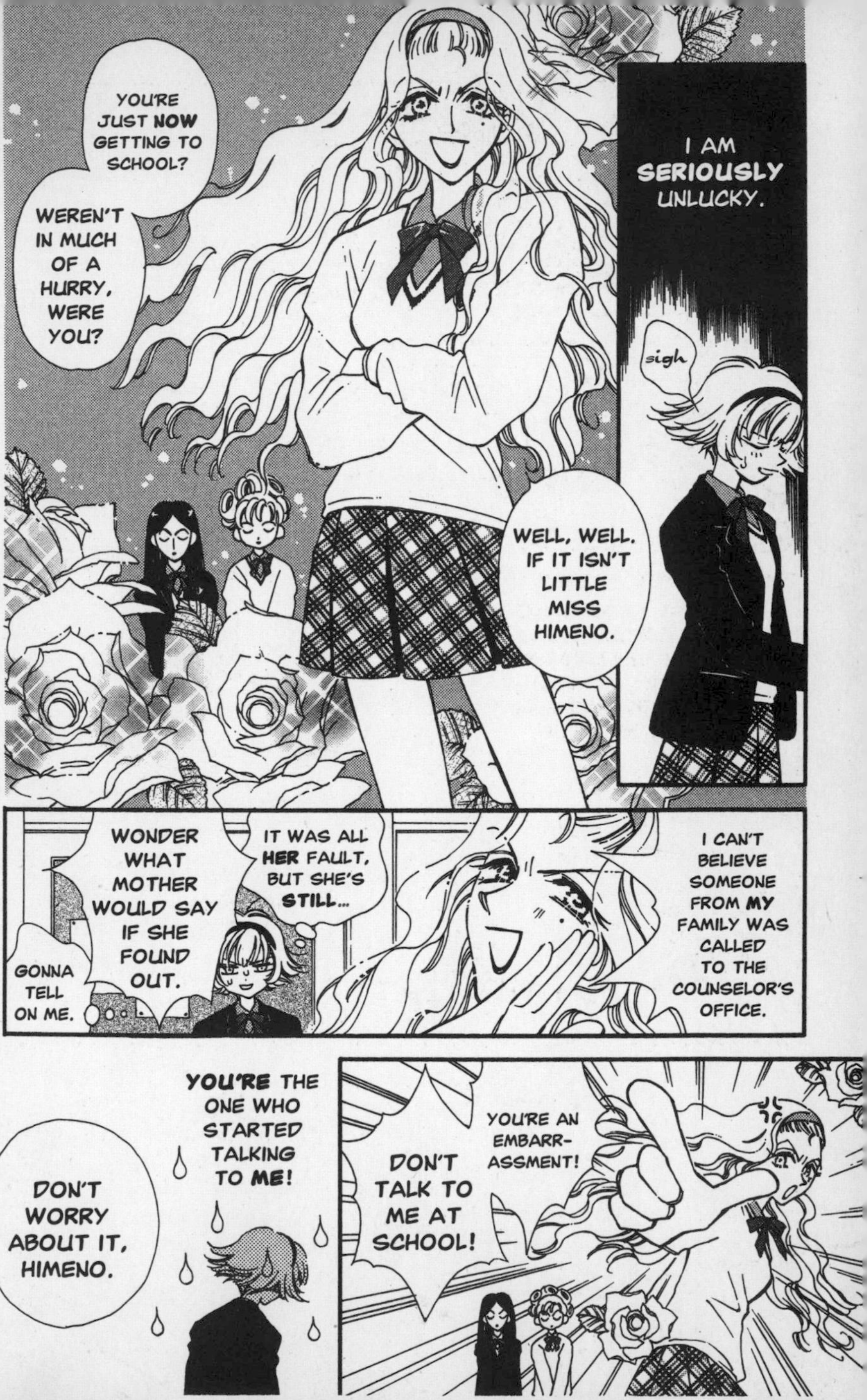
I AM SERIOUSLY UNLUCKY.
sigh
WELL, WELL. IF IT ISN'T LITTLE MISS HIMENO.
YOU'RE JUST NOW GETTING TO SCHOOL?
WEREN'T IN MUCH OF A HURRY, WERE YOU?
I CAN'T BELIEVE SOMEONE FROM MY FAMILY WAS CALLED TO THE COUNSELOR'S OFFICE.
IT WAS ALL HER FAULT, BUT SHE'S STILL...
WONDER WHAT MOTHER WOULD SAY IF SHE FOUND OUT.
GONNA TELL ON ME.
YOU'RE AN EMBARR-ASSMENT!
DON'T TALK TO ME AT SCHOOL!
YOU'RE THE ONE WHO STARTED TALKING TO ME!
DON'T WORRY ABOUT IT, HIMENO.

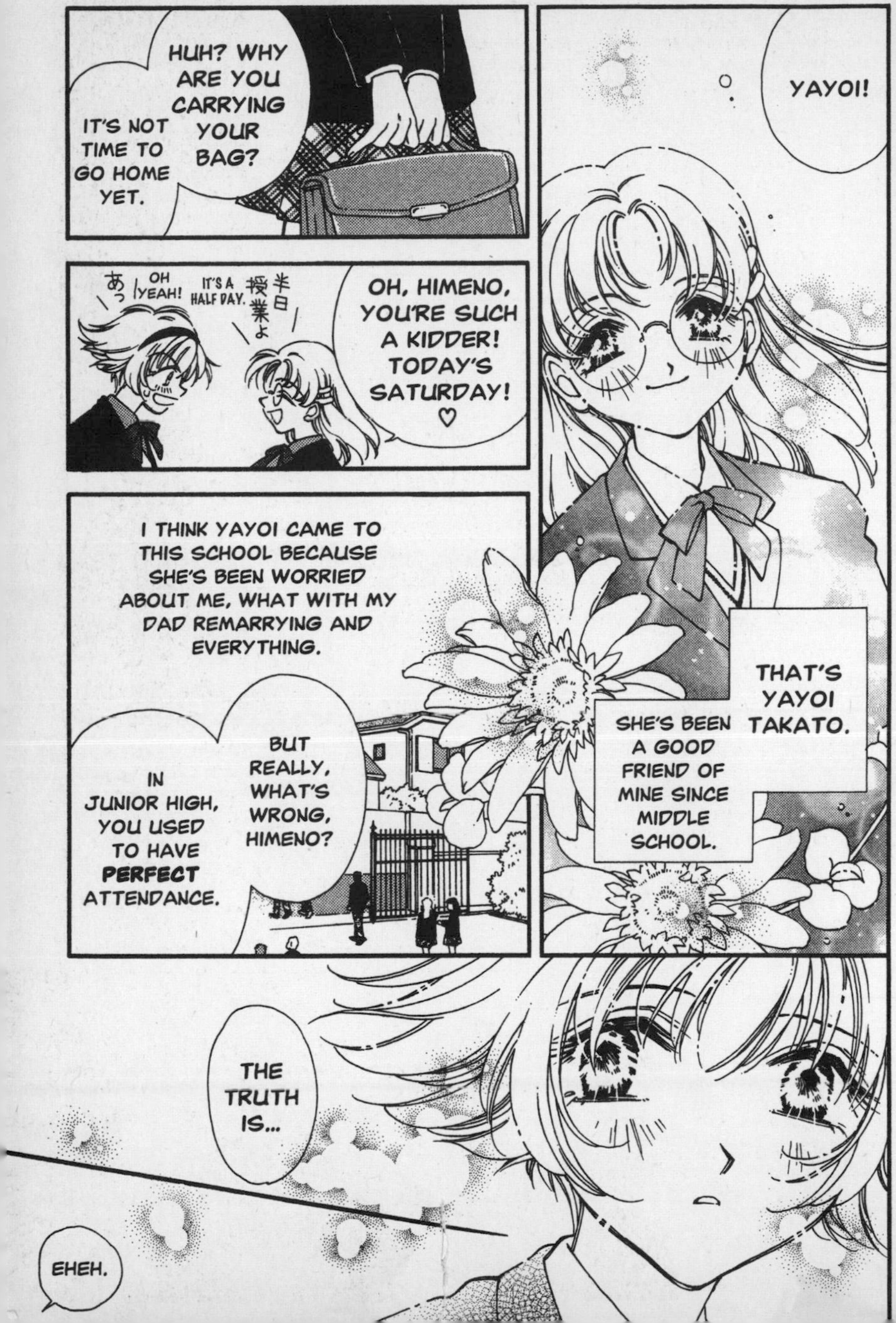
YAYOI!
THAT'S YAYOI TAKATO.
SHE'S BEEN A GOOD FRIEND OF MINE SINCE MIDDLE SCHOOL.
HUH? WHY ARE YOU CARRYING YOUR BAG?
IT'S NOT TIME TO GO HOME YET.
OH, HIMENO, YOU'RE SUCH A KIDDER! TODAY'S SATURDAY! ♡
半日授業よ
IT'S A HALF DAY.
あっ
OH YEAH!
I THINK YAYOI CAME TO THIS SCHOOL BECAUSE SHE'S BEEN WORRIED ABOUT ME, WHAT WITH MY DAD REMARRYING AND EVERYTHING.
BUT REALLY, WHAT'S WRONG, HIMENO?
IN JUNIOR HIGH, YOU USED TO HAVE PERFECT ATTENDANCE.
THE TRUTH IS...
EHEH.

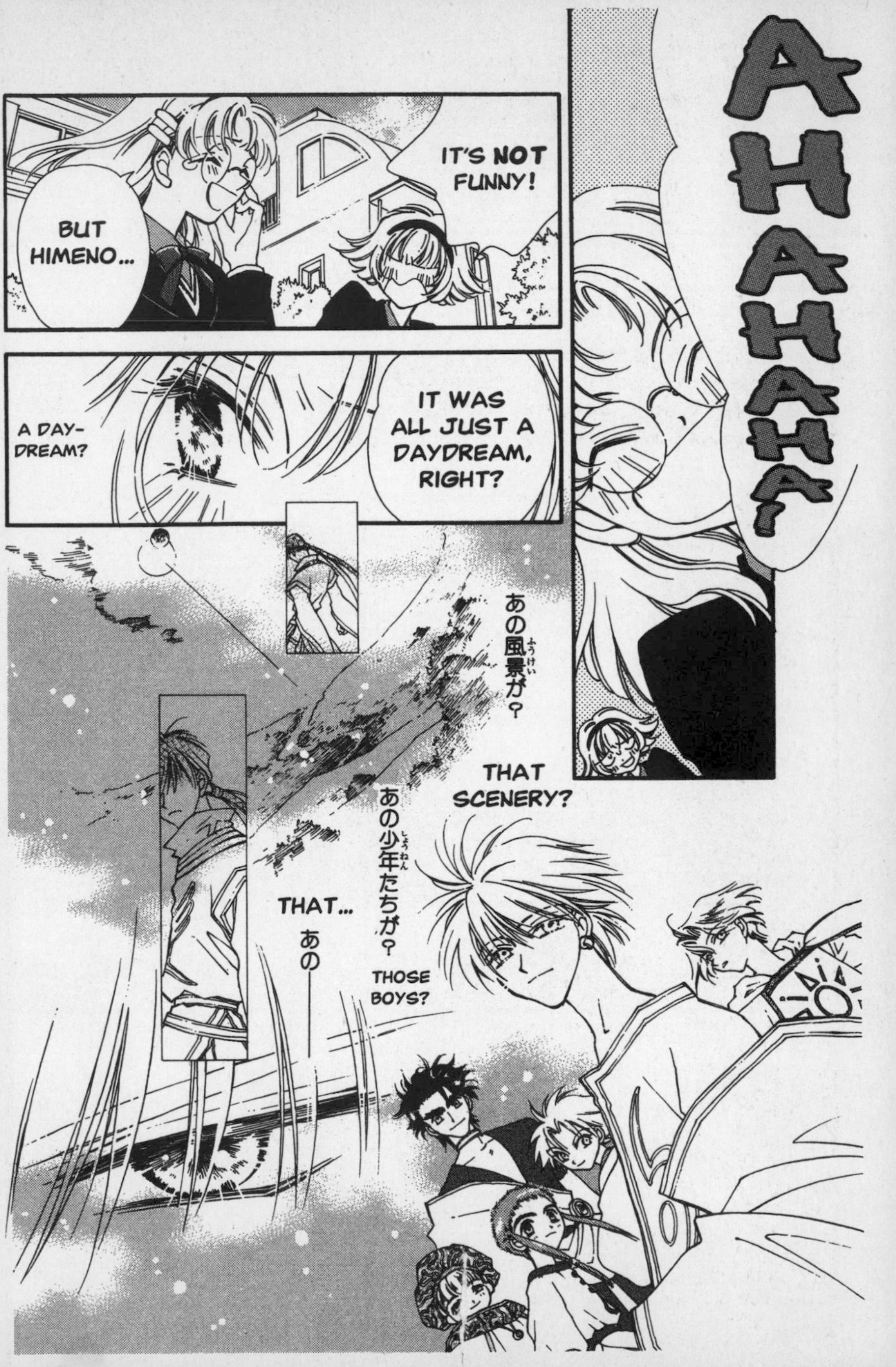
AHAHAHA!
IT'S NOT FUNNY!
BUT HIMENO...
IT WAS ALL JUST A DAYDREAM, RIGHT?
A DAY-DREAM?
あの風景が？
THAT SCENERY?
あの少年たちが？
THOSE BOYS?
あの――
THAT...

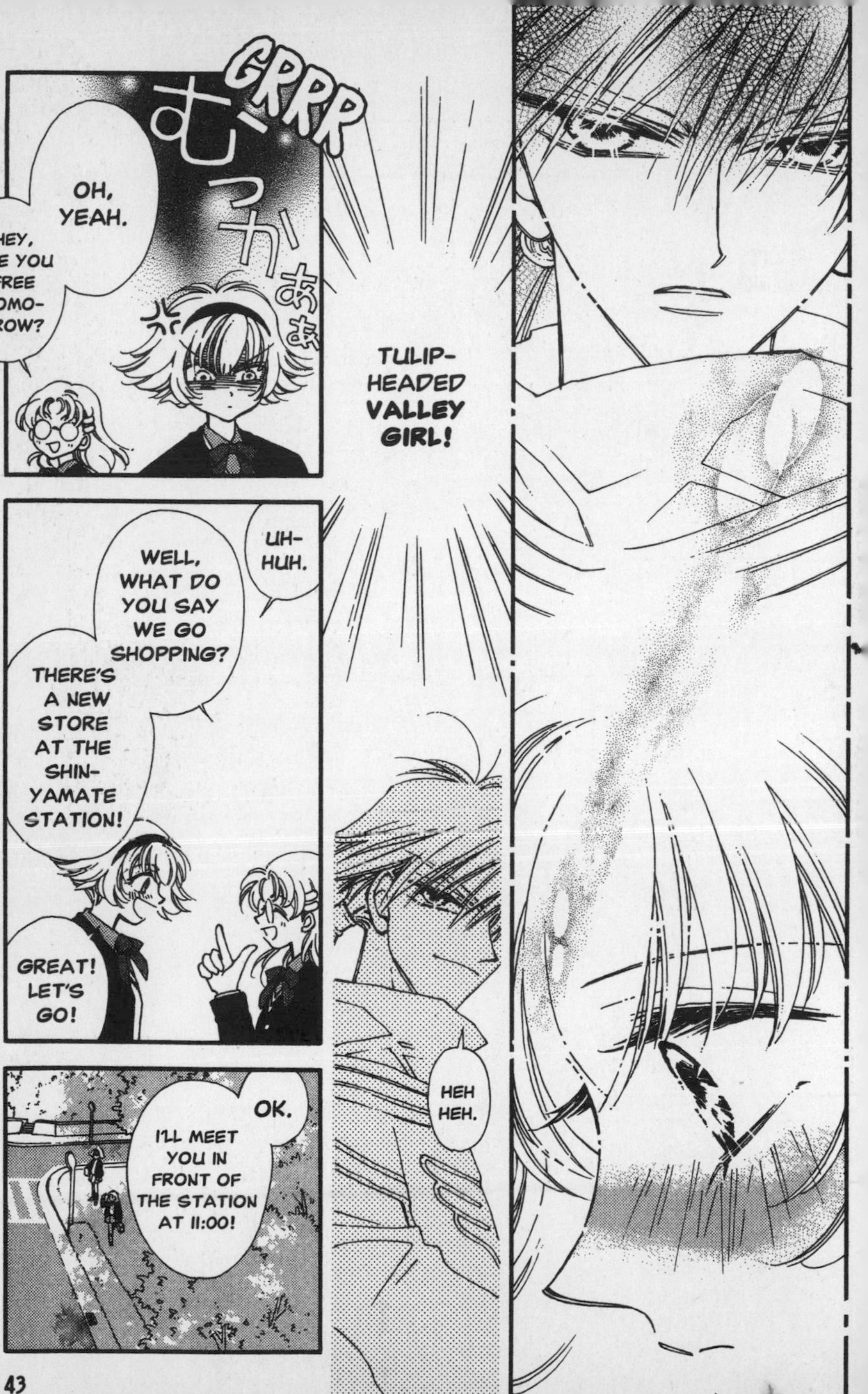
OH, YEAH.
HEY, ARE YOU FREE TOMORROW?
GRRR
むっかぁぁ
TULIP-HEADED VALLEY GIRL!
UH-HUH.
WELL, WHAT DO YOU SAY WE GO SHOPPING?
THERE'S A NEW STORE AT THE SHIN-YAMATE STATION!
GREAT! LET'S GO!
OK.
I'LL MEET YOU IN FRONT OF THE STATION AT 11:00!
HEH HEH.

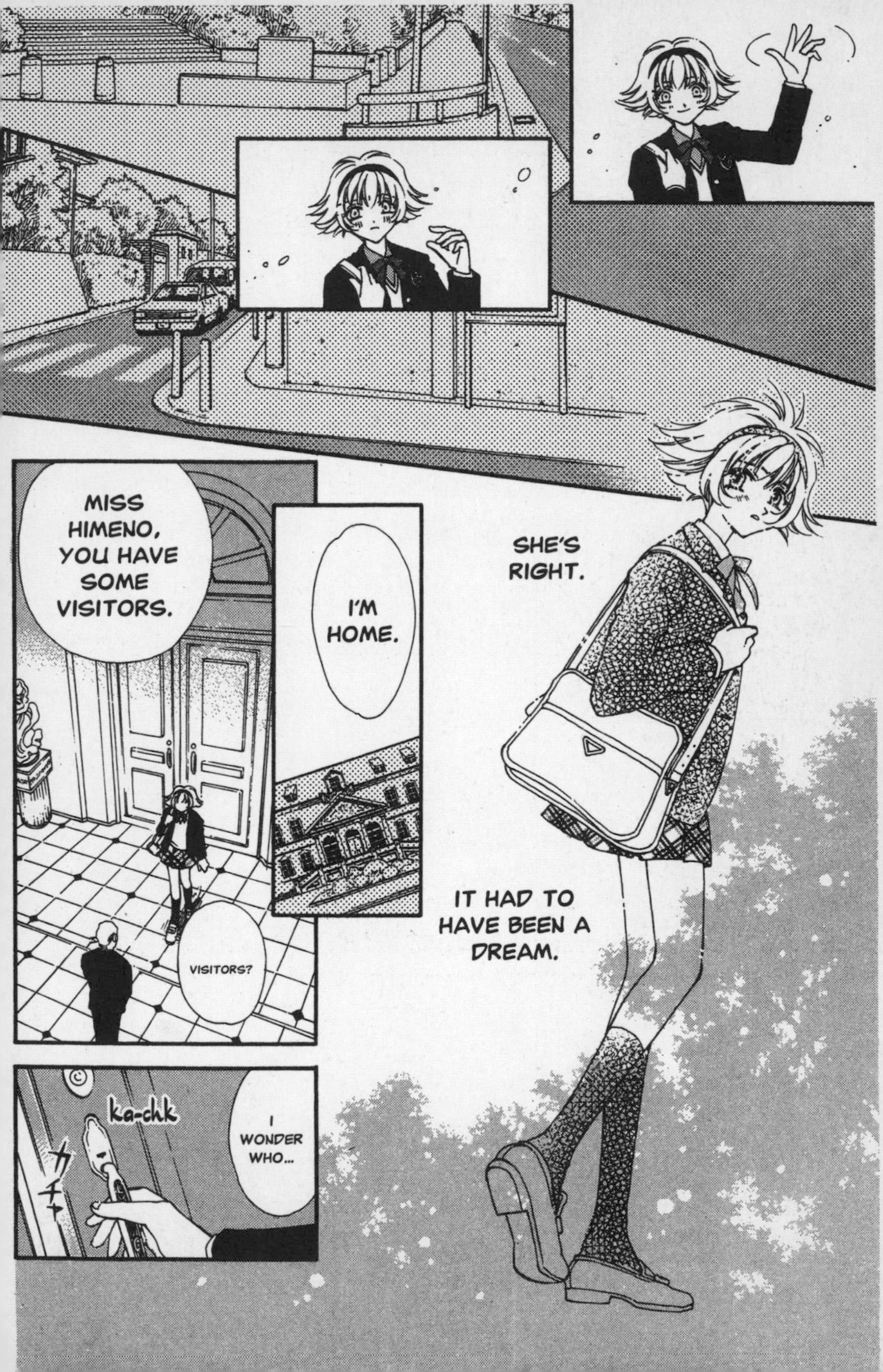
SHE'S RIGHT.
IT HAD TO HAVE BEEN A DREAM.
I'M HOME.
MISS HIMENO, YOU HAVE SOME VISITORS.
VISITORS?
I WONDER WHO...
ka-chk

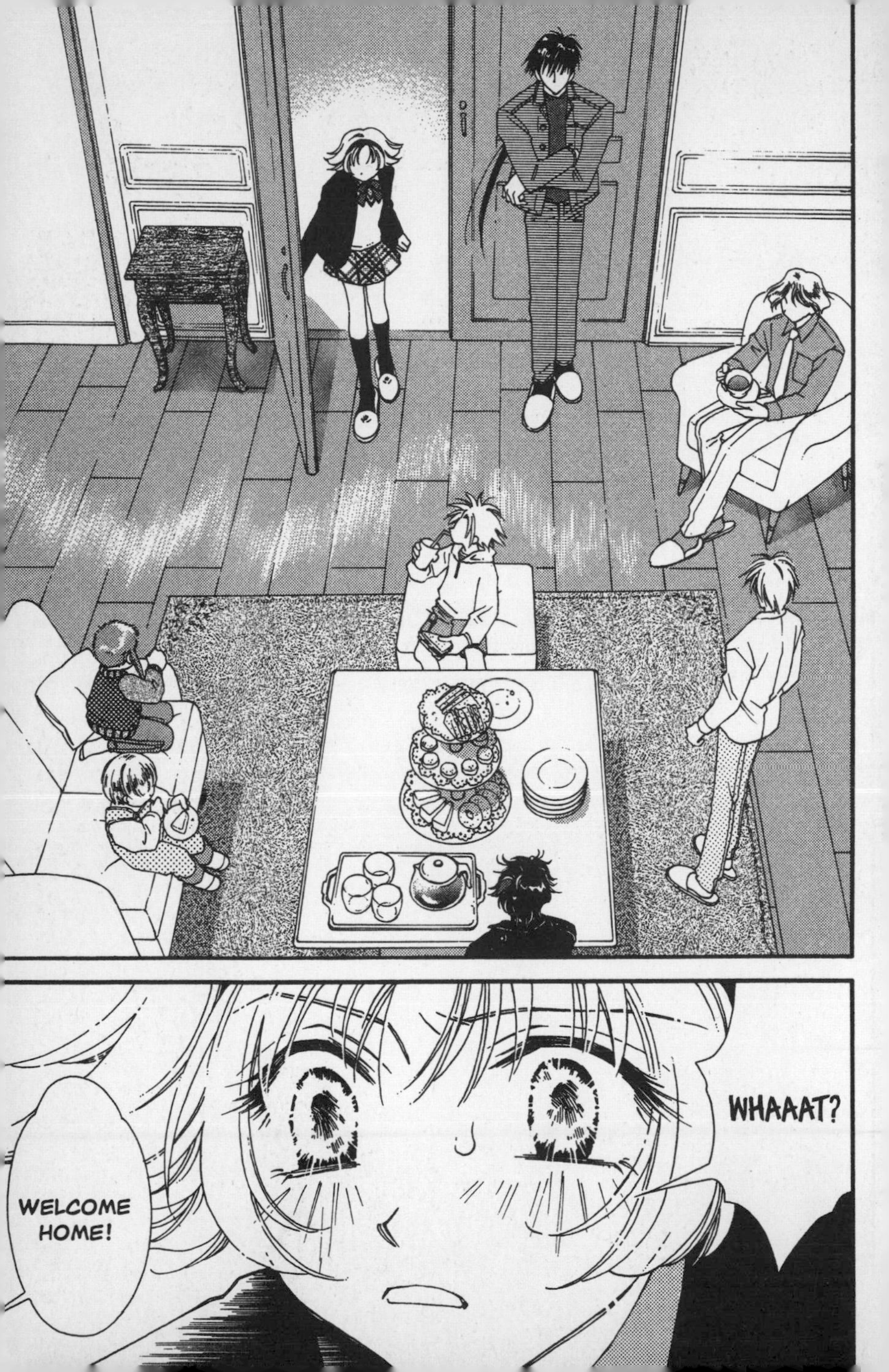
WHAAAT?
WELCOME HOME!

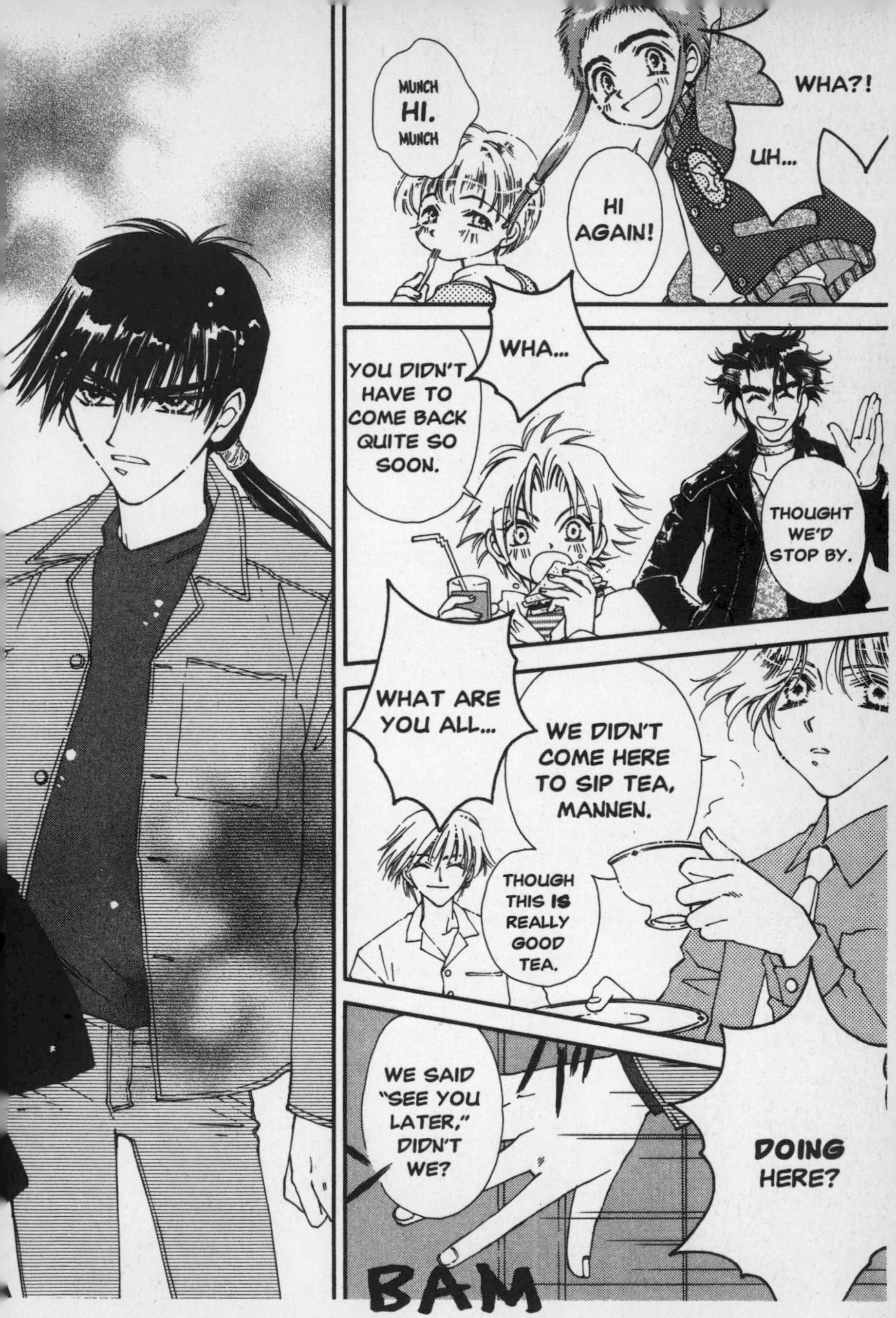
WHA?!
UH...
HI AGAIN!
MUNCH HI. MUNCH
THOUGHT WE'D STOP BY.
WHA...
YOU DIDN'T HAVE TO COME BACK QUITE SO SOON.
WE DIDN'T COME HERE TO SIP TEA, MANNEN.
THOUGH THIS IS REALLY GOOD TEA.
WHAT ARE YOU ALL...
DOING HERE?
WE SAID "SEE YOU LATER," DIDN'T WE?
BAM

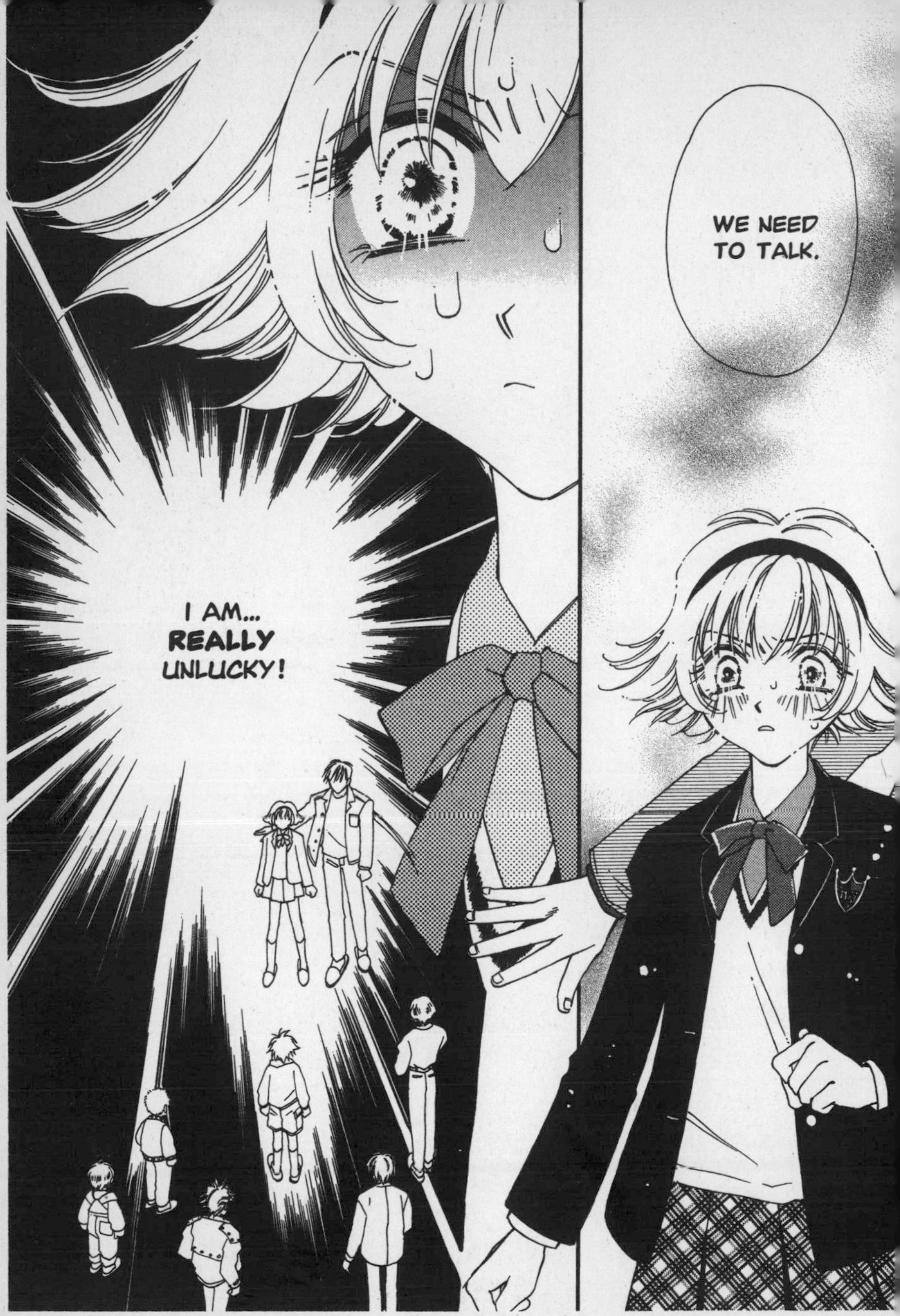
WE NEED TO TALK.
I AM... REALLY UNLUCKY!

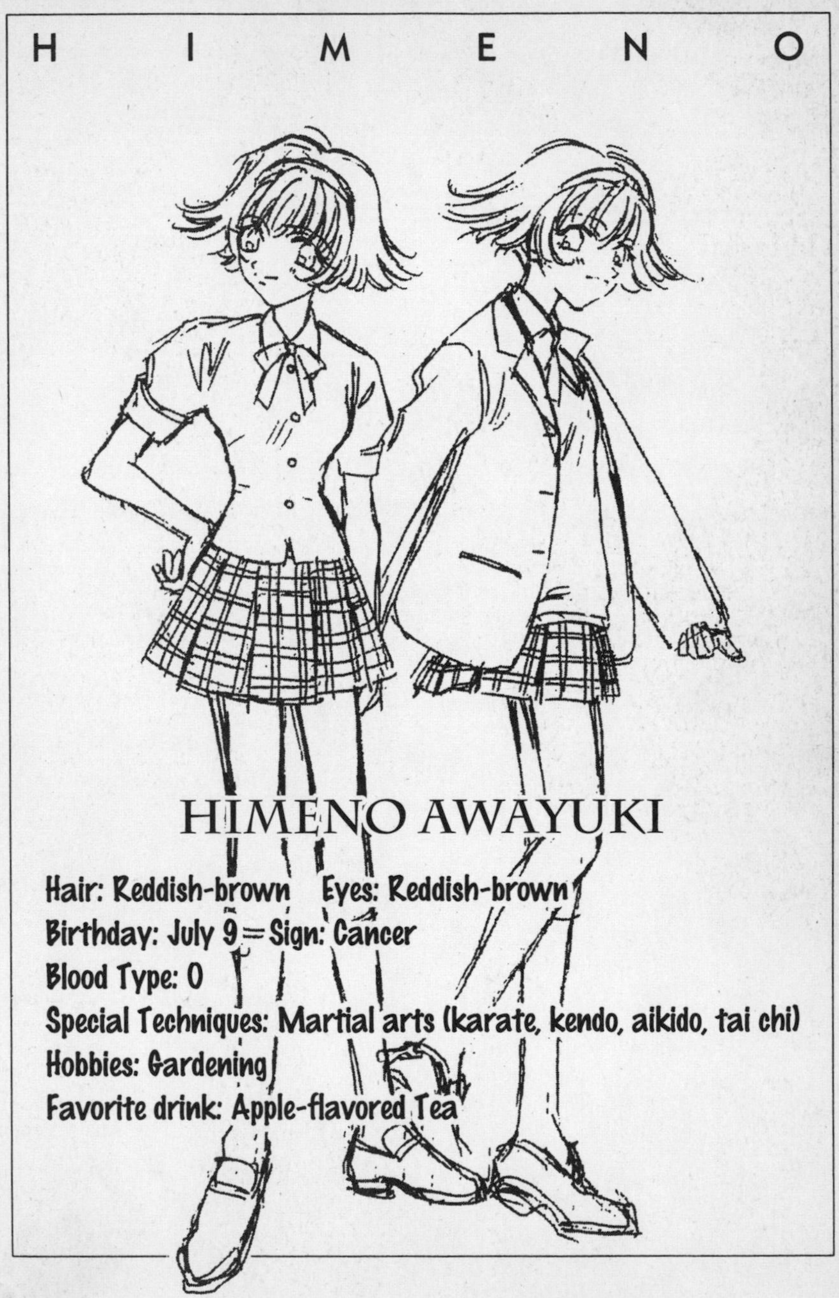

# HIMENO AWAYUKI

Hair: Reddish-brown Eyes: Reddish-brown
Birthday: July 9 = Sign: Cancer
Blood Type: O
Special Techniques: Martial arts (karate, kendo, aikido, tai chi)
Hobbies: Gardening
Favorite drink: Apple-flavored Tea

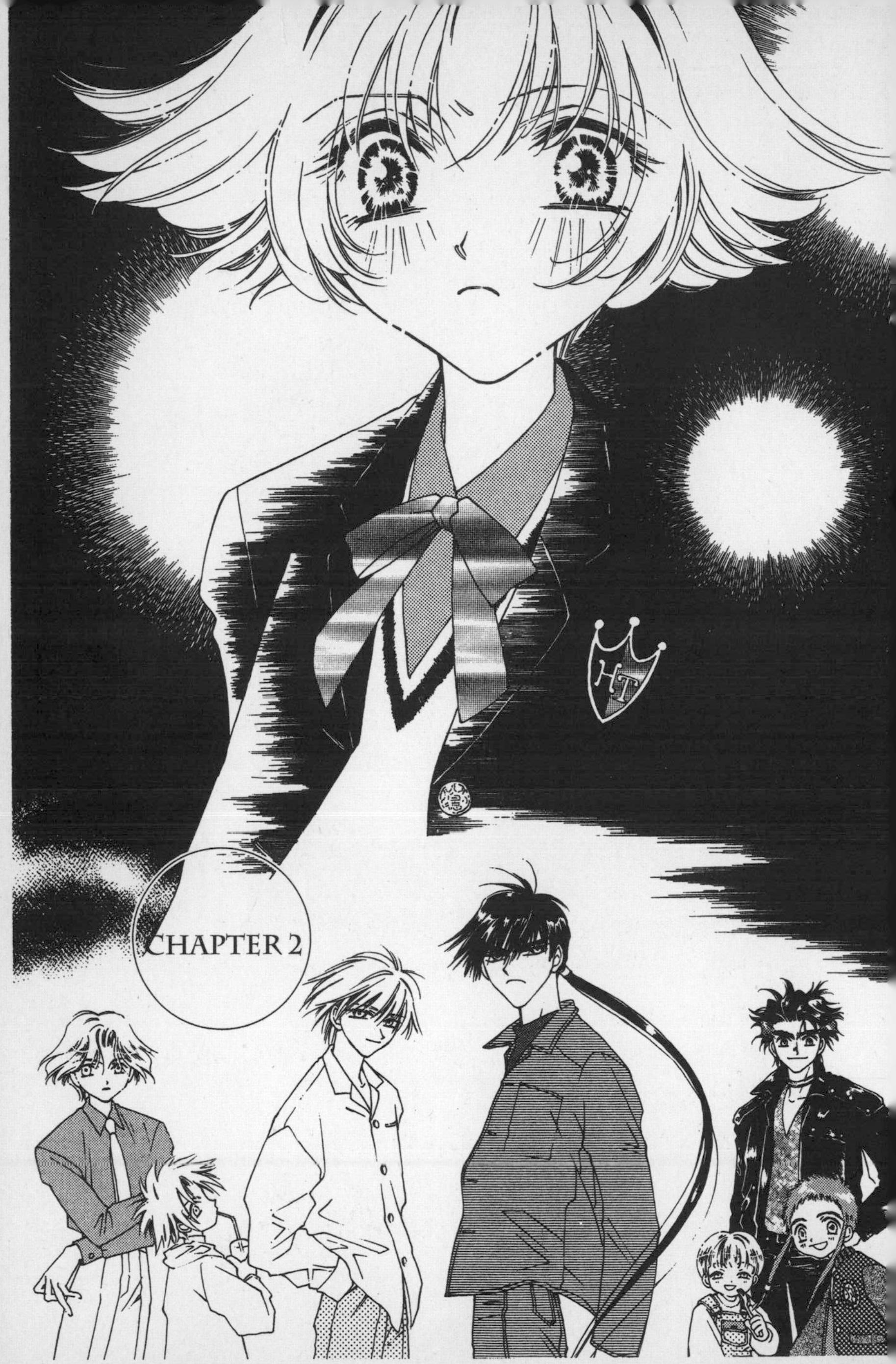
CHAPTER 2

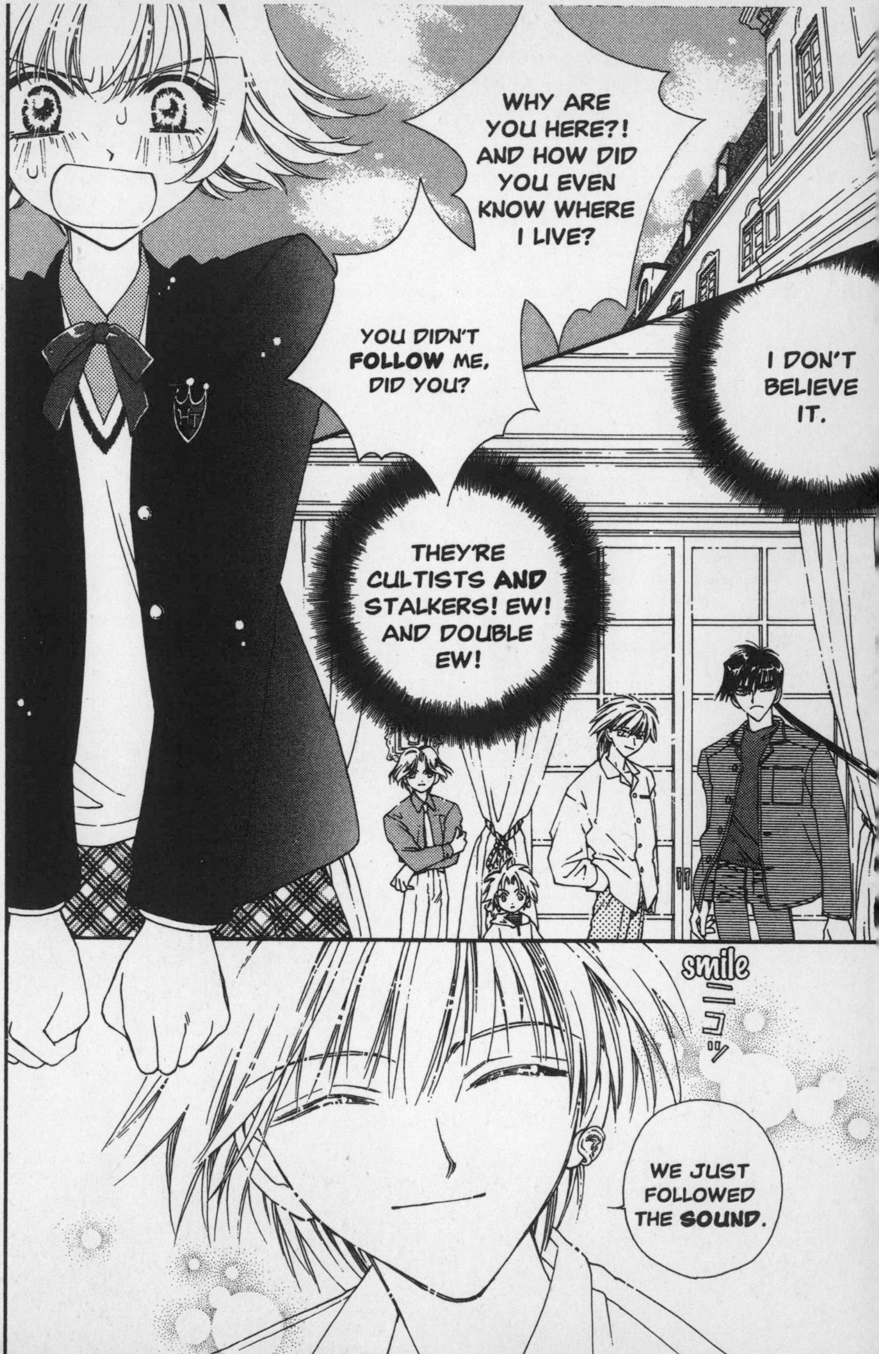
WHY ARE YOU HERE?! AND HOW DID YOU EVEN KNOW WHERE I LIVE?
I DON'T BELIEVE IT.
YOU DIDN'T **FOLLOW** ME, DID YOU?
THEY'RE CULTISTS **AND** STALKERS! EW! AND DOUBLE EW!
smile
ニコッ
WE JUST FOLLOWED THE **SOUND**.

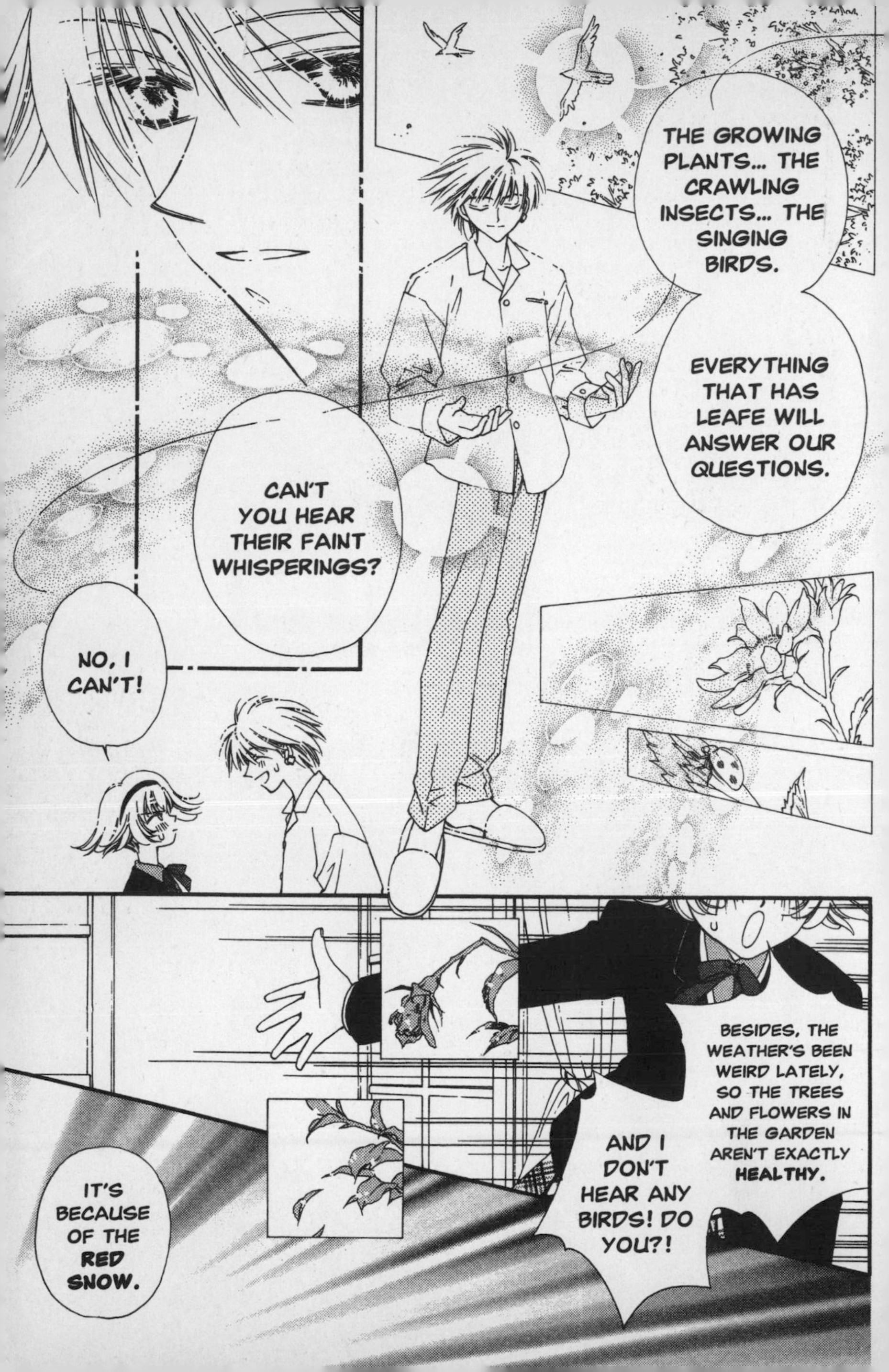
THE GROWING PLANTS... THE CRAWLING INSECTS... THE SINGING BIRDS.
EVERYTHING THAT HAS LEAFE WILL ANSWER OUR QUESTIONS.
CAN'T YOU HEAR THEIR FAINT WHISPERINGS?
NO, I CAN'T!
BESIDES, THE WEATHER'S BEEN WEIRD LATELY, SO THE TREES AND FLOWERS IN THE GARDEN AREN'T EXACTLY HEALTHY.
AND I DON'T HEAR ANY BIRDS! DO YOU?!
IT'S BECAUSE OF THE RED SNOW.

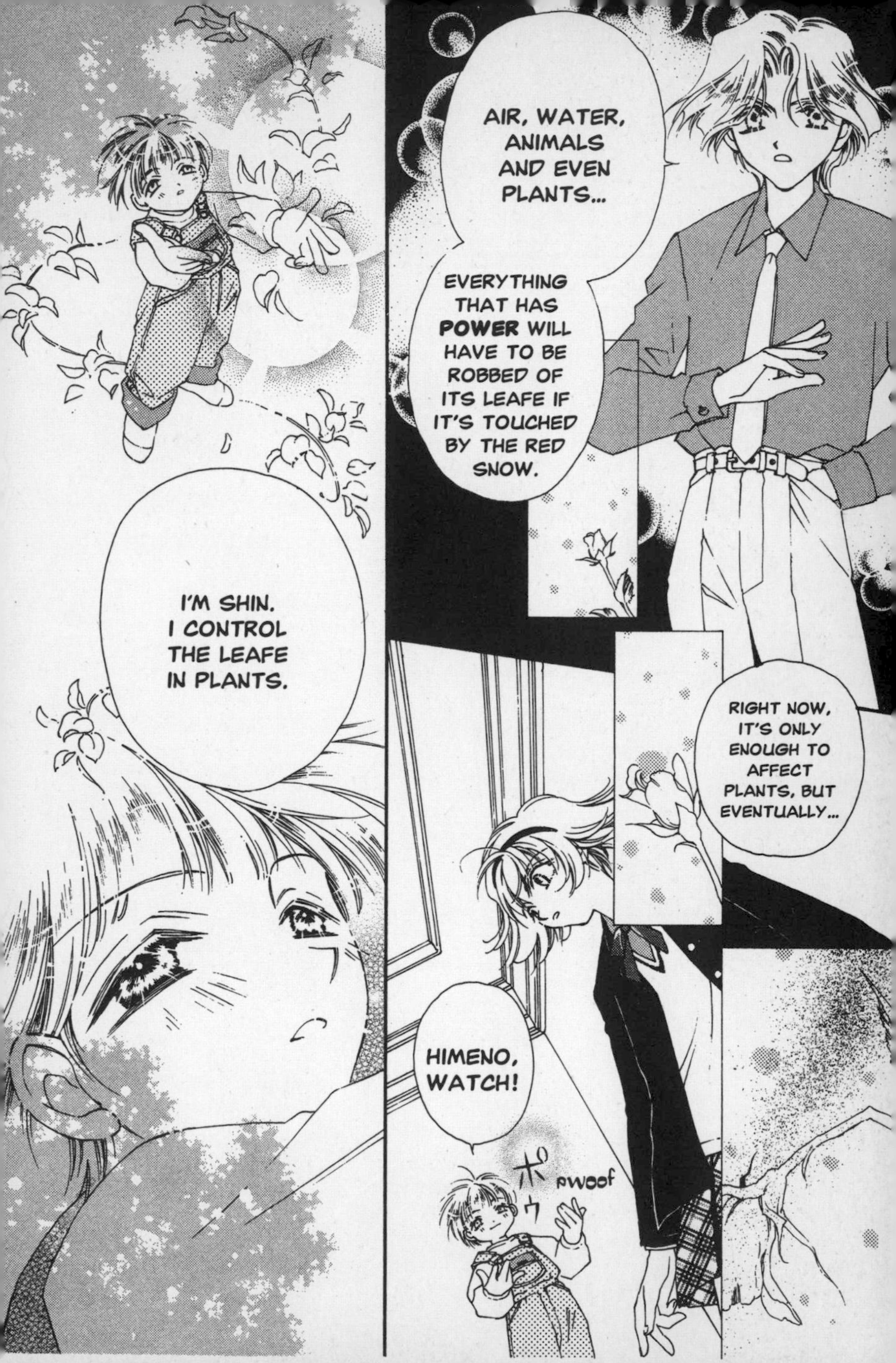
AIR, WATER, ANIMALS AND EVEN PLANTS...
EVERYTHING THAT HAS **POWER** WILL HAVE TO BE ROBBED OF ITS LEAFE IF IT'S TOUCHED BY THE RED SNOW.
RIGHT NOW, IT'S ONLY ENOUGH TO AFFECT PLANTS, BUT EVENTUALLY...
HIMENO, WATCH!
ポウ pwoof
I'M SHIN. I CONTROL THE LEAFE IN PLANTS.

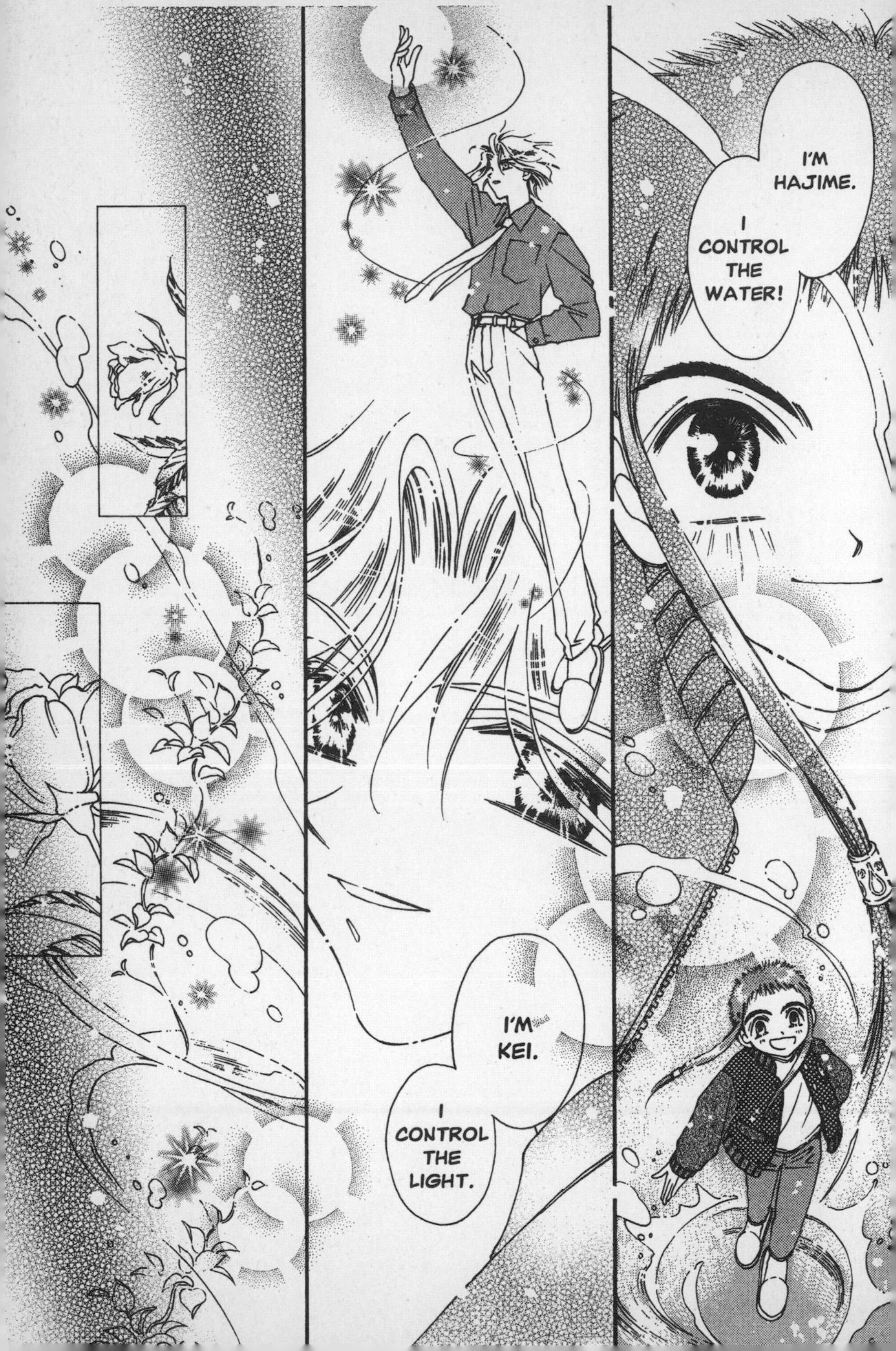
I'M HAJIME.
I CONTROL THE WATER!
I'M KEI.
I CONTROL THE LIGHT.

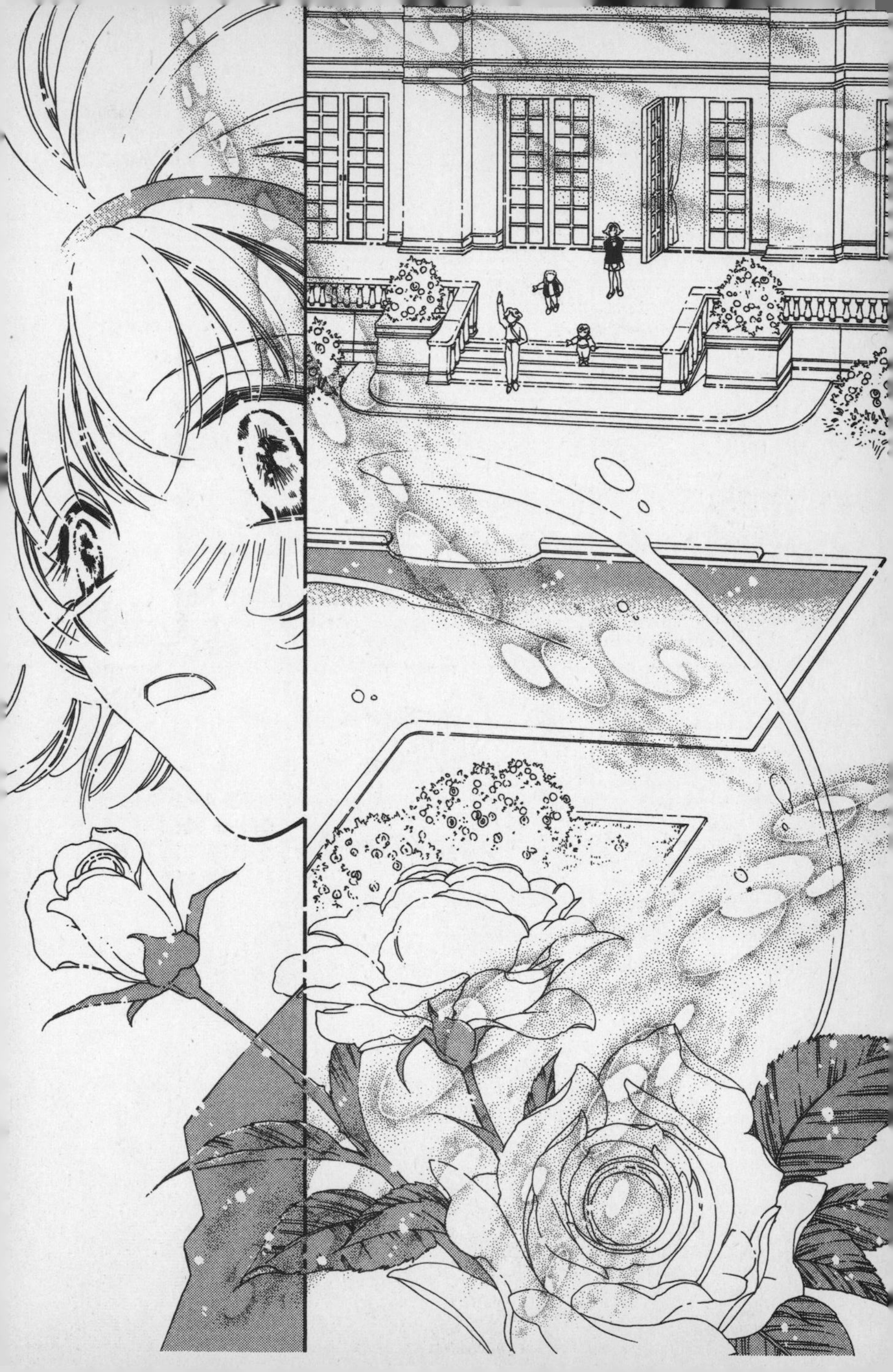

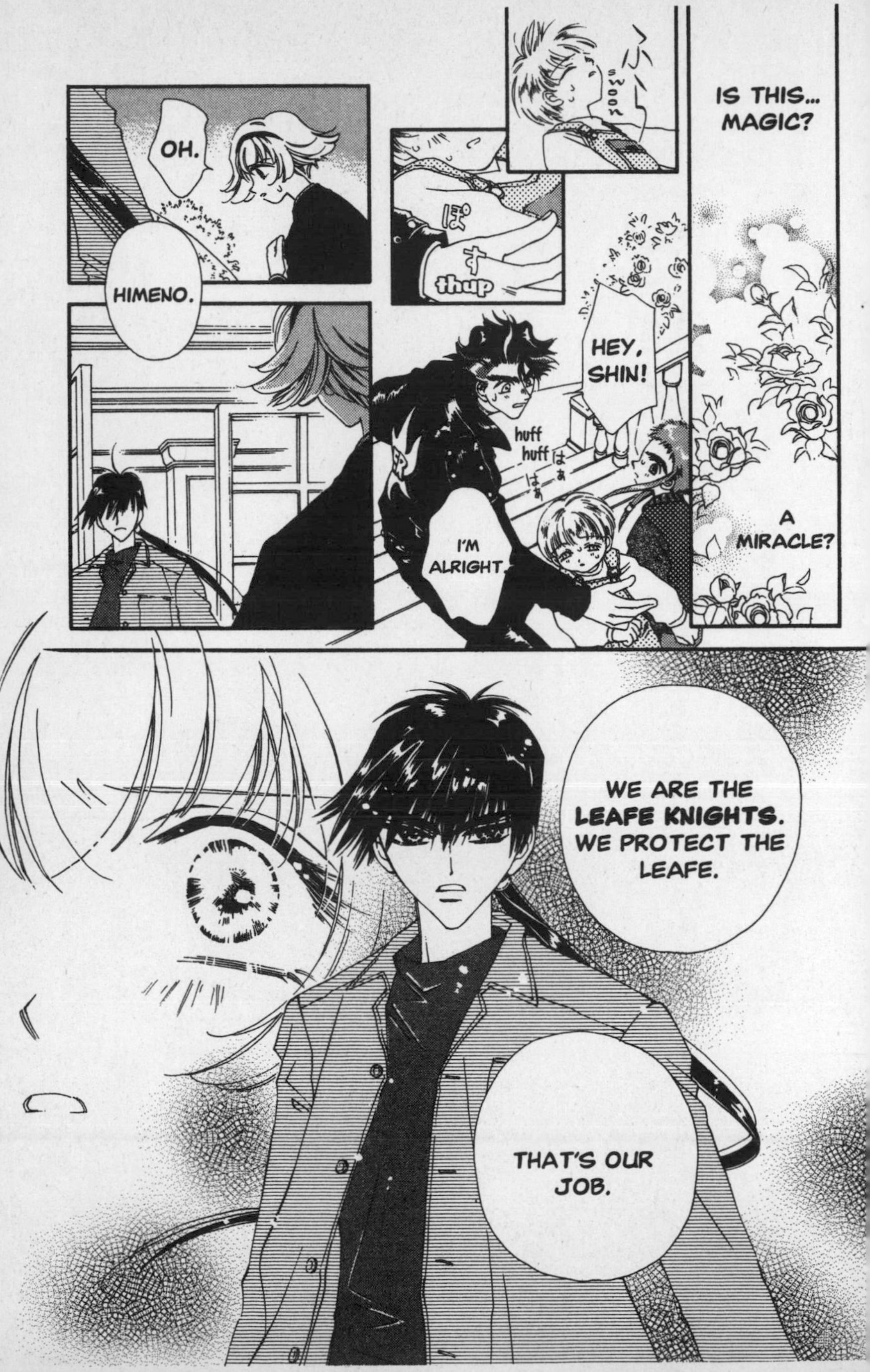
IS THIS... MAGIC?
swoon
ぽす
thup
OH.
HIMENO.
A MIRACLE?
HEY, SHIN!
huff huff
はぁ はぁ
I'M ALRIGHT.
WE ARE THE LEAFE KNIGHTS. WE PROTECT THE LEAFE.
THAT'S OUR JOB.

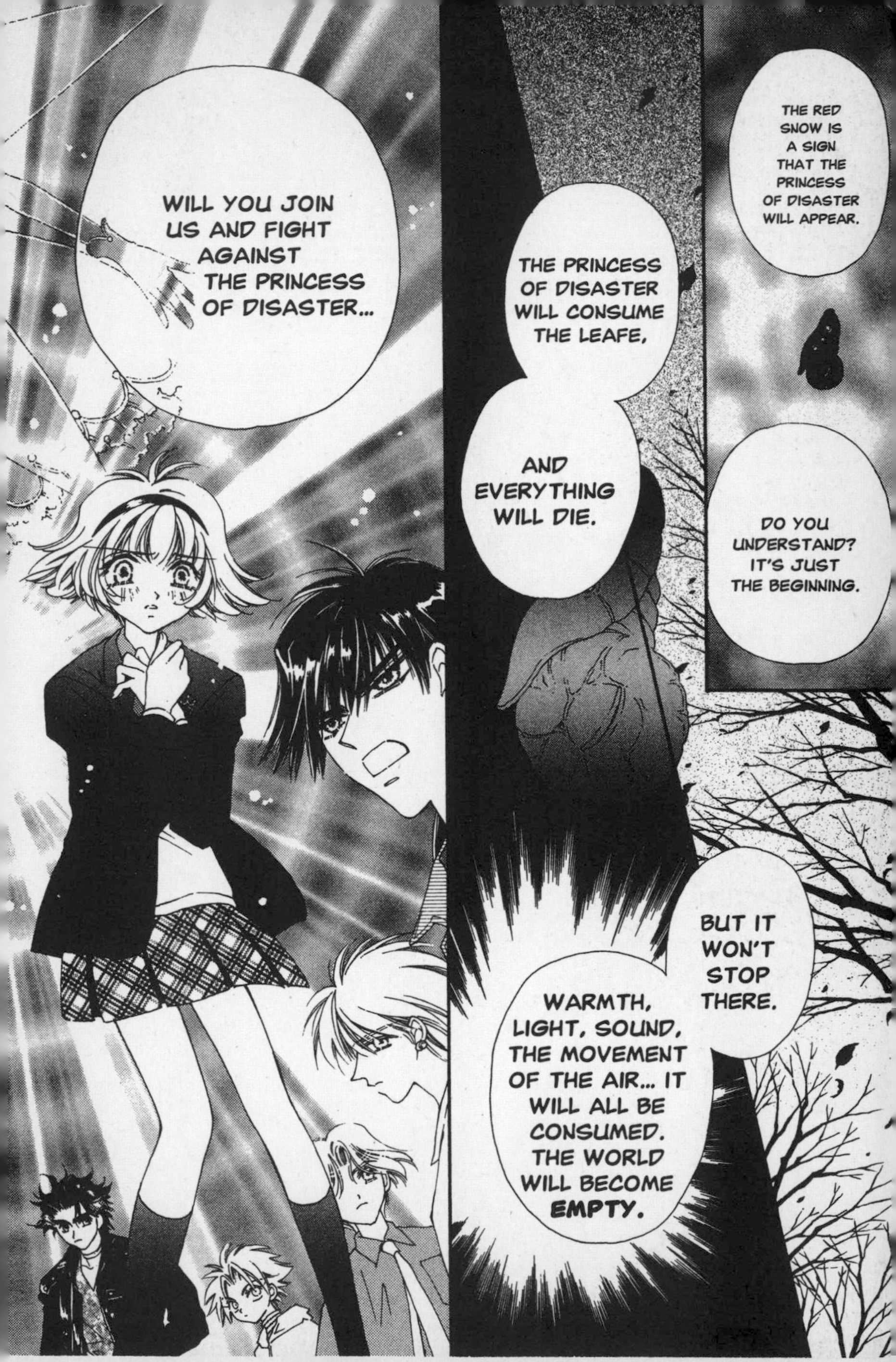
THE RED SNOW IS A SIGN THAT THE PRINCESS OF DISASTER WILL APPEAR.
DO YOU UNDERSTAND? IT'S JUST THE BEGINNING.
THE PRINCESS OF DISASTER WILL CONSUME THE LEAFE,
AND EVERYTHING WILL DIE.
BUT IT WON'T STOP THERE.
WARMTH, LIGHT, SOUND, THE MOVEMENT OF THE AIR... IT WILL ALL BE CONSUMED. THE WORLD WILL BECOME EMPTY.
WILL YOU JOIN US AND FIGHT AGAINST THE PRINCESS OF DISASTER...

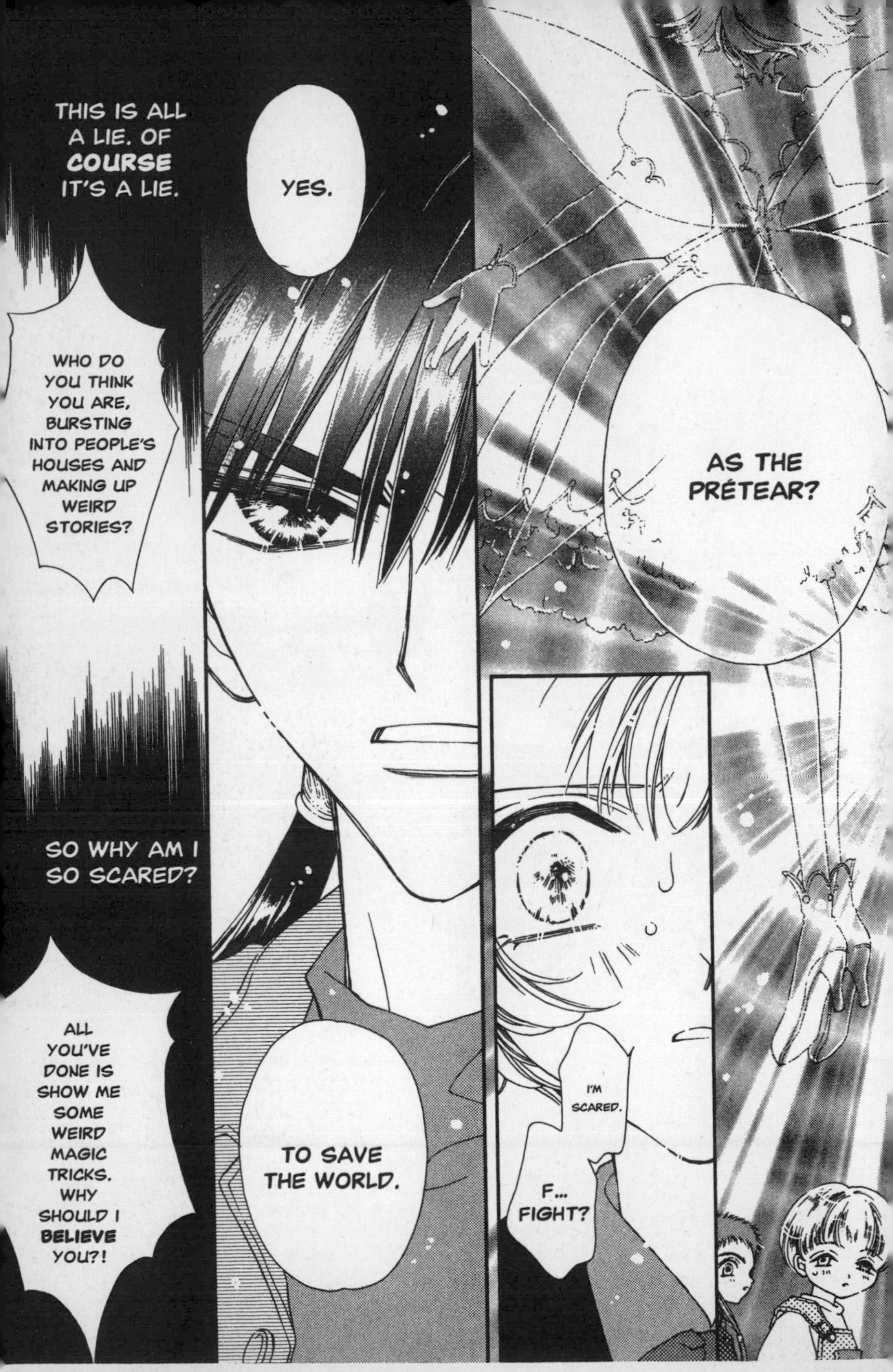
AS THE PRÉTEAR?
F... FIGHT?
I'M SCARED.
YES.
TO SAVE THE WORLD.
THIS IS ALL A LIE. OF COURSE IT'S A LIE.
WHO DO YOU THINK YOU ARE, BURSTING INTO PEOPLE'S HOUSES AND MAKING UP WEIRD STORIES?
SO WHY AM I SO SCARED?
ALL YOU'VE DONE IS SHOW ME SOME WEIRD MAGIC TRICKS. WHY SHOULD I BELIEVE YOU?!

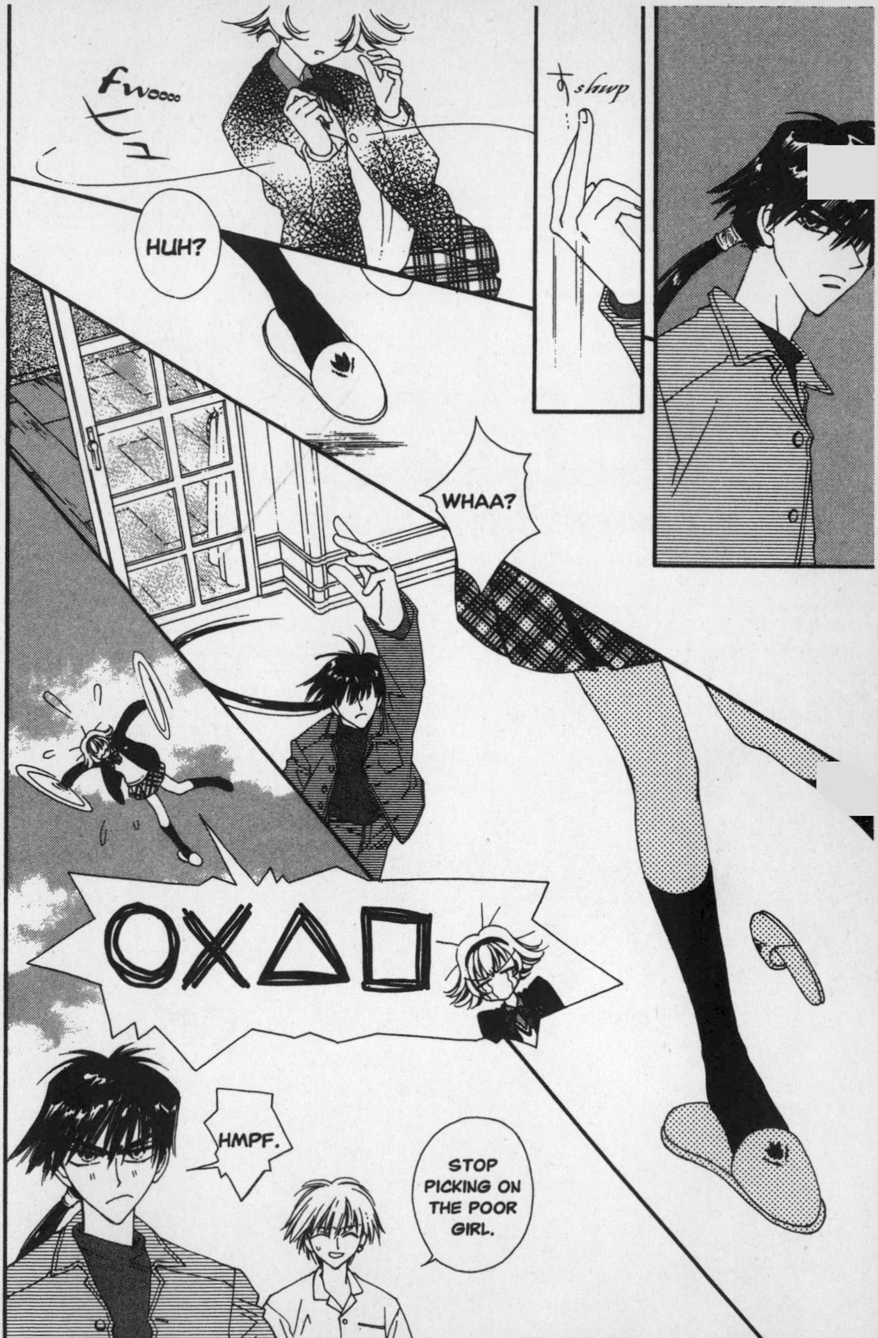

shwp
fwoooo
HUH?
WHAA?
OXΔ□
STOP PICKING ON THE POOR GIRL.
HMPF.

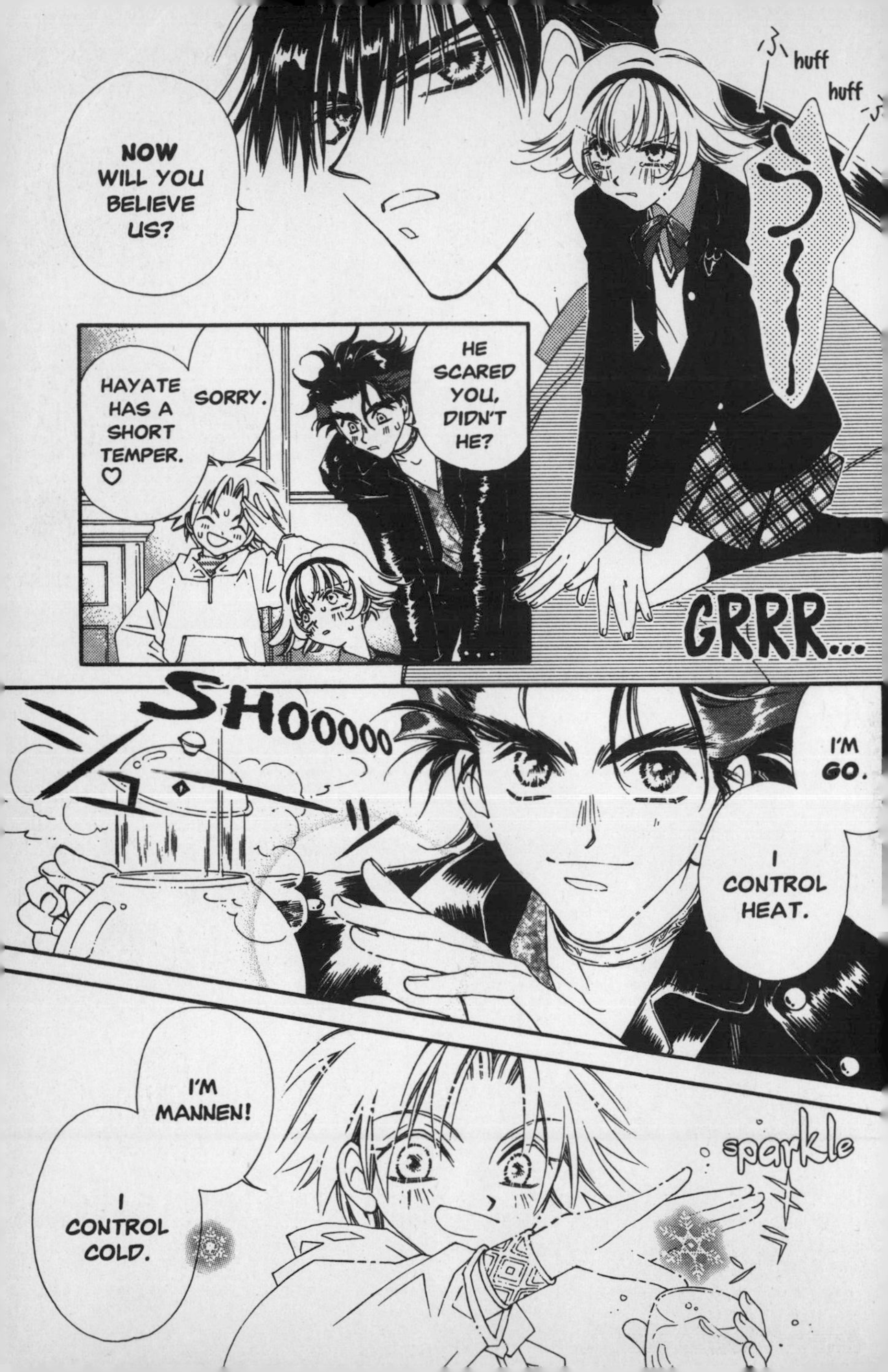
ふ huff
huff ふ
うー
NOW WILL YOU BELIEVE US?
GRRR...
HE SCARED YOU, DIDN'T HE?
SORRY.
HAYATE HAS A SHORT TEMPER. ♡
SHOOOOOO
I'M GO.
I CONTROL HEAT.
sparkle
I'M MANNEN!
I CONTROL COLD.

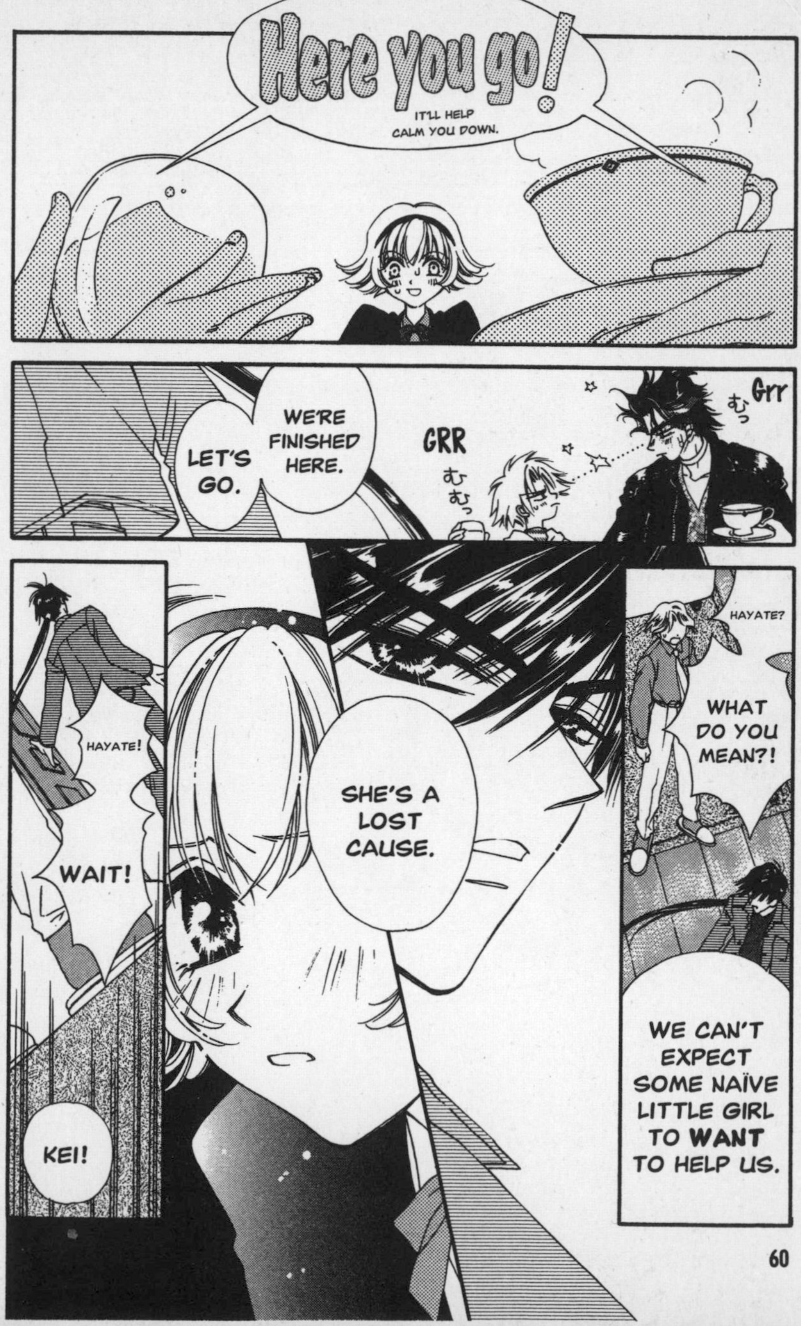
Here you go!
IT'LL HELP CALM YOU DOWN.
Grr
むっ
GRR
むむっ
WE'RE FINISHED HERE.
LET'S GO.
HAYATE?
WHAT DO YOU MEAN?!
WE CAN'T EXPECT SOME NAÏVE LITTLE GIRL TO WANT TO HELP US.
SHE'S A LOST CAUSE.
HAYATE!
WAIT!
KEI!

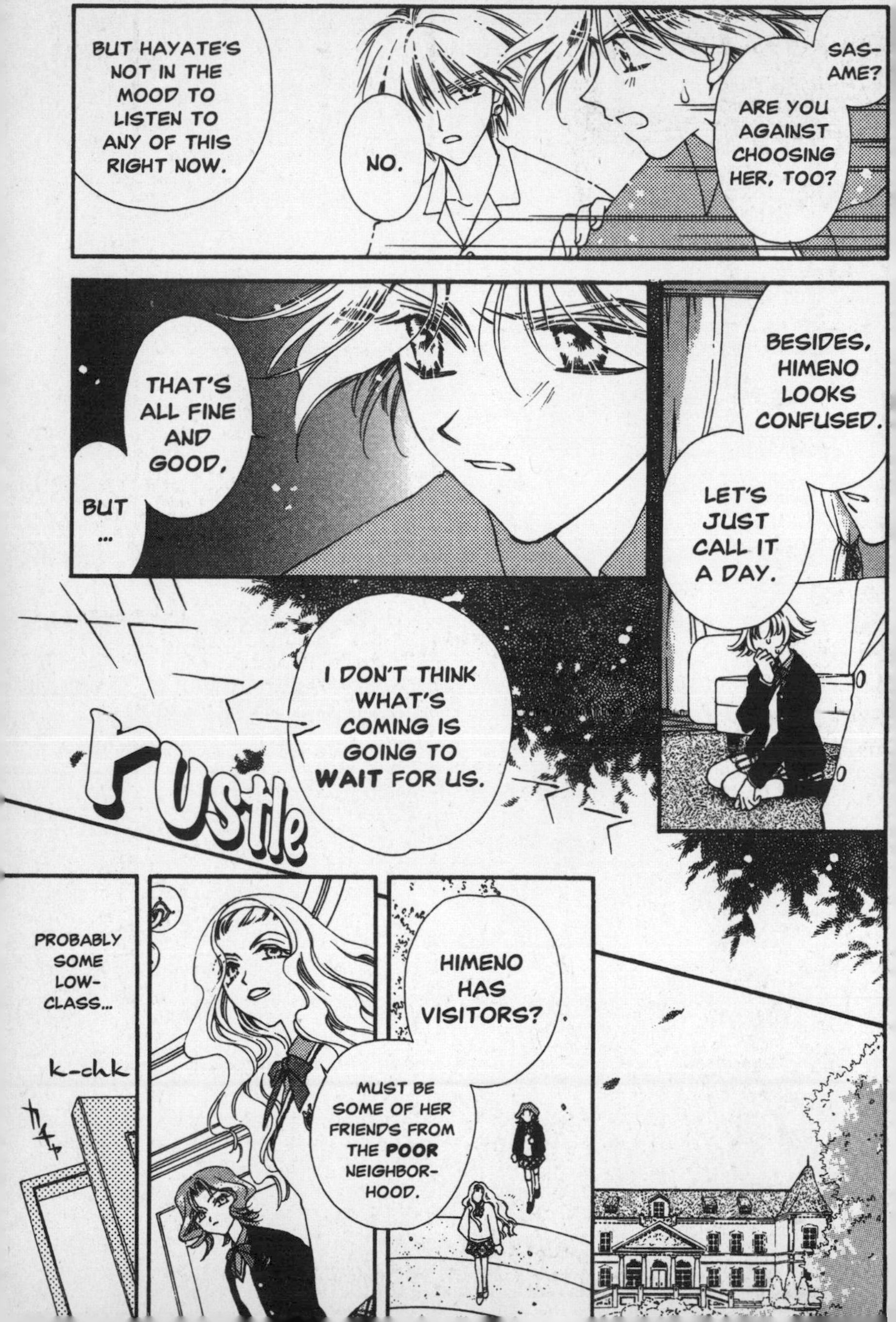
SAS-AME?
ARE YOU AGAINST CHOOSING HER, TOO?
NO.
BUT HAYATE'S NOT IN THE MOOD TO LISTEN TO ANY OF THIS RIGHT NOW.
BESIDES, HIMENO LOOKS CONFUSED.
LET'S JUST CALL IT A DAY.
THAT'S ALL FINE AND GOOD,
BUT ...
I DON'T THINK WHAT'S COMING IS GOING TO WAIT FOR US.
rustle
HIMENO HAS VISITORS?
MUST BE SOME OF HER FRIENDS FROM THE POOR NEIGHBOR-HOOD.
PROBABLY SOME LOW-CLASS...
k-chk

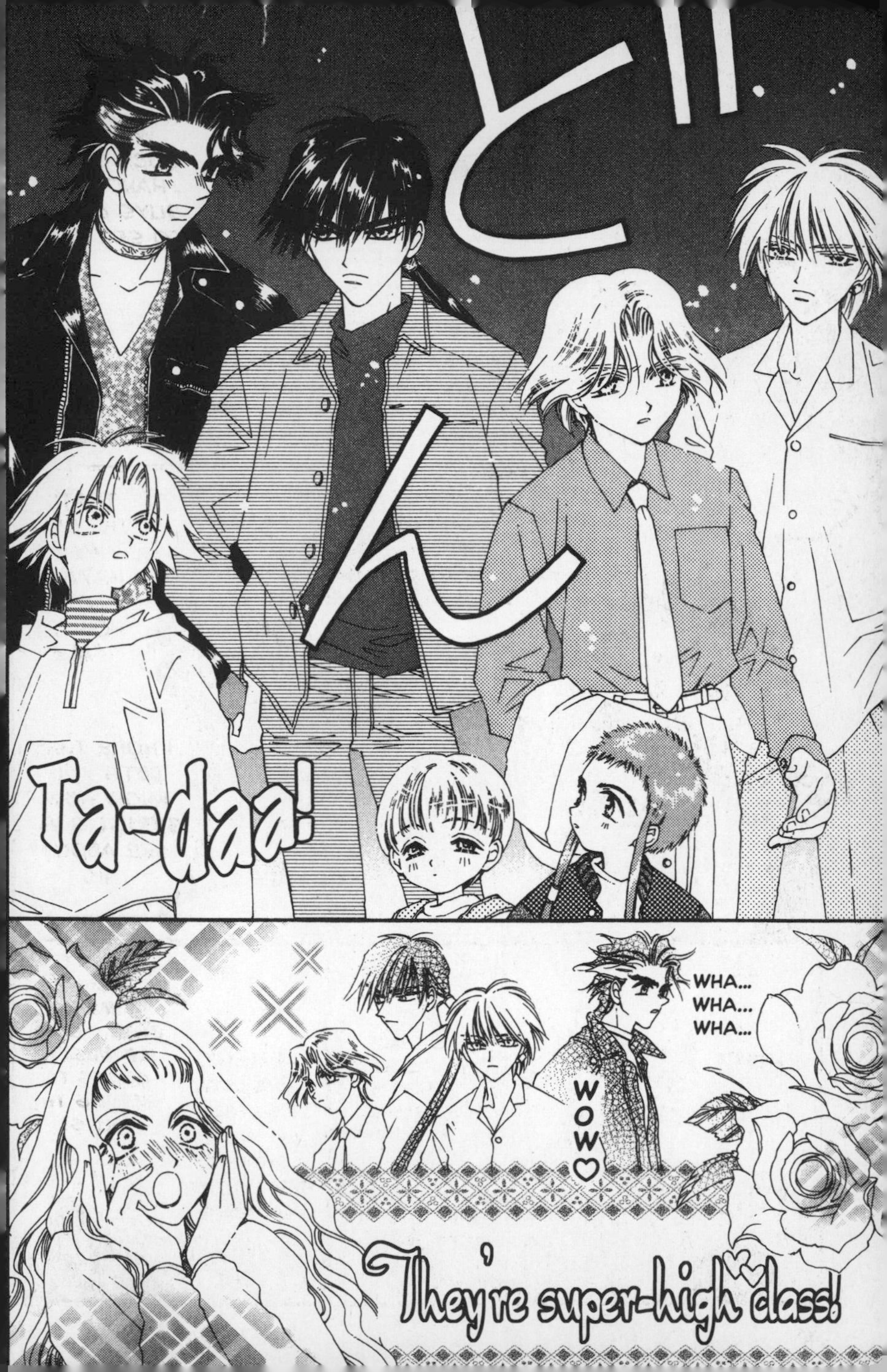
どーん
Ta-daa!
WHA... WHA... WHA...
WOW♡
They're super-high class!

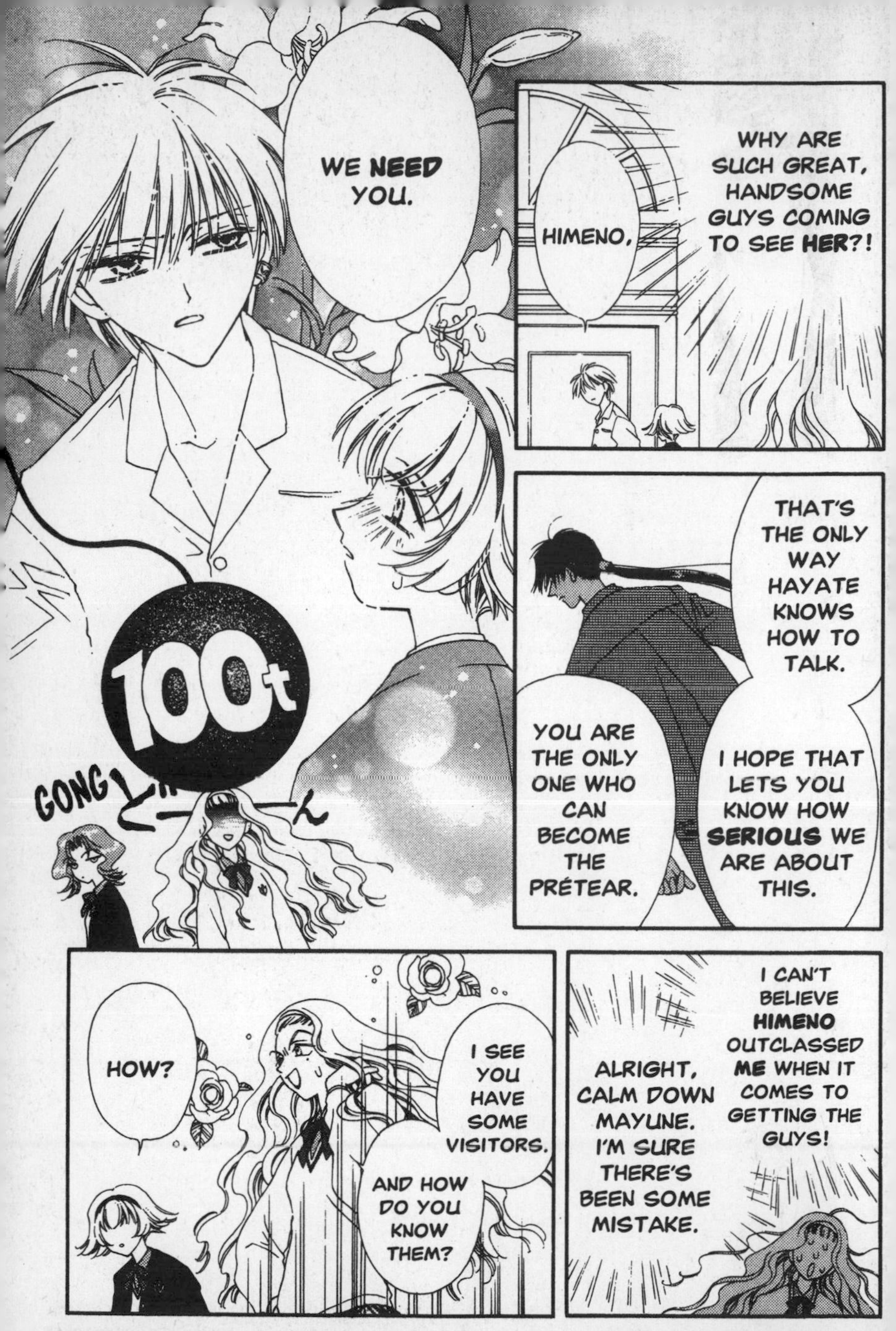
WHY ARE SUCH GREAT, HANDSOME GUYS COMING TO SEE HER?!
HIMENO,
WE NEED YOU.
THAT'S THE ONLY WAY HAYATE KNOWS HOW TO TALK.
I HOPE THAT LETS YOU KNOW HOW SERIOUS WE ARE ABOUT THIS.
YOU ARE THE ONLY ONE WHO CAN BECOME THE PRÉTEAR.
100t
GONG
I CAN'T BELIEVE HIMENO OUTCLASSED ME WHEN IT COMES TO GETTING THE GUYS!
ALRIGHT, CALM DOWN MAYUNE. I'M SURE THERE'S BEEN SOME MISTAKE.
I SEE YOU HAVE SOME VISITORS.
AND HOW DO YOU KNOW THEM?
HOW?

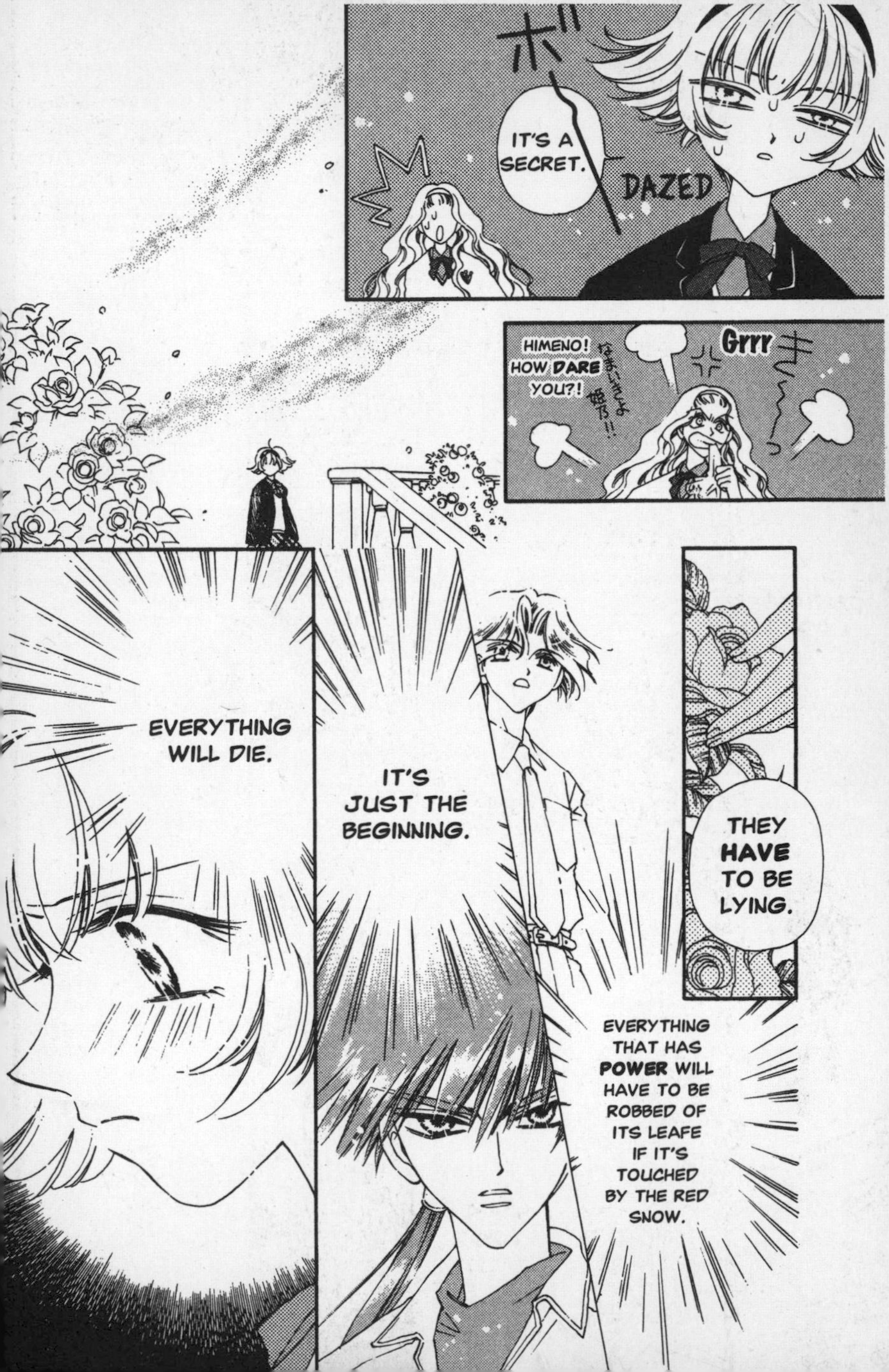
IT'S A SECRET.
DAZED
Grrr
HIMENO! HOW DARE YOU?!
THEY HAVE TO BE LYING.
IT'S JUST THE BEGINNING.
EVERYTHING THAT HAS POWER WILL HAVE TO BE ROBBED OF ITS LEAFE IF IT'S TOUCHED BY THE RED SNOW.
EVERYTHING WILL DIE.

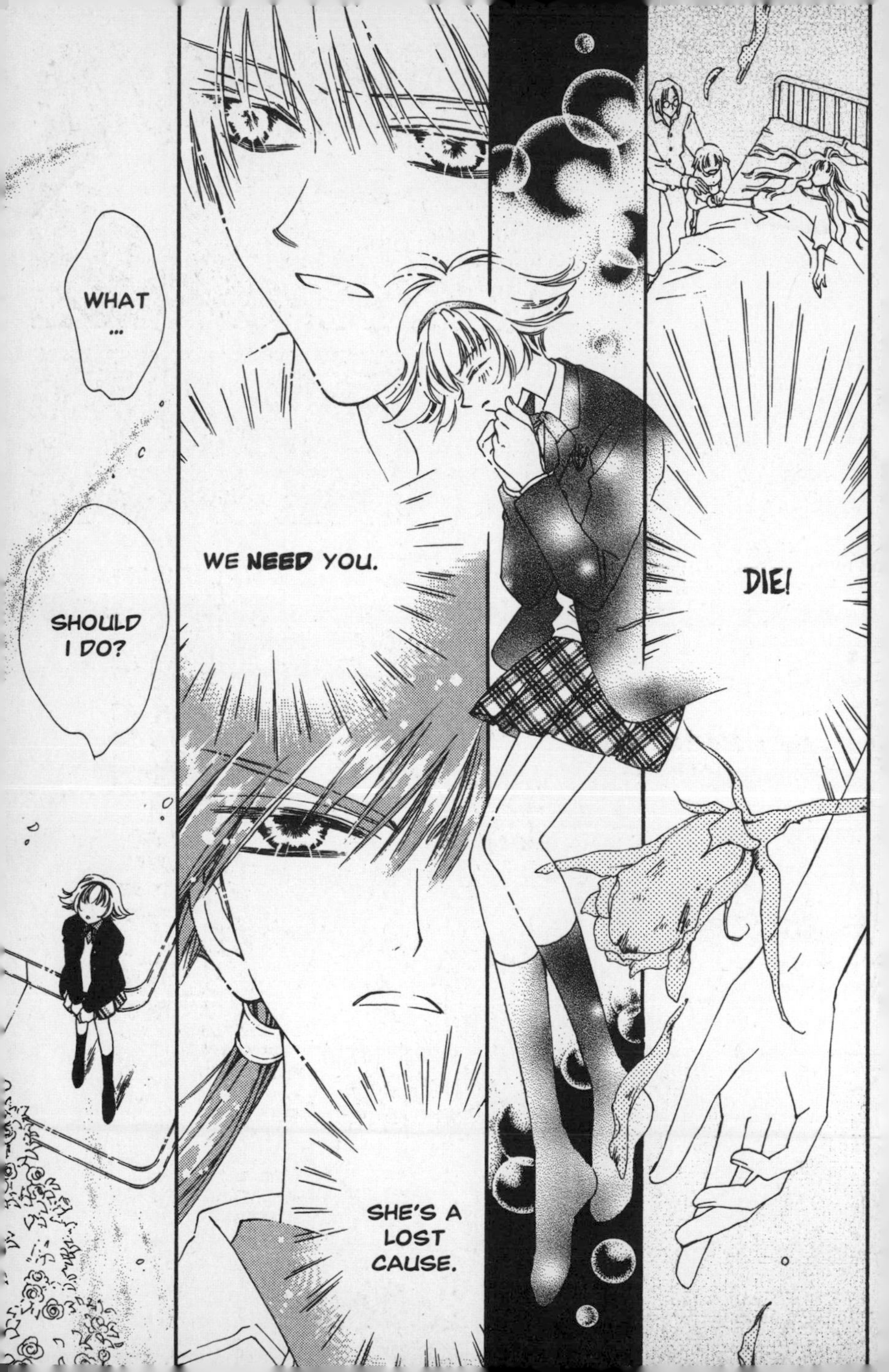
DIE!
WE NEED YOU.
SHE'S A LOST CAUSE.
WHAT ...
SHOULD I DO?

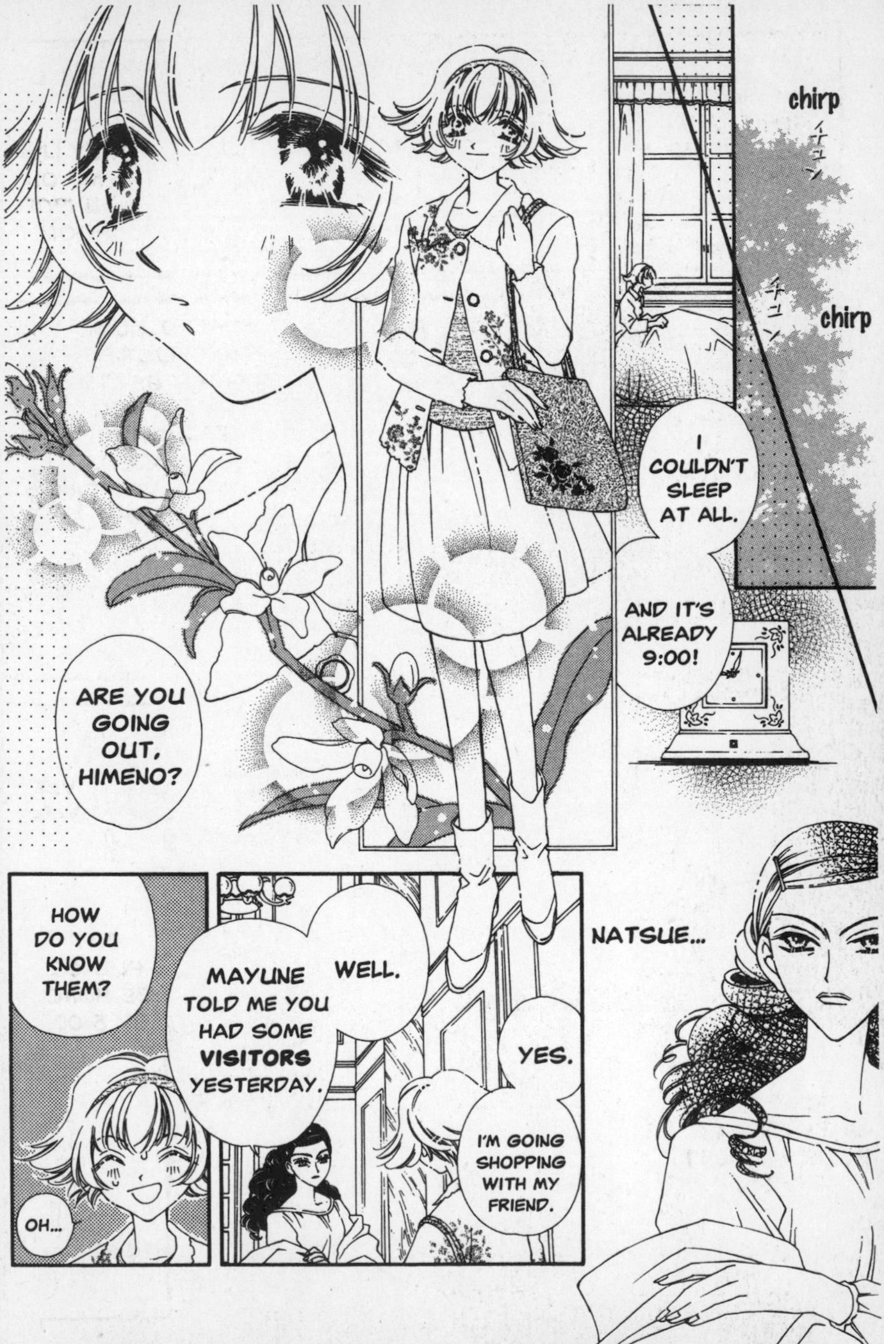
chirp
chirp
I COULDN'T SLEEP AT ALL.
AND IT'S ALREADY 9:00!
ARE YOU GOING OUT, HIMENO?
NATSUE...
YES.
I'M GOING SHOPPING WITH MY FRIEND.
WELL.
MAYUNE TOLD ME YOU HAD SOME **VISITORS** YESTERDAY.
HOW DO YOU KNOW THEM?
OH...

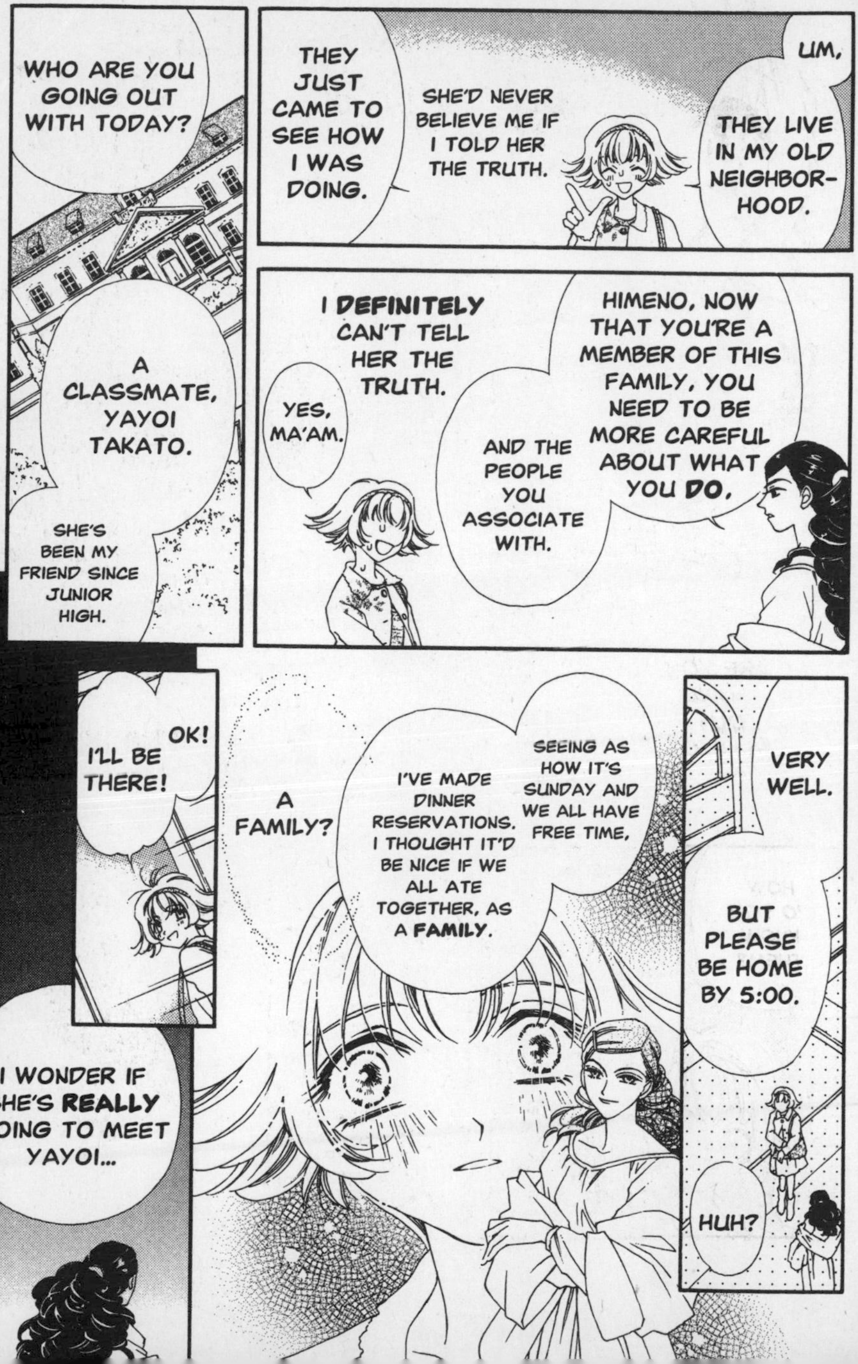
UM,
THEY LIVE IN MY OLD NEIGHBOR-HOOD.
SHE'D NEVER BELIEVE ME IF I TOLD HER THE TRUTH.
THEY JUST CAME TO SEE HOW I WAS DOING.
HIMENO, NOW THAT YOU'RE A MEMBER OF THIS FAMILY, YOU NEED TO BE MORE CAREFUL ABOUT WHAT YOU DO,
AND THE PEOPLE YOU ASSOCIATE WITH.
YES, MA'AM.
I DEFINITELY CAN'T TELL HER THE TRUTH.
WHO ARE YOU GOING OUT WITH TODAY?
A CLASSMATE, YAYOI TAKATO.
SHE'S BEEN MY FRIEND SINCE JUNIOR HIGH.
VERY WELL.
BUT PLEASE BE HOME BY 5:00.
HUH?
SEEING AS HOW IT'S SUNDAY AND WE ALL HAVE FREE TIME,
I'VE MADE DINNER RESERVATIONS. I THOUGHT IT'D BE NICE IF WE ALL ATE TOGETHER, AS A FAMILY.
A FAMILY?
OK! I'LL BE THERE!
I WONDER IF SHE'S REALLY GOING TO MEET YAYOI...

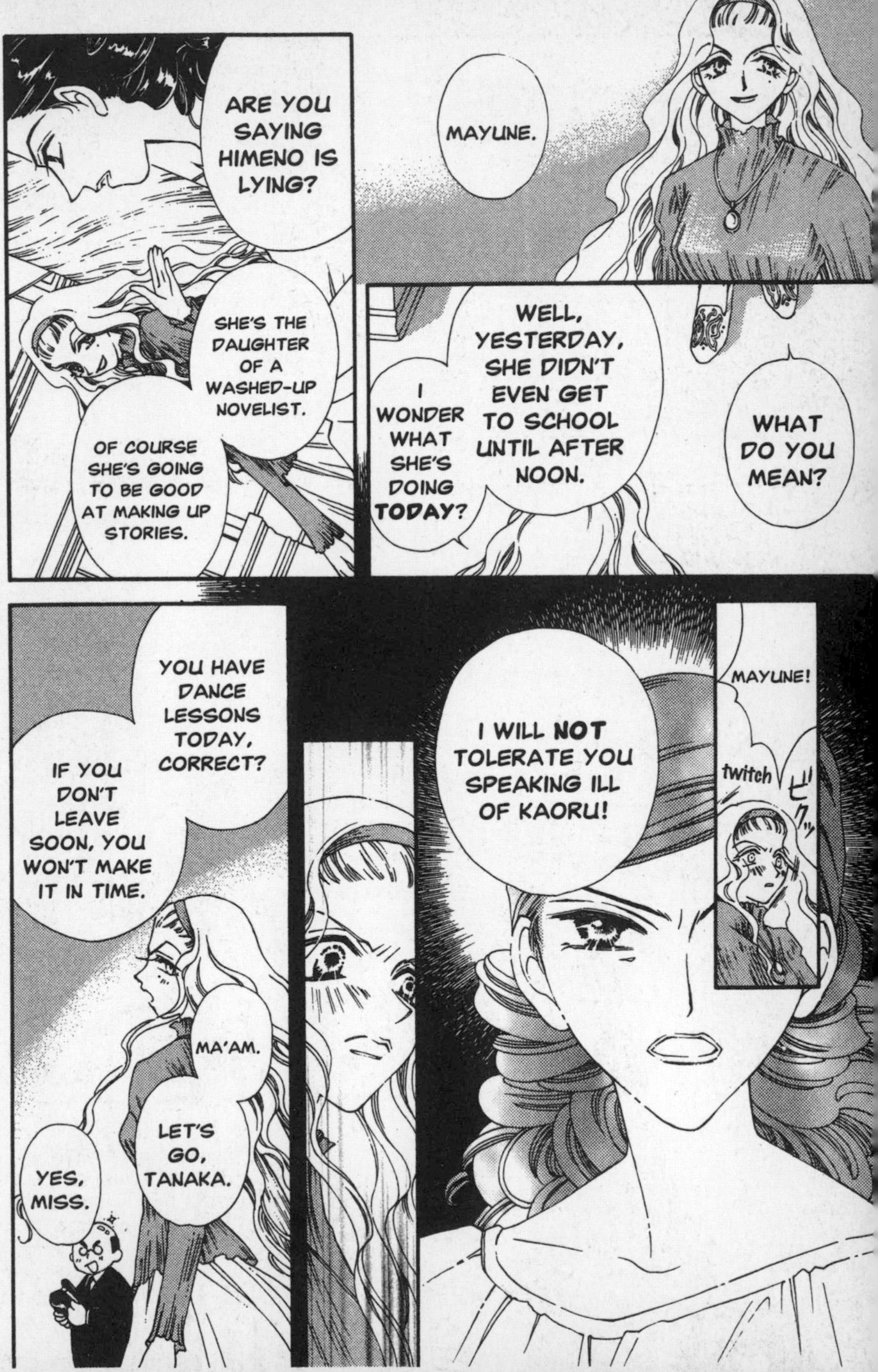
MAYUNE.
WHAT DO YOU MEAN?
WELL, YESTERDAY, SHE DIDN'T EVEN GET TO SCHOOL UNTIL AFTER NOON.
I WONDER WHAT SHE'S DOING **TODAY**?
ARE YOU SAYING HIMENO IS LYING?
SHE'S THE DAUGHTER OF A WASHED-UP NOVELIST.
OF COURSE SHE'S GOING TO BE GOOD AT MAKING UP STORIES.
MAYUNE!
twitch
ビクッ
I WILL **NOT** TOLERATE YOU SPEAKING ILL OF KAORU!
YOU HAVE DANCE LESSONS TODAY, CORRECT?
IF YOU DON'T LEAVE SOON, YOU WON'T MAKE IT IN TIME.
MA'AM.
LET'S GO, TANAKA.
YES, MISS.

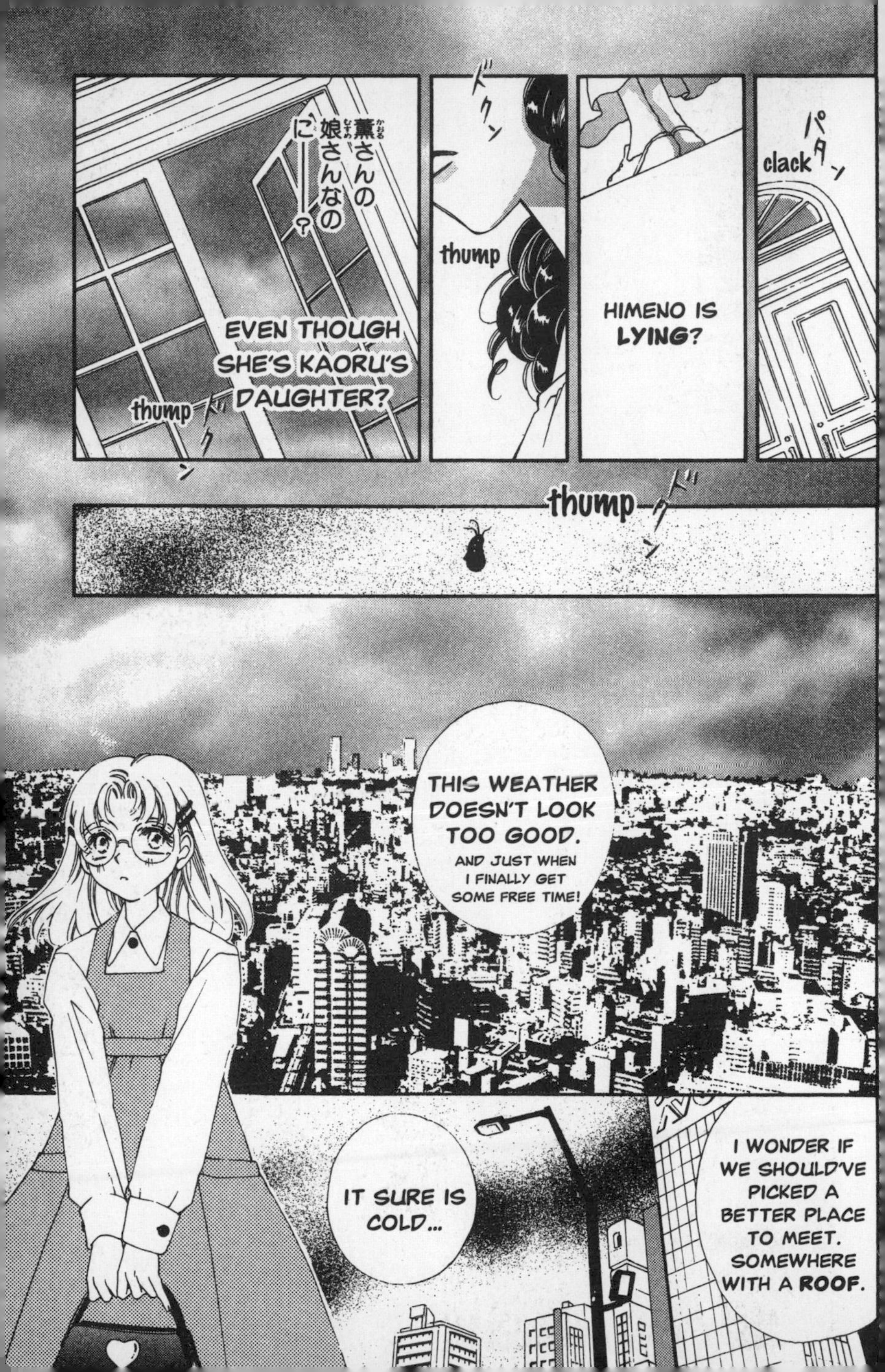
clack
パタン
HIMENO IS LYING?
thump
ドクン
薫さんの娘さんなのに――?
EVEN THOUGH SHE'S KAORU'S DAUGHTER?
thump
ドクン
thump
ドクン
THIS WEATHER DOESN'T LOOK TOO GOOD.
AND JUST WHEN I FINALLY GET SOME FREE TIME!
I WONDER IF WE SHOULD'VE PICKED A BETTER PLACE TO MEET. SOMEWHERE WITH A ROOF.
IT SURE IS COLD...

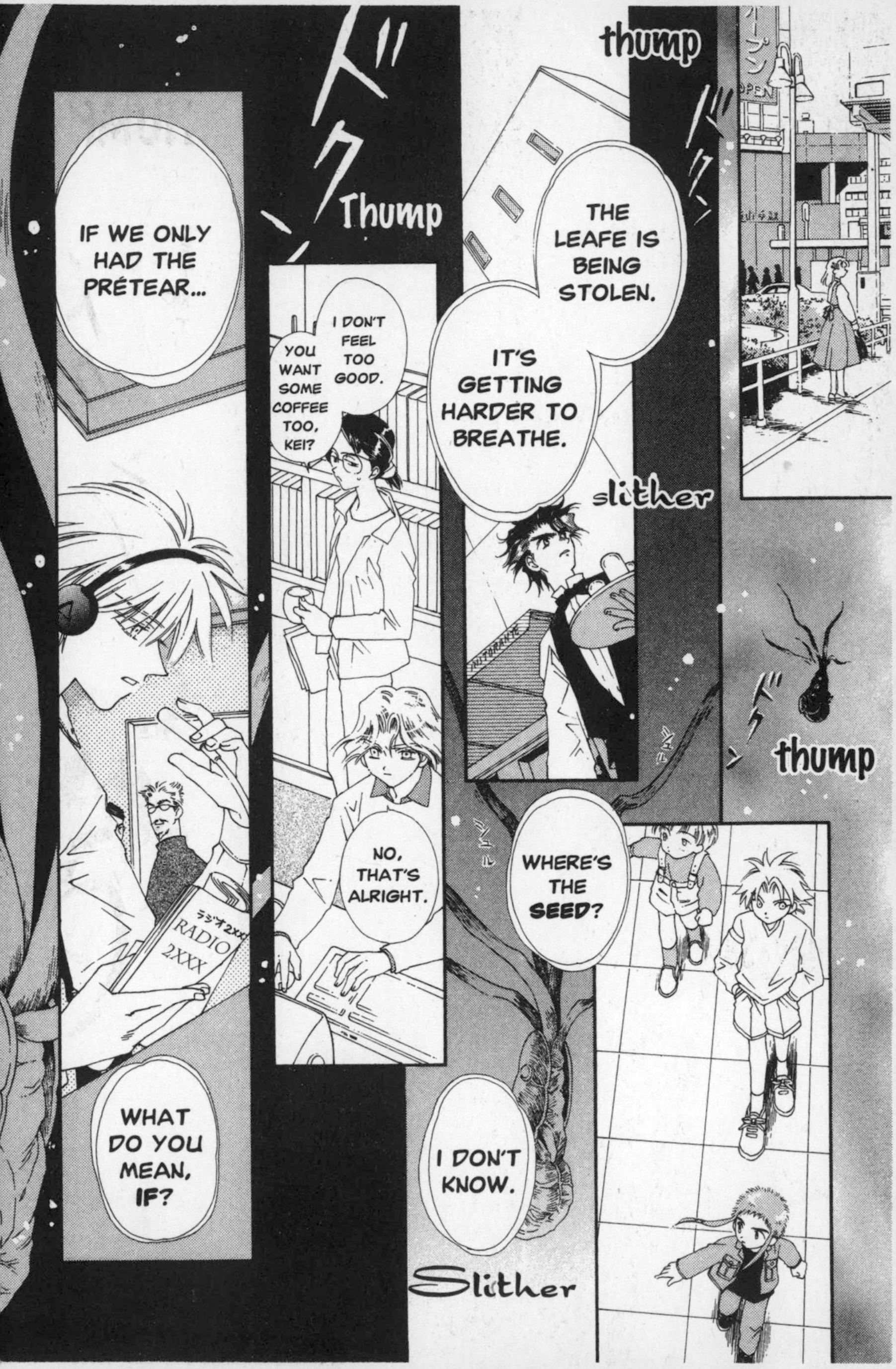
thump
THE LEAFE IS BEING STOLEN.
IT'S GETTING HARDER TO BREATHE.
slither
Thump
I DON'T FEEL TOO GOOD.
YOU WANT SOME COFFEE TOO, KEI?
NO, THAT'S ALRIGHT.
IF WE ONLY HAD THE PRÉTEAR...
RADIO 2XXX
WHAT DO YOU MEAN, IF?
thump
WHERE'S THE SEED?
I DON'T KNOW.
Slither

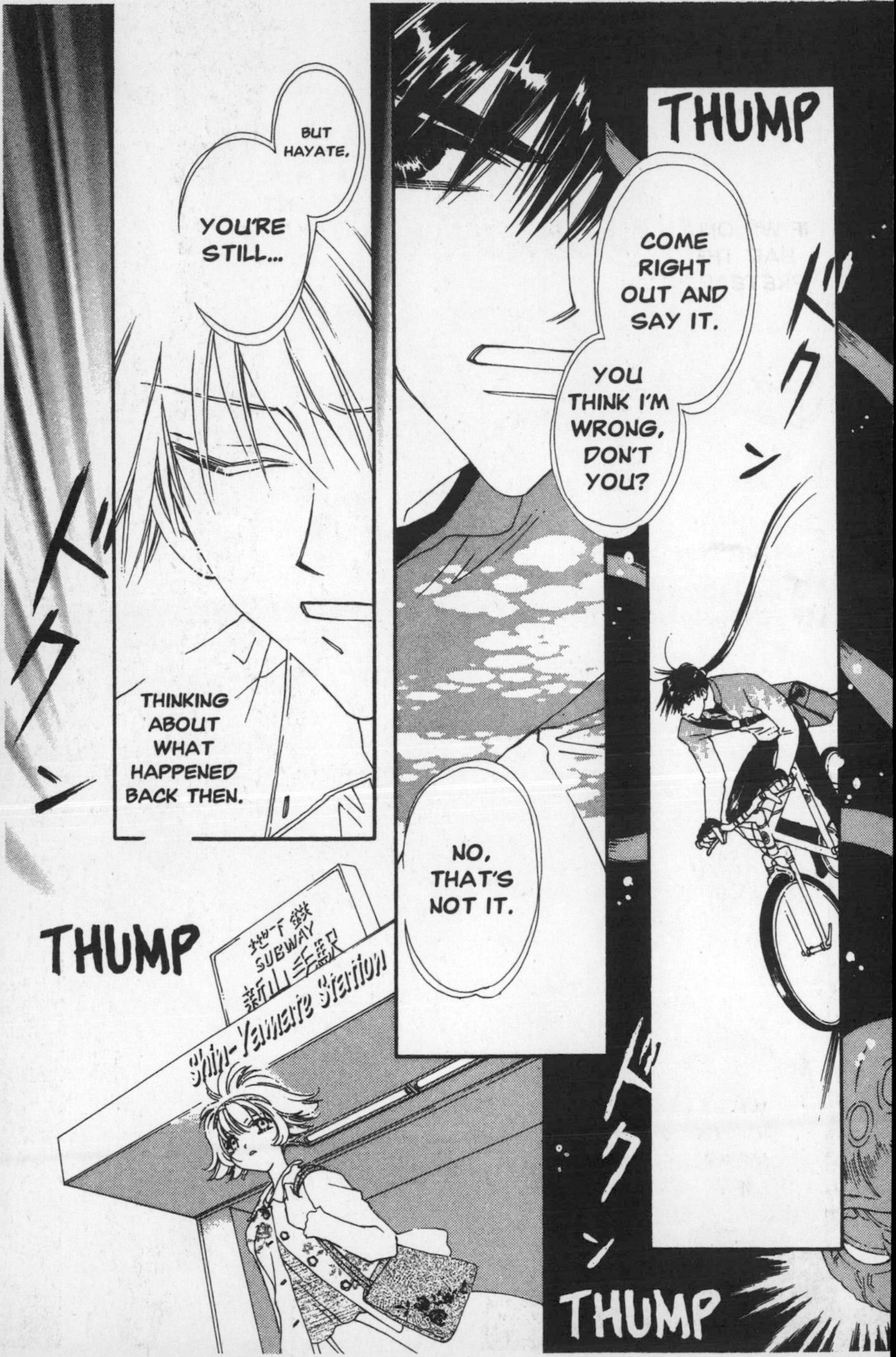
THUMP
ドクン
COME RIGHT OUT AND SAY IT.
YOU THINK I'M WRONG, DON'T YOU?
BUT HAYATE,
YOU'RE STILL...
THINKING ABOUT WHAT HAPPENED BACK THEN.
ドクン
NO, THAT'S NOT IT.
ドクン
THUMP
THUMP
地下鉄
SUBWAY
新山手駅
Shin-Yamate Station

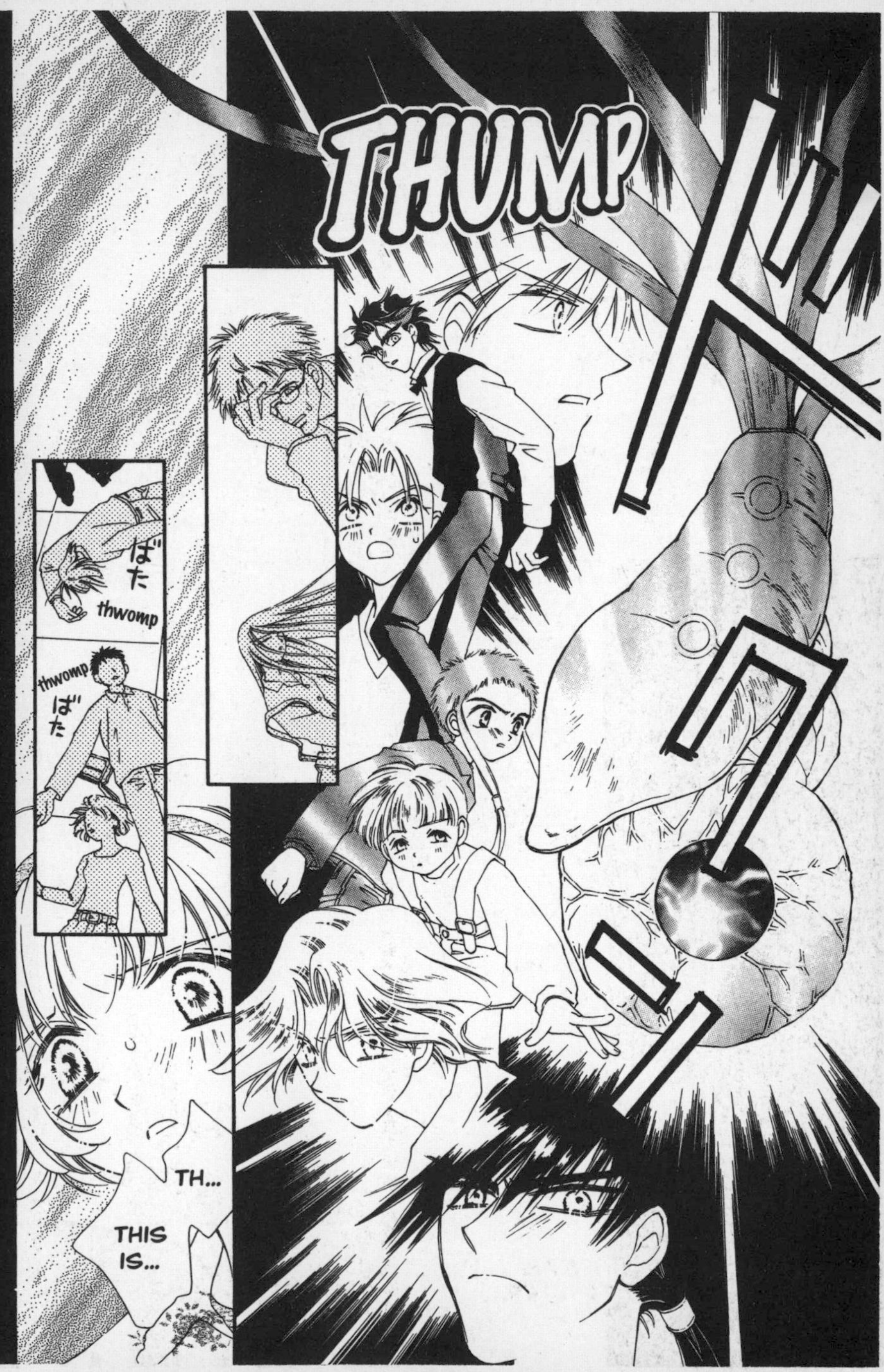

THUMP
ばた
thwomp
thwomp
ばた
TH...
THIS IS...

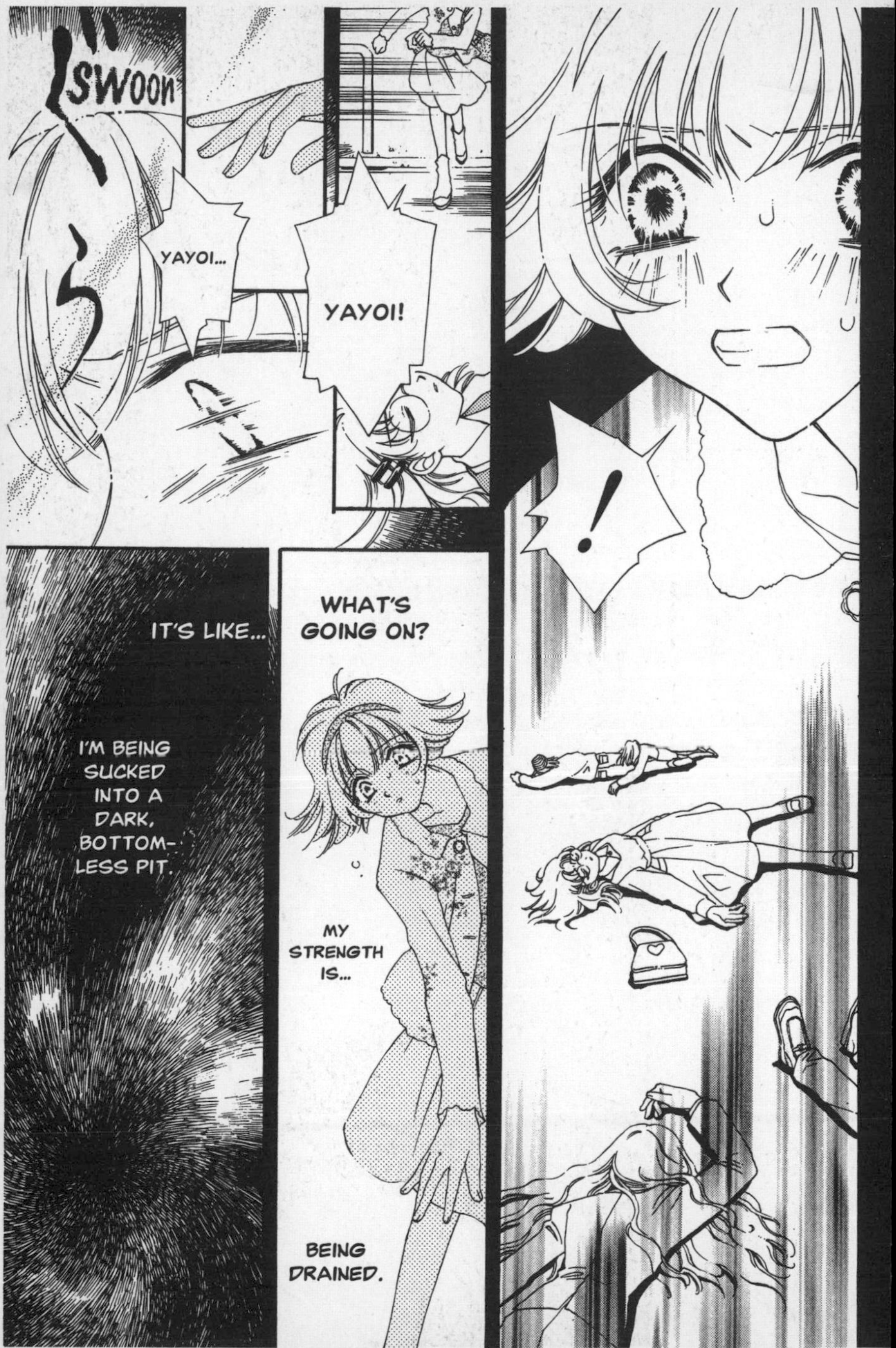
SWOON
YAYOI!
YAYOI...
!
WHAT'S GOING ON?
IT'S LIKE...
I'M BEING SUCKED INTO A DARK, BOTTOMLESS PIT.
MY STRENGTH IS...
BEING DRAINED.

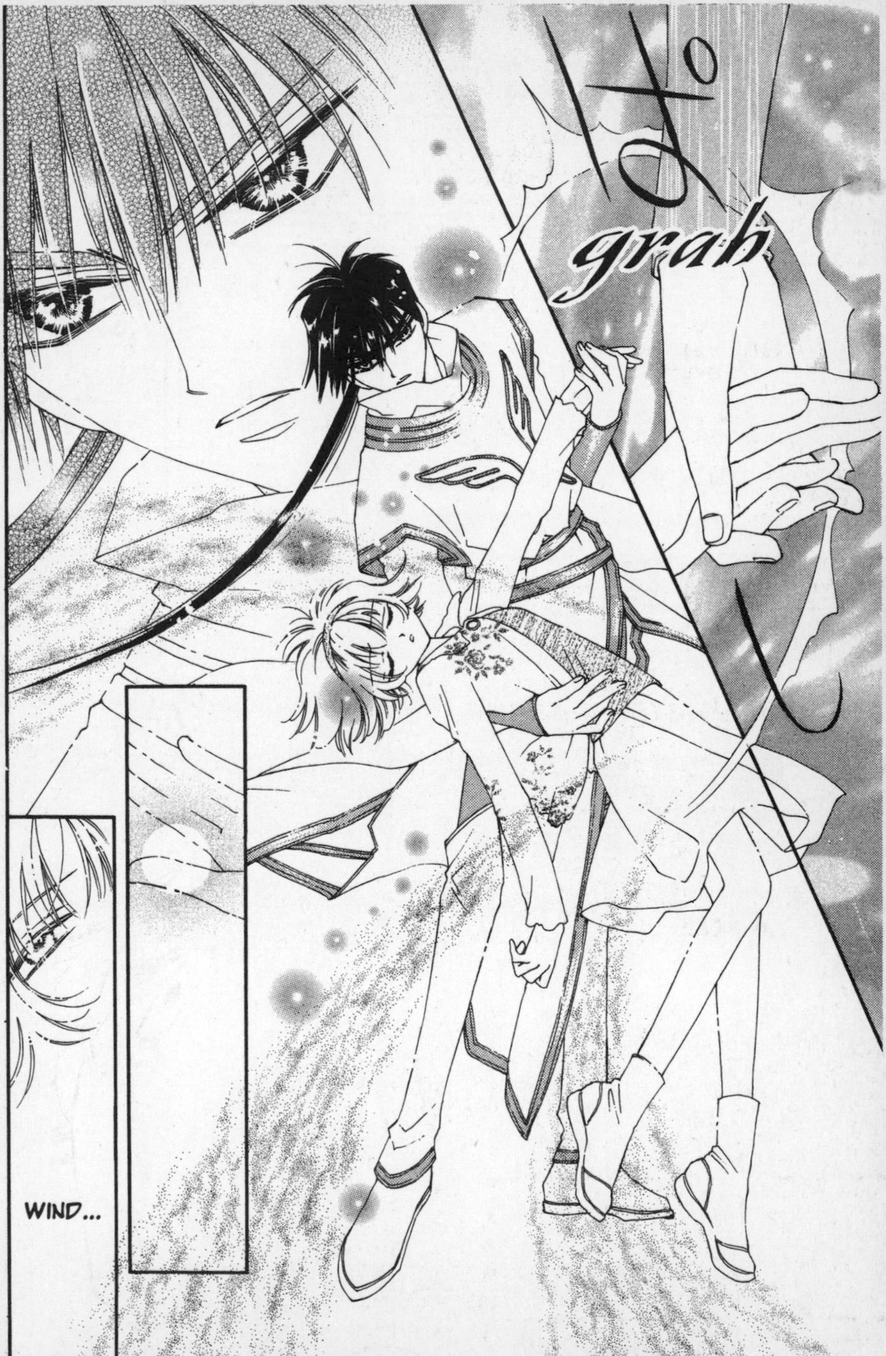
grab
WIND...

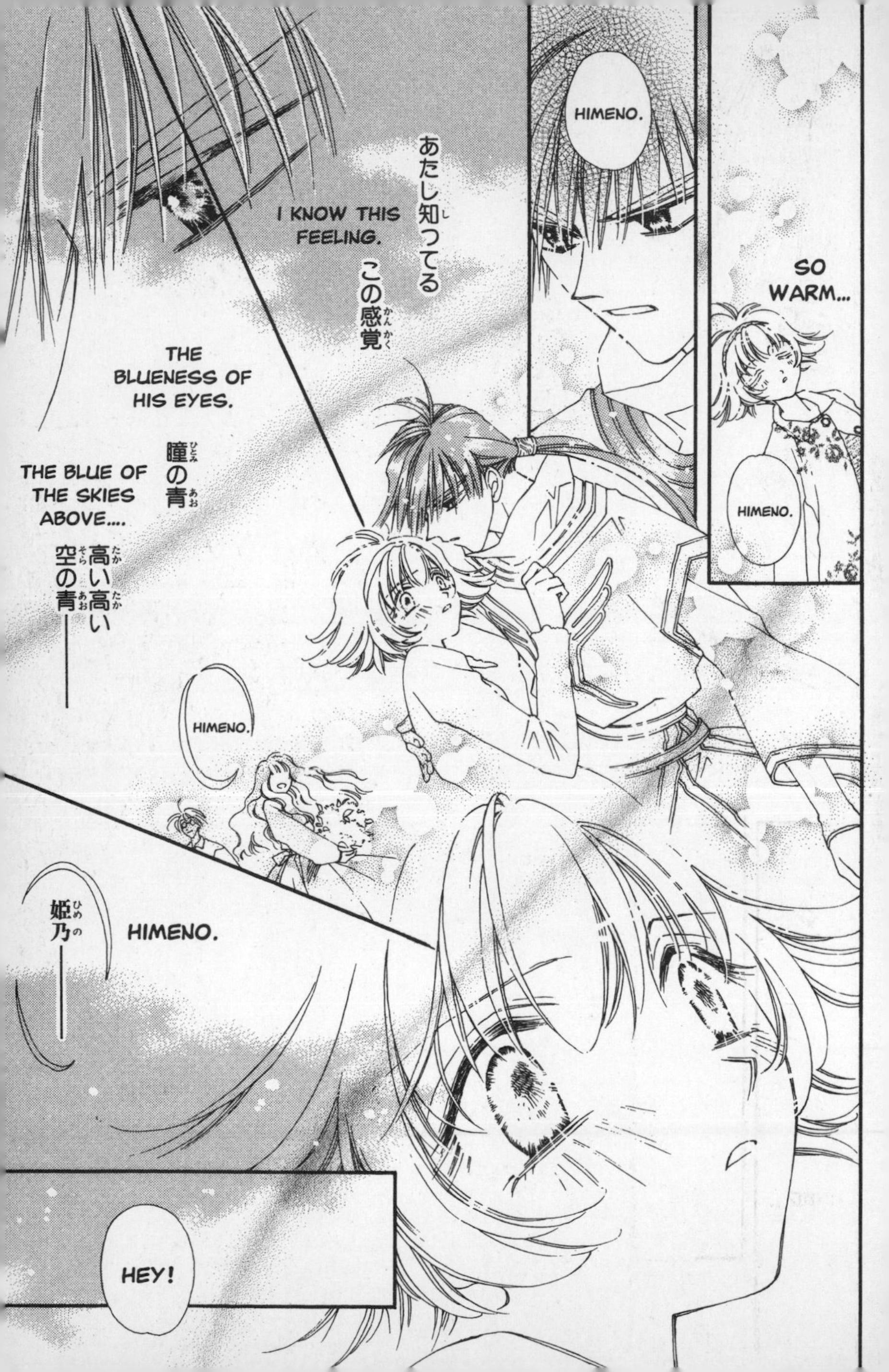

HIMENO.
SO WARM...
HIMENO.
あたし知ってる
I KNOW THIS FEELING.
この感覚
THE BLUENESS OF HIS EYES.
瞳の青
THE BLUE OF THE SKIES ABOVE....
高い高い空の青——
HIMENO.
姫乃——
HIMENO.
HEY!

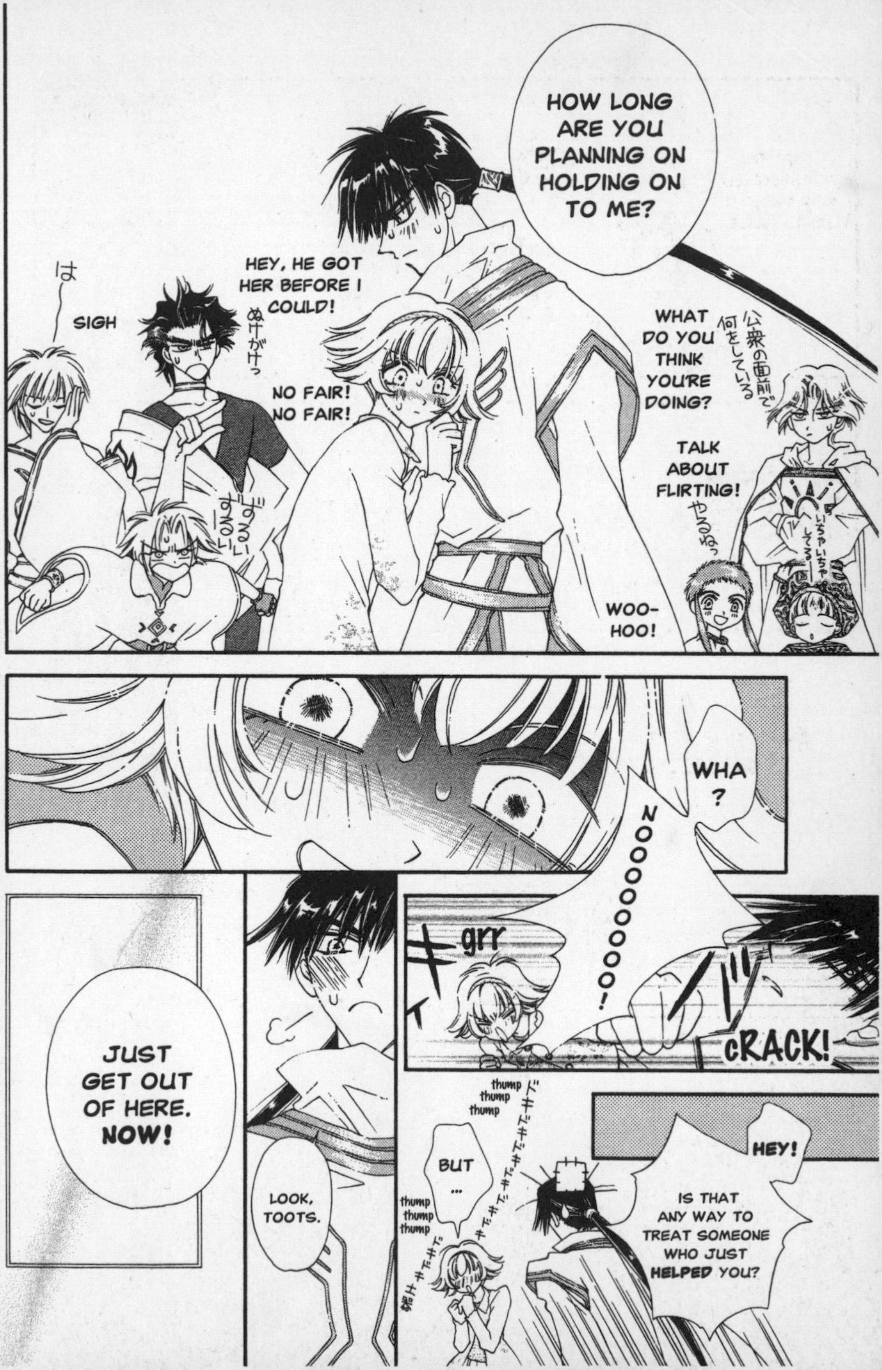
HOW LONG ARE YOU PLANNING ON HOLDING ON TO ME?
WHAT DO YOU THINK YOU'RE DOING?
公衆の面前で何をしている
TALK ABOUT FLIRTING!
いちゃいちゃしてる
やるねっ
WOO-HOO!
HEY, HE GOT HER BEFORE I COULD!
ぬけがけっ
NO FAIR! NO FAIR!
ずるいずるい
SIGH
は～
WHA?
NOOOOOOOOOO!
grr
CRACK!
JUST GET OUT OF HERE. NOW!
LOOK, TOOTS.
HEY!
IS THAT ANY WAY TO TREAT SOMEONE WHO JUST HELPED YOU?
thump thump thump
BUT ...
thump thump thump

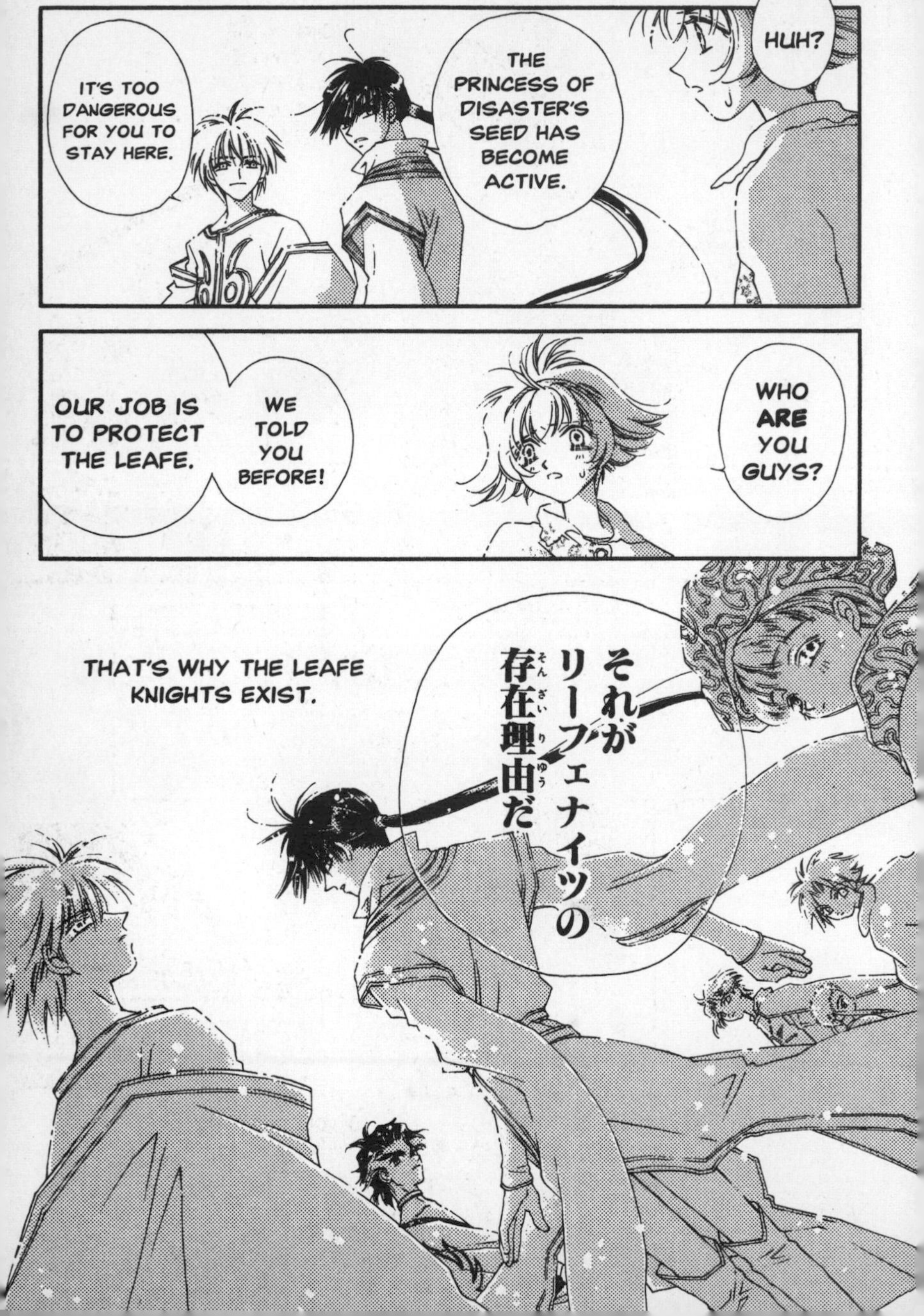
HUH?
THE PRINCESS OF DISASTER'S SEED HAS BECOME ACTIVE.
IT'S TOO DANGEROUS FOR YOU TO STAY HERE.
WHO ARE YOU GUYS?
WE TOLD YOU BEFORE!
OUR JOB IS TO PROTECT THE LEAFE.
それがリーフェナイツの存在理由だ
THAT'S WHY THE LEAFE KNIGHTS EXIST.

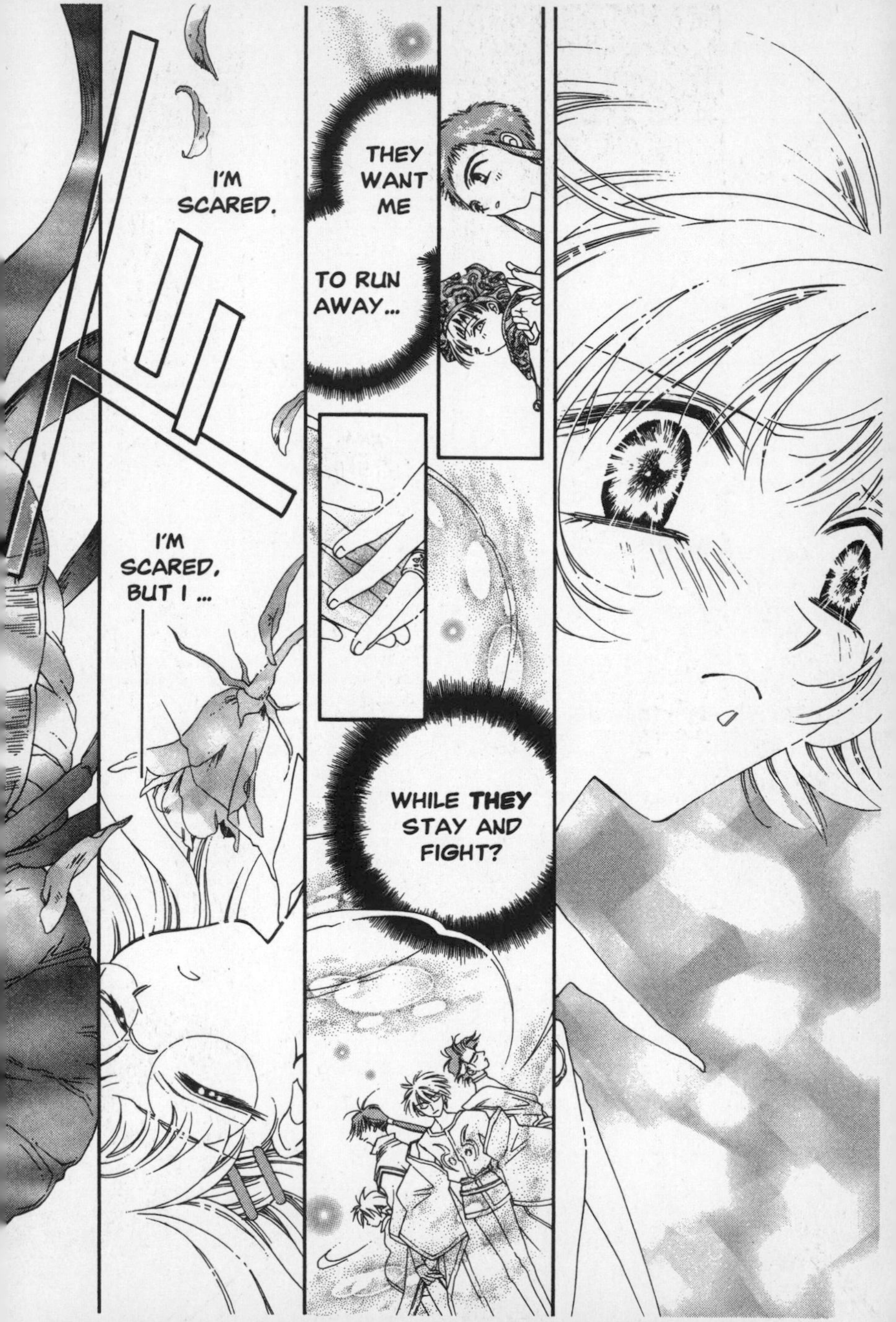
THEY WANT ME
TO RUN AWAY...
WHILE THEY STAY AND FIGHT?
I'M SCARED.
I'M SCARED, BUT I ...

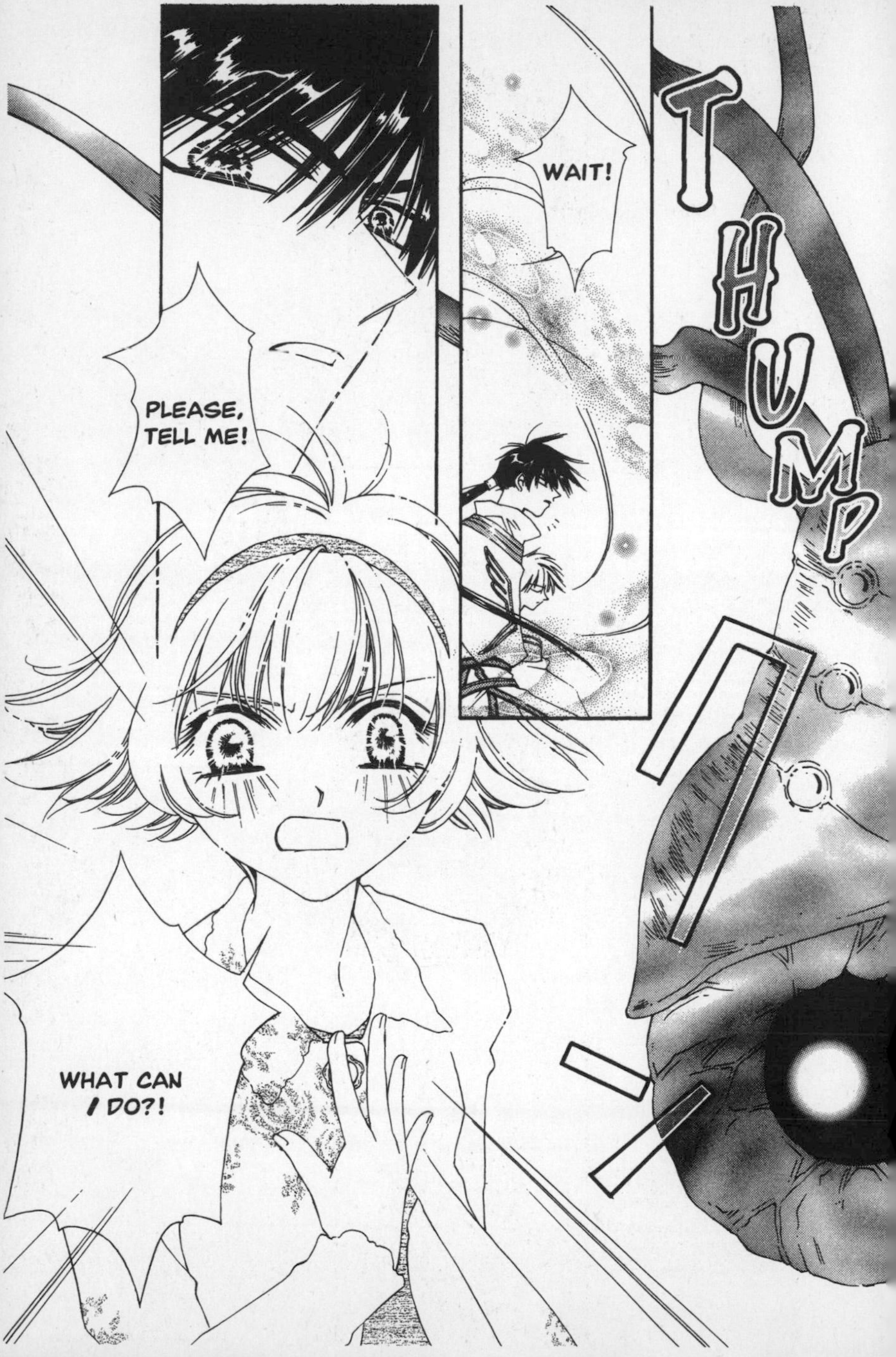
THUMP
WAIT!
PLEASE, TELL ME!
WHAT CAN I DO?!

# H A Y A T E

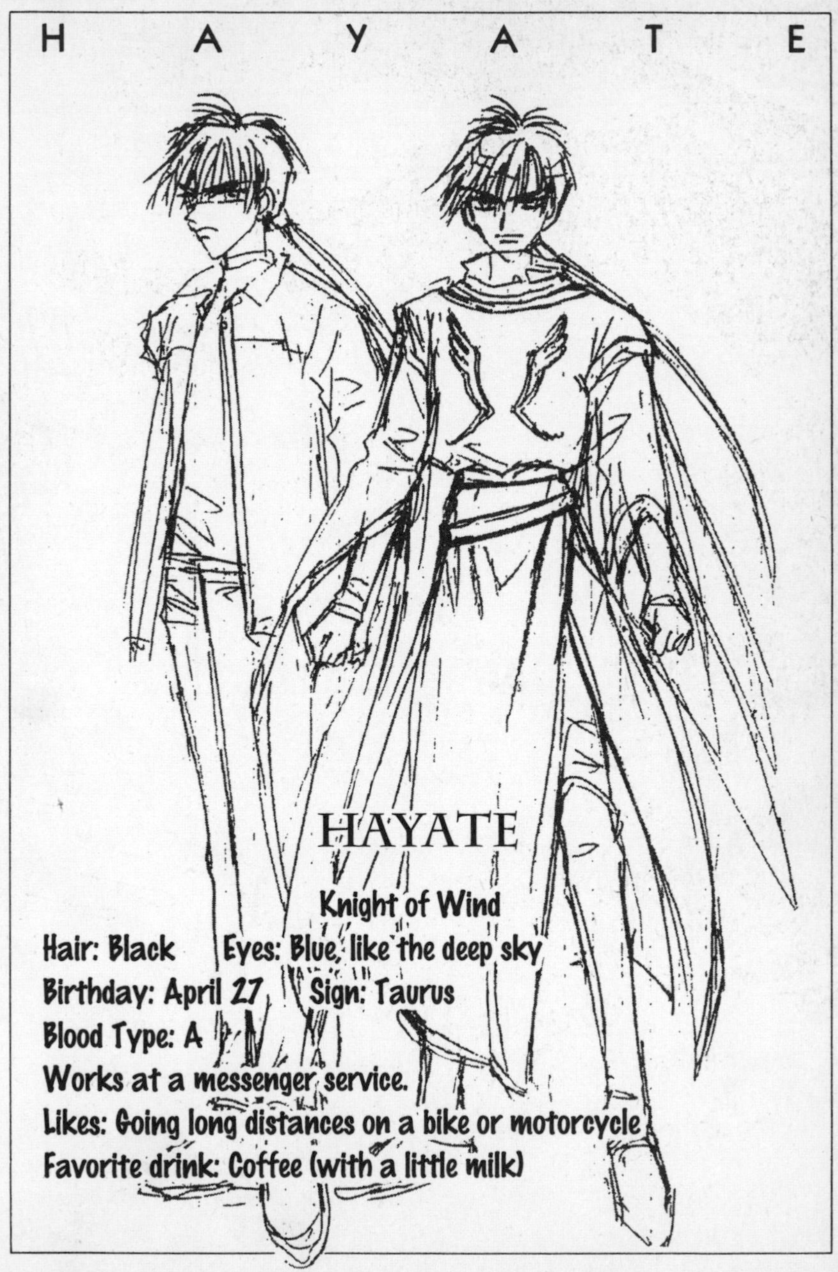

## HAYATE

**Knight of Wind**

**Hair: Black Eyes: Blue, like the deep sky**

**Birthday: April 27 Sign: Taurus**

**Blood Type: A**

**Works at a messenger service.**

**Likes: Going long distances on a bike or motorcycle**

**Favorite drink: Coffee (with a little milk)**

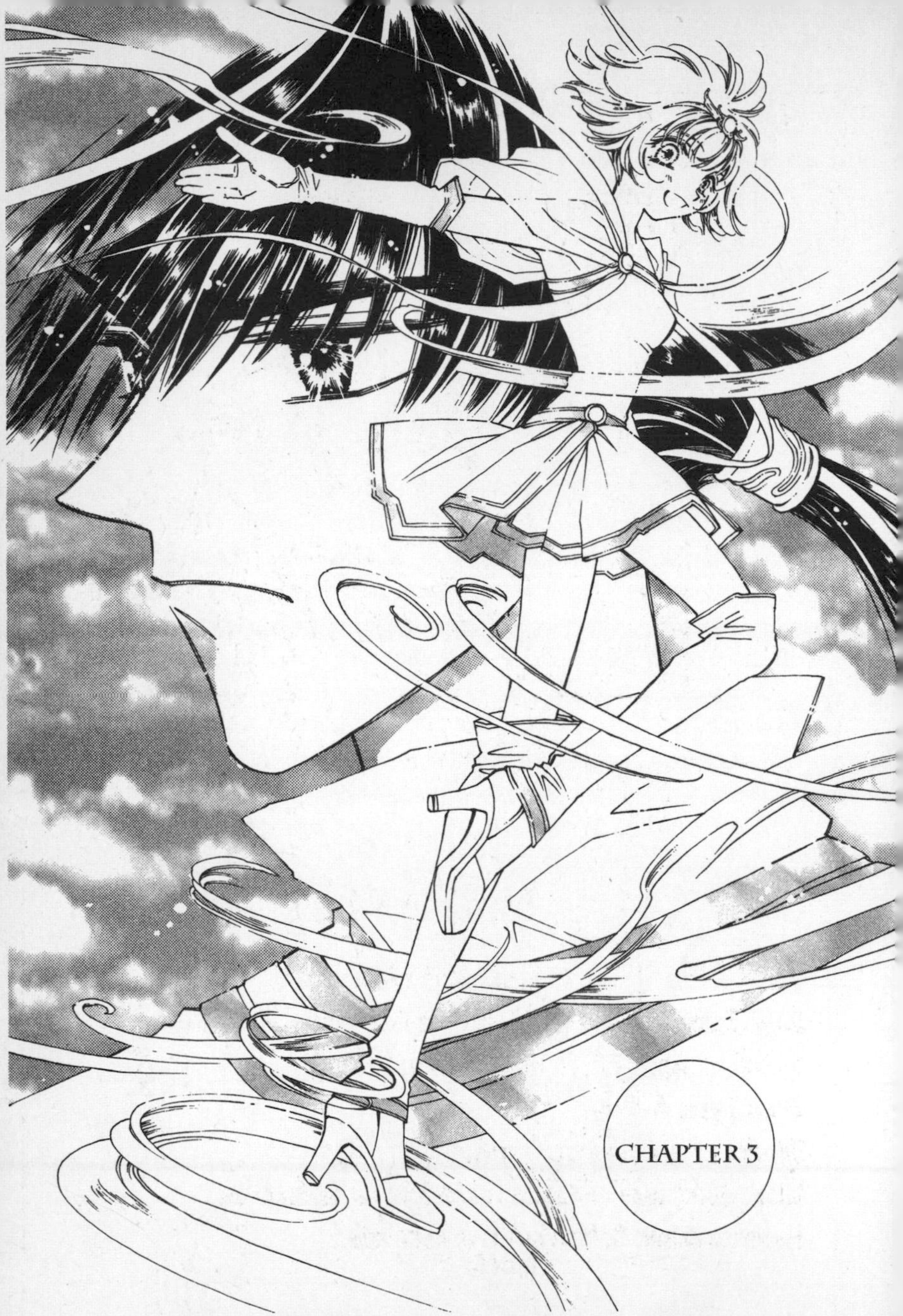
CHAPTER 3

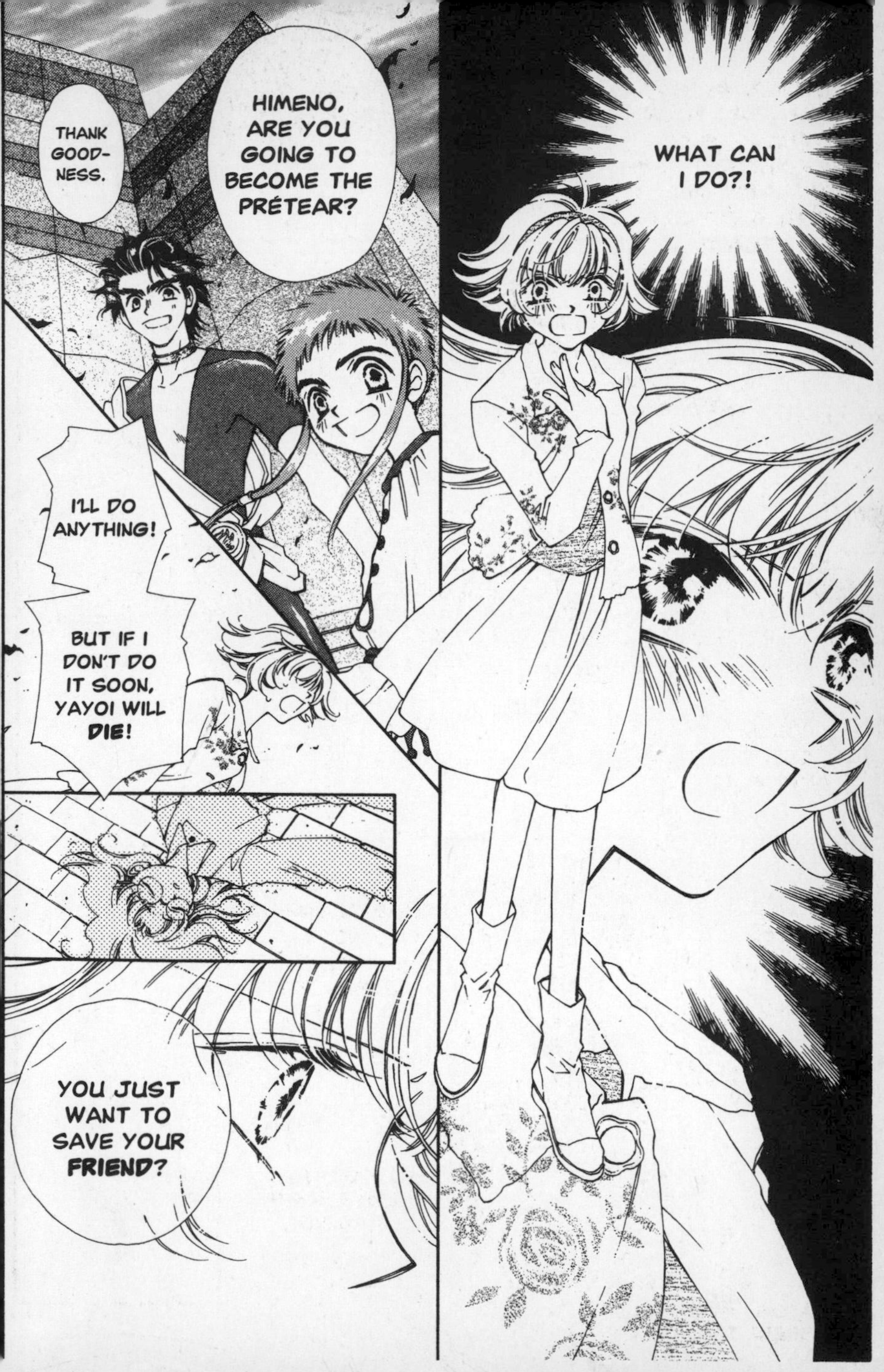
HIMENO, ARE YOU GOING TO BECOME THE PRÉTEAR?
THANK GOODNESS.
I'LL DO ANYTHING!
BUT IF I DON'T DO IT SOON, YAYOI WILL DIE!
YOU JUST WANT TO SAVE YOUR FRIEND?
WHAT CAN I DO?!

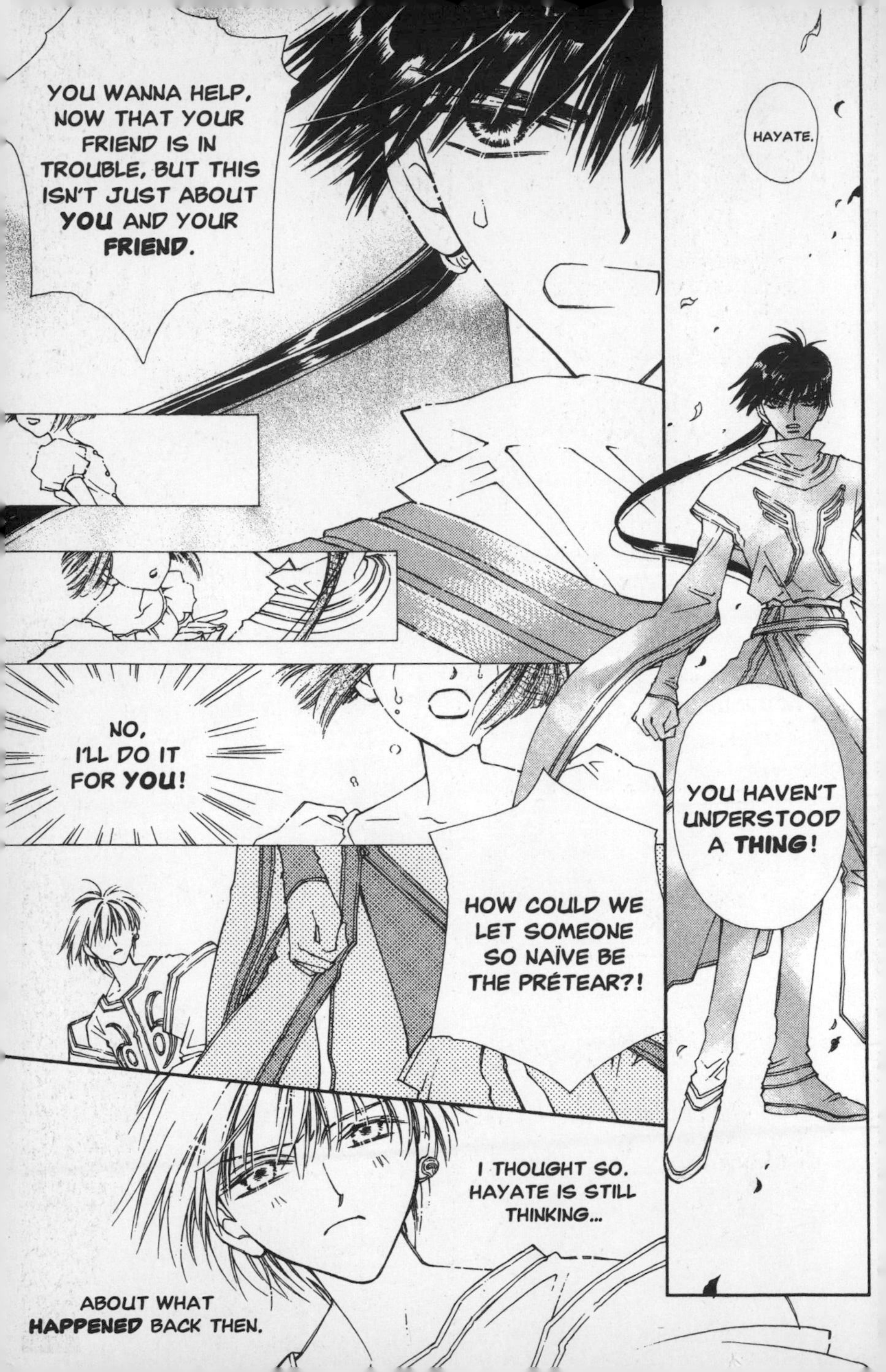
HAYATE.
YOU WANNA HELP, NOW THAT YOUR FRIEND IS IN TROUBLE, BUT THIS ISN'T JUST ABOUT **YOU** AND YOUR **FRIEND**.
NO, I'LL DO IT FOR **YOU**!
YOU HAVEN'T UNDERSTOOD A **THING**!
HOW COULD WE LET SOMEONE SO NAÏVE BE THE PRÉTEAR?!
I THOUGHT SO. HAYATE IS STILL THINKING...
ABOUT WHAT **HAPPENED** BACK THEN.

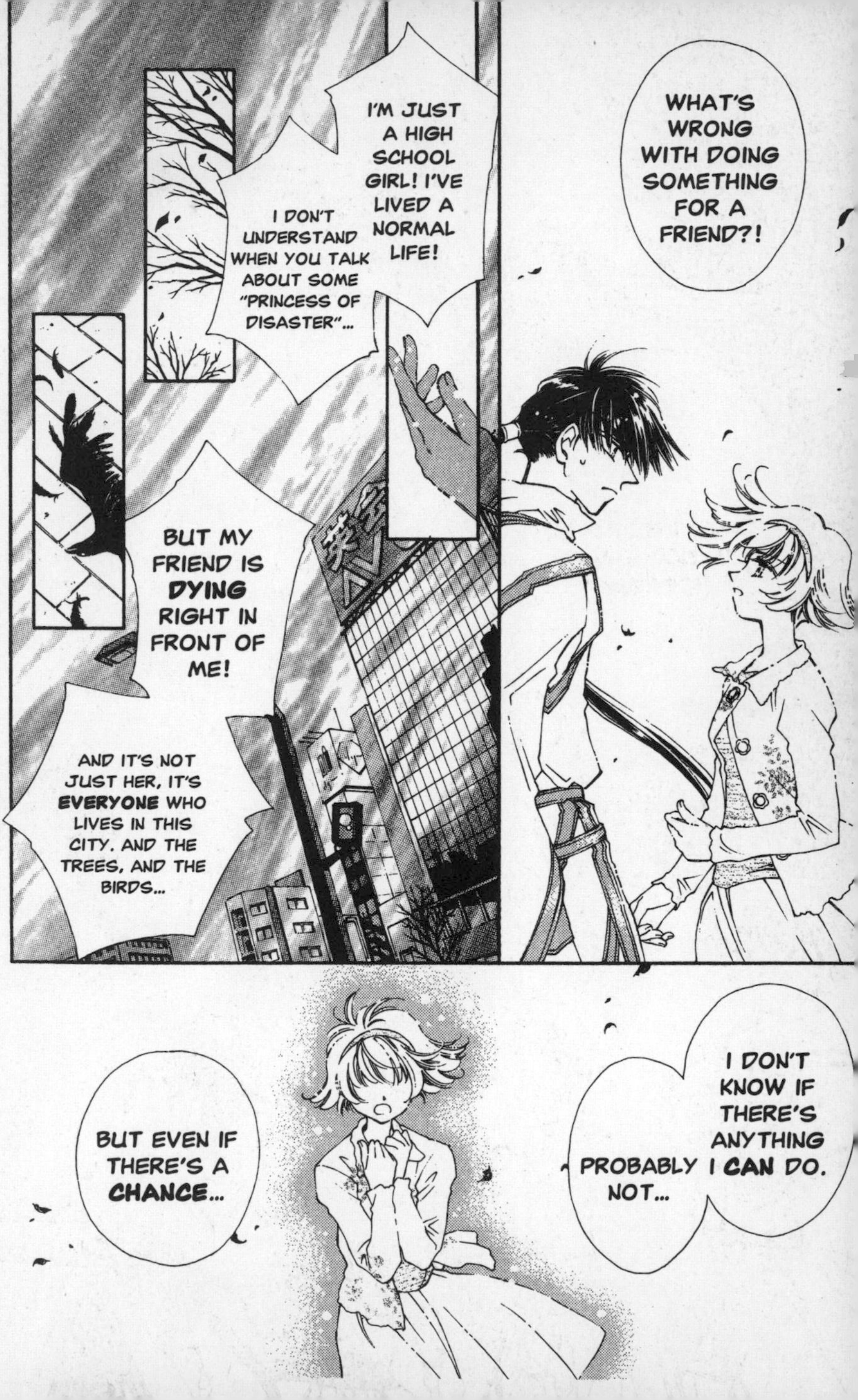
WHAT'S WRONG WITH DOING SOMETHING FOR A FRIEND?!
I'M JUST A HIGH SCHOOL GIRL! I'VE LIVED A NORMAL LIFE!
I DON'T UNDERSTAND WHEN YOU TALK ABOUT SOME "PRINCESS OF DISASTER"...
BUT MY FRIEND IS **DYING** RIGHT IN FRONT OF ME!
AND IT'S NOT JUST HER, IT'S **EVERYONE** WHO LIVES IN THIS CITY. AND THE TREES, AND THE BIRDS...
I DON'T KNOW IF THERE'S ANYTHING I **CAN** DO.
PROBABLY NOT...
BUT EVEN IF THERE'S A **CHANCE**...

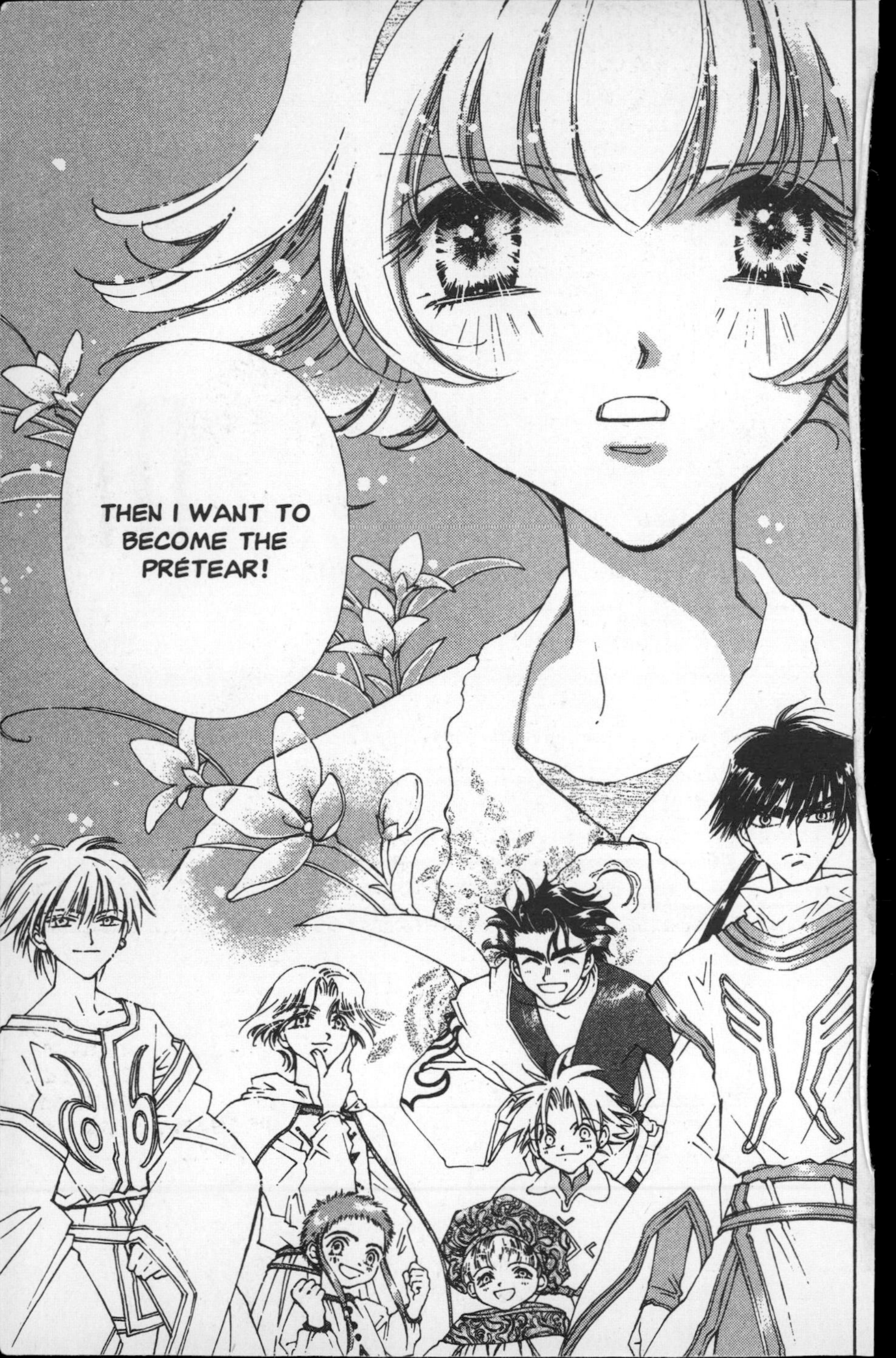
THEN I WANT TO BECOME THE PRÉTEAR!

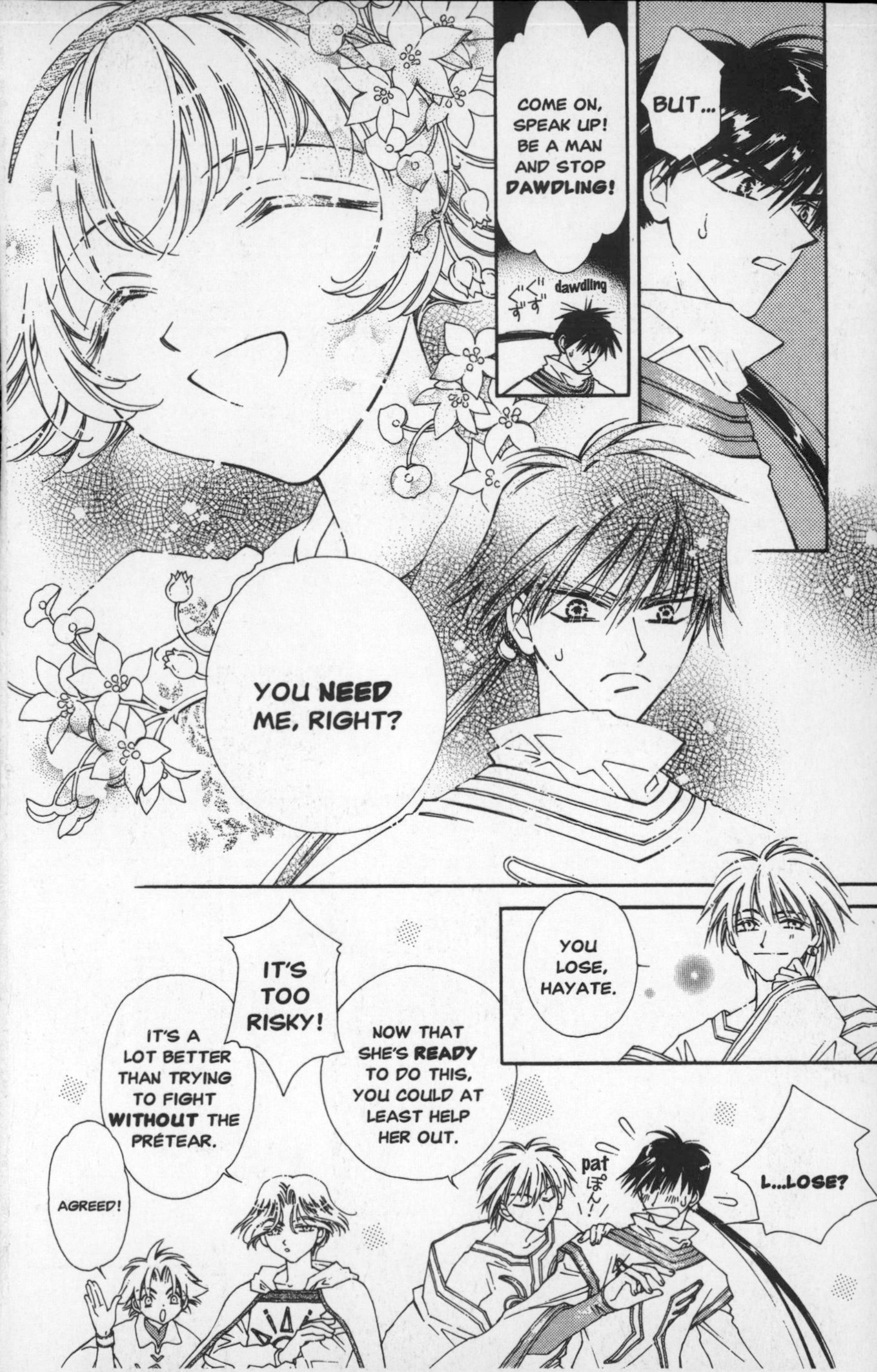
BUT...
COME ON, SPEAK UP! BE A MAN AND STOP DAWDLING!
dawdling
ぐずぐず
YOU NEED ME, RIGHT?
YOU LOSE, HAYATE.
L...LOSE?
pat
ぽん!
NOW THAT SHE'S READY TO DO THIS, YOU COULD AT LEAST HELP HER OUT.
IT'S TOO RISKY!
IT'S A LOT BETTER THAN TRYING TO FIGHT WITHOUT THE PRÉTEAR.
AGREED!

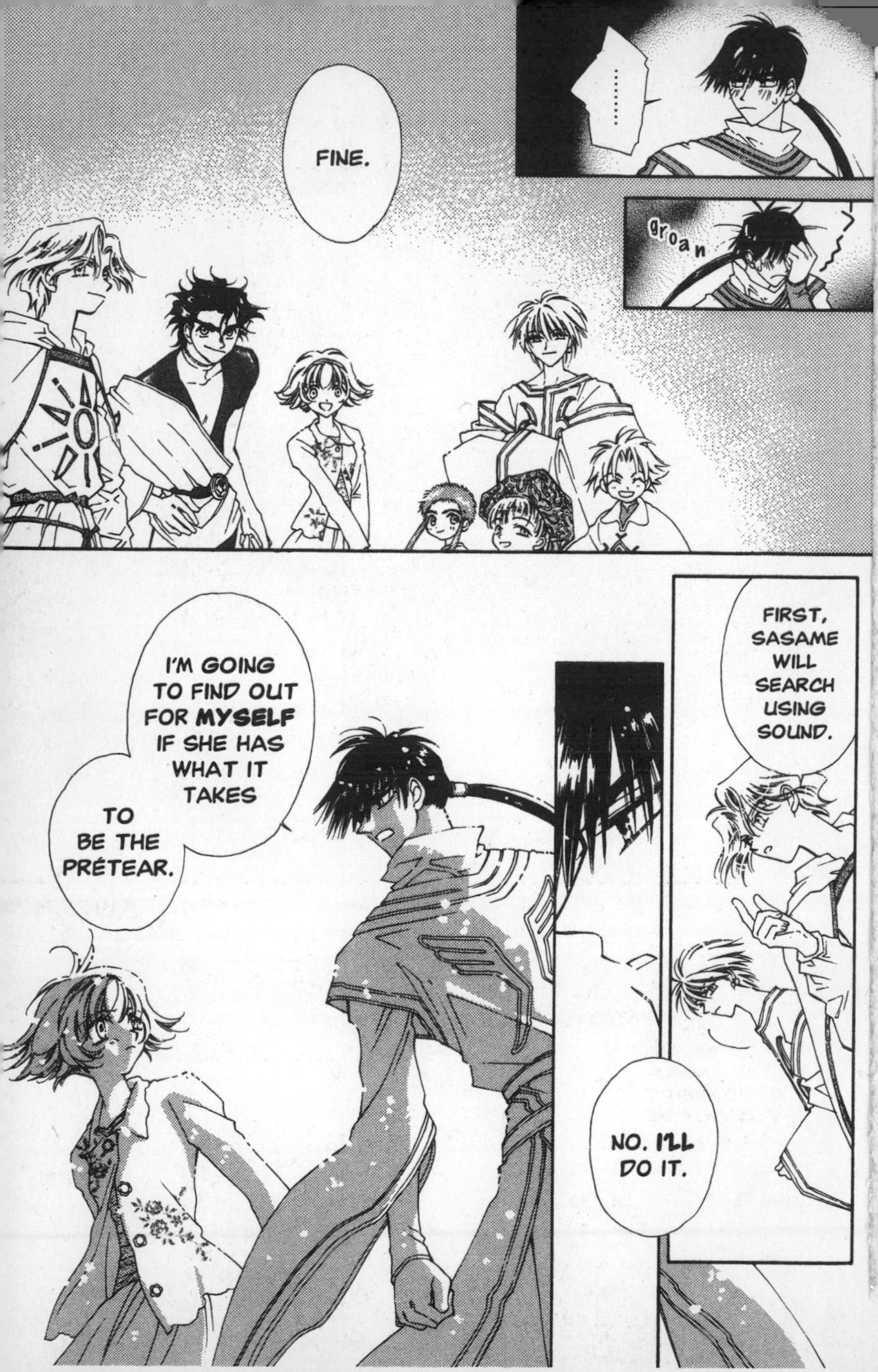
......
groan
FINE.
FIRST, SASAME WILL SEARCH USING SOUND.
NO. I'LL DO IT.
I'M GOING TO FIND OUT FOR MYSELF IF SHE HAS WHAT IT TAKES
TO BE THE PRÉTEAR.

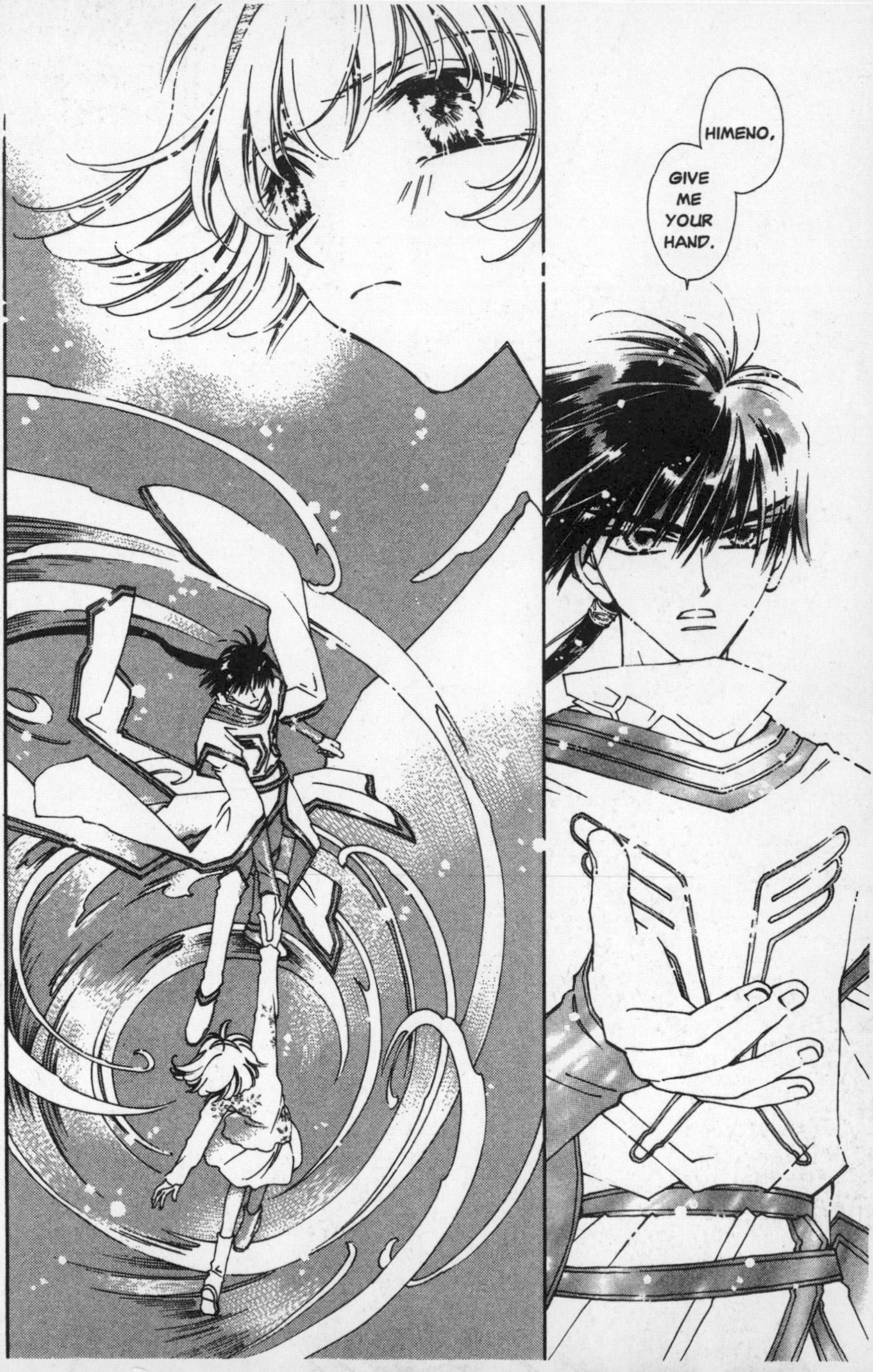
HIMENO,
GIVE ME YOUR HAND.

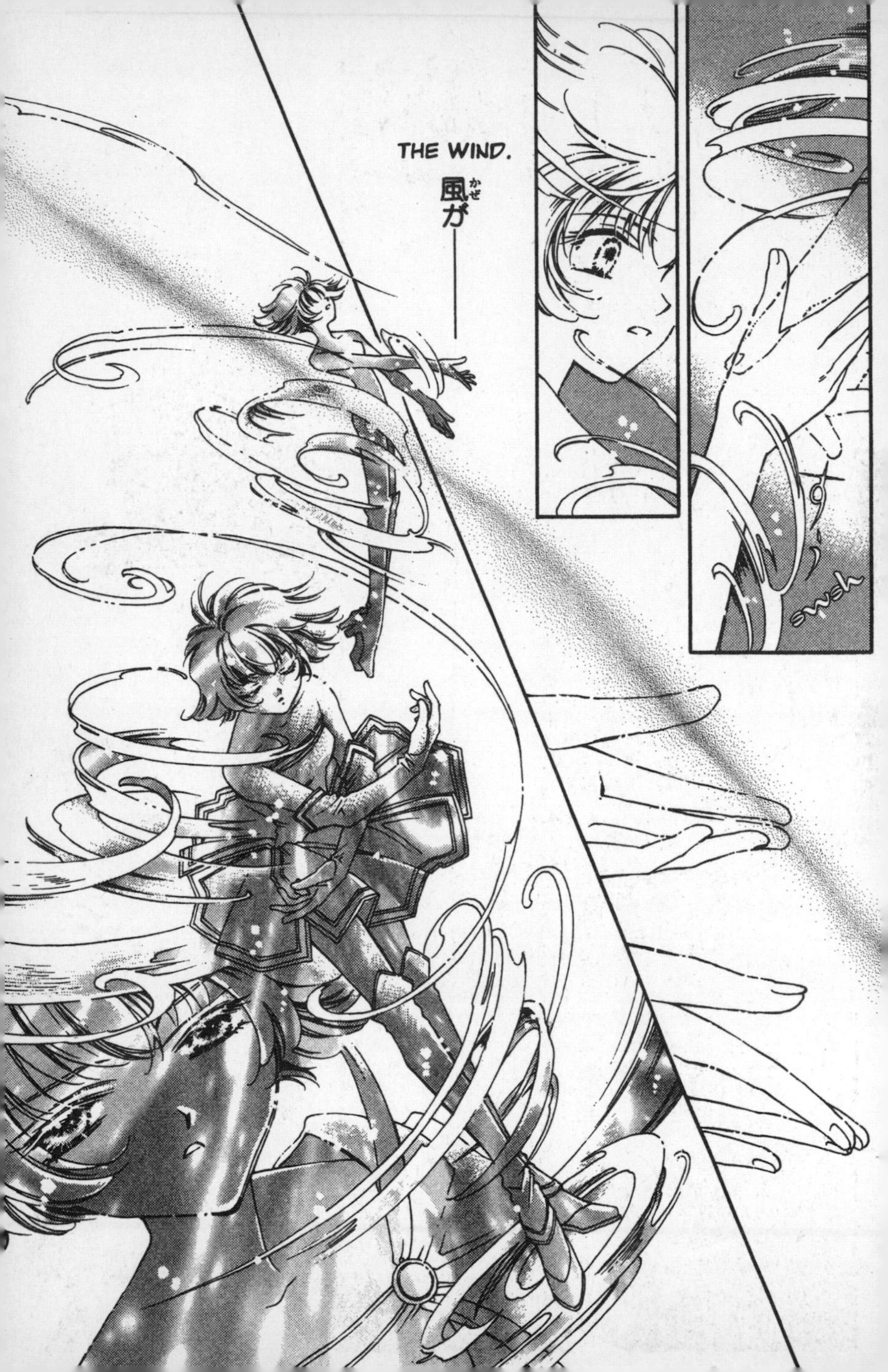
THE WIND.
風ガ——
swsh

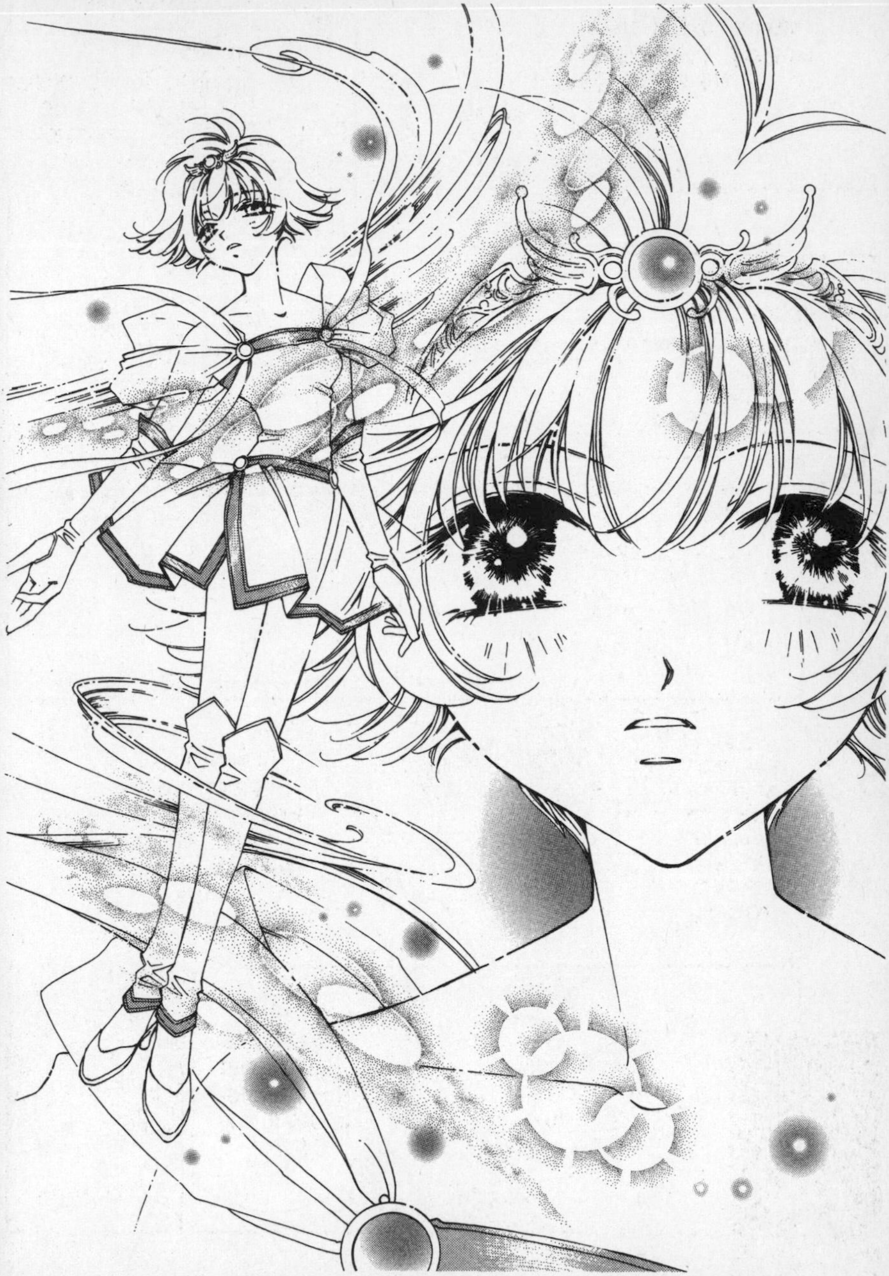

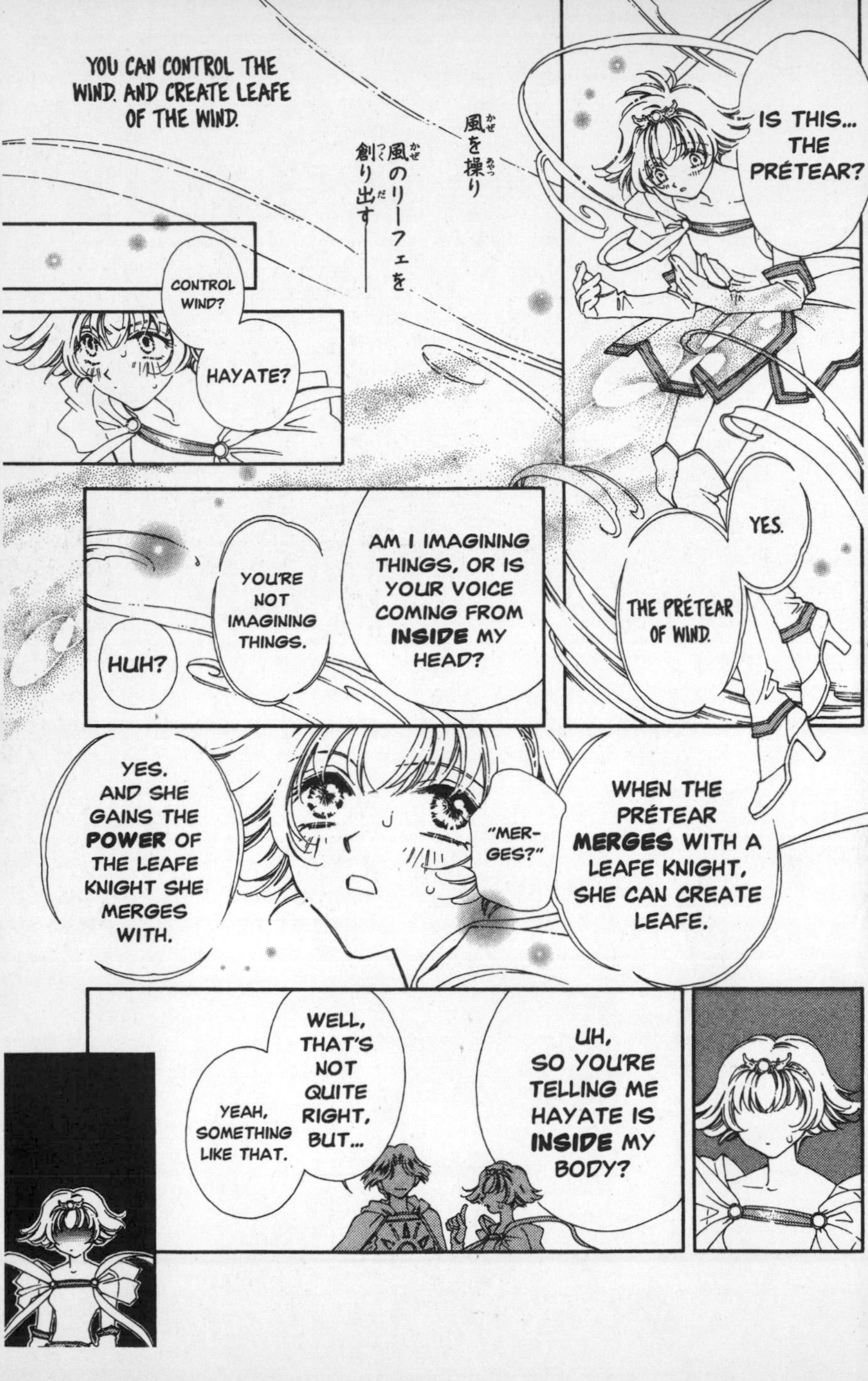
IS THIS... THE PRÉTEAR?
YOU CAN CONTROL THE WIND. AND CREATE LEAFE OF THE WIND.
風を操り
風のリーフェを創り出す
CONTROL WIND?
HAYATE?
YES.
THE PRÉTEAR OF WIND.
AM I IMAGINING THINGS, OR IS YOUR VOICE COMING FROM INSIDE MY HEAD?
YOU'RE NOT IMAGINING THINGS.
HUH?
WHEN THE PRÉTEAR MERGES WITH A LEAFE KNIGHT, SHE CAN CREATE LEAFE.
"MER-GES?"
YES. AND SHE GAINS THE POWER OF THE LEAFE KNIGHT SHE MERGES WITH.
UH, SO YOU'RE TELLING ME HAYATE IS INSIDE MY BODY?
WELL, THAT'S NOT QUITE RIGHT, BUT...
YEAH, SOMETHING LIKE THAT.

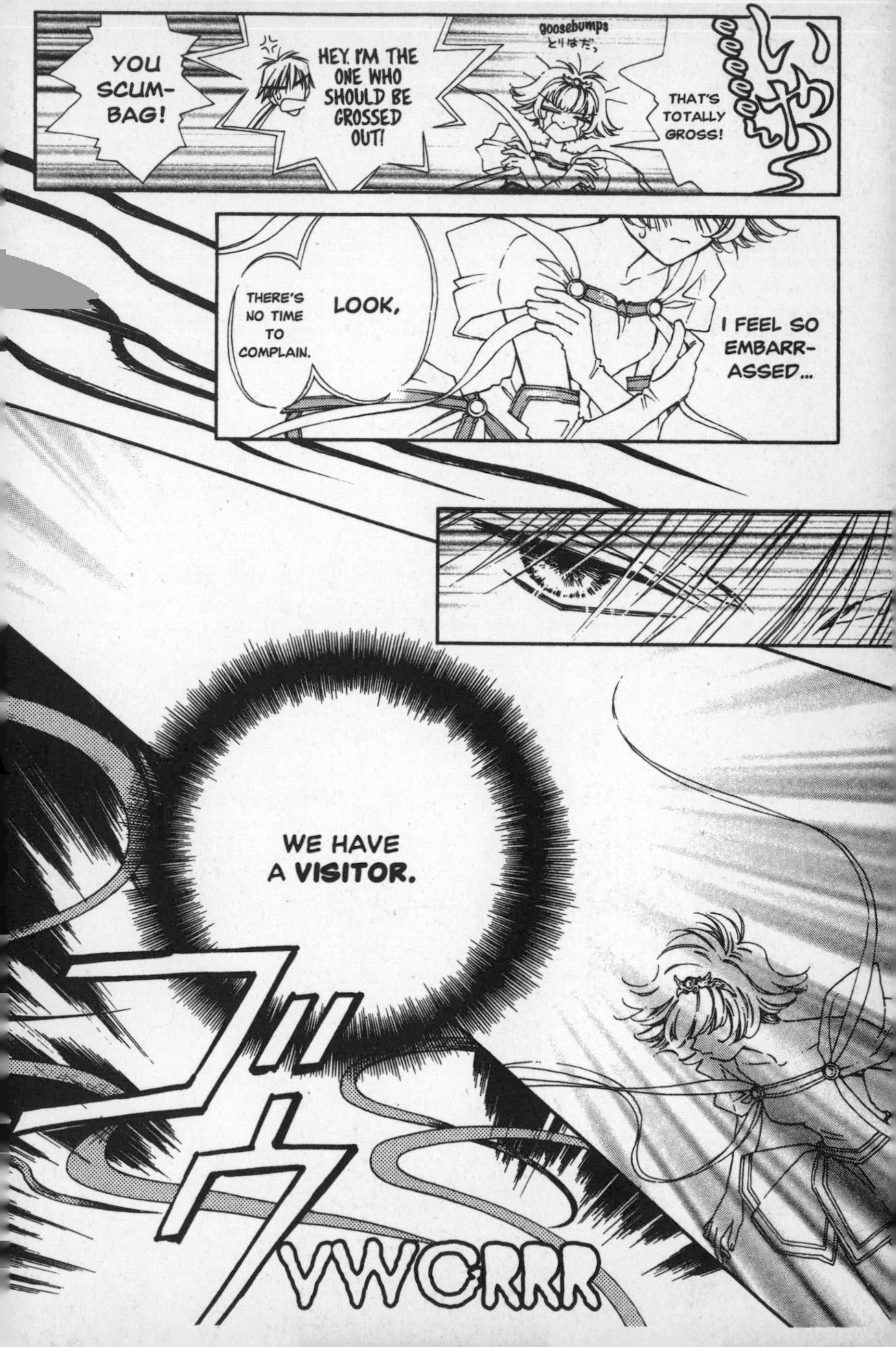
THAT'S TOTALLY GROSS!
goosebumps
とりはだっ
HEY. I'M THE ONE WHO SHOULD BE GROSSED OUT!
YOU SCUM-BAG!
I FEEL SO EMBARR-ASSED...
LOOK,
THERE'S NO TIME TO COMPLAIN.
WE HAVE A VISITOR.
VWORRR

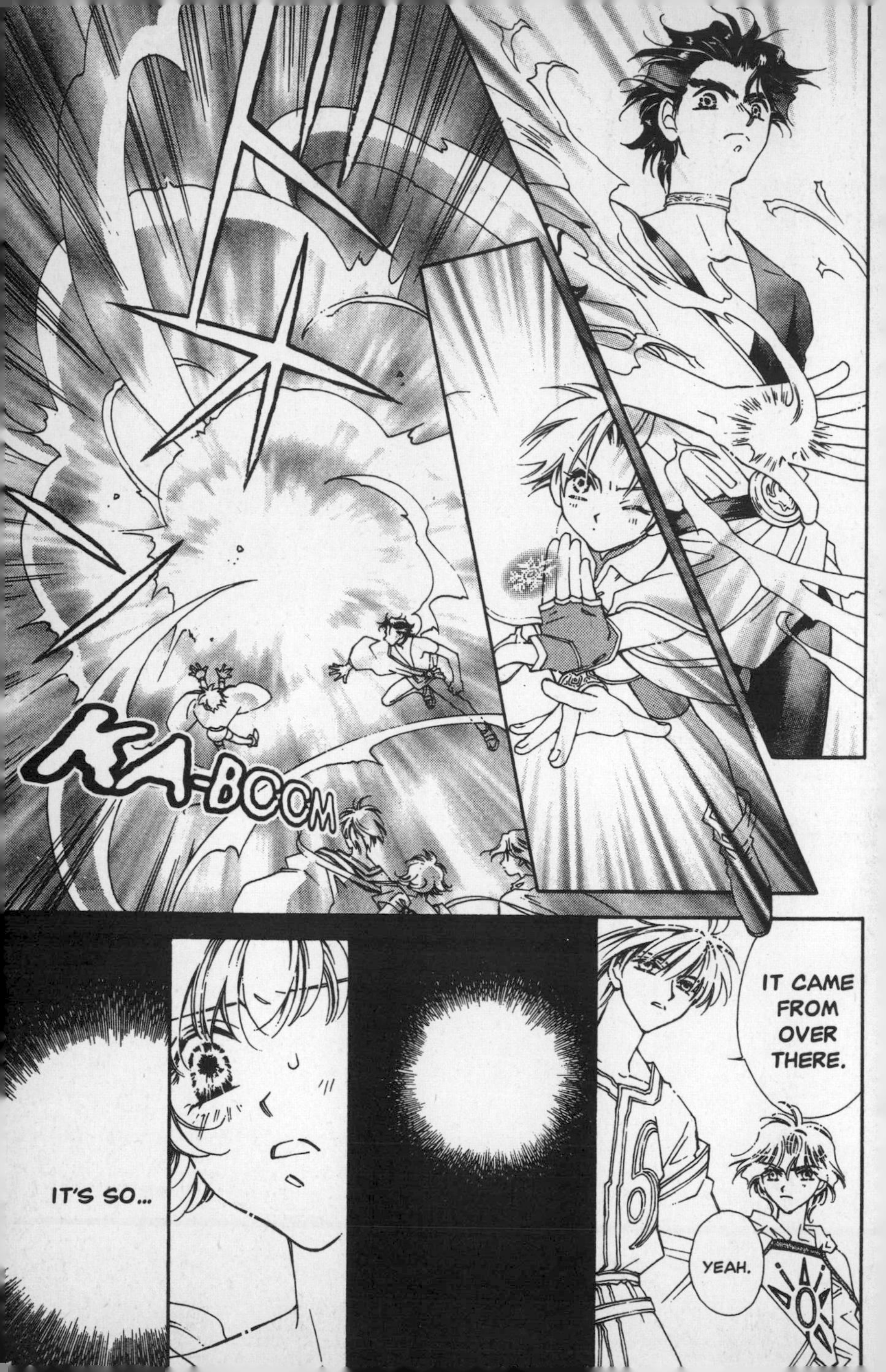
KA-BOOM
IT CAME FROM OVER THERE.
YEAH.
IT'S SO...

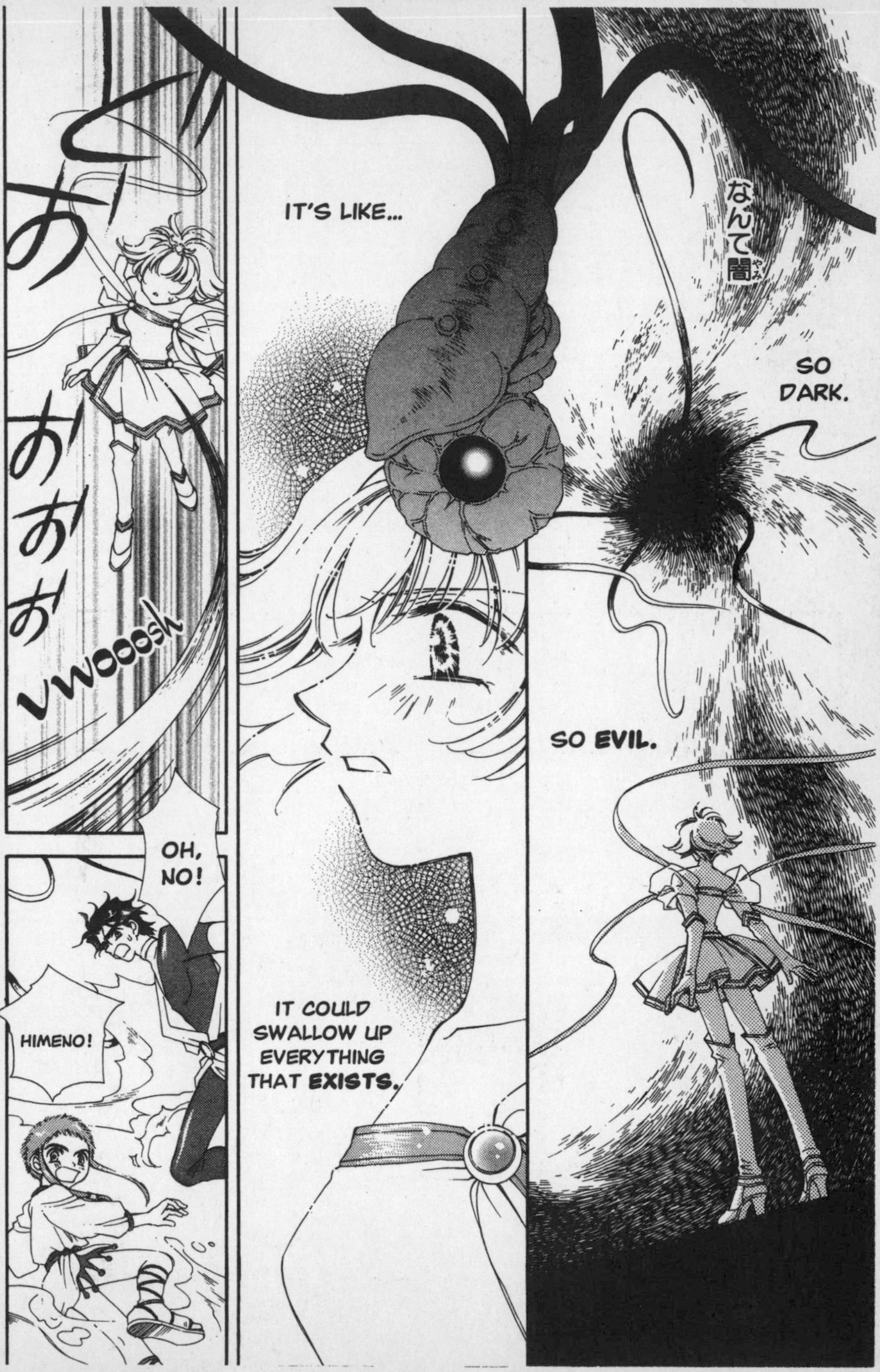
なんて闇
SO DARK.
SO EVIL.
IT'S LIKE...
IT COULD SWALLOW UP EVERYTHING THAT EXISTS.
おおおお
WOOOSH
OH, NO!
HIMENO!

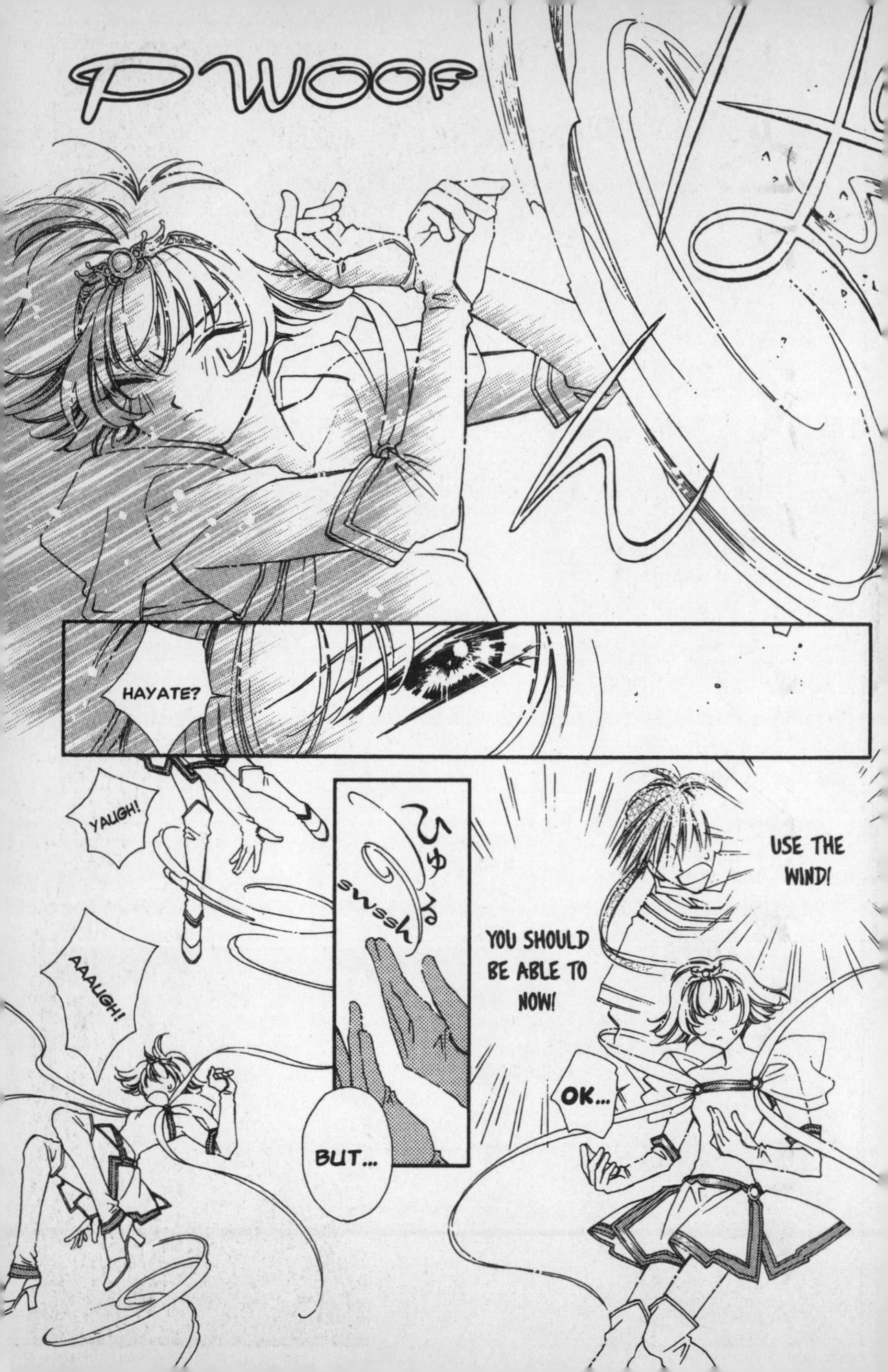
PWOOF
HAYATE?
ひゅる
SWSSH
USE THE WIND!
YOU SHOULD BE ABLE TO NOW!
YAUGH!
AAAUGH!
OK...
BUT...

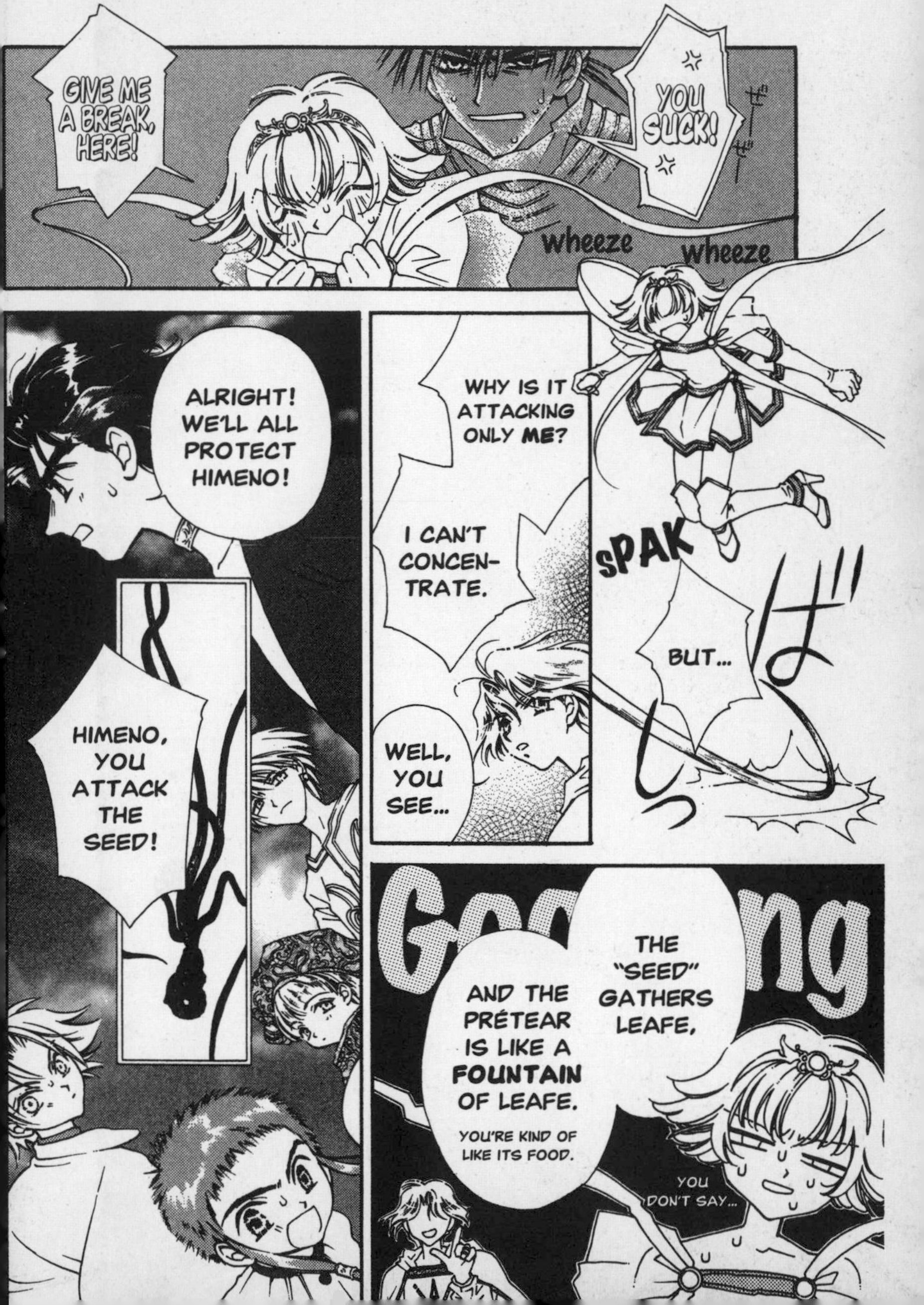
GIVE ME A BREAK, HERE!
YOU SUCK!
wheeze
wheeze
ALRIGHT! WE'LL ALL PROTECT HIMENO!
HIMENO, YOU ATTACK THE SEED!
WHY IS IT ATTACKING ONLY ME?
I CAN'T CONCENTRATE.
SPAK
BUT...
WELL, YOU SEE...
THE "SEED" GATHERS LEAFE,
AND THE PRÉTEAR IS LIKE A FOUNTAIN OF LEAFE.
YOU'RE KIND OF LIKE ITS FOOD.
YOU DON'T SAY...

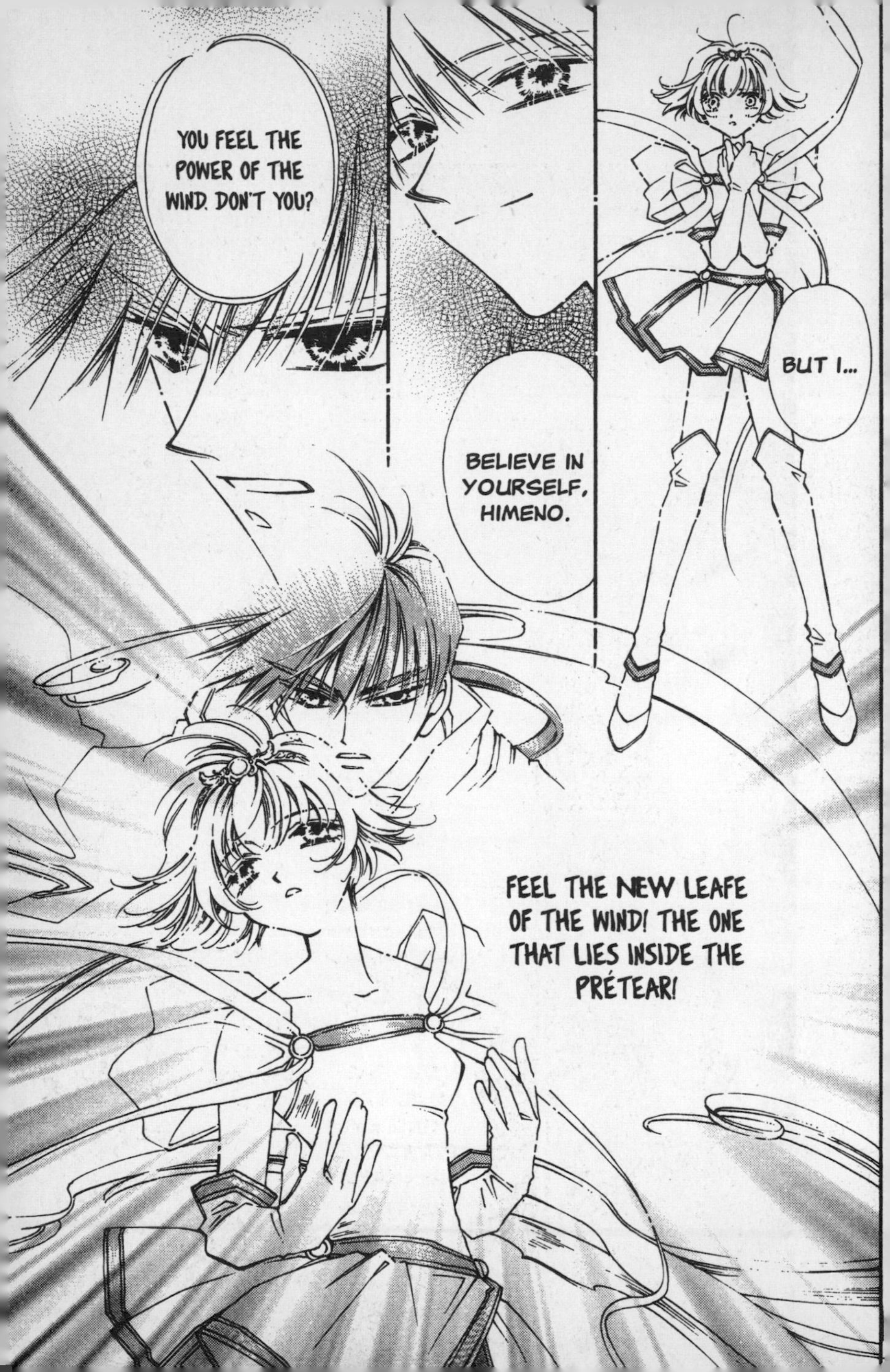
BUT I...
BELIEVE IN YOURSELF, HIMENO.
YOU FEEL THE POWER OF THE WIND. DON'T YOU?
FEEL THE NEW LEAFE OF THE WIND! THE ONE THAT LIES INSIDE THE PRÉTEAR!

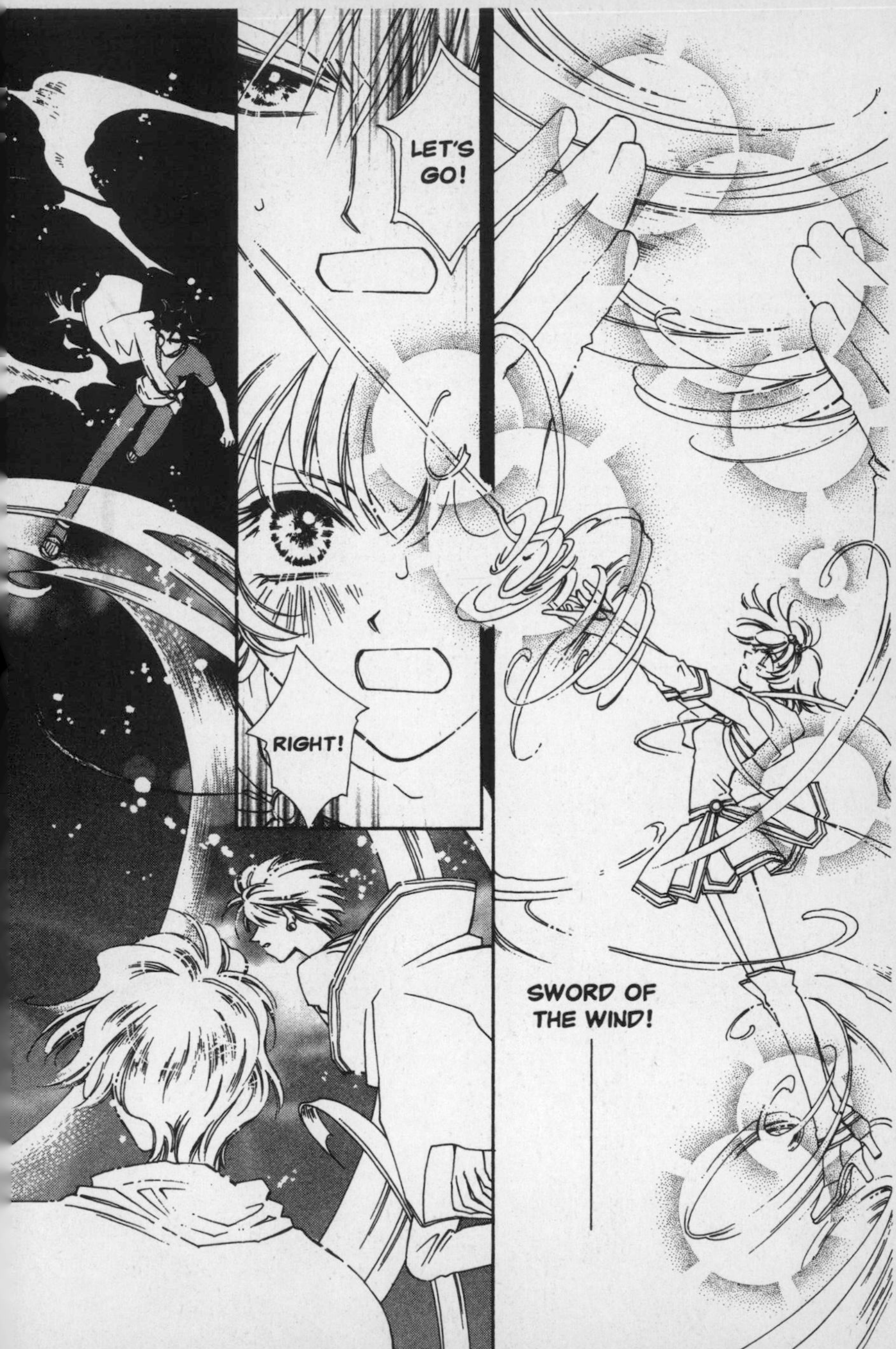
SWORD OF THE WIND!
LET'S GO!
RIGHT!

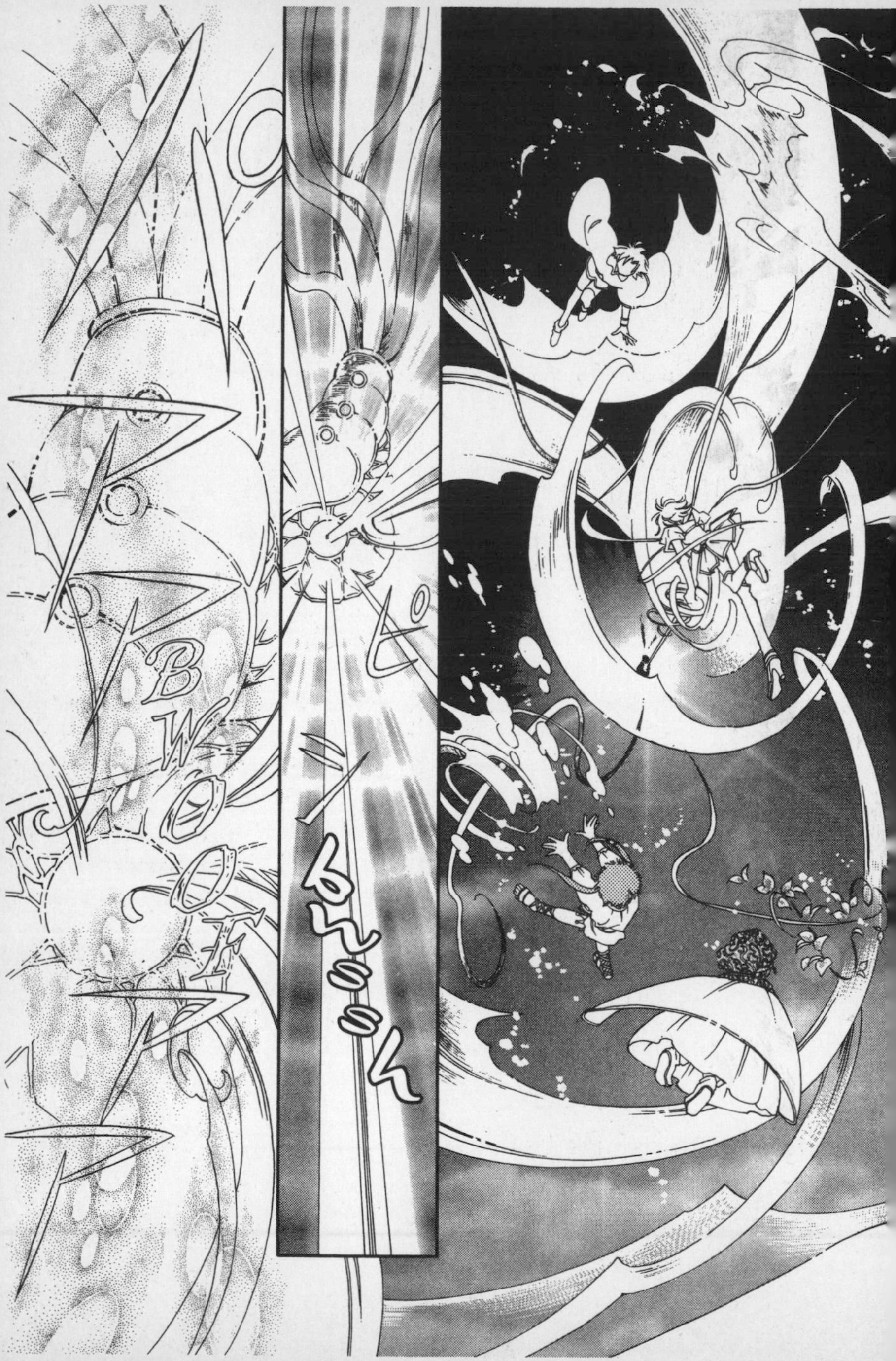
BWOOF
fwoosh

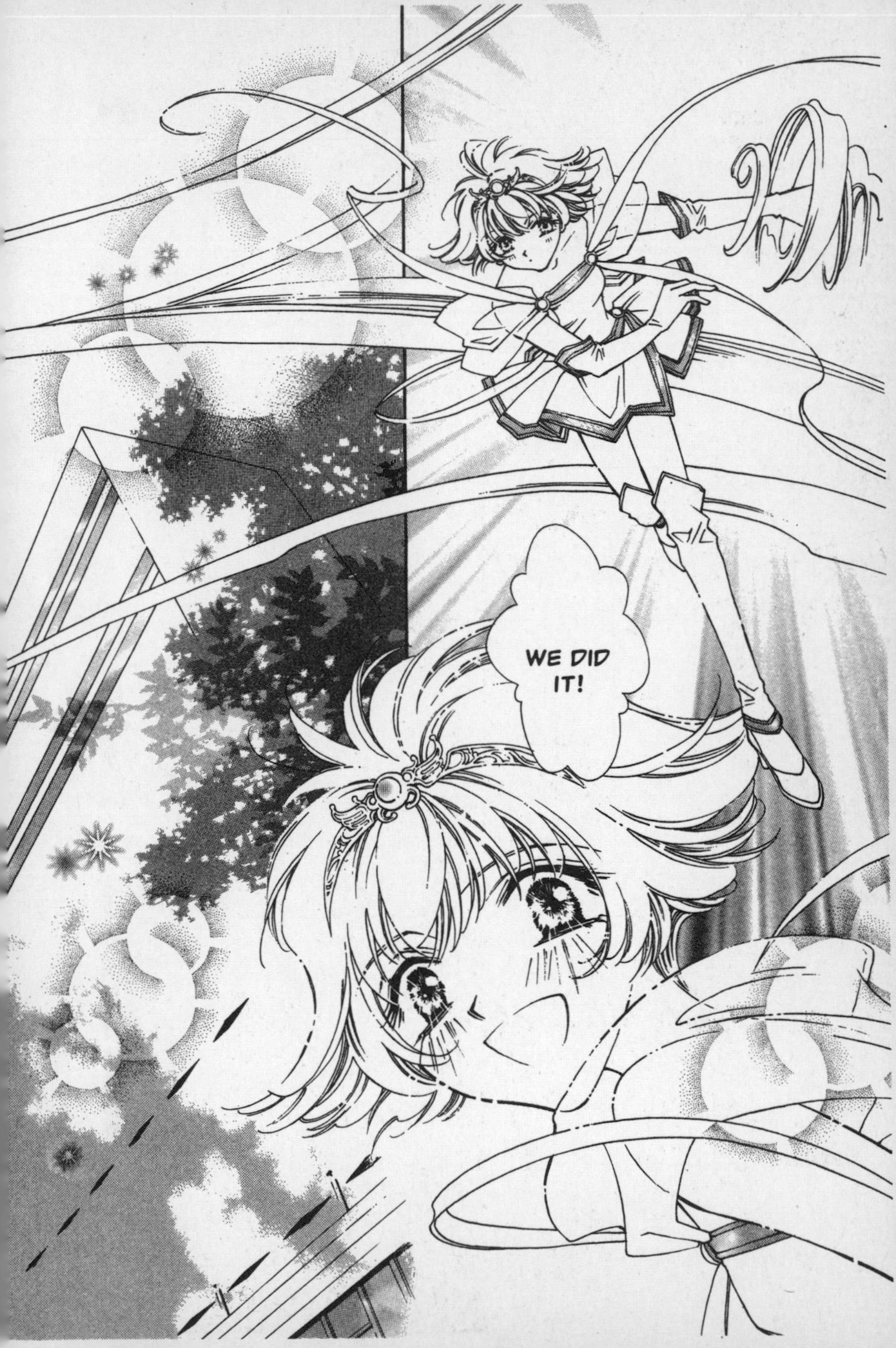
WE DID
IT!

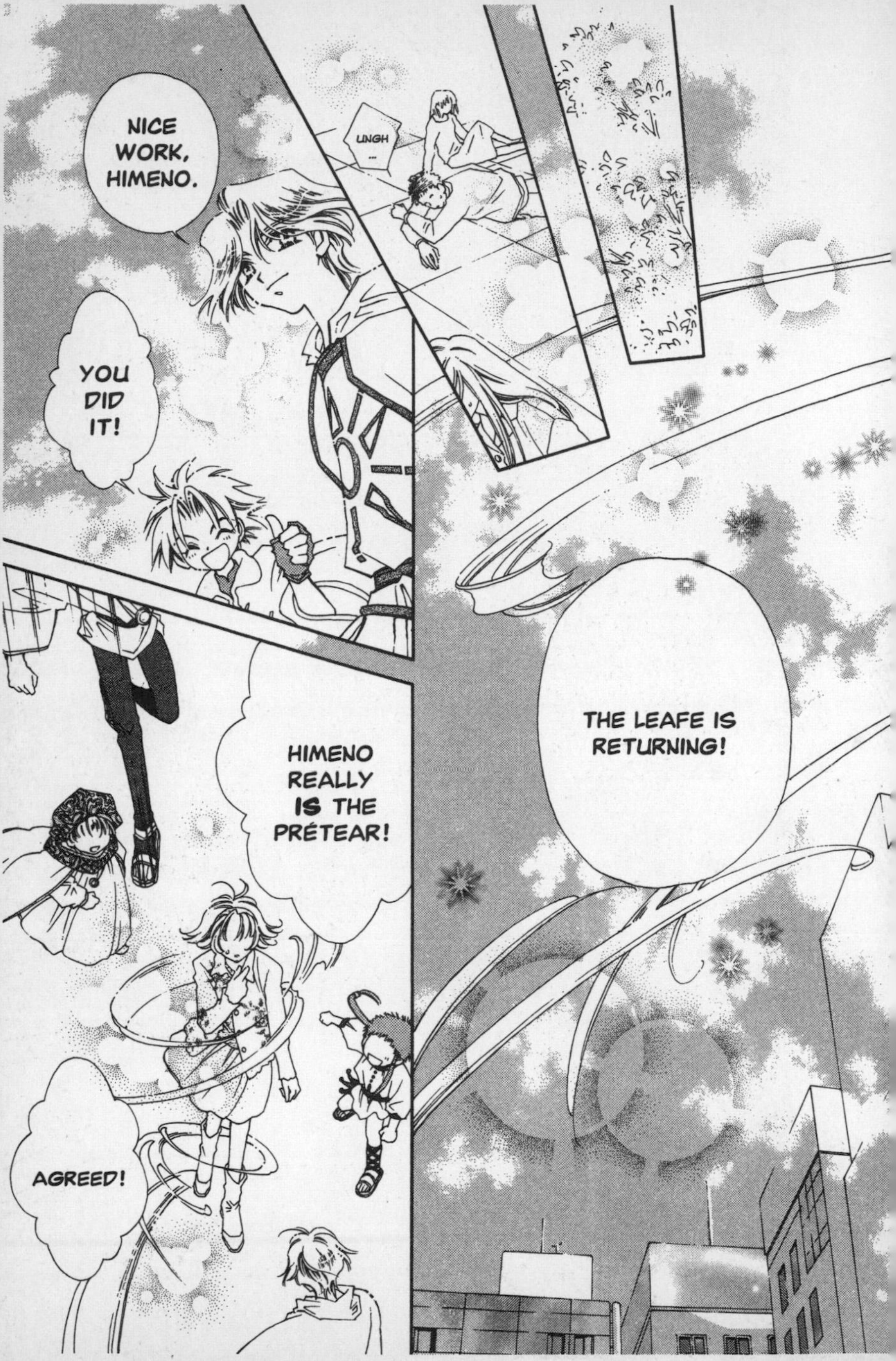
UNGH ...
THE LEAFE IS RETURNING!
NICE WORK, HIMENO.
YOU DID IT!
HIMENO REALLY IS THE PRÉTEAR!
AGREED!

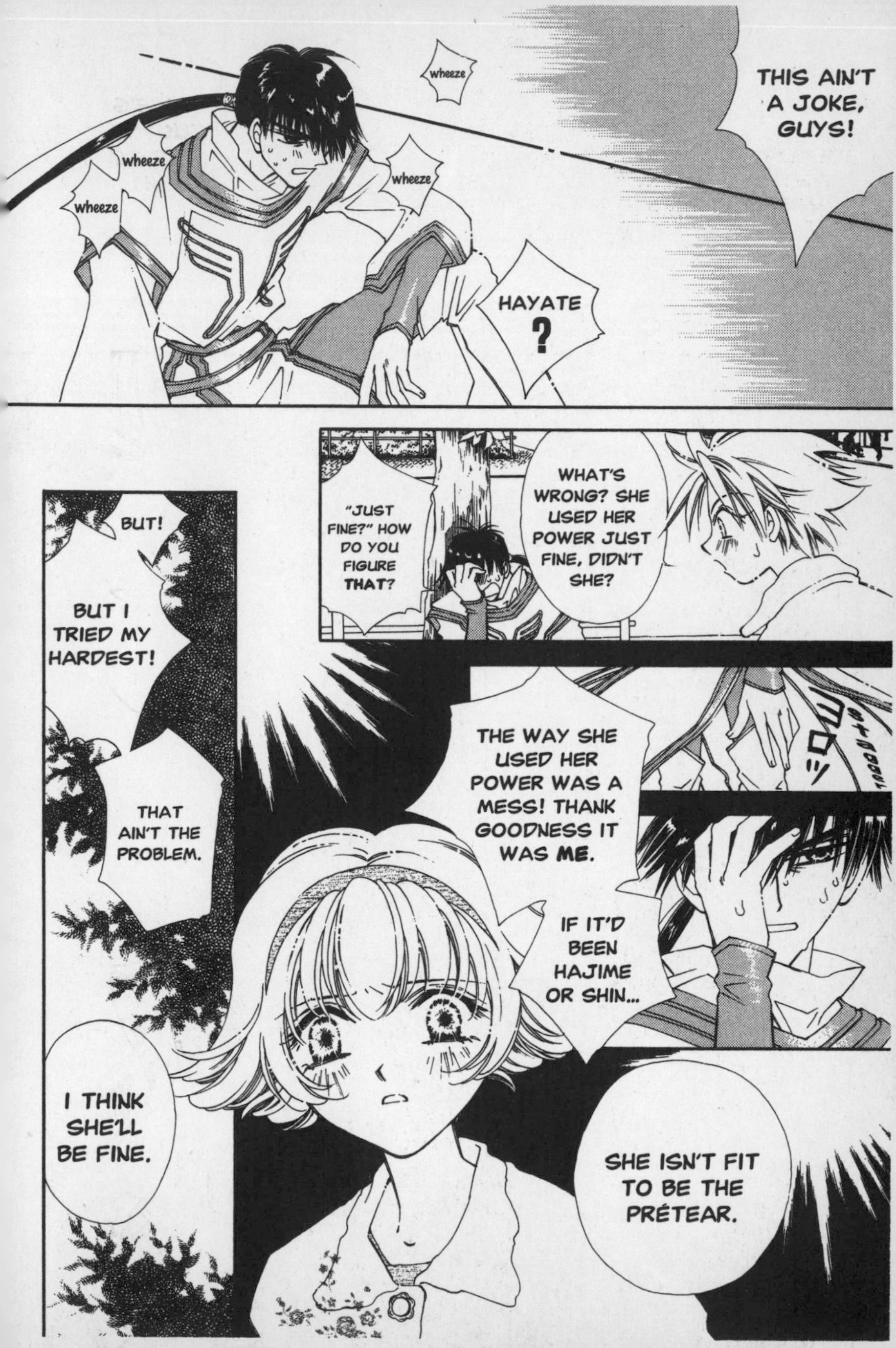

THIS AIN'T A JOKE, GUYS!
wheeze
wheeze
wheeze
wheeze
HAYATE ?
WHAT'S WRONG? SHE USED HER POWER JUST FINE, DIDN'T SHE?
"JUST FINE?" HOW DO YOU FIGURE THAT?
THE WAY SHE USED HER POWER WAS A MESS! THANK GOODNESS IT WAS ME.
IF IT'D BEEN HAJIME OR SHIN...
SHE ISN'T FIT TO BE THE PRÉTEAR.
I THINK SHE'LL BE FINE.
BUT!
BUT I TRIED MY HARDEST!
THAT AIN'T THE PROBLEM.

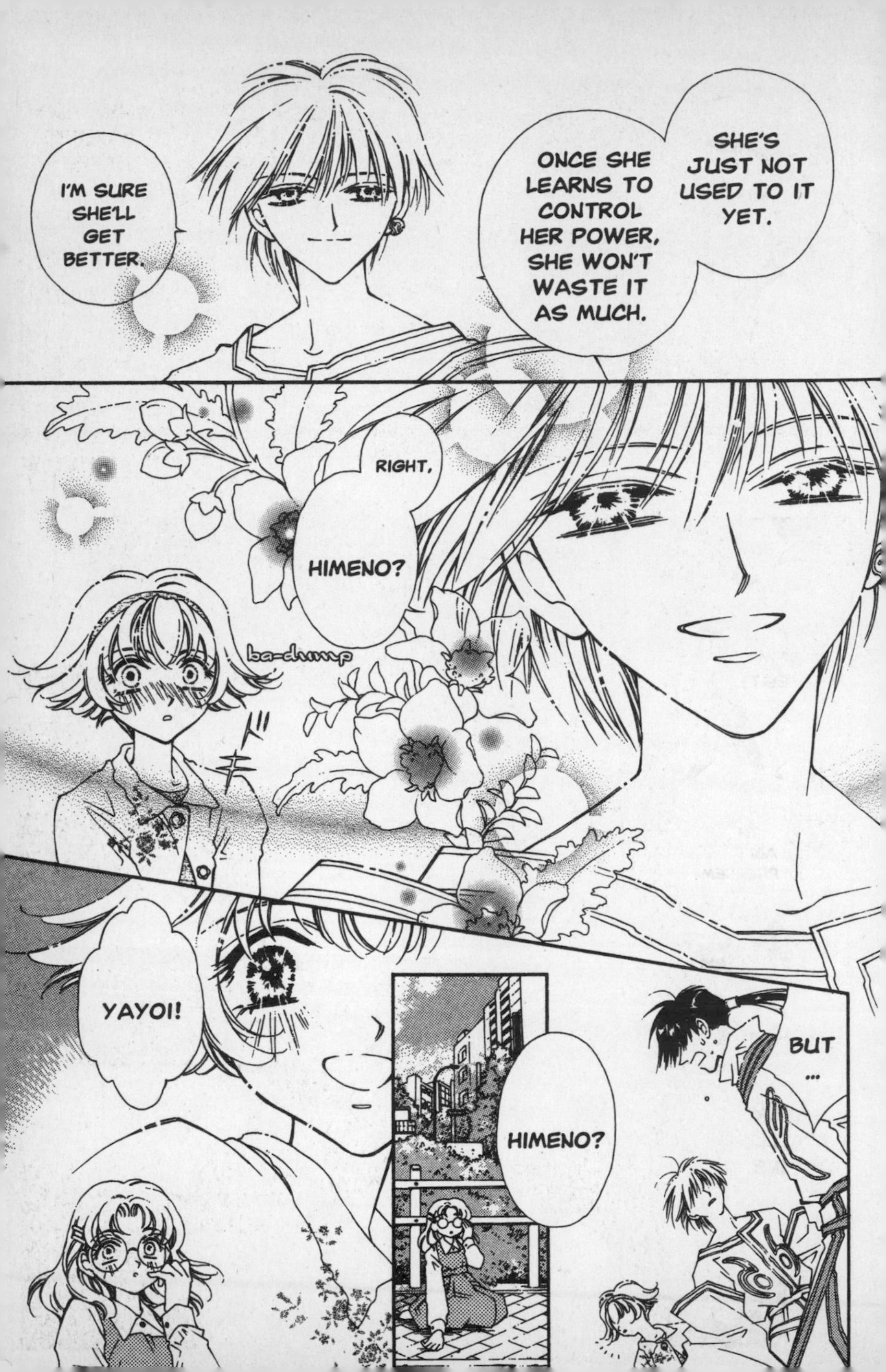
SHE'S JUST NOT USED TO IT YET.
ONCE SHE LEARNS TO CONTROL HER POWER, SHE WON'T WASTE IT AS MUCH.
I'M SURE SHE'LL GET BETTER.
RIGHT,
HIMENO?
ba-dump
ドキ
BUT ...
HIMENO?
YAYOI!

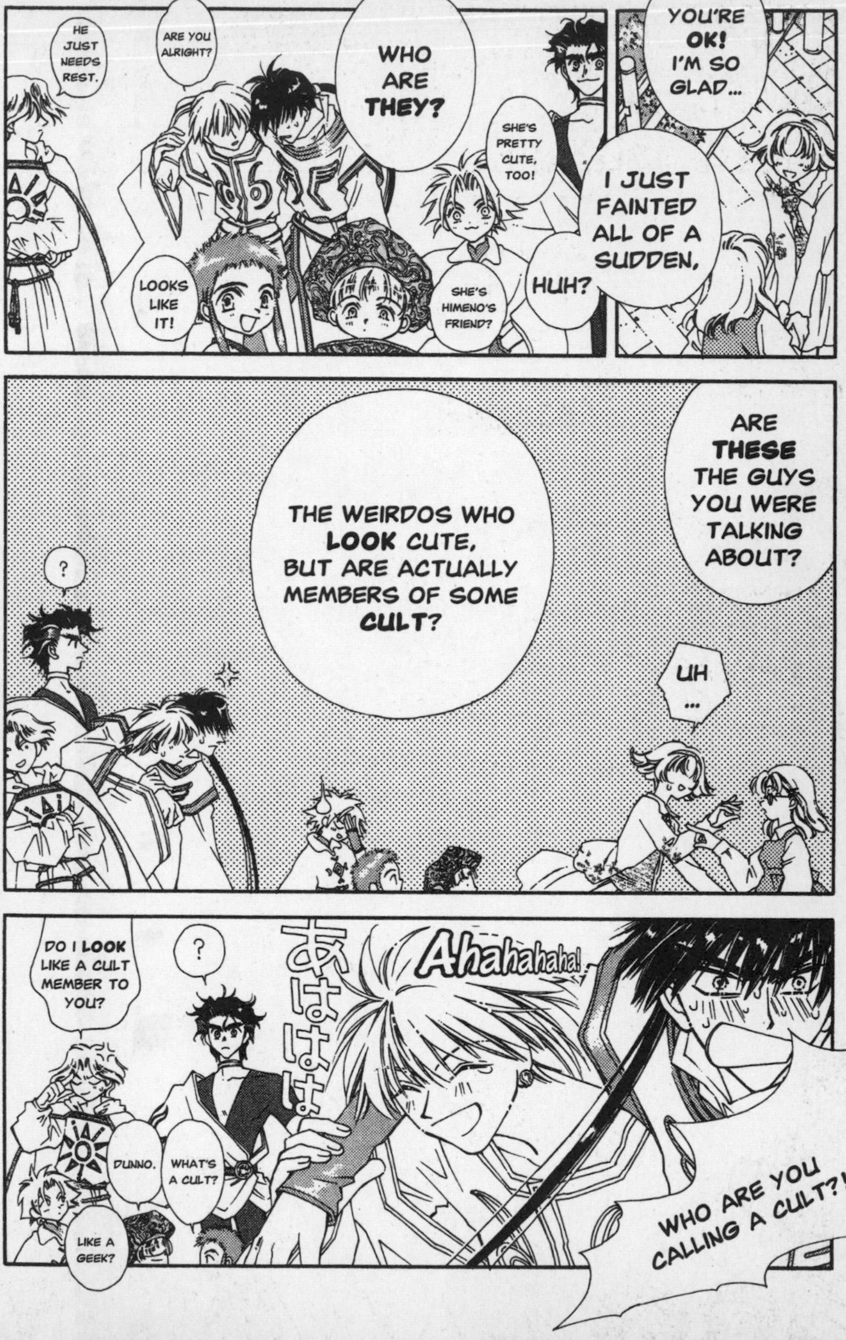

YOU'RE OK! I'M SO GLAD...
I JUST FAINTED ALL OF A SUDDEN,
HUH?
WHO ARE THEY?
SHE'S PRETTY CUTE, TOO!
SHE'S HIMENO'S FRIEND?
ARE YOU ALRIGHT?
HE JUST NEEDS REST.
LOOKS LIKE IT!
ARE THESE THE GUYS YOU WERE TALKING ABOUT?
THE WEIRDOS WHO LOOK CUTE, BUT ARE ACTUALLY MEMBERS OF SOME CULT?
UH ...
?
WHO ARE YOU CALLING A CULT?!
Ahahahaha!
あははは
DO I LOOK LIKE A CULT MEMBER TO YOU?
?
WHAT'S A CULT?
DUNNO.
LIKE A GEEK?

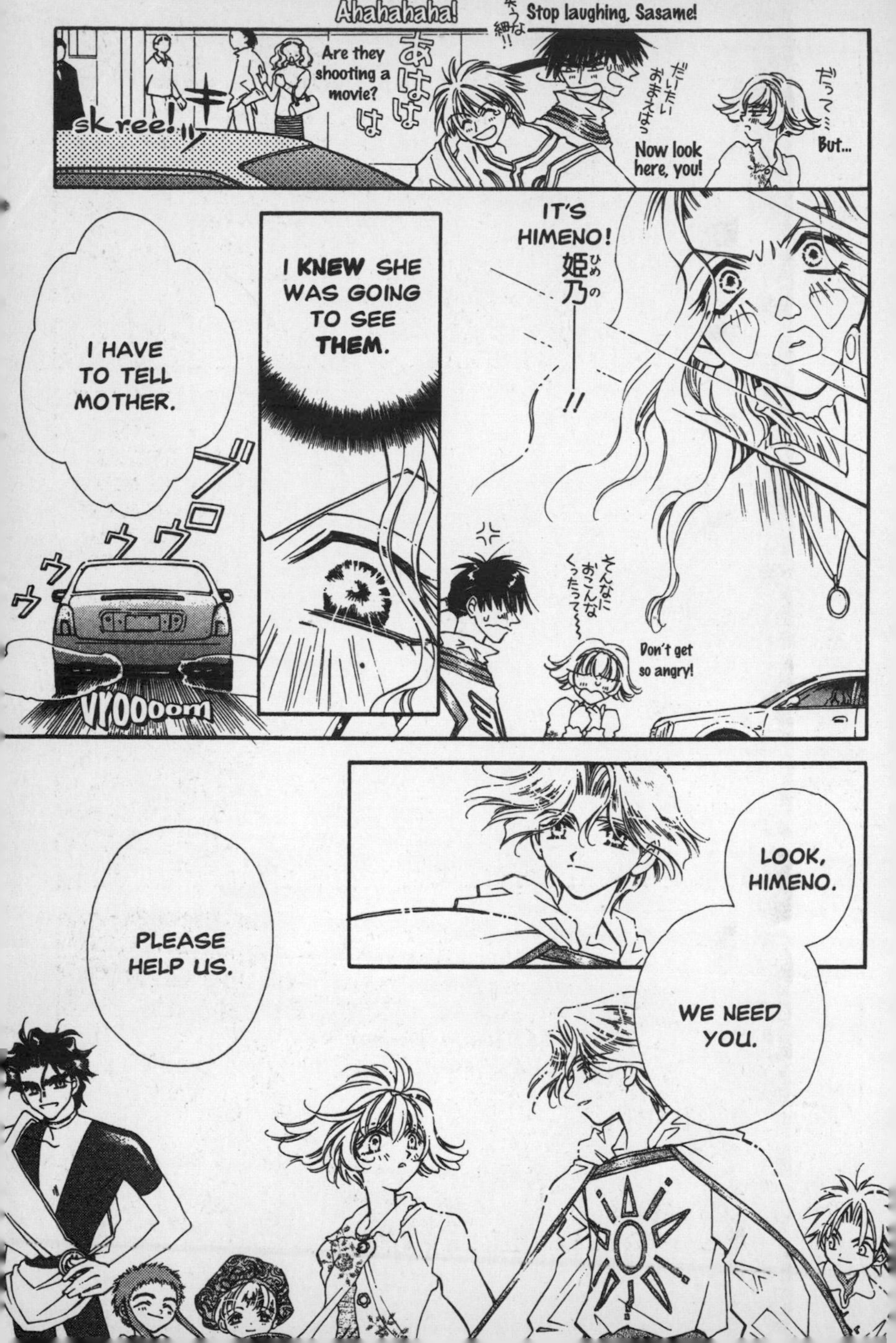

Stop laughing, Sasame!
笑うな細!!
Ahahahaha!
だってミ
But...
だいたいおまえはっ
Now look here, you!
あははは
Are they shooting a movie?
キ
skree!
IT'S HIMENO!
姫乃―!!
I KNEW SHE WAS GOING TO SEE THEM.
I HAVE TO TELL MOTHER.
ブロロウウウ
VROOOom
そんなにおこんなくったって~~
Don't get so angry!
LOOK, HIMENO.
WE NEED YOU.
PLEASE HELP US.

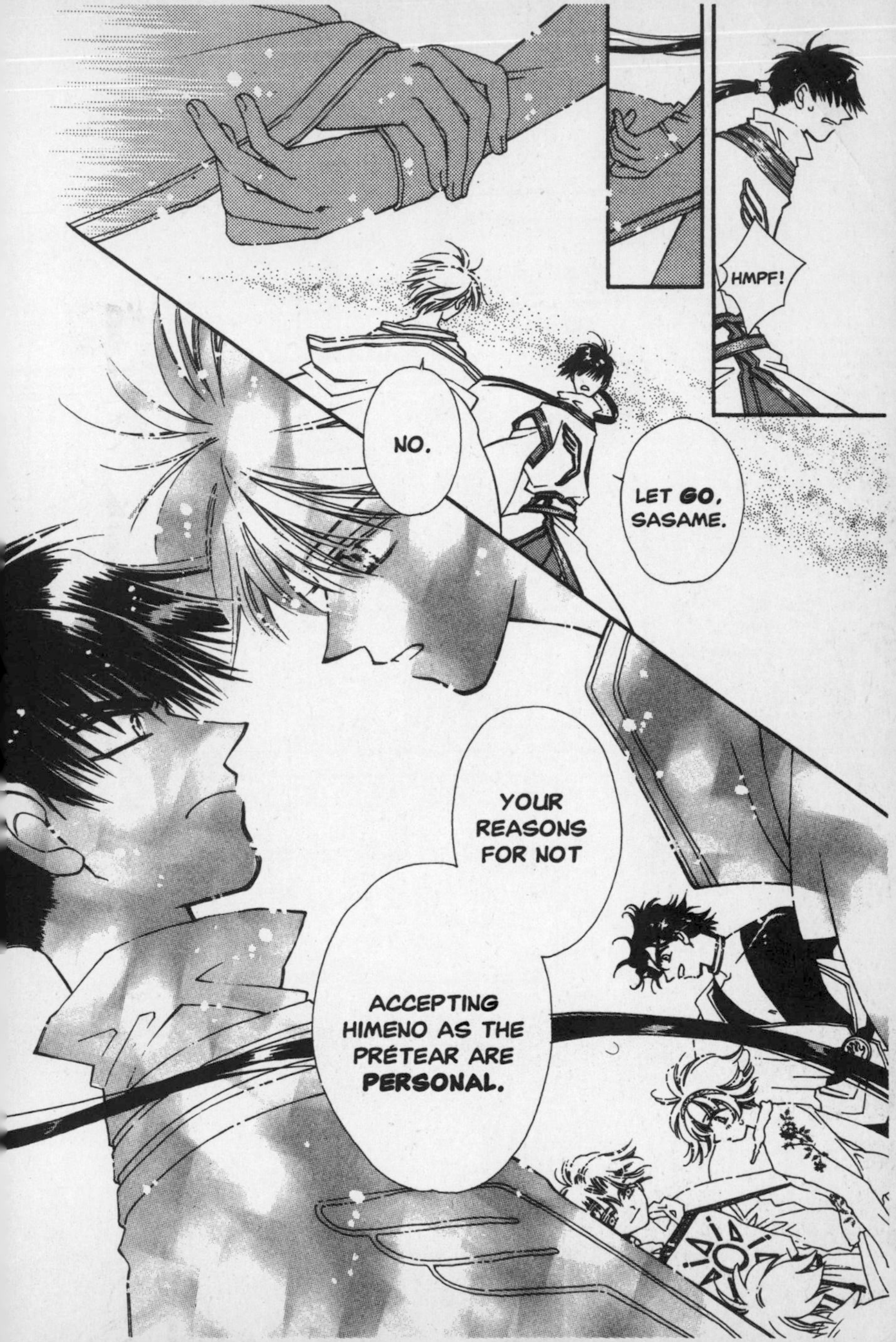
HMPF!
LET GO, SASAME.
NO.
YOUR REASONS FOR NOT
ACCEPTING HIMENO AS THE PRÉTEAR ARE PERSONAL.

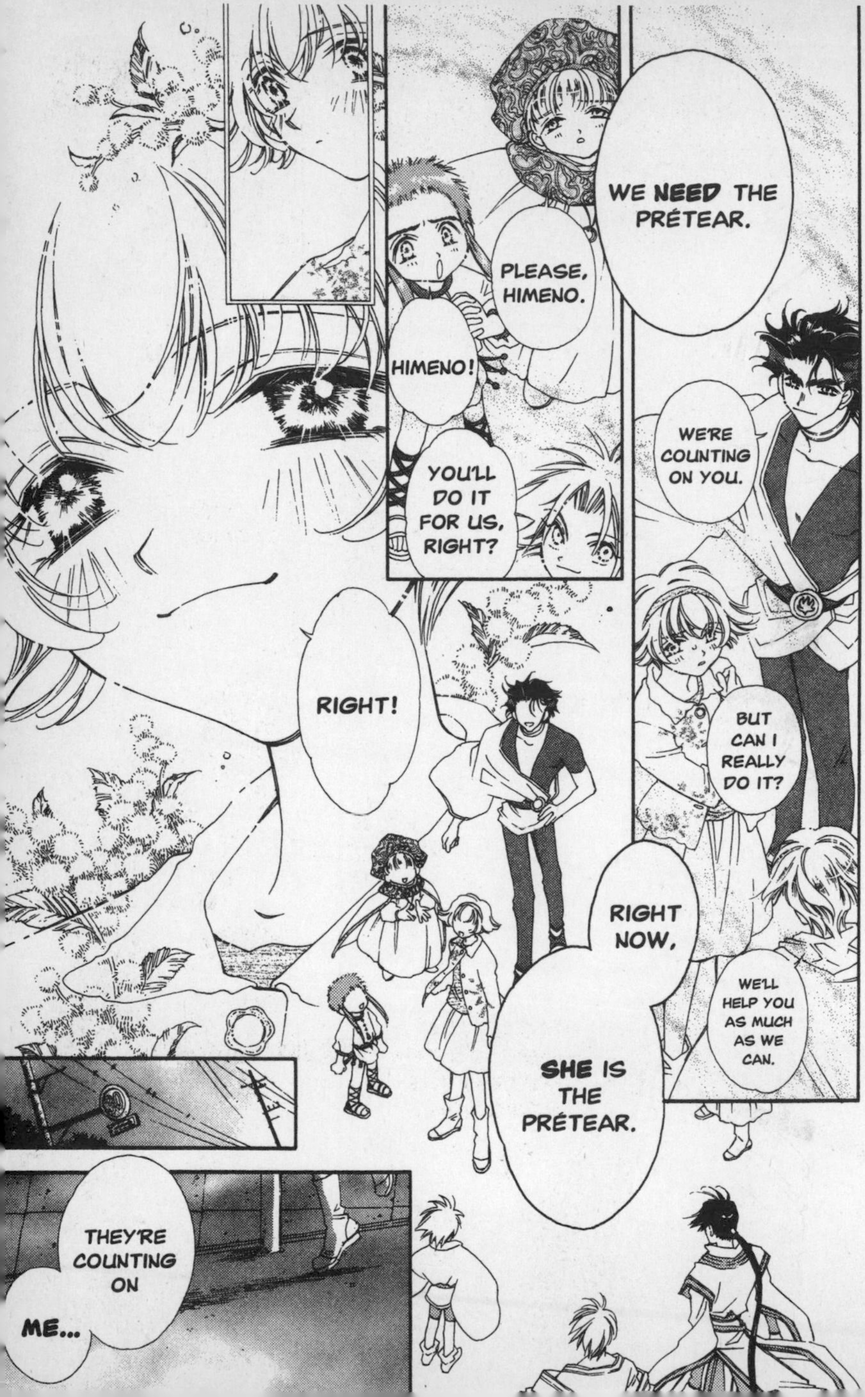
WE NEED THE PRÉTEAR.
PLEASE, HIMENO.
HIMENO!
WE'RE COUNTING ON YOU.
YOU'LL DO IT FOR US, RIGHT?
BUT CAN I REALLY DO IT?
WE'LL HELP YOU AS MUCH AS WE CAN.
RIGHT NOW,
SHE IS THE PRÉTEAR.
RIGHT!
THEY'RE COUNTING ON
ME...

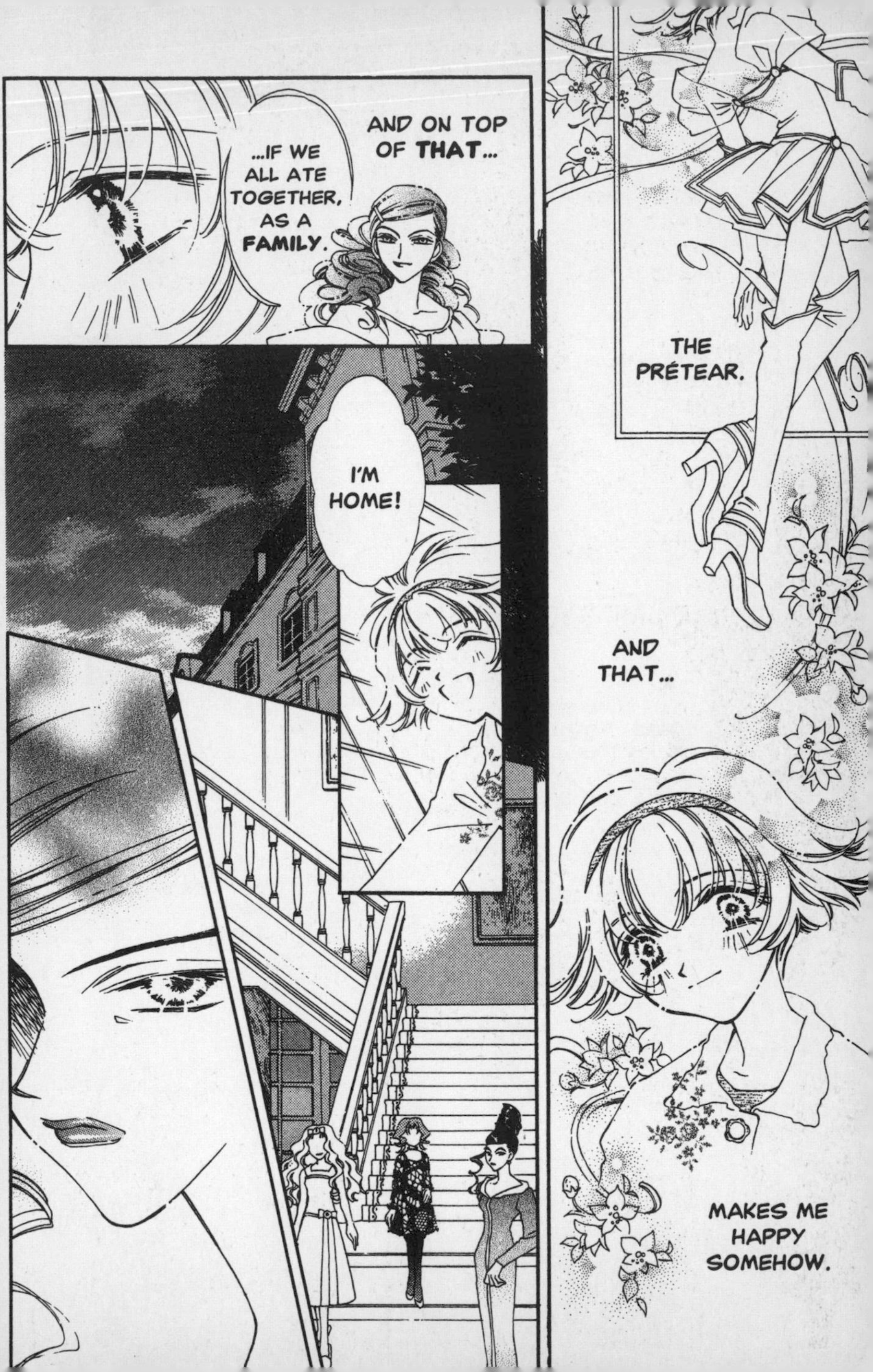
...IF WE ALL ATE TOGETHER, AS A FAMILY.
AND ON TOP OF THAT...
I'M HOME!
THE PRÉTEAR.
AND THAT...
MAKES ME HAPPY SOMEHOW.

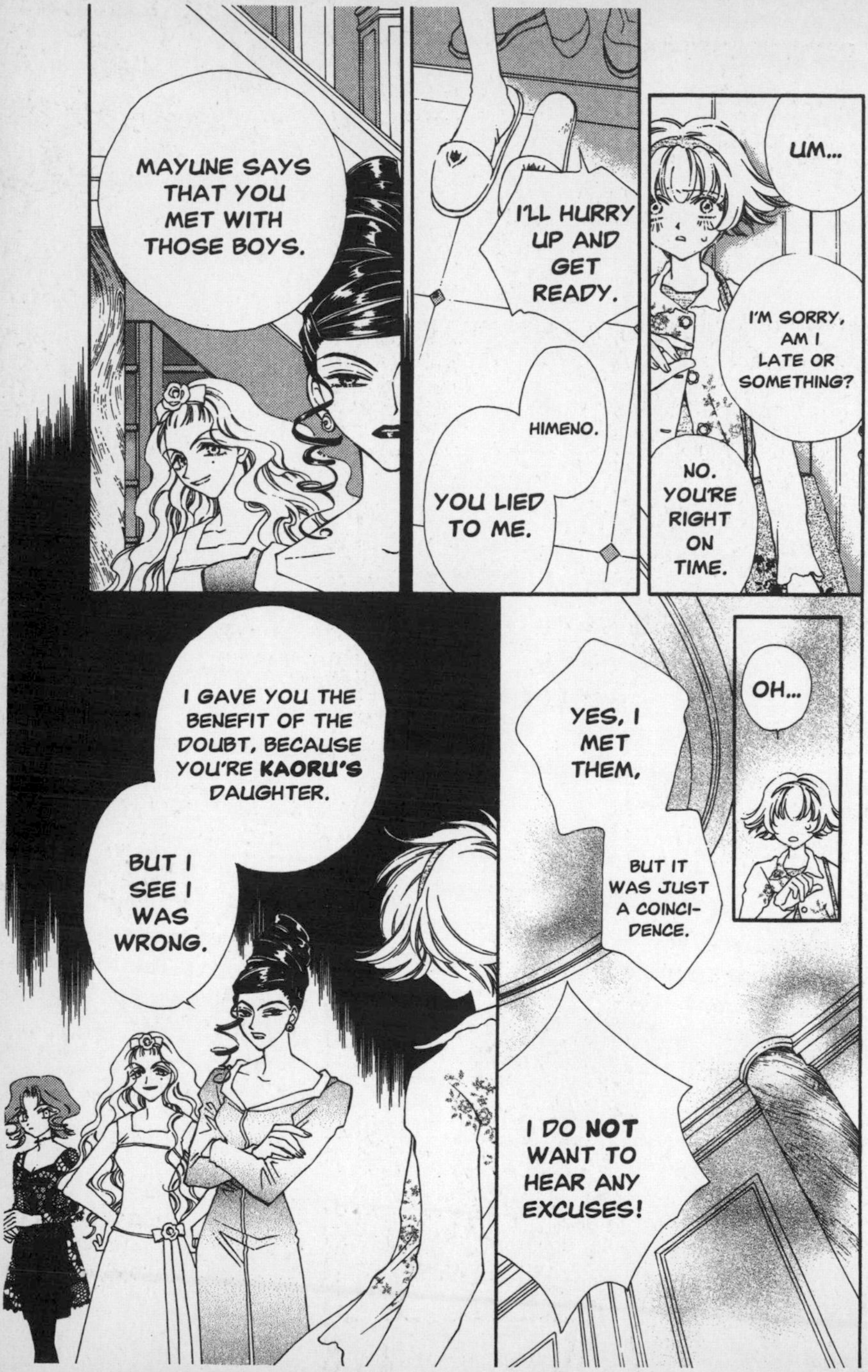
UM...
I'M SORRY, AM I LATE OR SOMETHING?
NO. YOU'RE RIGHT ON TIME.
I'LL HURRY UP AND GET READY.
HIMENO.
YOU LIED TO ME.
MAYUNE SAYS THAT YOU MET WITH THOSE BOYS.
OH...
YES, I MET THEM,
BUT IT WAS JUST A COINCI-DENCE.
I DO **NOT** WANT TO HEAR ANY EXCUSES!
I GAVE YOU THE BENEFIT OF THE DOUBT, BECAUSE YOU'RE **KAORU'S** DAUGHTER.
BUT I SEE I WAS WRONG.

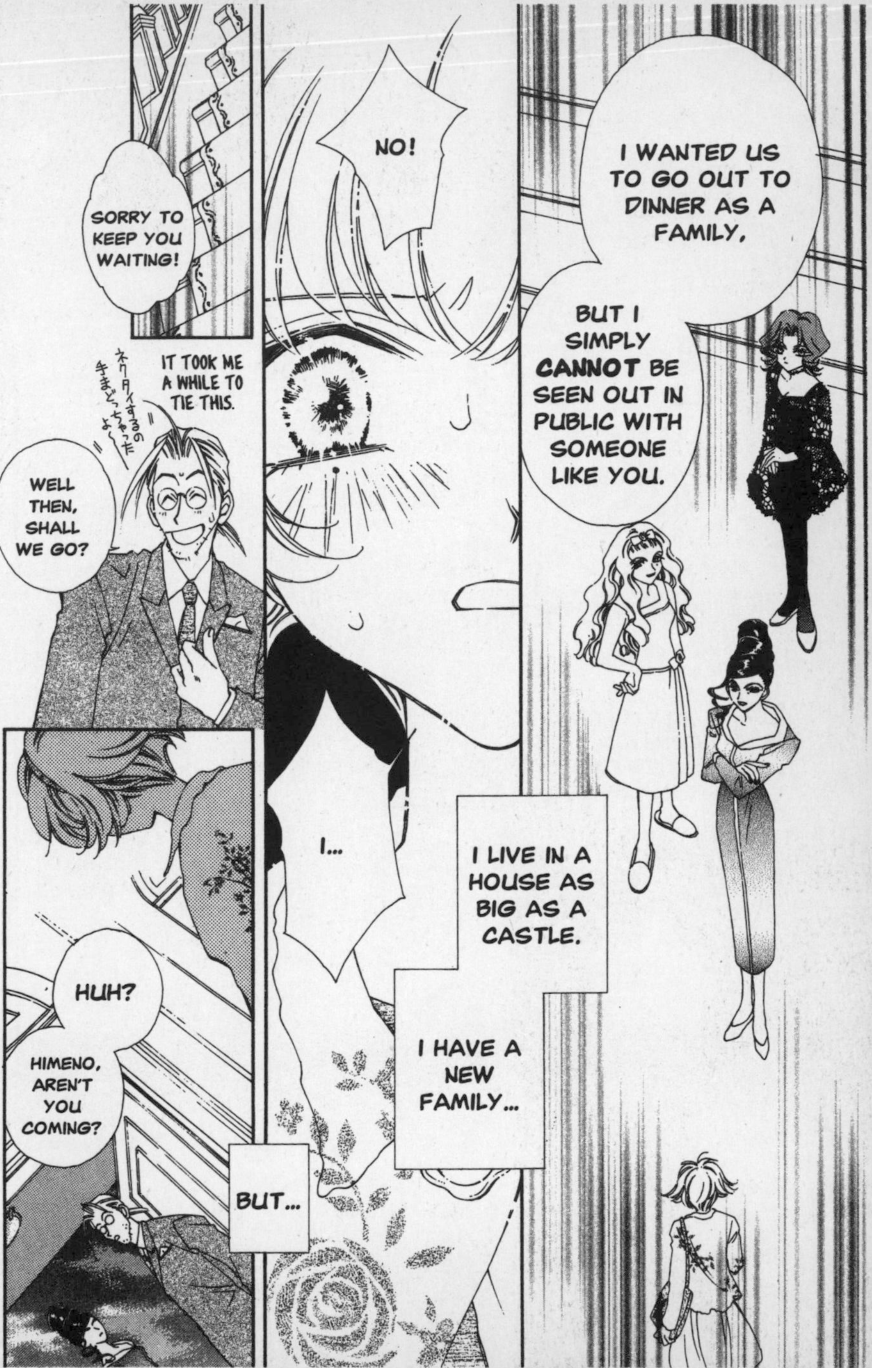
I WANTED US TO GO OUT TO DINNER AS A FAMILY,
BUT I SIMPLY **CANNOT** BE SEEN OUT IN PUBLIC WITH SOMEONE LIKE YOU.
NO!
I...
I LIVE IN A HOUSE AS BIG AS A CASTLE.
I HAVE A NEW FAMILY...
BUT...
SORRY TO KEEP YOU WAITING!
IT TOOK ME A WHILE TO TIE THIS.
ネクタイするの手まどっちゃったよ〜
WELL THEN, SHALL WE GO?
HUH?
HIMENO, AREN'T YOU COMING?

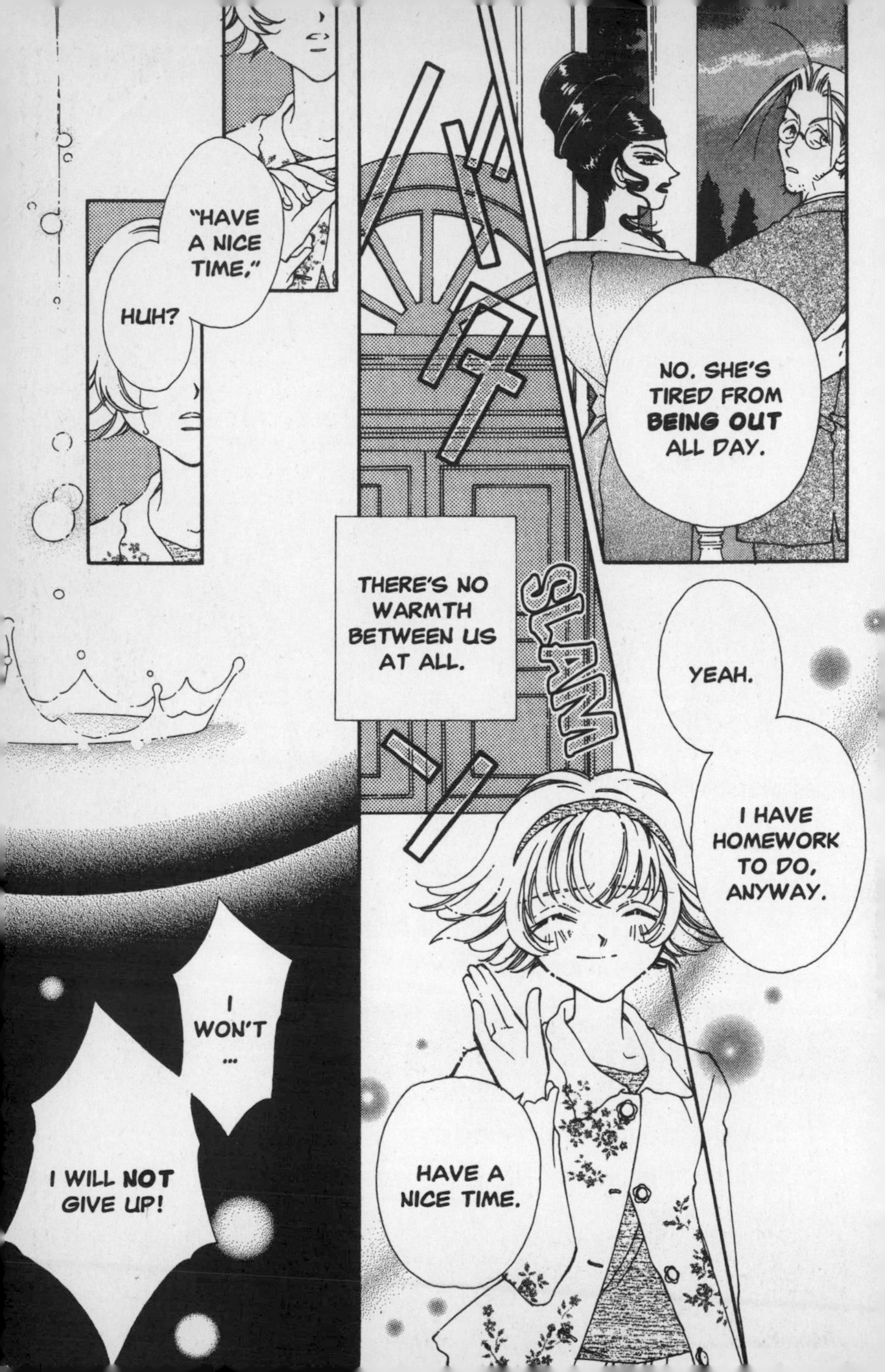
NO. SHE'S TIRED FROM BEING OUT ALL DAY.
SLAM
THERE'S NO WARMTH BETWEEN US AT ALL.
"HAVE A NICE TIME,"
HUH?
YEAH.
I HAVE HOMEWORK TO DO, ANYWAY.
HAVE A NICE TIME.
I WON'T ...
I WILL NOT GIVE UP!

S A S A M E

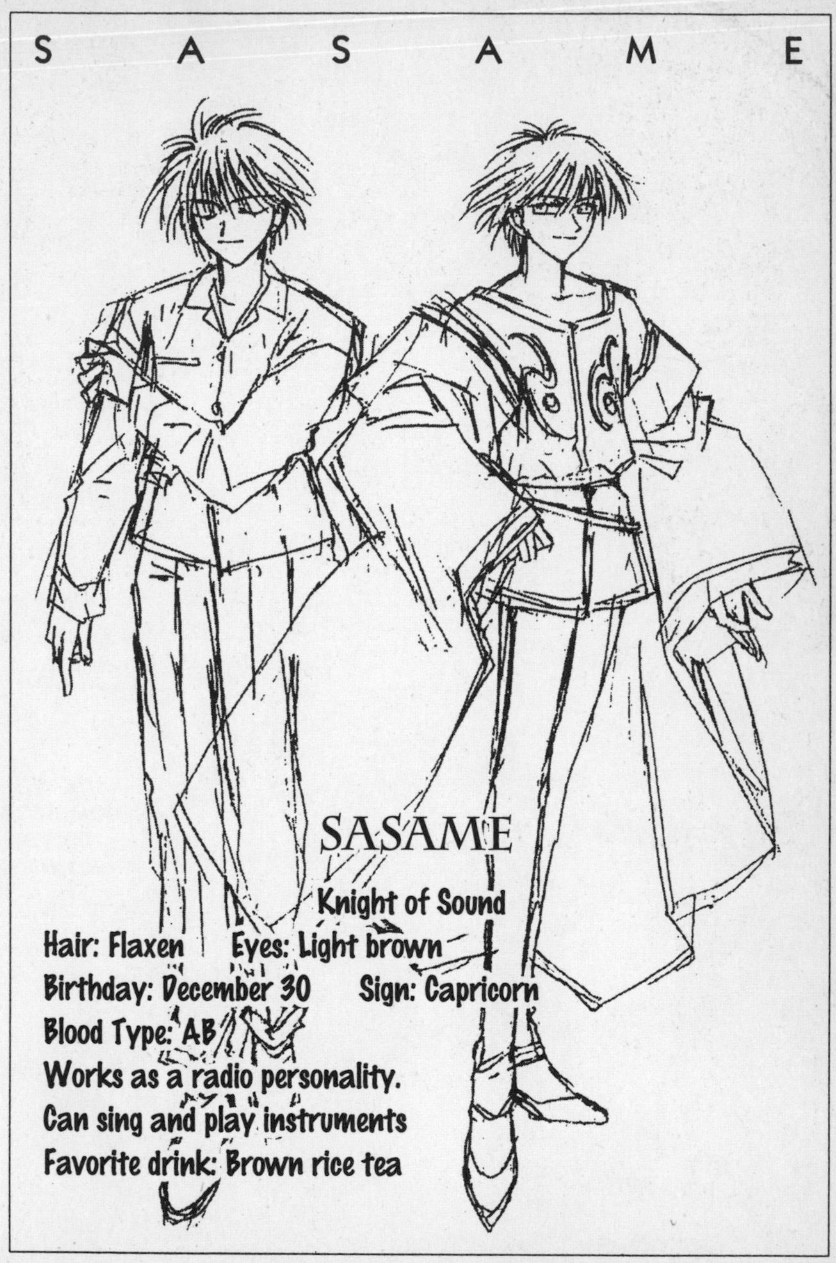

## SASAME

Knight of Sound

Hair: Flaxen  Eyes: Light brown

Birthday: December 30  Sign: Capricorn

Blood Type: AB

Works as a radio personality.

Can sing and play instruments

Favorite drink: Brown rice tea

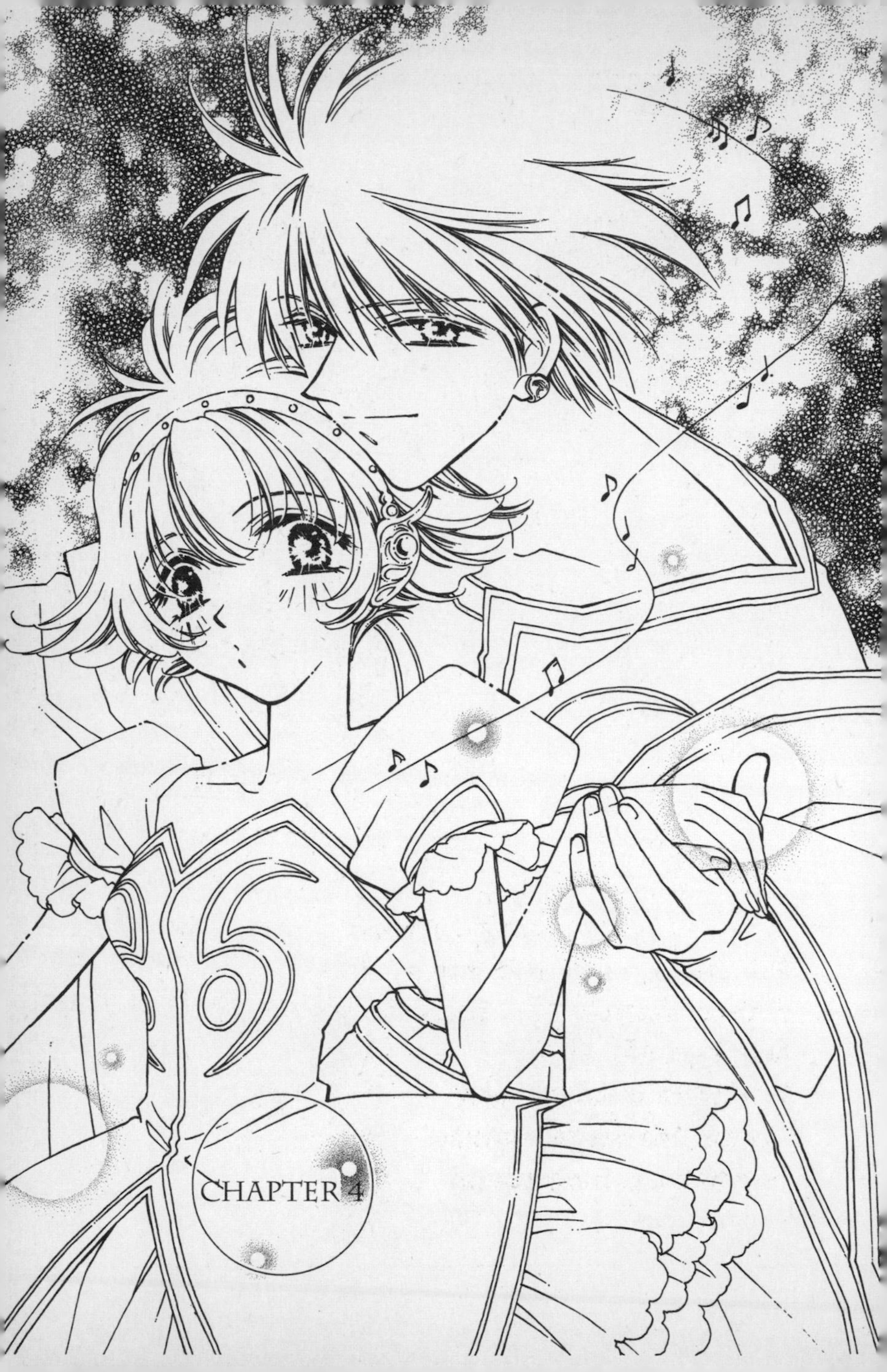
CHAPTER 4

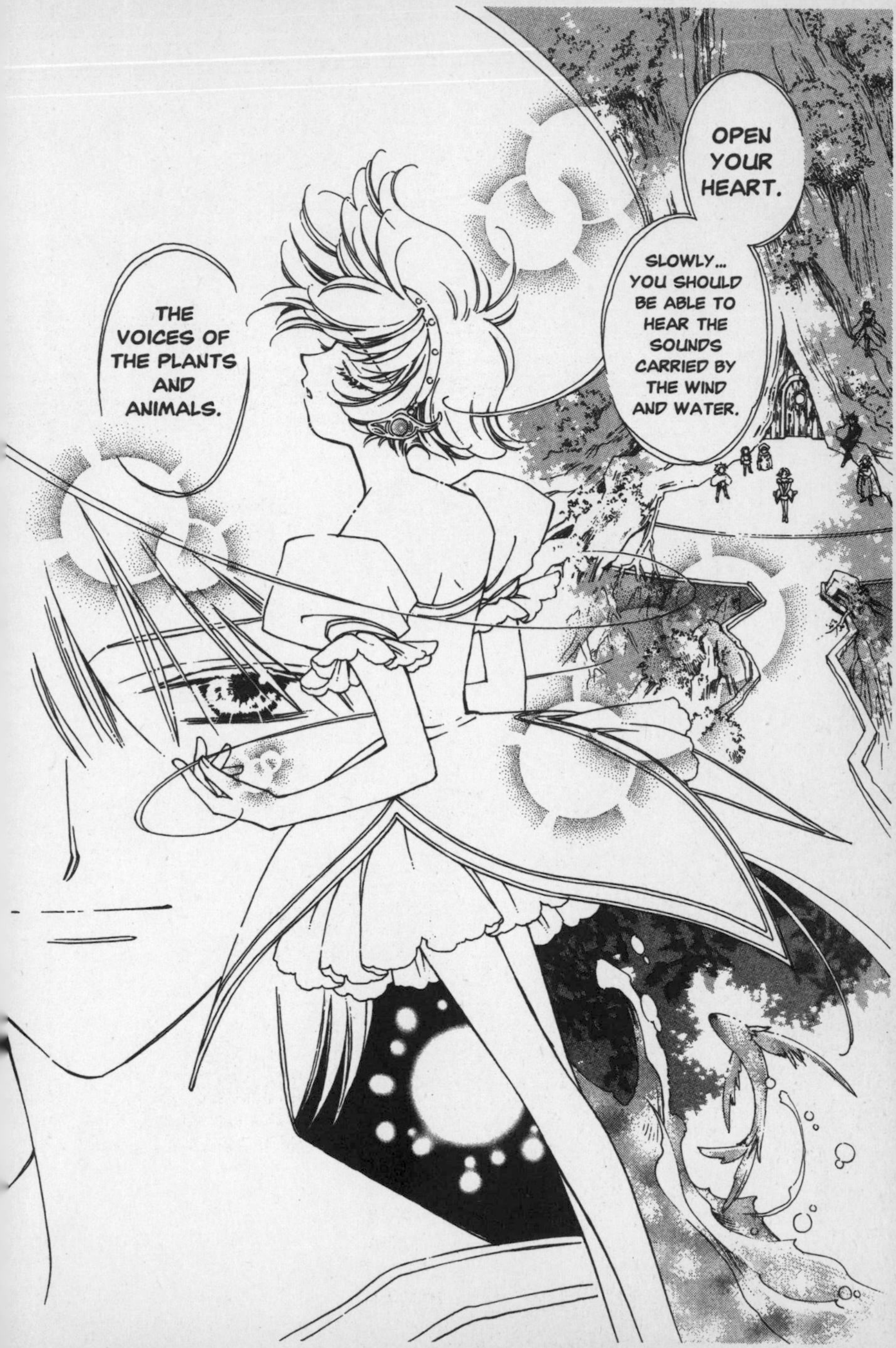
OPEN YOUR HEART.
SLOWLY... YOU SHOULD BE ABLE TO HEAR THE SOUNDS CARRIED BY THE WIND AND WATER.
THE VOICES OF THE PLANTS AND ANIMALS.

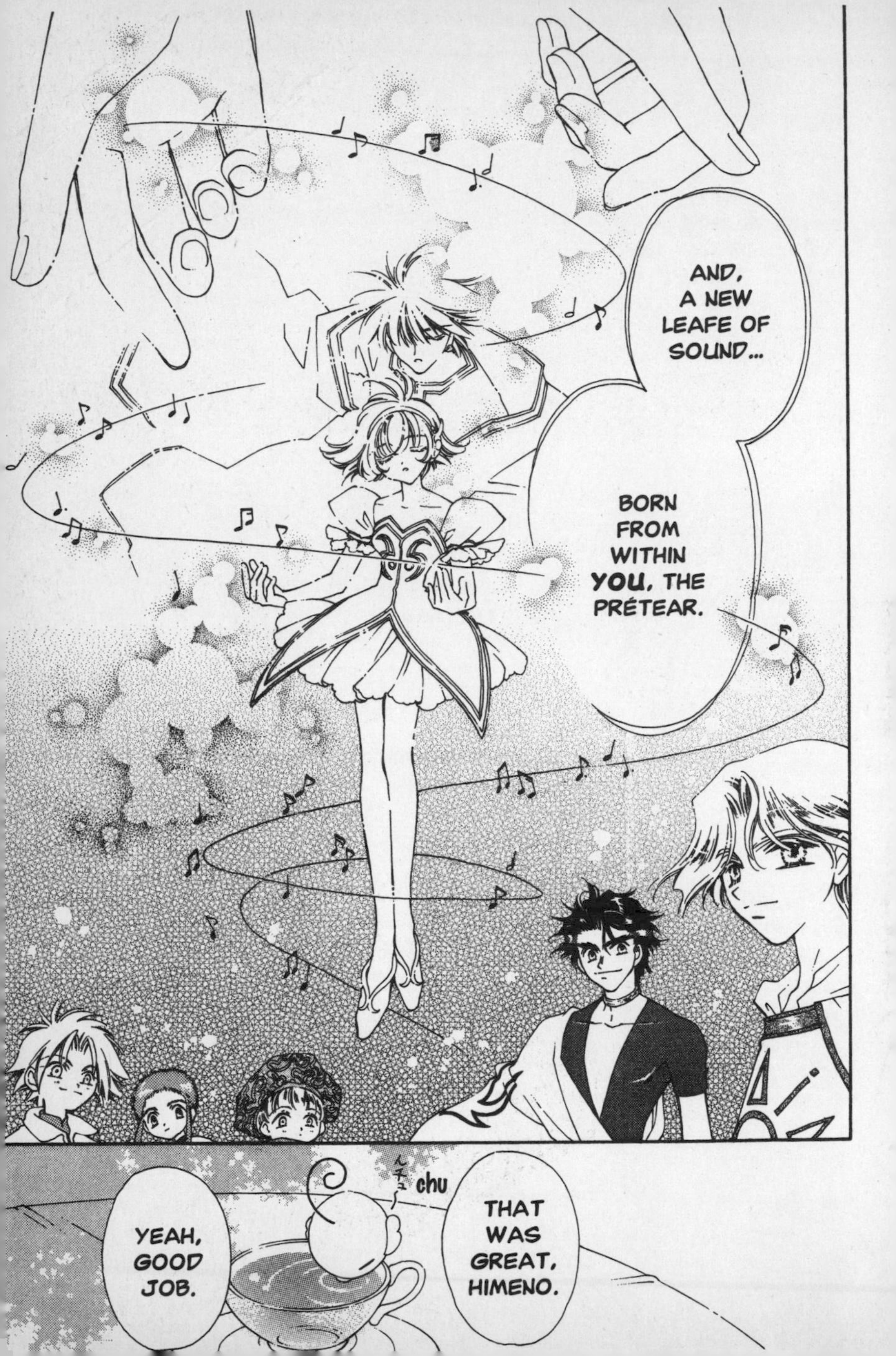
AND, A NEW LEAFE OF SOUND...
BORN FROM WITHIN YOU, THE PRÉTEAR.
THAT WAS GREAT, HIMENO.
chu
YEAH, GOOD JOB.

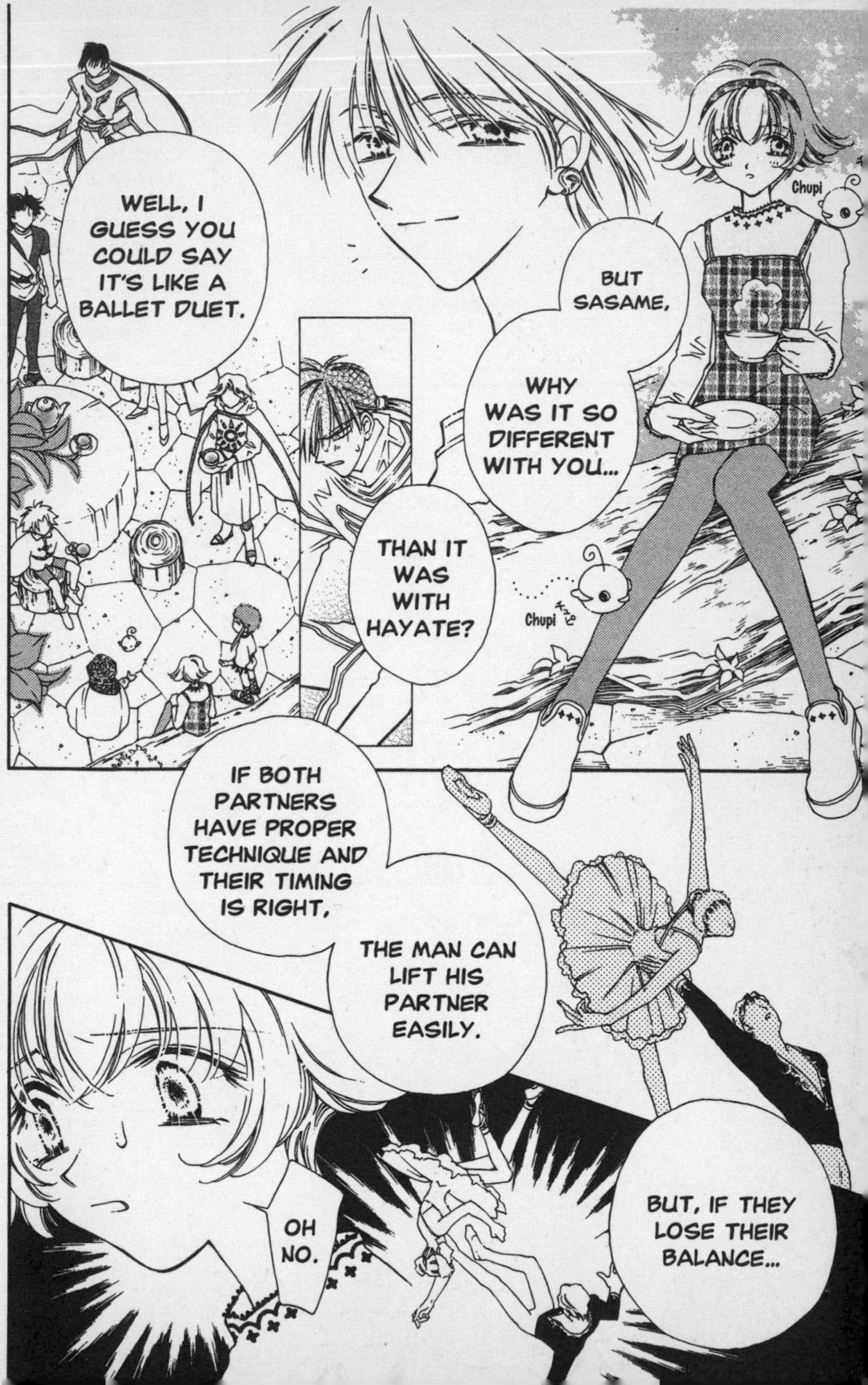
Chupi
BUT SASAME,
WHY WAS IT SO DIFFERENT WITH YOU...
THAN IT WAS WITH HAYATE?
Chupi
WELL, I GUESS YOU COULD SAY IT'S LIKE A BALLET DUET.
IF BOTH PARTNERS HAVE PROPER TECHNIQUE AND THEIR TIMING IS RIGHT,
THE MAN CAN LIFT HIS PARTNER EASILY.
BUT, IF THEY LOSE THEIR BALANCE...
OH NO.

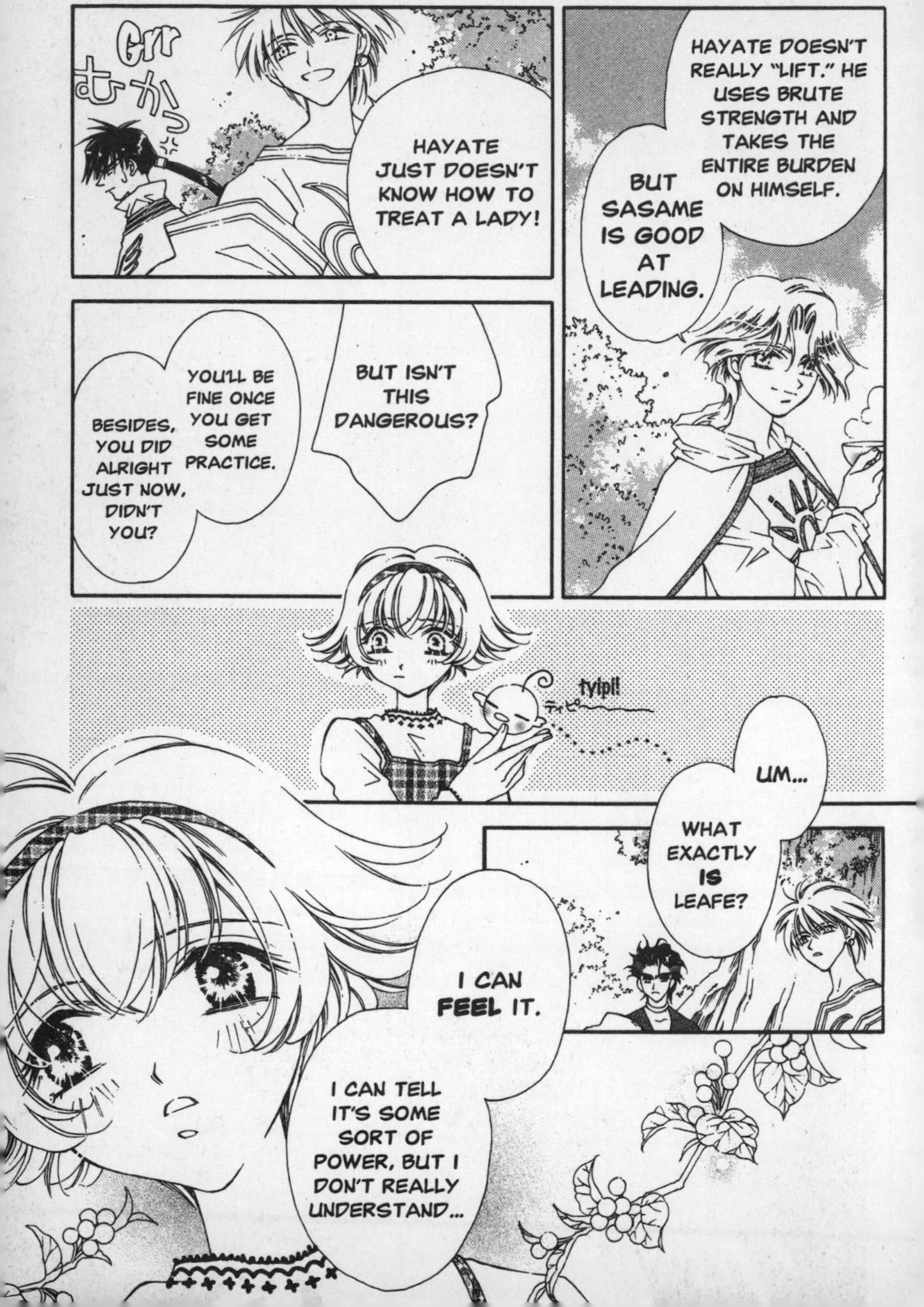
HAYATE DOESN'T REALLY "LIFT." HE USES BRUTE STRENGTH AND TAKES THE ENTIRE BURDEN ON HIMSELF.
BUT SASAME IS GOOD AT LEADING.
Grr
むかっ
HAYATE JUST DOESN'T KNOW HOW TO TREAT A LADY!
BUT ISN'T THIS DANGEROUS?
YOU'LL BE FINE ONCE YOU GET SOME PRACTICE.
BESIDES, YOU DID ALRIGHT JUST NOW, DIDN'T YOU?
tyipi!
UM...
WHAT EXACTLY IS LEAFE?
I CAN FEEL IT.
I CAN TELL IT'S SOME SORT OF POWER, BUT I DON'T REALLY UNDERSTAND...

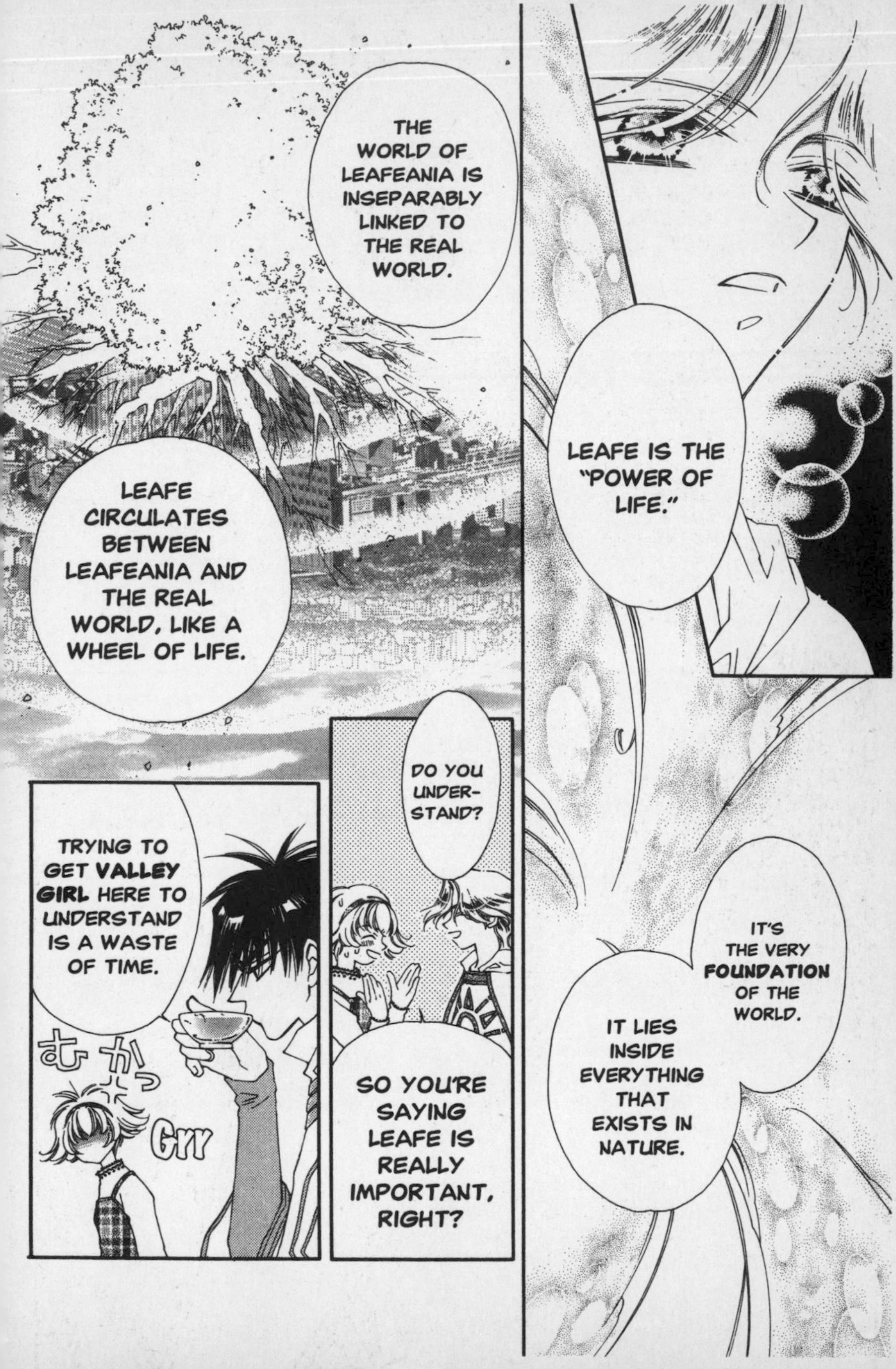
LEAFE IS THE "POWER OF LIFE."
IT'S THE VERY FOUNDATION OF THE WORLD.
IT LIES INSIDE EVERYTHING THAT EXISTS IN NATURE.
THE WORLD OF LEAFEANIA IS INSEPARABLY LINKED TO THE REAL WORLD.
LEAFE CIRCULATES BETWEEN LEAFEANIA AND THE REAL WORLD, LIKE A WHEEL OF LIFE.
DO YOU UNDER-STAND?
SO YOU'RE SAYING LEAFE IS REALLY IMPORTANT, RIGHT?
TRYING TO GET VALLEY GIRL HERE TO UNDERSTAND IS A WASTE OF TIME.
むかっ
Grr

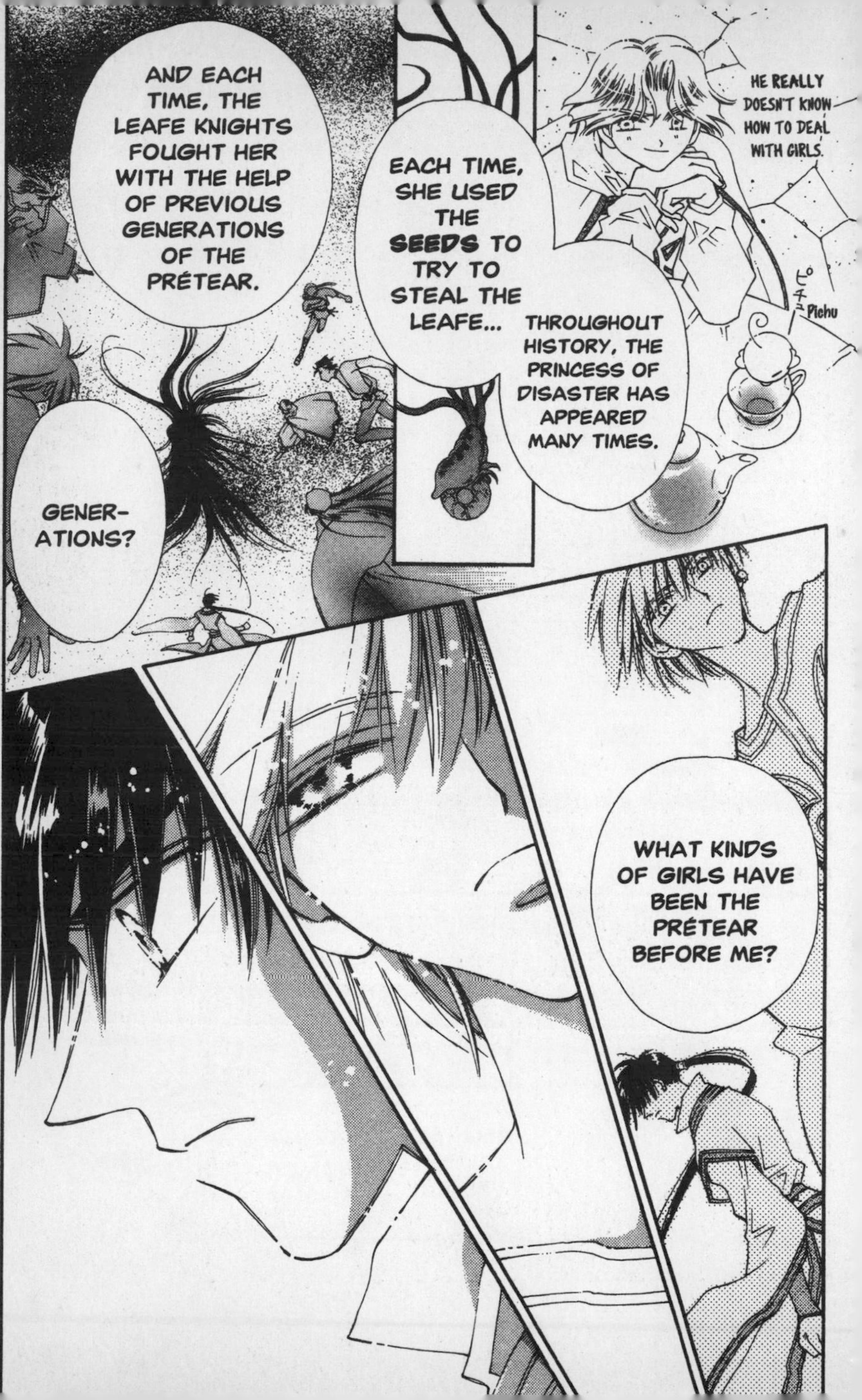
HE REALLY DOESN'T KNOW HOW TO DEAL WITH GIRLS.
ピチュ Pichu
THROUGHOUT HISTORY, THE PRINCESS OF DISASTER HAS APPEARED MANY TIMES.
EACH TIME, SHE USED THE SEEDS TO TRY TO STEAL THE LEAFE...
AND EACH TIME, THE LEAFE KNIGHTS FOUGHT HER WITH THE HELP OF PREVIOUS GENERATIONS OF THE PRÉTEAR.
GENER-ATIONS?
WHAT KINDS OF GIRLS HAVE BEEN THE PRÉTEAR BEFORE ME?

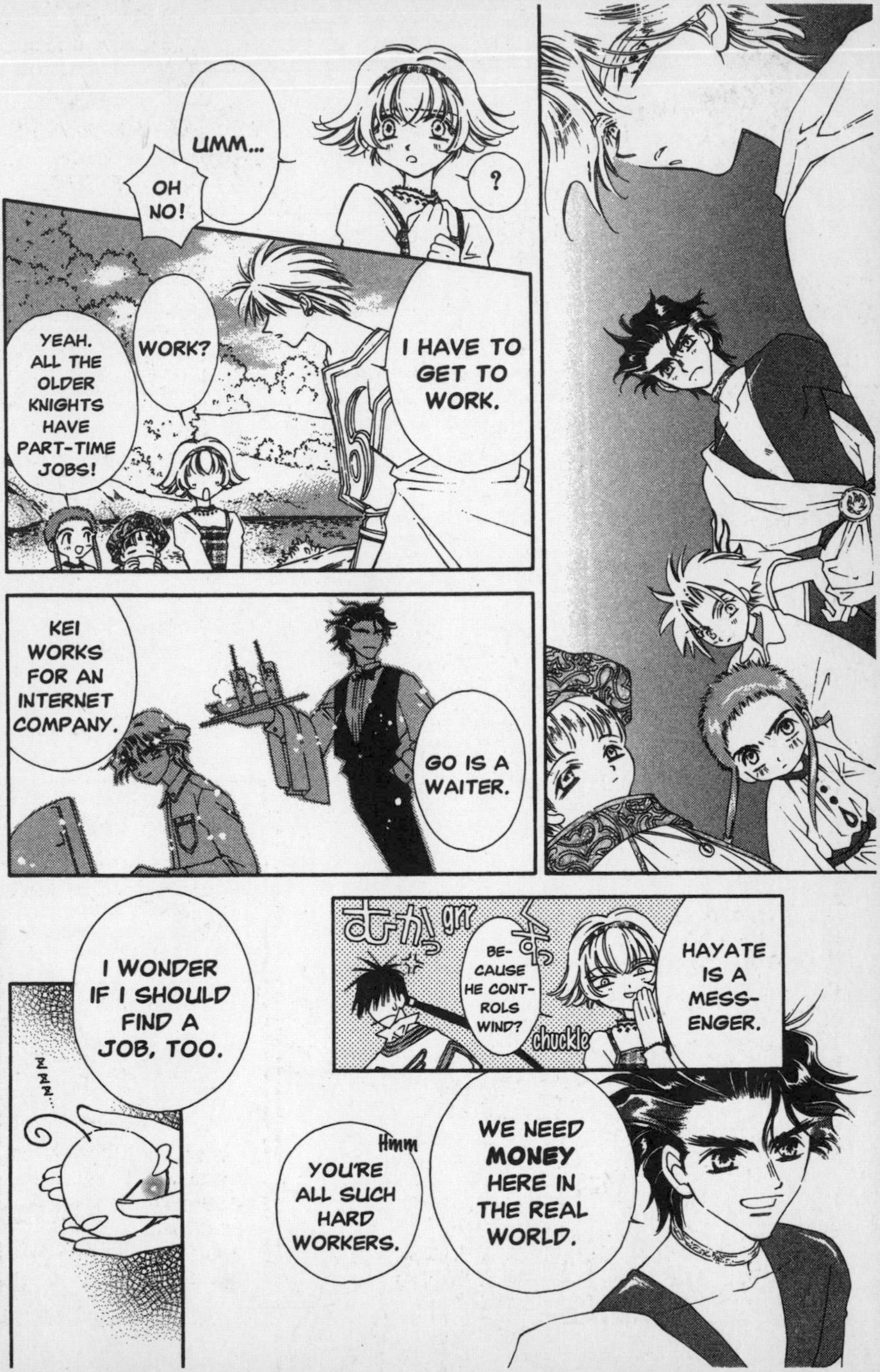
?
UMM...
OH NO!
I HAVE TO GET TO WORK.
WORK?
YEAH. ALL THE OLDER KNIGHTS HAVE PART-TIME JOBS!
GO IS A WAITER.
KEI WORKS FOR AN INTERNET COMPANY.
HAYATE IS A MESS-ENGER.
くすっ chuckle
BE-CAUSE HE CONT-ROLS WIND?
むかっ grr
WE NEED MONEY HERE IN THE REAL WORLD.
Hmm
YOU'RE ALL SUCH HARD WORKERS.
I WONDER IF I SHOULD FIND A JOB, TOO.
ZZZ...

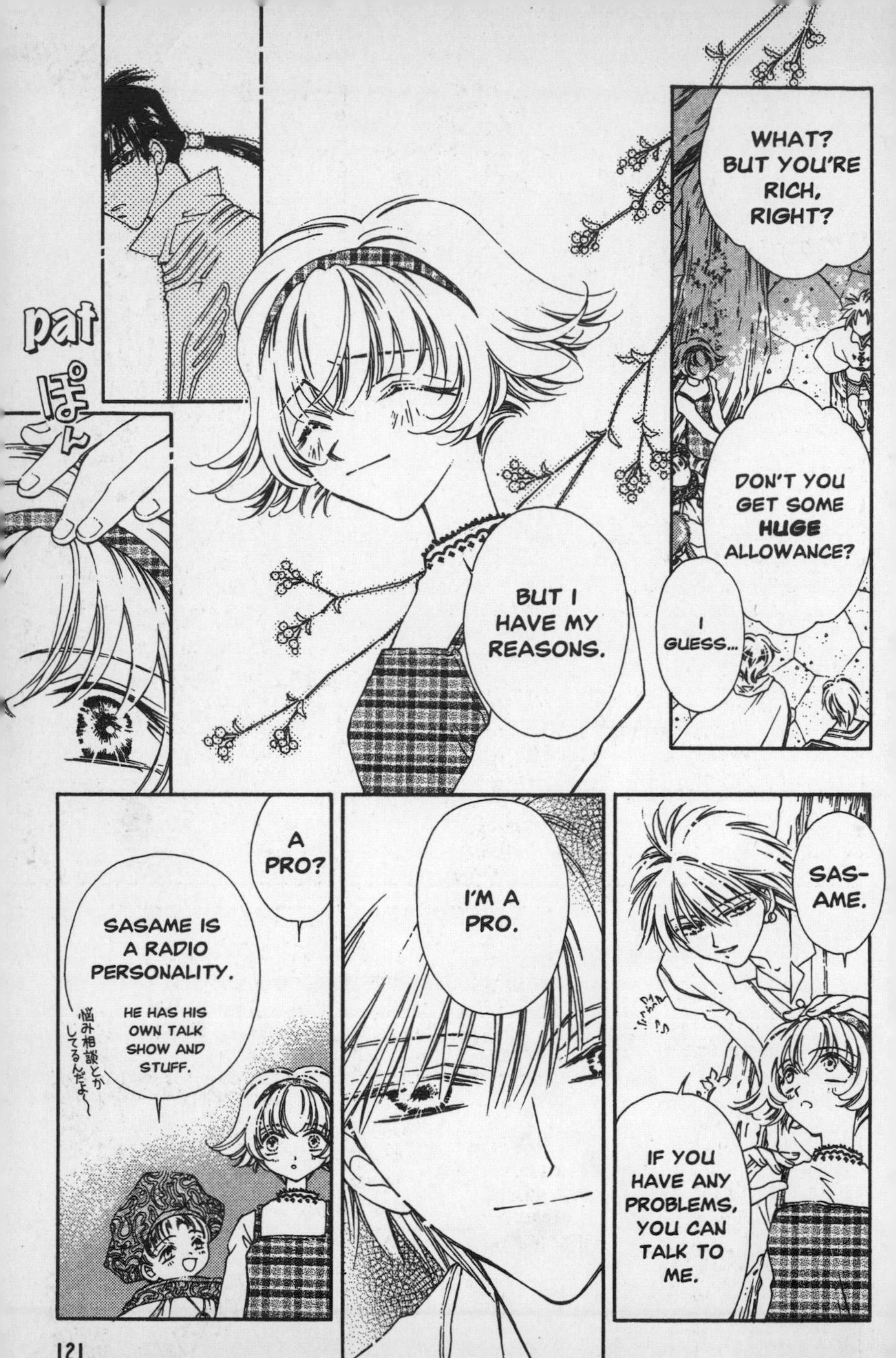
WHAT? BUT YOU'RE RICH, RIGHT?
DON'T YOU GET SOME **HUGE** ALLOWANCE?
I GUESS...
BUT I HAVE MY REASONS.
pat
ぽん
SAS-AME.
IF YOU HAVE ANY PROBLEMS, YOU CAN TALK TO ME.
I'M A PRO.
A PRO?
SASAME IS A RADIO PERSONALITY.
HE HAS HIS OWN TALK SHOW AND STUFF.
悩み相談とかしてるんだよ～

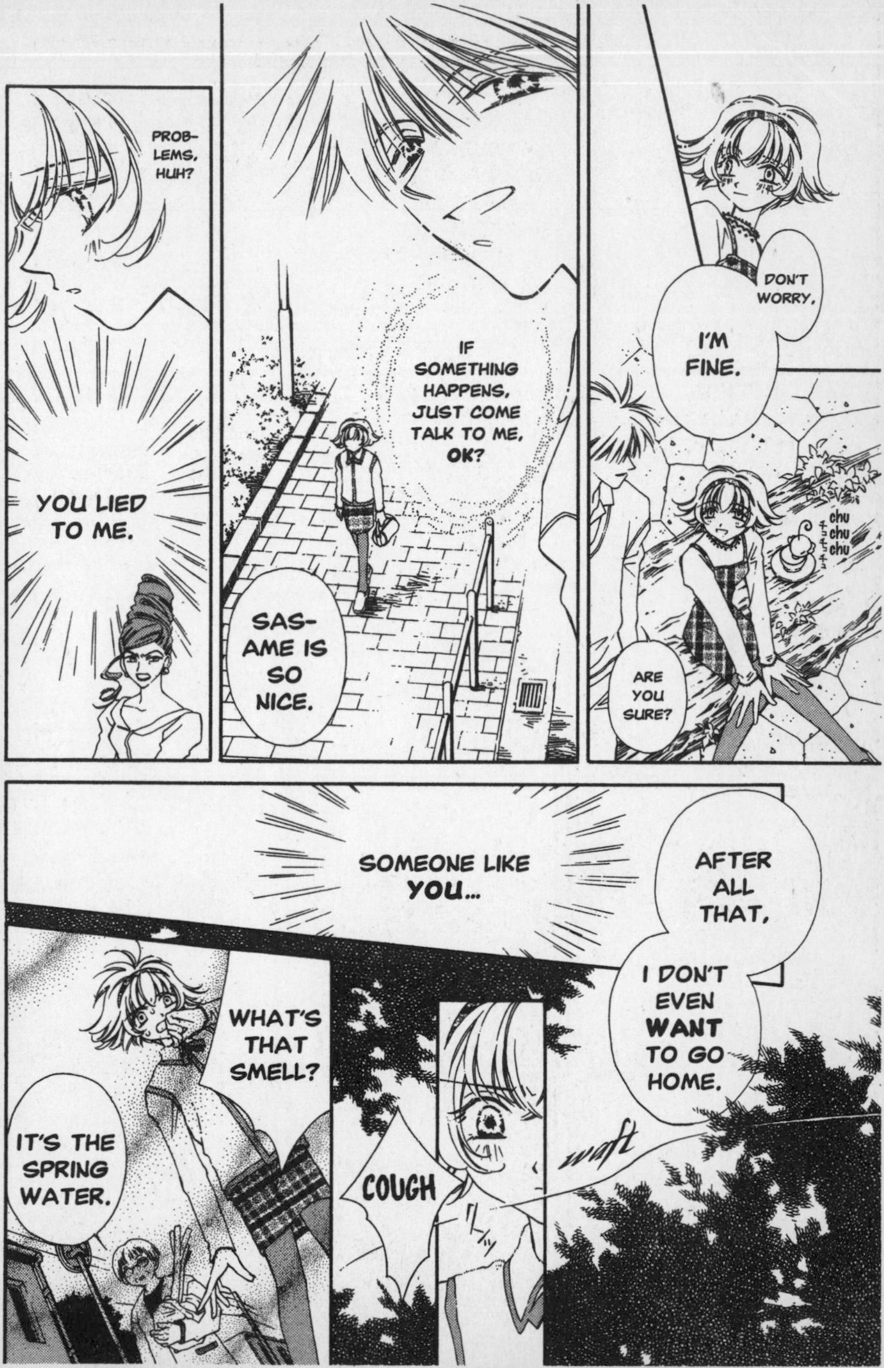
DON'T WORRY,
I'M FINE.
ARE YOU SURE?
chu chu chu
IF SOMETHING HAPPENS, JUST COME TALK TO ME, OK?
SAS-AME IS SO NICE.
PROB-LEMS, HUH?
YOU LIED TO ME.
AFTER ALL THAT,
SOMEONE LIKE YOU...
I DON'T EVEN WANT TO GO HOME.
waft
COUGH
WHAT'S THAT SMELL?
IT'S THE SPRING WATER.

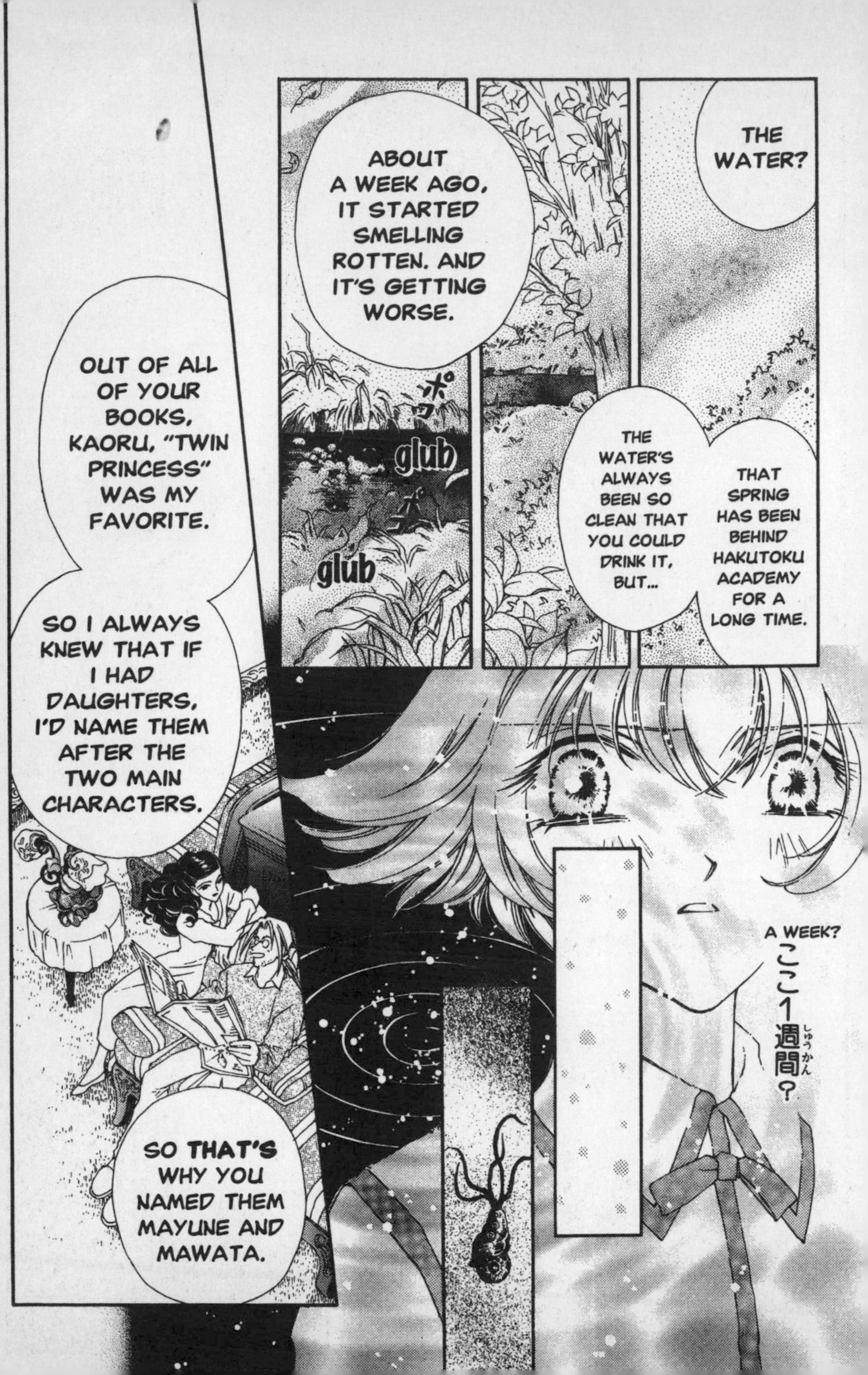
THE WATER?
THAT SPRING HAS BEEN BEHIND HAKUTOKU ACADEMY FOR A LONG TIME.
THE WATER'S ALWAYS BEEN SO CLEAN THAT YOU COULD DRINK IT, BUT...
ABOUT A WEEK AGO, IT STARTED SMELLING ROTTEN. AND IT'S GETTING WORSE.
glub
glub
A WEEK?
ここ1週間?
OUT OF ALL OF YOUR BOOKS, KAORU, "TWIN PRINCESS" WAS MY FAVORITE.
SO I ALWAYS KNEW THAT IF I HAD DAUGHTERS, I'D NAME THEM AFTER THE TWO MAIN CHARACTERS.
SO THAT'S WHY YOU NAMED THEM MAYUNE AND MAWATA.

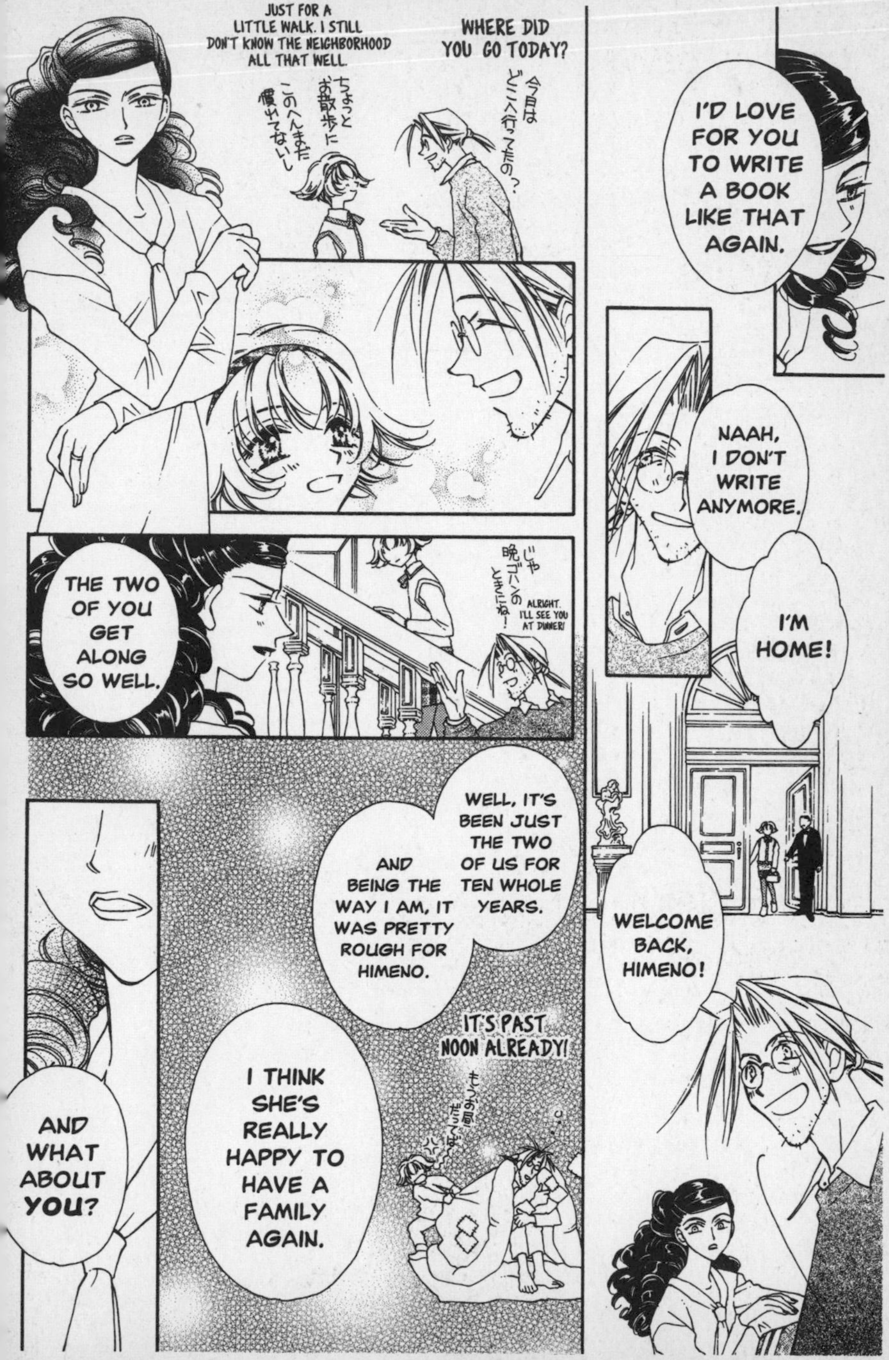
I'D LOVE FOR YOU TO WRITE A BOOK LIKE THAT AGAIN.
NAAH, I DON'T WRITE ANYMORE.
I'M HOME!
WELCOME BACK, HIMENO!
WHERE DID YOU GO TODAY?
今日はどこへ行ってたの？
JUST FOR A LITTLE WALK. I STILL DON'T KNOW THE NEIGHBORHOOD ALL THAT WELL.
ちょっとお散歩に このへんまだ慣れてないし
ALRIGHT. I'LL SEE YOU AT DINNER!
じゃ晩ゴハンのときにね！
THE TWO OF YOU GET ALONG SO WELL.
WELL, IT'S BEEN JUST THE TWO OF US FOR TEN WHOLE YEARS.
AND BEING THE WAY I AM, IT WAS PRETTY ROUGH FOR HIMENO.
IT'S PAST NOON ALREADY!
もうお昼だってば～
I THINK SHE'S REALLY HAPPY TO HAVE A FAMILY AGAIN.
AND WHAT ABOUT YOU?

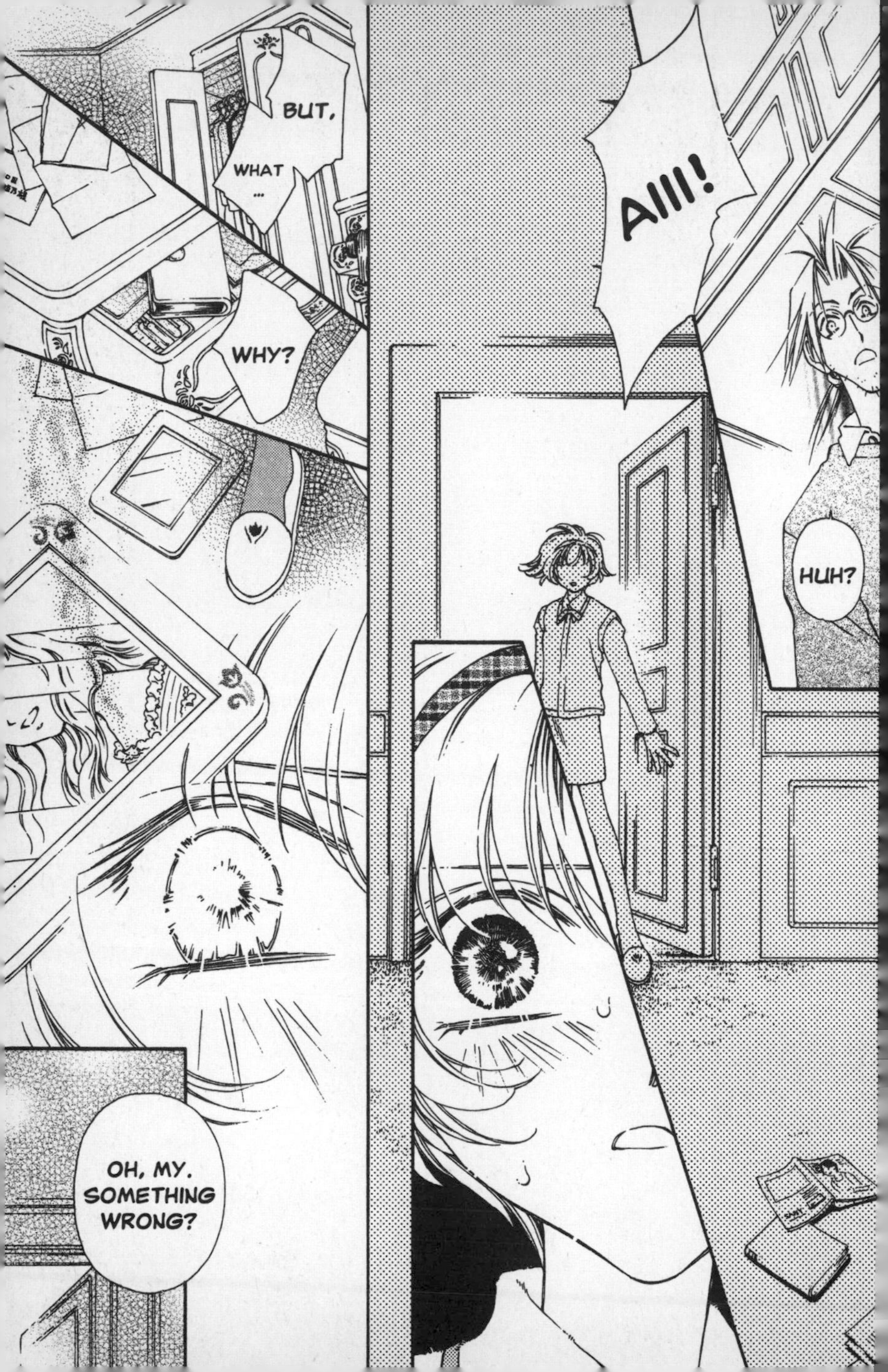
Alll!
HUH?
BUT,
WHAT ...
WHY?
OH, MY. SOMETHING WRONG?

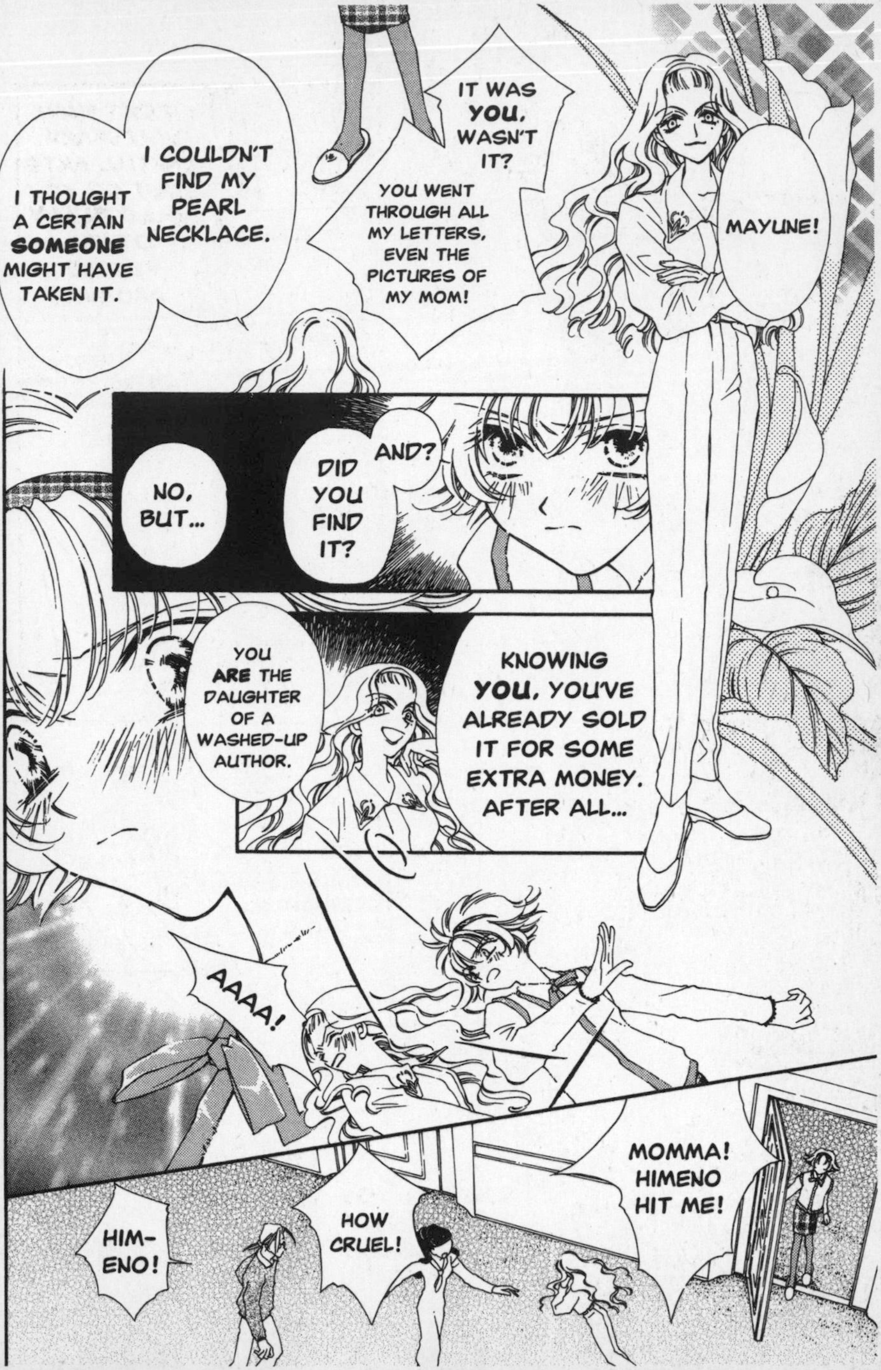
MAYUNE!
IT WAS YOU, WASN'T IT?
YOU WENT THROUGH ALL MY LETTERS, EVEN THE PICTURES OF MY MOM!
I COULDN'T FIND MY PEARL NECKLACE.
I THOUGHT A CERTAIN SOMEONE MIGHT HAVE TAKEN IT.
AND?
DID YOU FIND IT?
NO, BUT...
KNOWING YOU, YOU'VE ALREADY SOLD IT FOR SOME EXTRA MONEY. AFTER ALL...
YOU ARE THE DAUGHTER OF A WASHED-UP AUTHOR.
AAAA!
MOMMA! HIMENO HIT ME!
HOW CRUEL!
HIM-ENO!

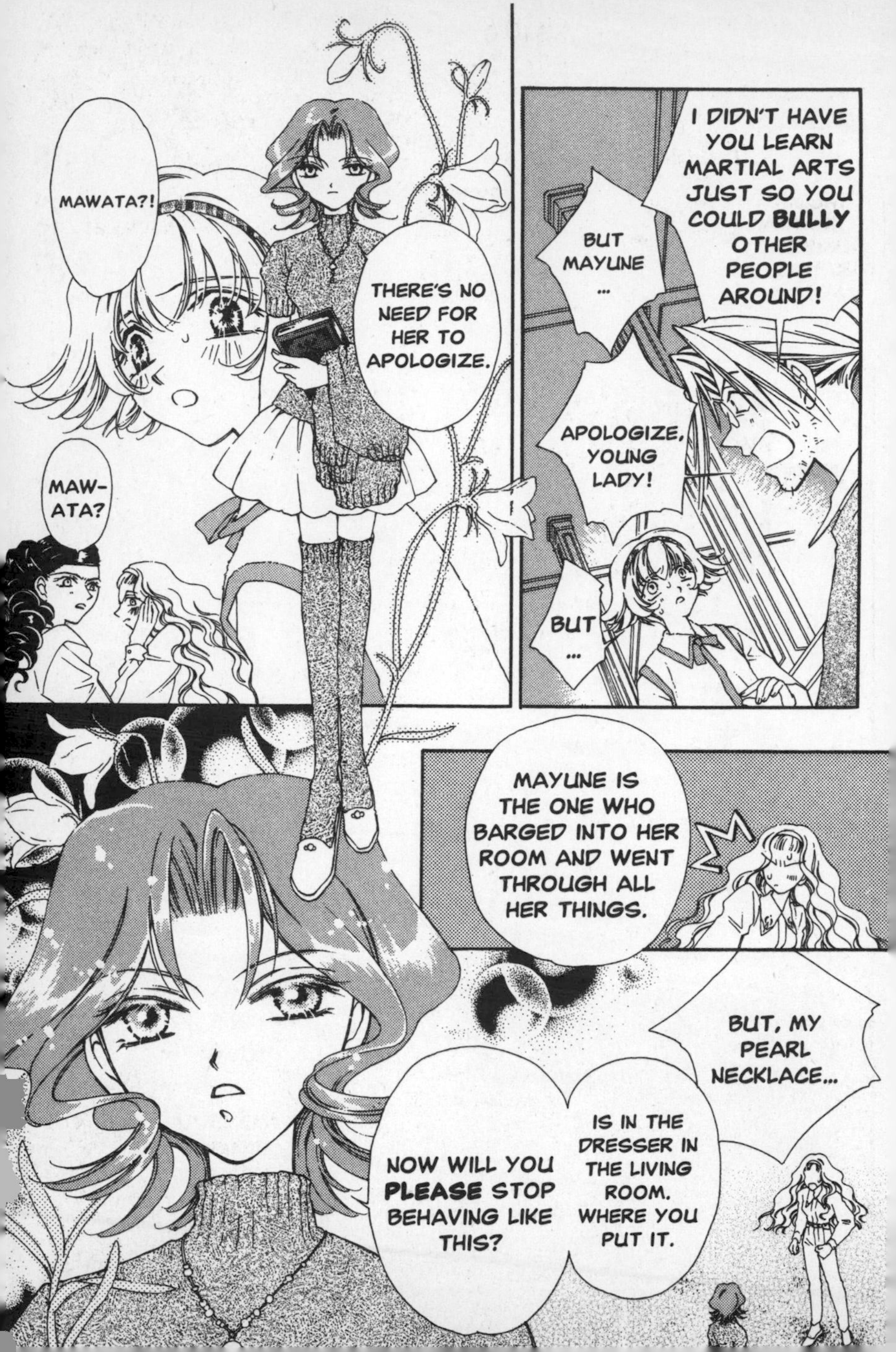
I DIDN'T HAVE YOU LEARN MARTIAL ARTS JUST SO YOU COULD BULLY OTHER PEOPLE AROUND!
BUT MAYUNE ...
APOLOGIZE, YOUNG LADY!
BUT ...
THERE'S NO NEED FOR HER TO APOLOGIZE.
MAWATA?!
MAW-ATA?
MAYUNE IS THE ONE WHO BARGED INTO HER ROOM AND WENT THROUGH ALL HER THINGS.
BUT, MY PEARL NECKLACE...
IS IN THE DRESSER IN THE LIVING ROOM. WHERE YOU PUT IT.
NOW WILL YOU PLEASE STOP BEHAVING LIKE THIS?

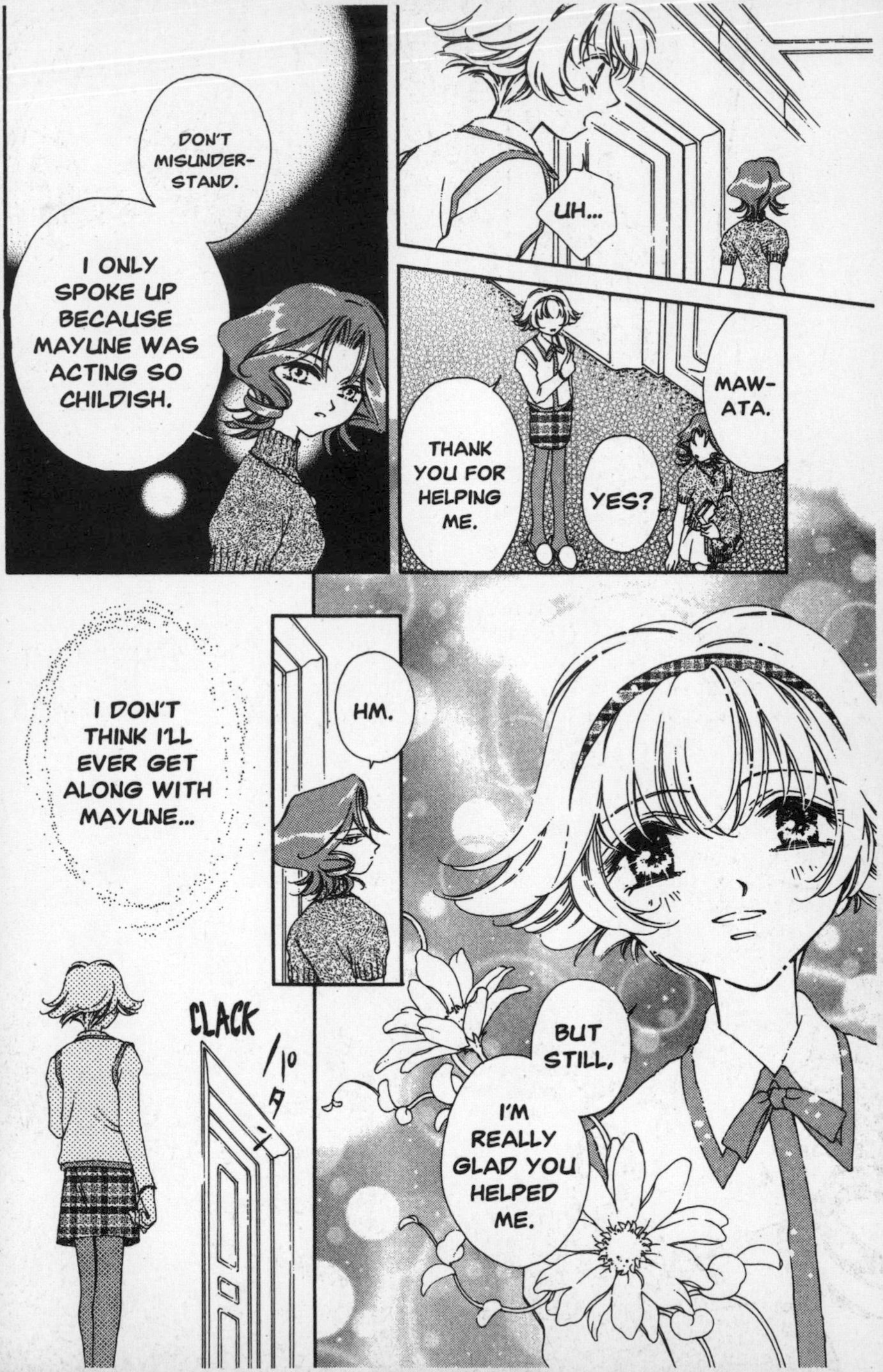

UH...
DON'T MISUNDERSTAND.
I ONLY SPOKE UP BECAUSE MAYUNE WAS ACTING SO CHILDISH.
MAW-ATA.
YES?
THANK YOU FOR HELPING ME.
HM.
I DON'T THINK I'LL EVER GET ALONG WITH MAYUNE...
CLACK
BUT STILL,
I'M REALLY GLAD YOU HELPED ME.

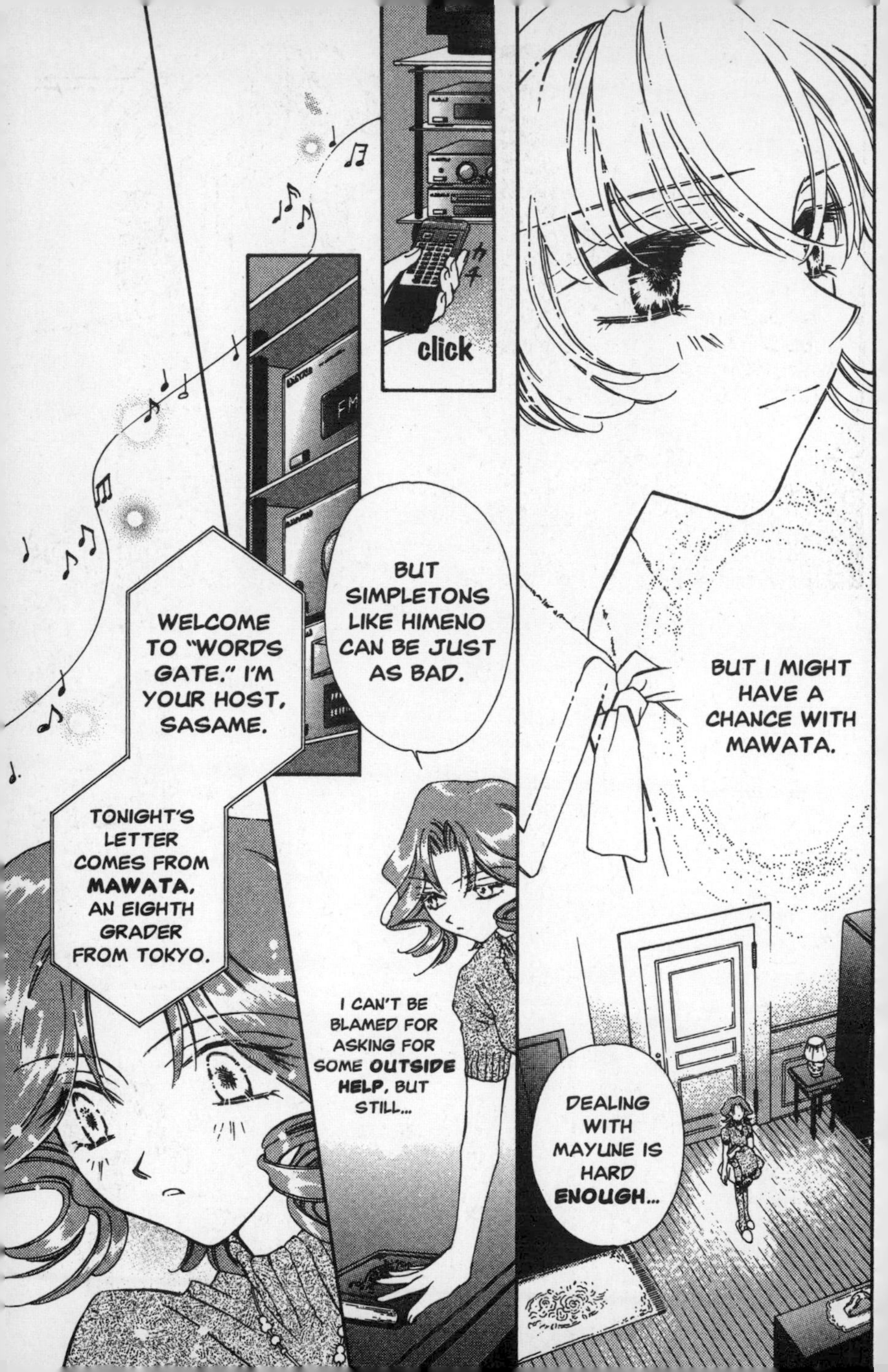

BUT I MIGHT HAVE A CHANCE WITH MAWATA.
DEALING WITH MAYUNE IS HARD ENOUGH...
click
BUT SIMPLETONS LIKE HIMENO CAN BE JUST AS BAD.
I CAN'T BE BLAMED FOR ASKING FOR SOME **OUTSIDE HELP**, BUT STILL...
WELCOME TO "WORDS GATE." I'M YOUR HOST, SASAME.
TONIGHT'S LETTER COMES FROM **MAWATA**, AN EIGHTH GRADER FROM TOKYO.

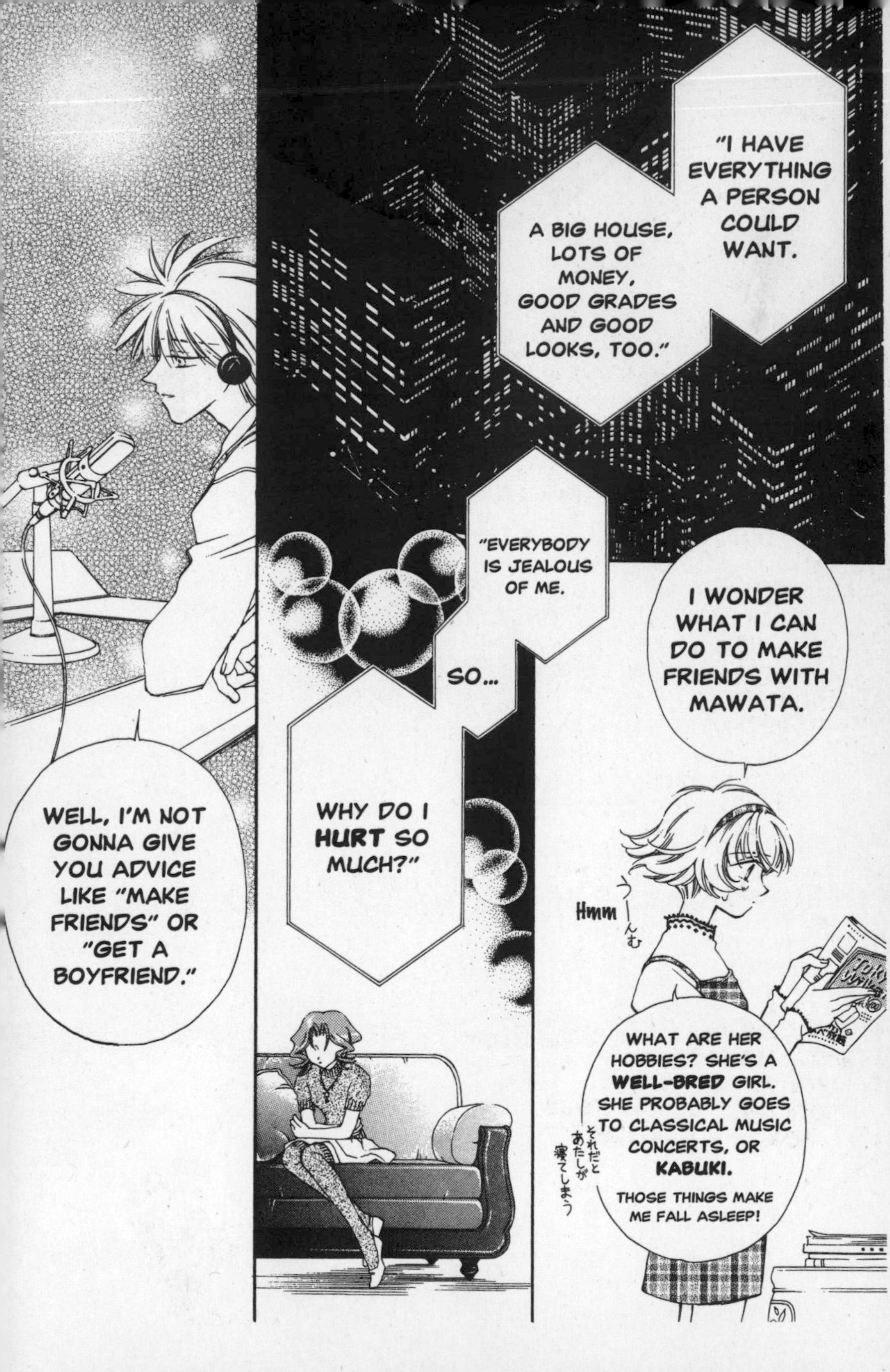
"I HAVE EVERYTHING A PERSON COULD WANT.
A BIG HOUSE, LOTS OF MONEY, GOOD GRADES AND GOOD LOOKS, TOO."
"EVERYBODY IS JEALOUS OF ME.
SO...
WHY DO I **HURT** SO MUCH?"
WELL, I'M NOT GONNA GIVE YOU ADVICE LIKE "MAKE FRIENDS" OR "GET A BOYFRIEND."
I WONDER WHAT I CAN DO TO MAKE FRIENDS WITH MAWATA.
Hmm
うーんむ
WHAT ARE HER HOBBIES? SHE'S A **WELL-BRED** GIRL. SHE PROBABLY GOES TO CLASSICAL MUSIC CONCERTS, OR **KABUKI.**
THOSE THINGS MAKE ME FALL ASLEEP!
それだとあたしが寝てしまう

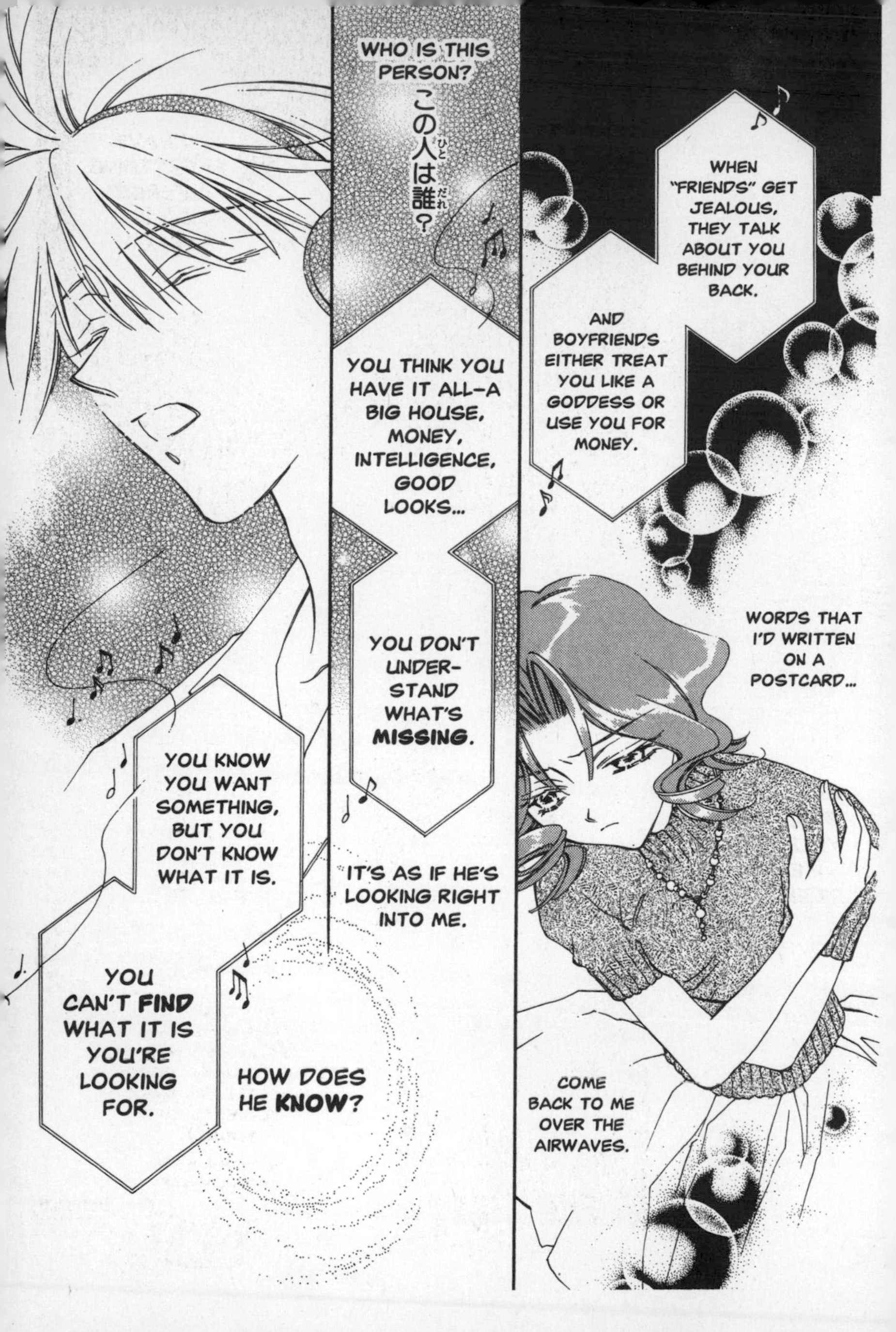
WHEN "FRIENDS" GET JEALOUS, THEY TALK ABOUT YOU BEHIND YOUR BACK.
AND BOYFRIENDS EITHER TREAT YOU LIKE A GODDESS OR USE YOU FOR MONEY.
WORDS THAT I'D WRITTEN ON A POSTCARD...
COME BACK TO ME OVER THE AIRWAVES.
WHO IS THIS PERSON?
この人は誰？
YOU THINK YOU HAVE IT ALL—A BIG HOUSE, MONEY, INTELLIGENCE, GOOD LOOKS...
YOU DON'T UNDERSTAND WHAT'S **MISSING**.
IT'S AS IF HE'S LOOKING RIGHT INTO ME.
YOU KNOW YOU WANT SOMETHING, BUT YOU DON'T KNOW WHAT IT IS.
YOU CAN'T **FIND** WHAT IT IS YOU'RE LOOKING FOR.
HOW DOES HE **KNOW**?

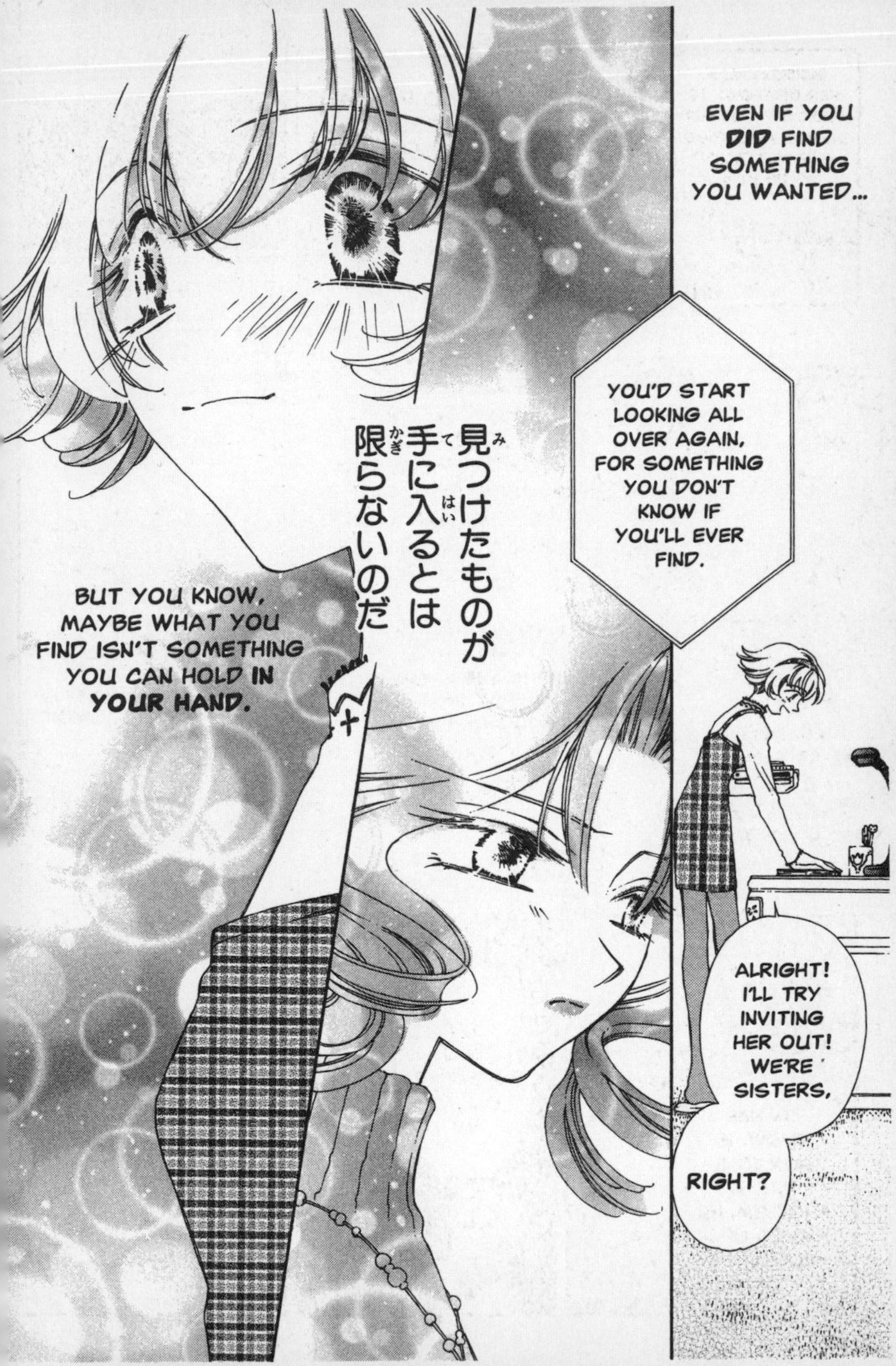
EVEN IF YOU DID FIND SOMETHING YOU WANTED...
YOU'D START LOOKING ALL OVER AGAIN, FOR SOMETHING YOU DON'T KNOW IF YOU'LL EVER FIND.
見つけたものが手に入るとは限らないのだ
BUT YOU KNOW, MAYBE WHAT YOU FIND ISN'T SOMETHING YOU CAN HOLD IN YOUR HAND.
ALRIGHT! I'LL TRY INVITING HER OUT! WE'RE SISTERS,
RIGHT?

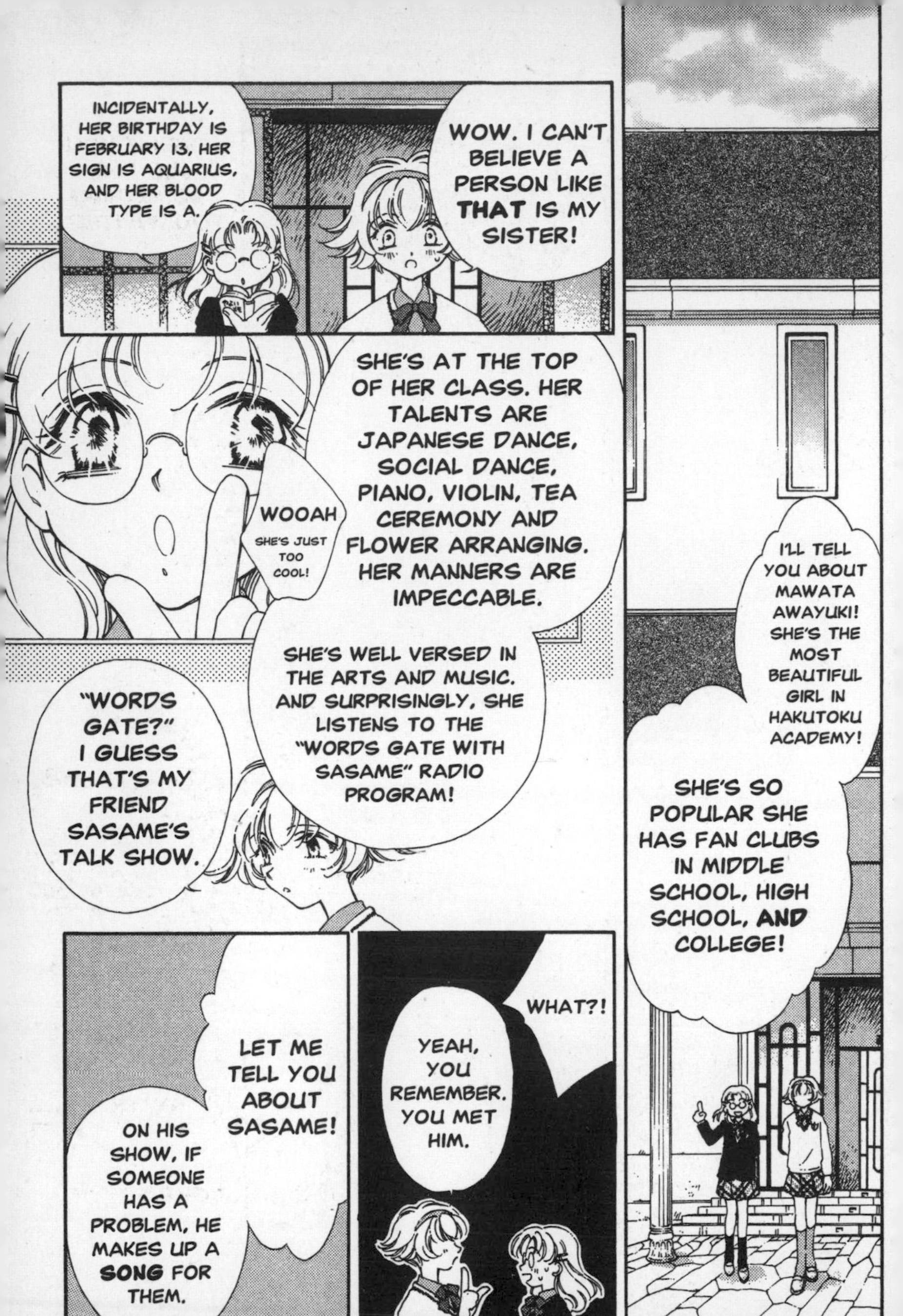

I'LL TELL YOU ABOUT MAWATA AWAYUKI! SHE'S THE MOST BEAUTIFUL GIRL IN HAKUTOKU ACADEMY!
SHE'S SO POPULAR SHE HAS FAN CLUBS IN MIDDLE SCHOOL, HIGH SCHOOL, AND COLLEGE!
WOW. I CAN'T BELIEVE A PERSON LIKE THAT IS MY SISTER!
INCIDENTALLY, HER BIRTHDAY IS FEBRUARY 13, HER SIGN IS AQUARIUS, AND HER BLOOD TYPE IS A.
SHE'S AT THE TOP OF HER CLASS. HER TALENTS ARE JAPANESE DANCE, SOCIAL DANCE, PIANO, VIOLIN, TEA CEREMONY AND FLOWER ARRANGING. HER MANNERS ARE IMPECCABLE.
WOOAH
SHE'S JUST TOO COOL!
SHE'S WELL VERSED IN THE ARTS AND MUSIC. AND SURPRISINGLY, SHE LISTENS TO THE "WORDS GATE WITH SASAME" RADIO PROGRAM!
"WORDS GATE?" I GUESS THAT'S MY FRIEND SASAME'S TALK SHOW.
WHAT?!
YEAH, YOU REMEMBER. YOU MET HIM.
LET ME TELL YOU ABOUT SASAME!
ON HIS SHOW, IF SOMEONE HAS A PROBLEM, HE MAKES UP A SONG FOR THEM.

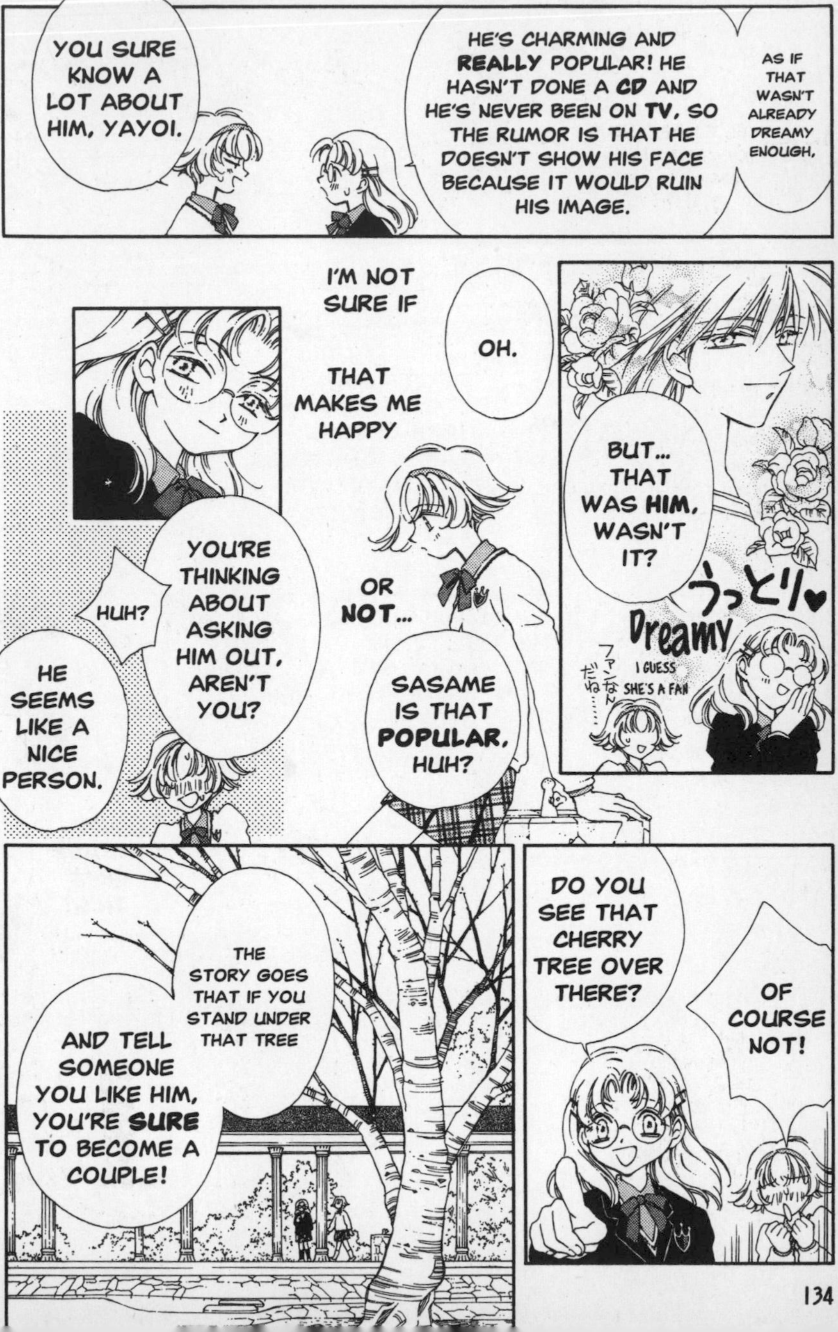
AS IF THAT WASN'T ALREADY DREAMY ENOUGH,
HE'S CHARMING AND REALLY POPULAR! HE HASN'T DONE A CD AND HE'S NEVER BEEN ON TV, SO THE RUMOR IS THAT HE DOESN'T SHOW HIS FACE BECAUSE IT WOULD RUIN HIS IMAGE.
YOU SURE KNOW A LOT ABOUT HIM, YAYOI.
BUT... THAT WAS HIM, WASN'T IT?
うっとり♥
Dreamy
ファンなんだね……
I GUESS SHE'S A FAN
OH.
I'M NOT SURE IF
THAT MAKES ME HAPPY
OR NOT...
SASAME IS THAT POPULAR, HUH?
YOU'RE THINKING ABOUT ASKING HIM OUT, AREN'T YOU?
HUH?
HE SEEMS LIKE A NICE PERSON.
DO YOU SEE THAT CHERRY TREE OVER THERE?
OF COURSE NOT!
THE STORY GOES THAT IF YOU STAND UNDER THAT TREE
AND TELL SOMEONE YOU LIKE HIM, YOU'RE SURE TO BECOME A COUPLE!

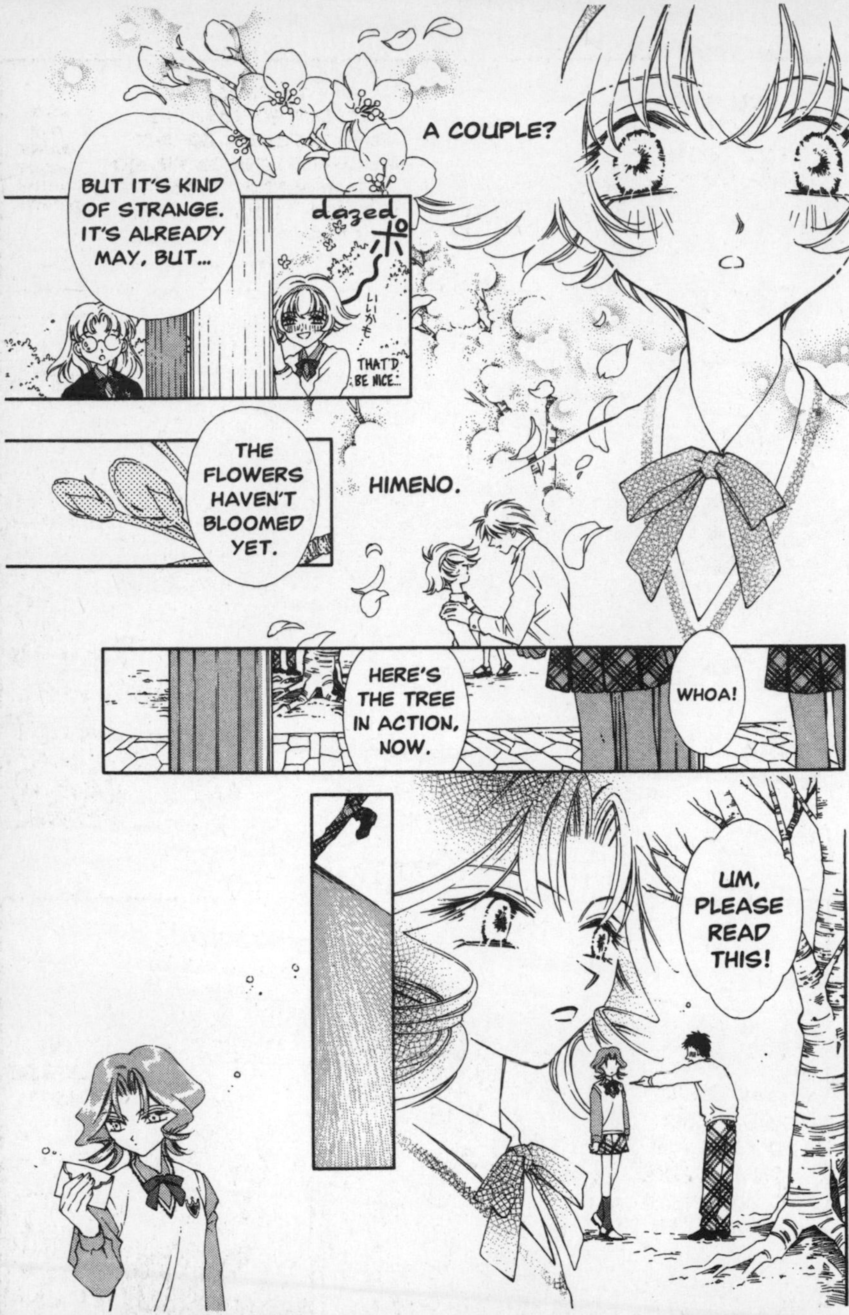
A COUPLE?
BUT IT'S KIND OF STRANGE. IT'S ALREADY MAY, BUT...
dazed
ポ
いいかも
THAT'D BE NICE...
HIMENO.
THE FLOWERS HAVEN'T BLOOMED YET.
WHOA!
HERE'S THE TREE IN ACTION, NOW.
UM, PLEASE READ THIS!

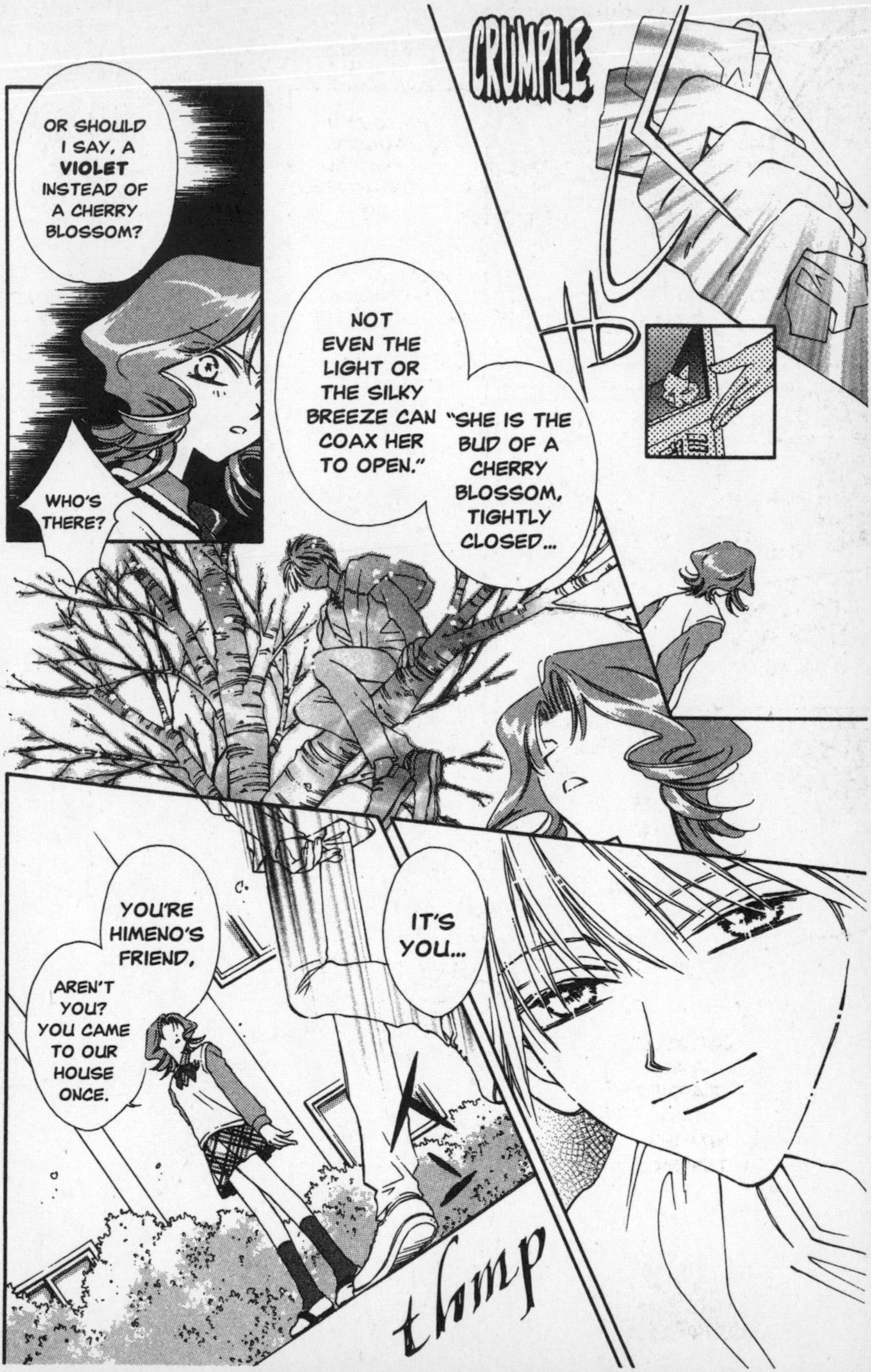
CRUMPLE
"SHE IS THE BUD OF A CHERRY BLOSSOM, TIGHTLY CLOSED...
NOT EVEN THE LIGHT OR THE SILKY BREEZE CAN COAX HER TO OPEN."
OR SHOULD I SAY, A **VIOLET** INSTEAD OF A CHERRY BLOSSOM?
WHO'S THERE?
IT'S YOU...
YOU'RE HIMENO'S FRIEND,
AREN'T YOU? YOU CAME TO OUR HOUSE ONCE.
thmp

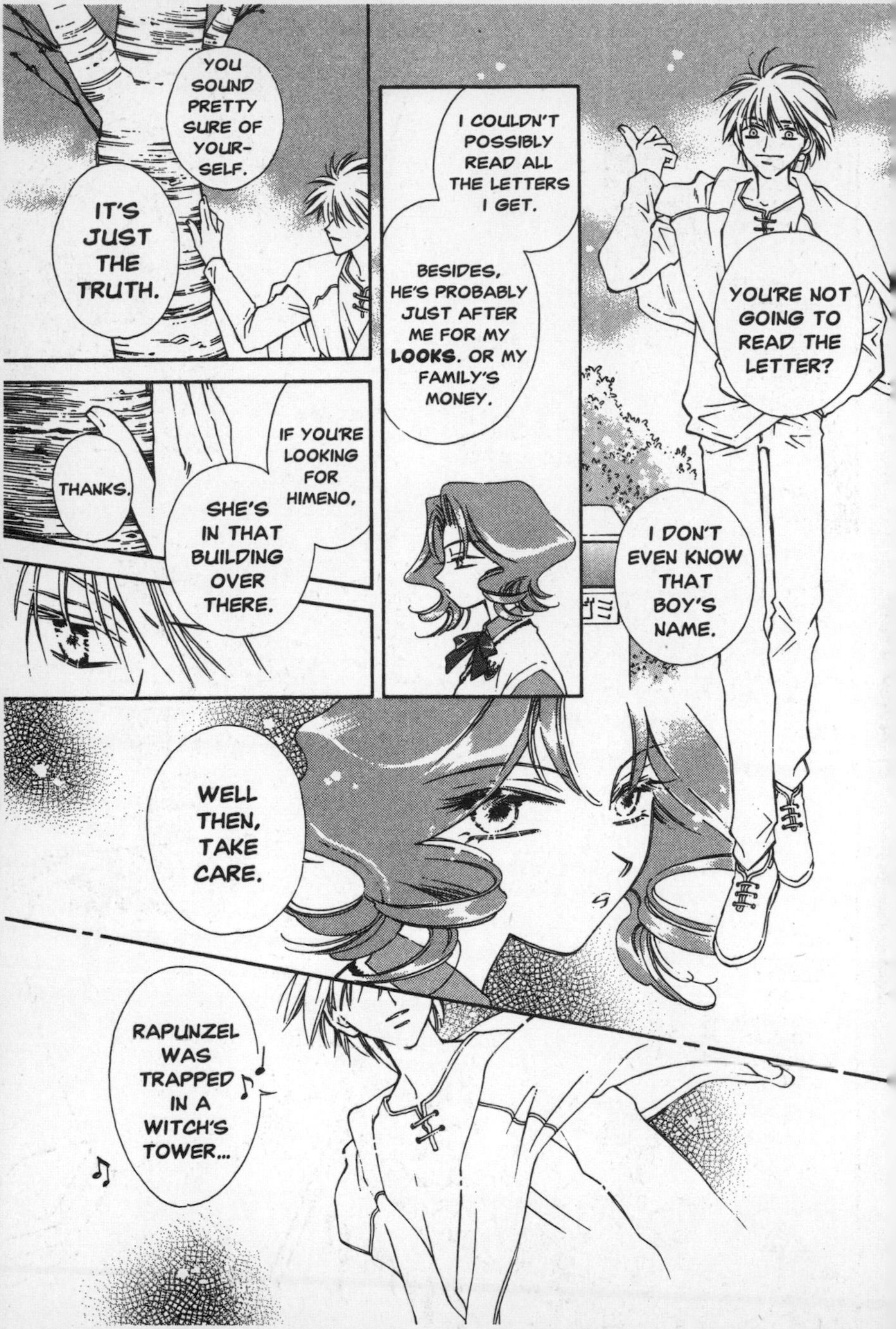
YOU'RE NOT GOING TO READ THE LETTER?
I DON'T EVEN KNOW THAT BOY'S NAME.
I COULDN'T POSSIBLY READ ALL THE LETTERS I GET.
BESIDES, HE'S PROBABLY JUST AFTER ME FOR MY **LOOKS**. OR MY FAMILY'S MONEY.
YOU SOUND PRETTY SURE OF YOUR-SELF.
IT'S JUST THE TRUTH.
IF YOU'RE LOOKING FOR HIMENO,
SHE'S IN THAT BUILDING OVER THERE.
THANKS.
WELL THEN, TAKE CARE.
RAPUNZEL WAS TRAPPED IN A WITCH'S TOWER...

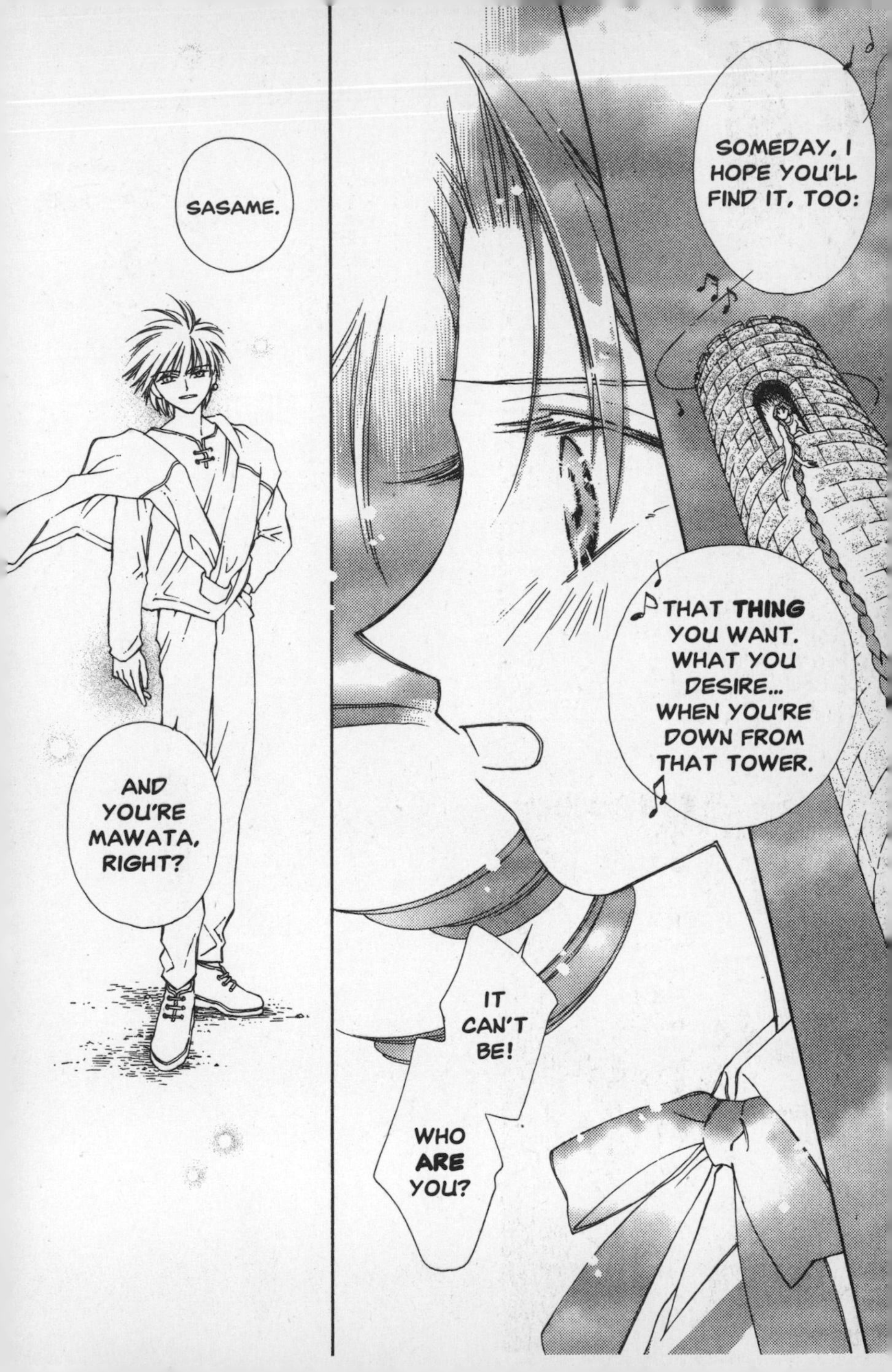
SOMEDAY, I HOPE YOU'LL FIND IT, TOO:
THAT **THING** YOU WANT. WHAT YOU DESIRE... WHEN YOU'RE DOWN FROM THAT TOWER.
IT CAN'T BE!
WHO **ARE** YOU?
SASAME.
AND YOU'RE MAWATA, RIGHT?

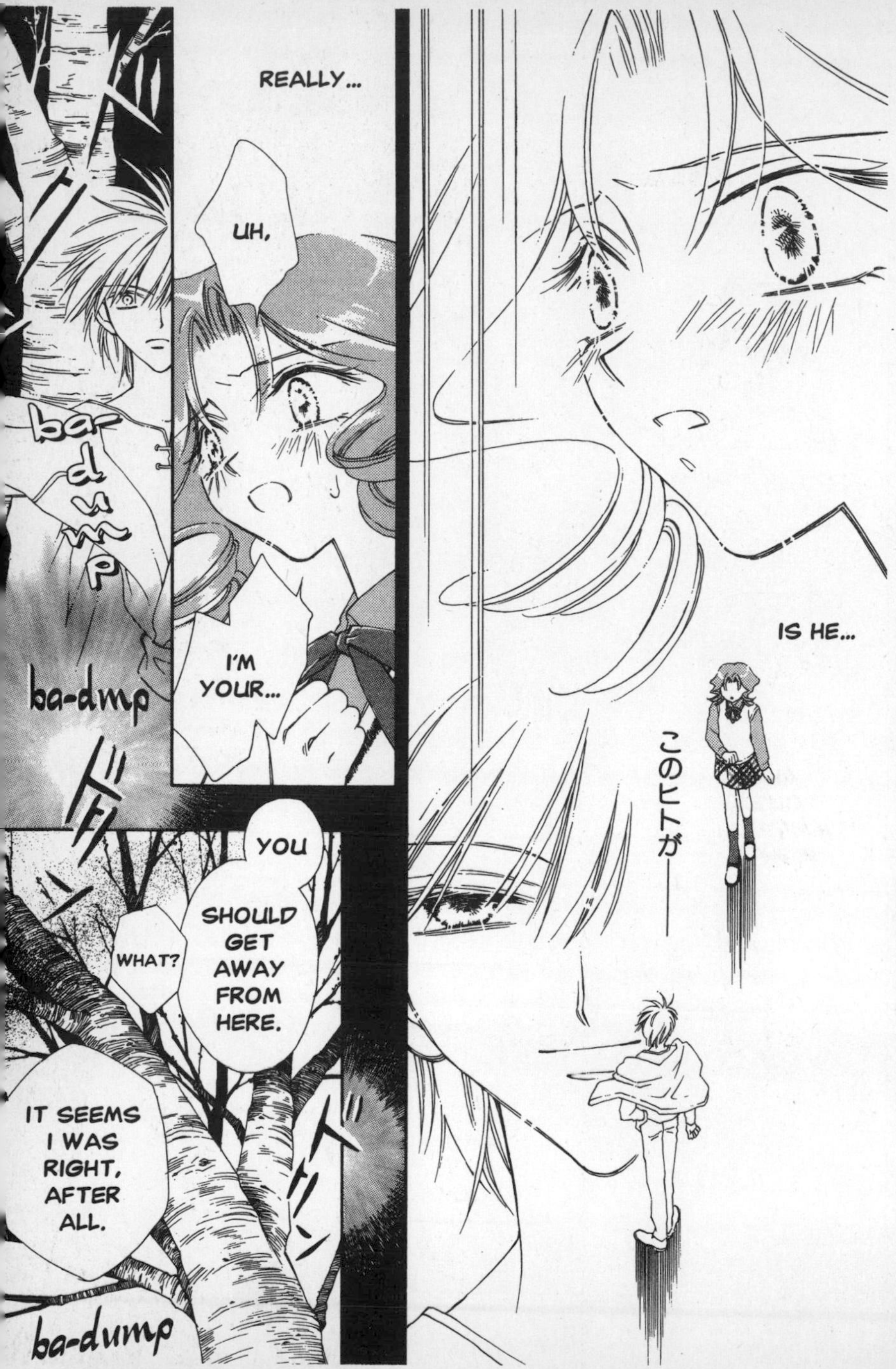
IS HE...
このヒトが——
REALLY...
UH,
I'M YOUR...
ba-dump
ba-dmp
YOU SHOULD GET AWAY FROM HERE.
WHAT?
IT SEEMS I WAS RIGHT, AFTER ALL.
ba-dump

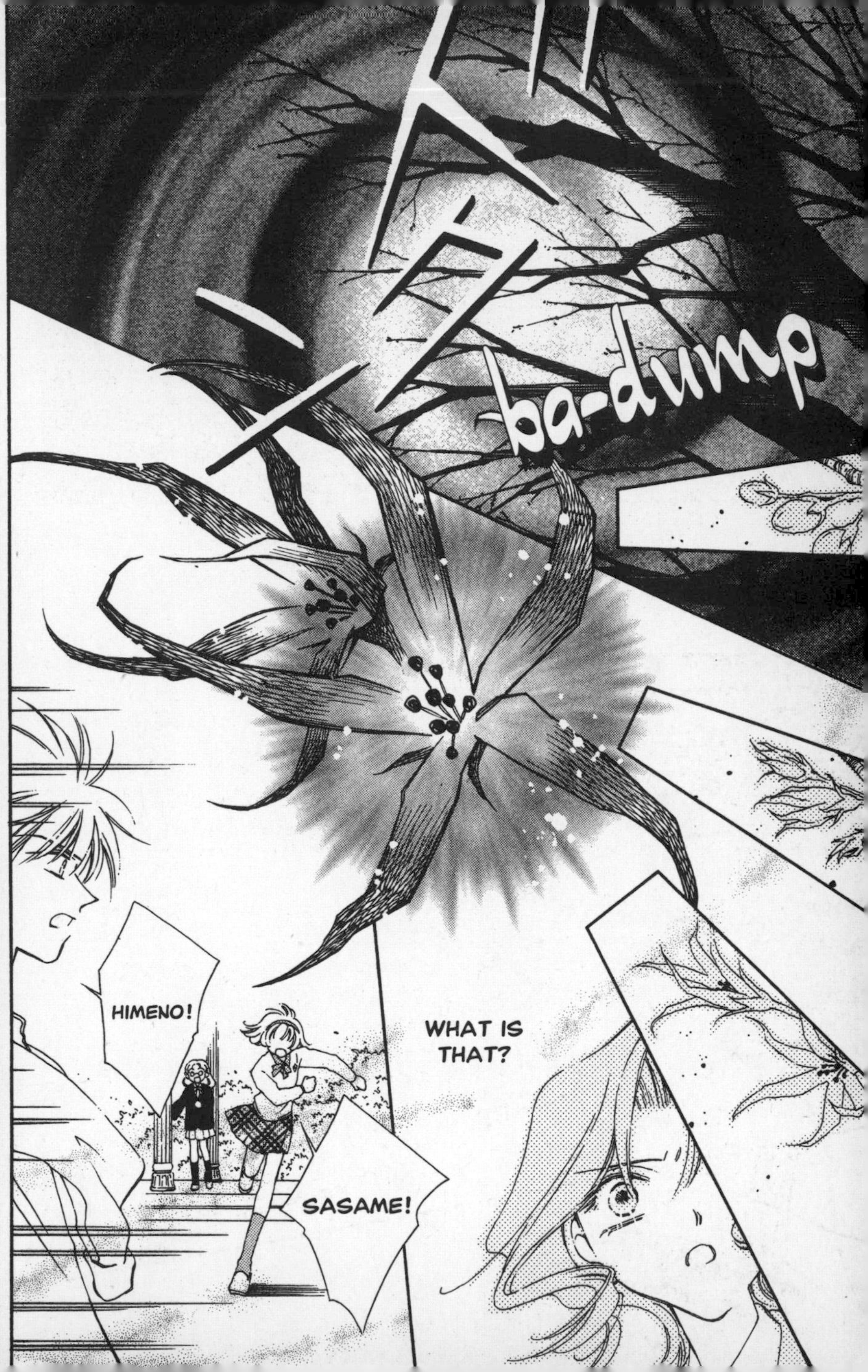
ba-dump
WHAT IS THAT?
SASAME!
HIMENO!

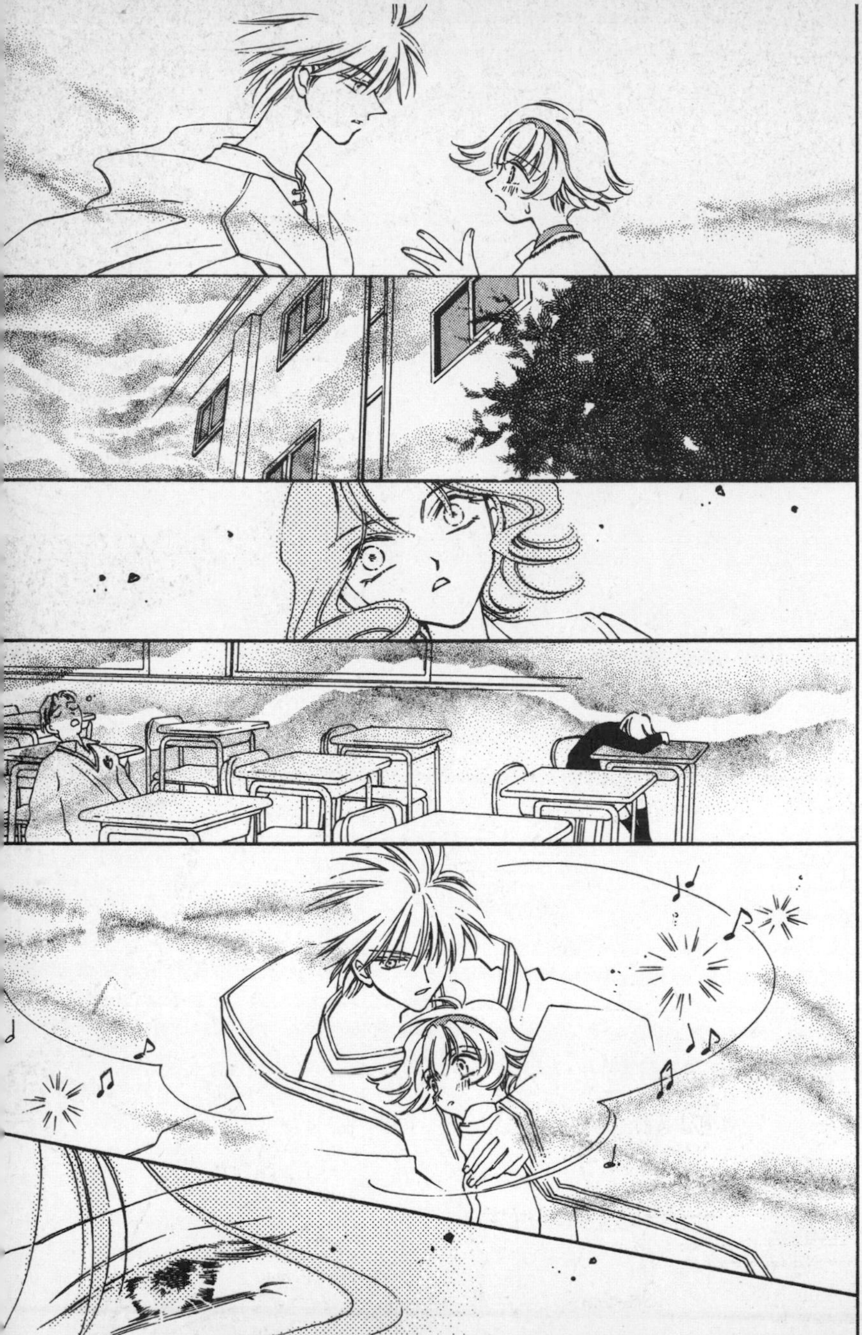

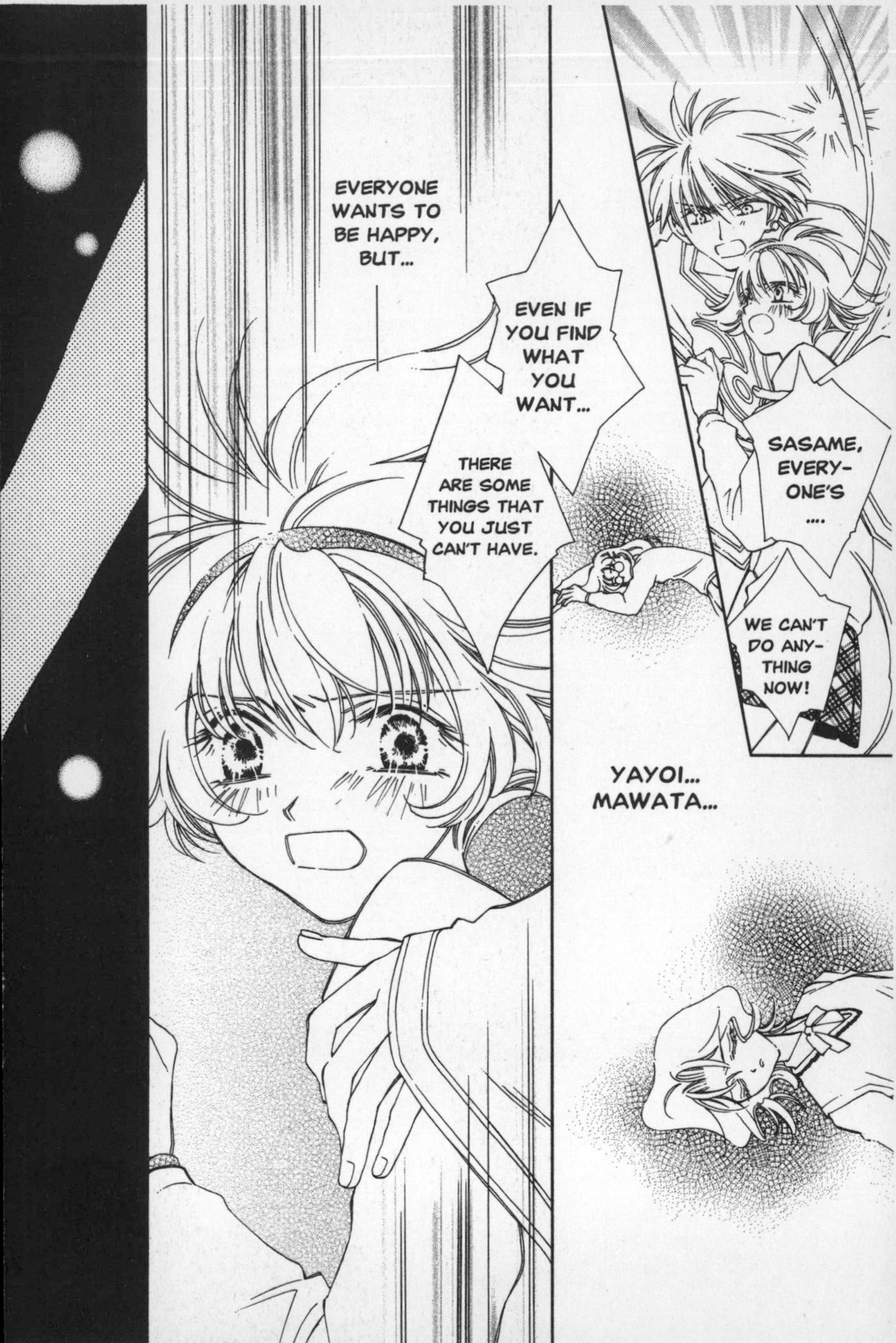
SASAME, EVERYONE'S ....
WE CAN'T DO ANYTHING NOW!
YAYOI... MAWATA...
EVERYONE WANTS TO BE HAPPY, BUT...
EVEN IF YOU FIND WHAT YOU WANT...
THERE ARE SOME THINGS THAT YOU JUST CAN'T HAVE.

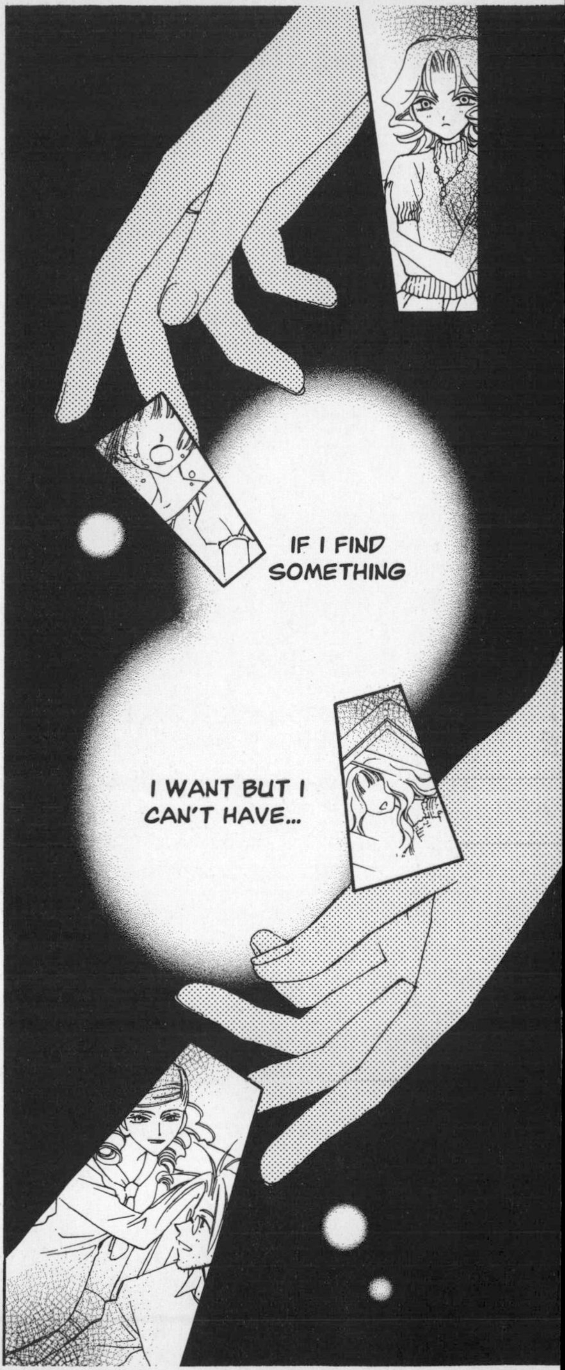
IF I FIND SOMETHING
I WANT BUT I CAN'T HAVE...

THAT FACT WILL HAUNT ME...

UNTIL THE VERY END.

H A J I M E

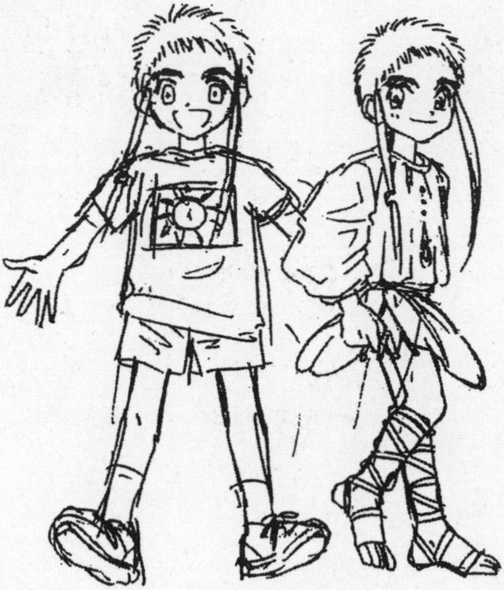

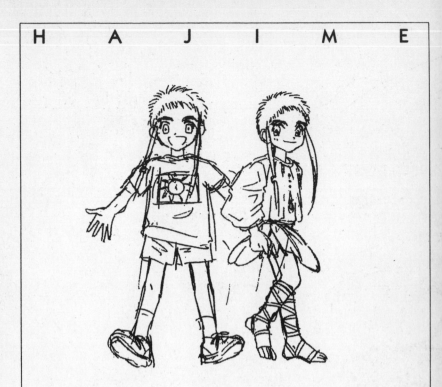

# HAJIME

Knight of Water

Hair: Orange Eyes: Aquamarine

Birthday: April 8 Sign: Aries

Blood Type: O

Good at making models

Favorite drink: Orange juice

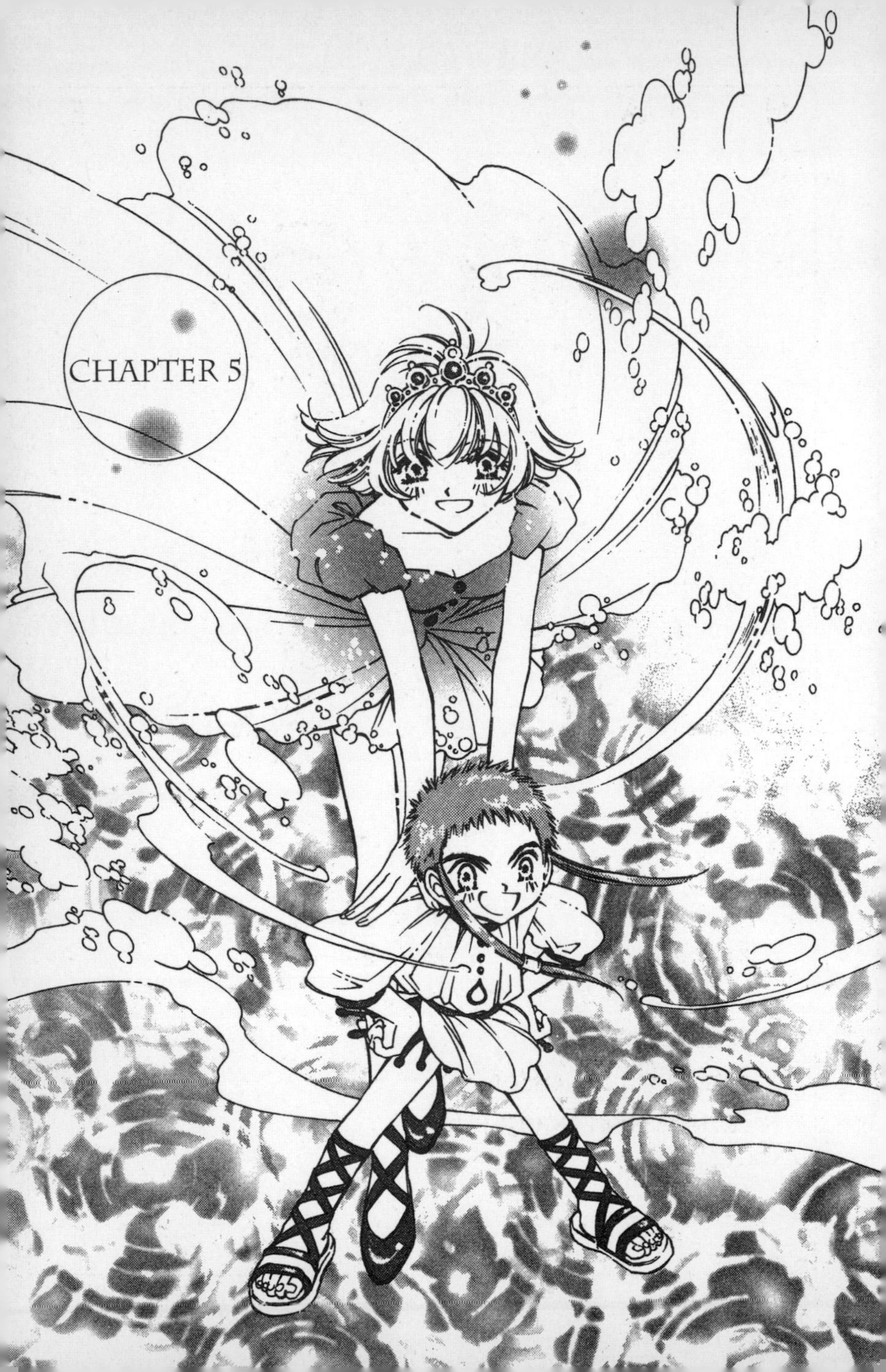
CHAPTER 5

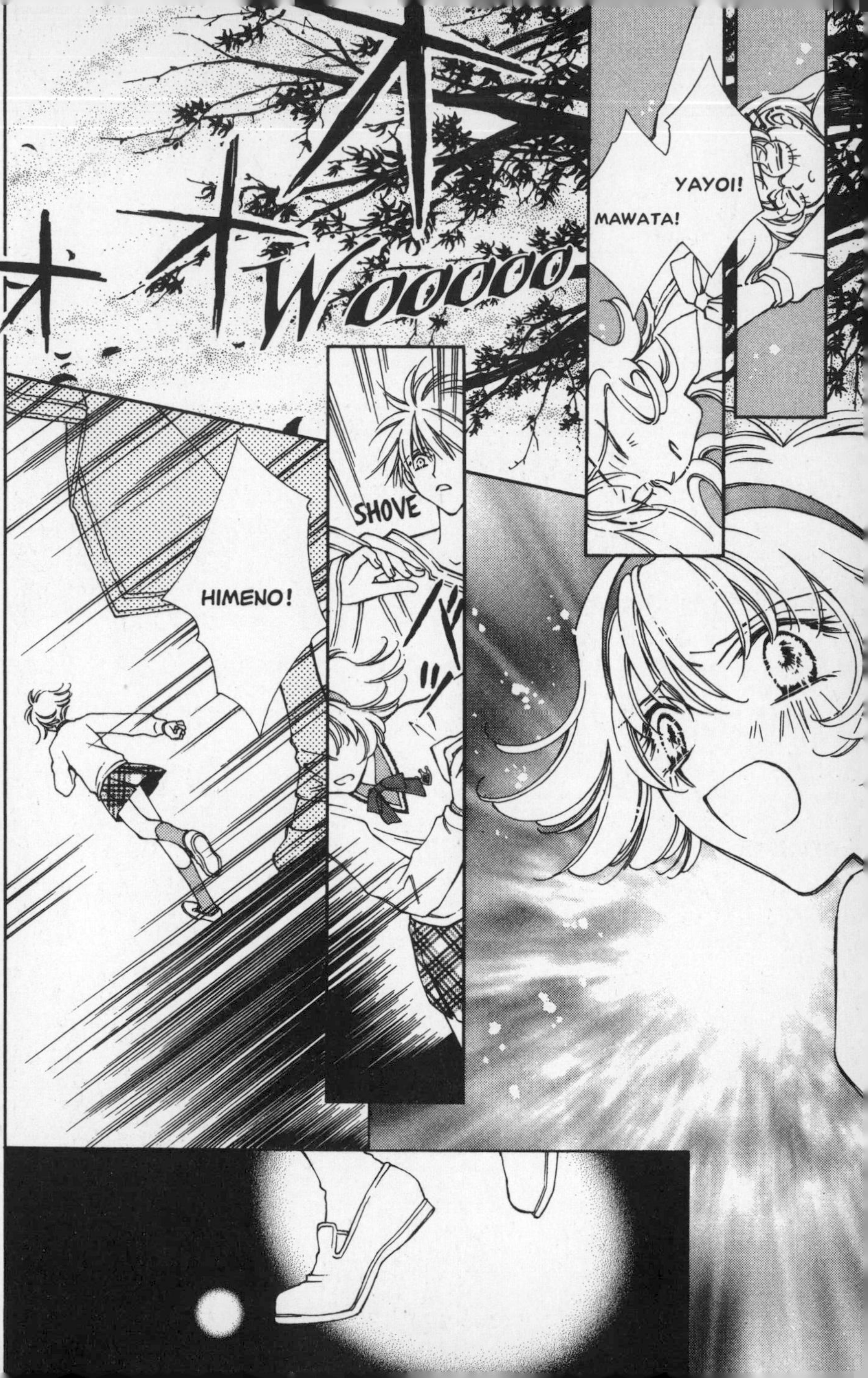
WOOOOOO
YAYOI!
MAWATA!
SHOVE
HIMENO!

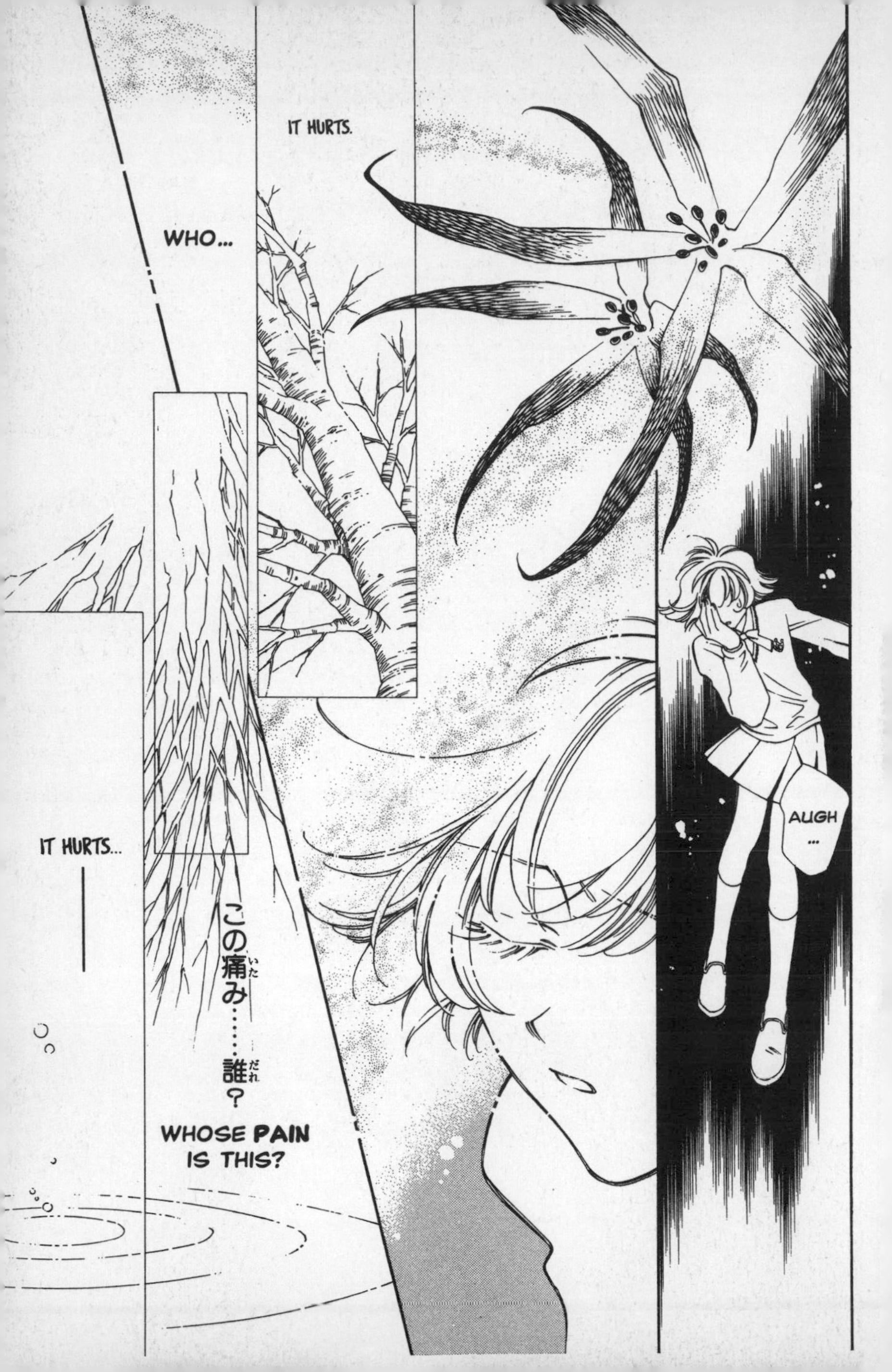
AUGH ...
IT HURTS.
WHO...
IT HURTS...
この痛み……誰？
WHOSE PAIN IS THIS?

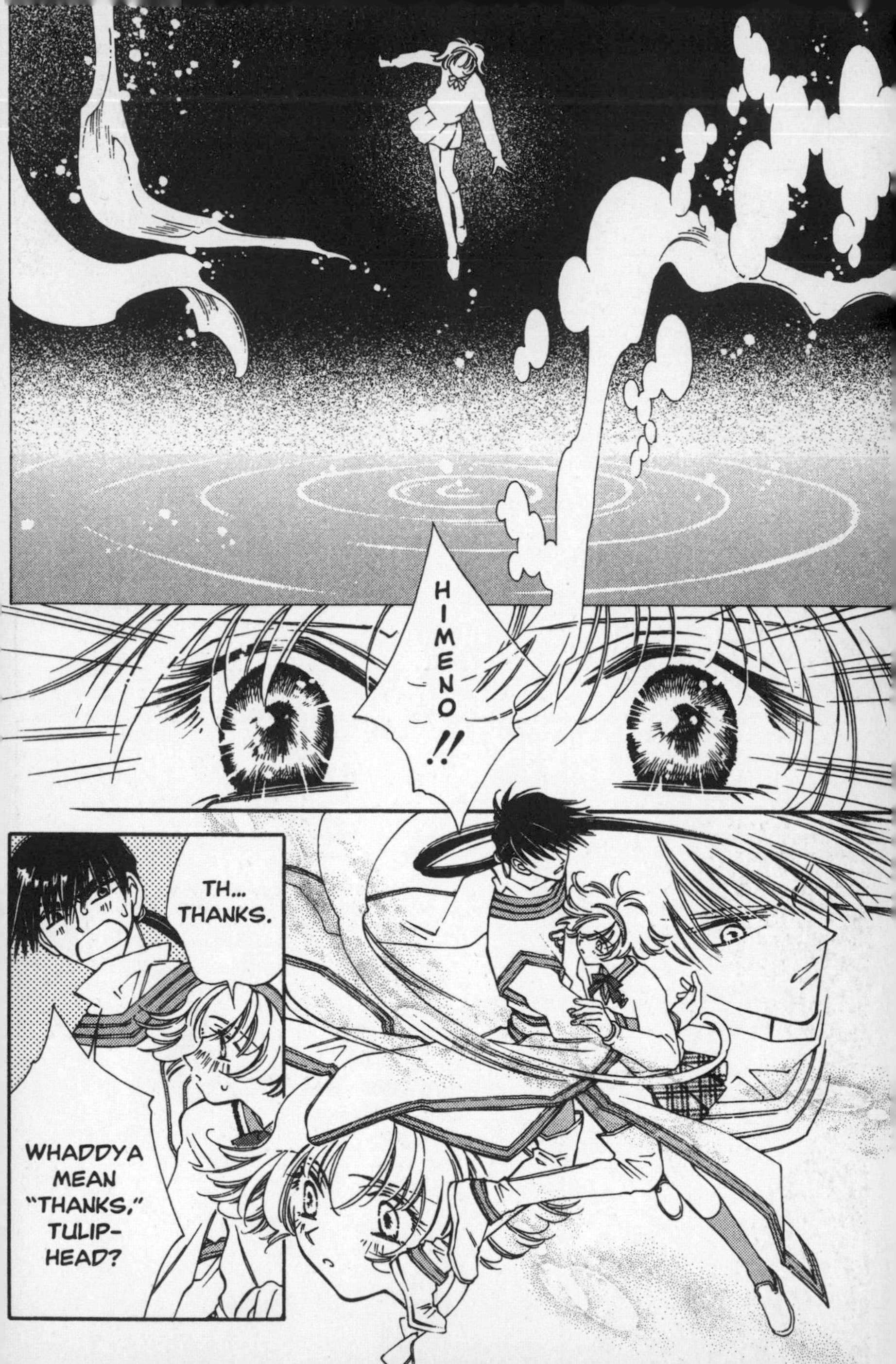
HIMENO!!
TH... THANKS.
WHADDYA MEAN "THANKS," TULIP-HEAD?

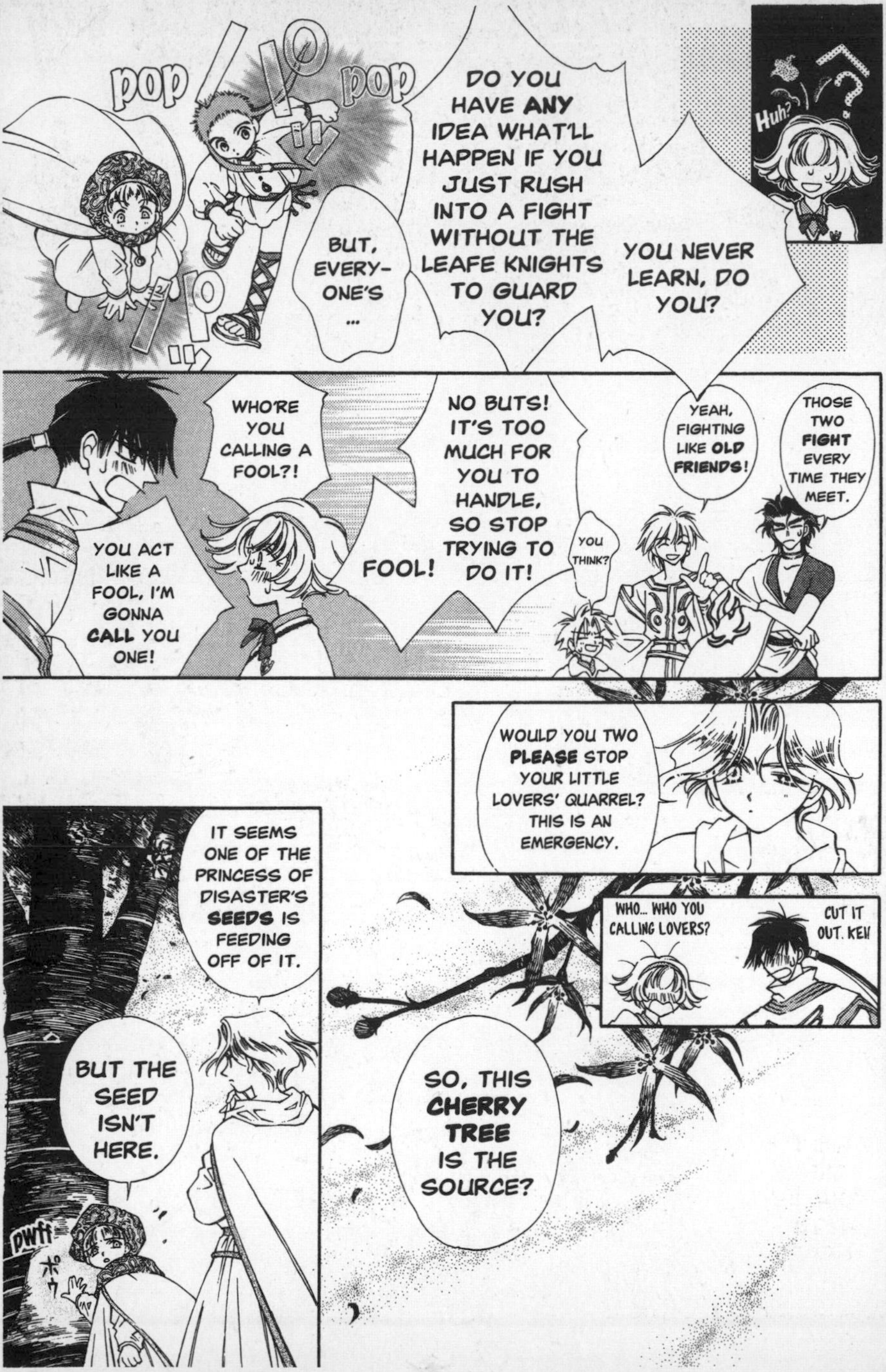
Huh?
YOU NEVER LEARN, DO YOU?
DO YOU HAVE ANY IDEA WHAT'LL HAPPEN IF YOU JUST RUSH INTO A FIGHT WITHOUT THE LEAFE KNIGHTS TO GUARD YOU?
pop
pop
BUT, EVERY-ONE'S ...
THOSE TWO FIGHT EVERY TIME THEY MEET.
YEAH, FIGHTING LIKE OLD FRIENDS!
YOU THINK?
NO BUTS! IT'S TOO MUCH FOR YOU TO HANDLE, SO STOP TRYING TO DO IT!
FOOL!
WHO'RE YOU CALLING A FOOL?!
YOU ACT LIKE A FOOL, I'M GONNA CALL YOU ONE!
WOULD YOU TWO PLEASE STOP YOUR LITTLE LOVERS' QUARREL? THIS IS AN EMERGENCY.
CUT IT OUT. KEI!
WHO... WHO YOU CALLING LOVERS?
SO, THIS CHERRY TREE IS THE SOURCE?
IT SEEMS ONE OF THE PRINCESS OF DISASTER'S SEEDS IS FEEDING OFF OF IT.
BUT THE SEED ISN'T HERE.
pwff
ポウ

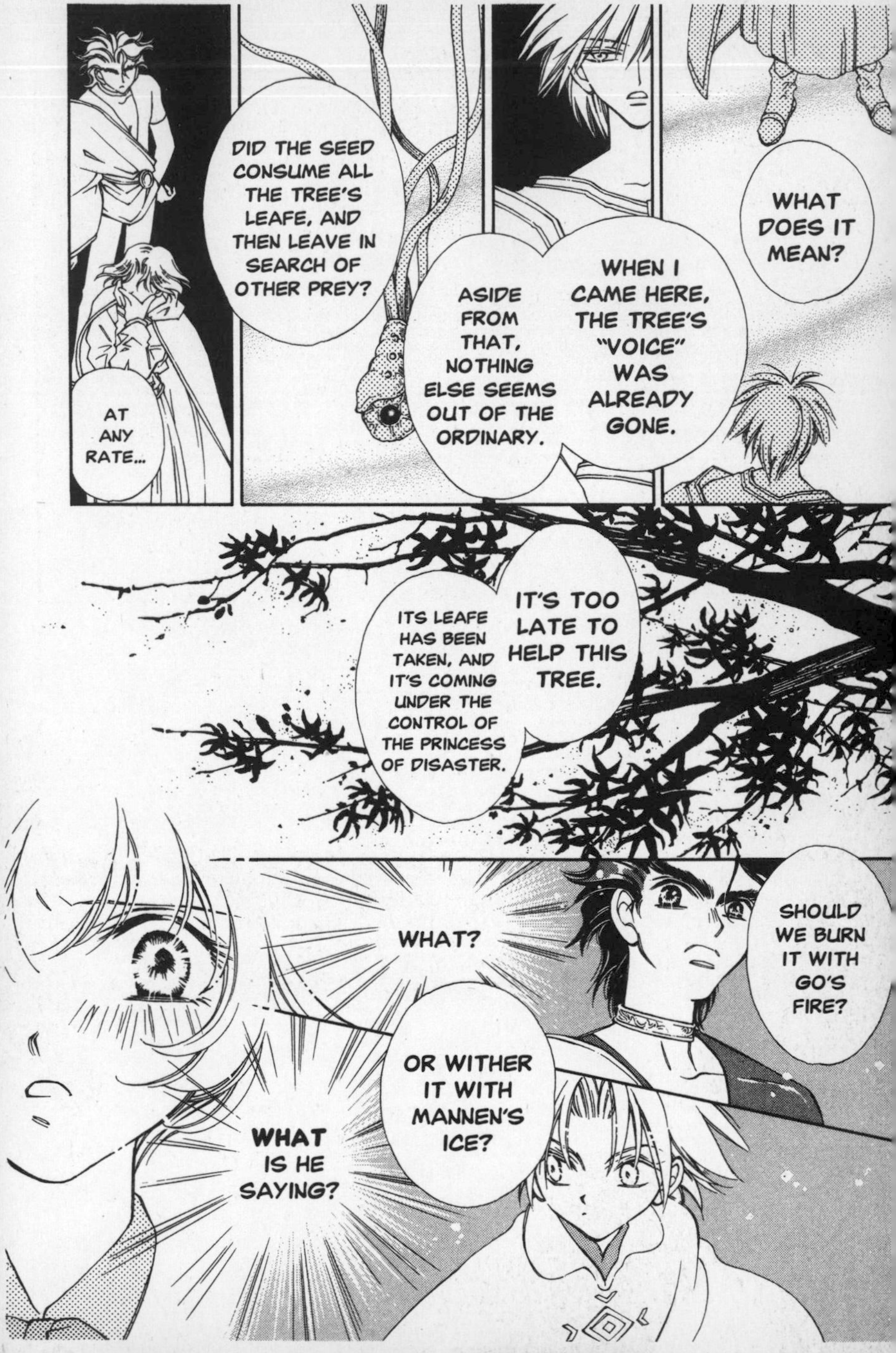
WHAT DOES IT MEAN?
WHEN I CAME HERE, THE TREE'S "VOICE" WAS ALREADY GONE.
ASIDE FROM THAT, NOTHING ELSE SEEMS OUT OF THE ORDINARY.
DID THE SEED CONSUME ALL THE TREE'S LEAFE, AND THEN LEAVE IN SEARCH OF OTHER PREY?
AT ANY RATE...
IT'S TOO LATE TO HELP THIS TREE.
ITS LEAFE HAS BEEN TAKEN, AND IT'S COMING UNDER THE CONTROL OF THE PRINCESS OF DISASTER.
SHOULD WE BURN IT WITH GO'S FIRE?
OR WITHER IT WITH MANNEN'S ICE?
WHAT?
WHAT IS HE SAYING?

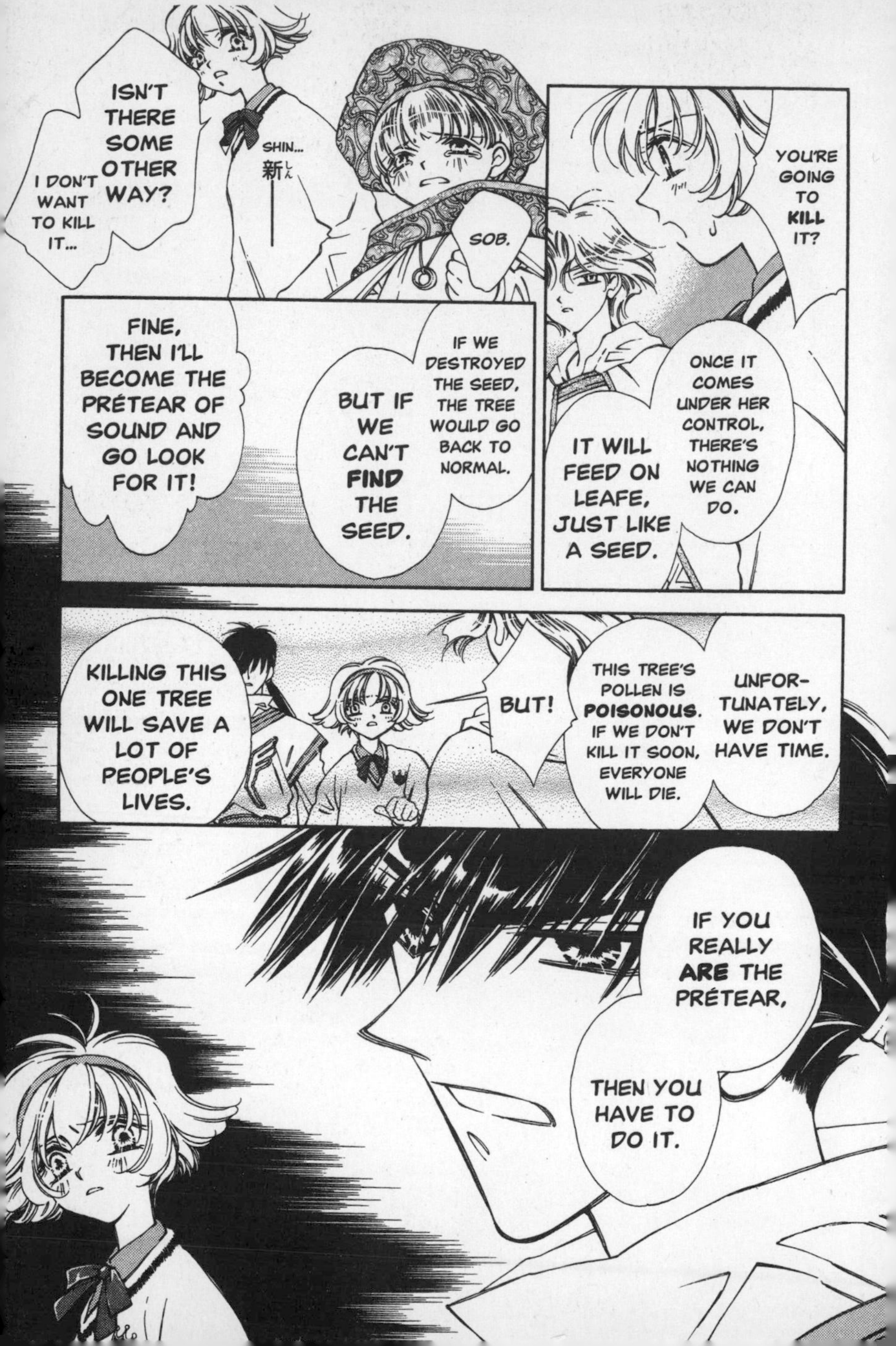

SOB.
SHIN... 新しん
ISN'T THERE SOME OTHER WAY?
I DON'T WANT TO KILL IT...
YOU'RE GOING TO KILL IT?
ONCE IT COMES UNDER HER CONTROL, THERE'S NOTHING WE CAN DO.
IT WILL FEED ON LEAFE, JUST LIKE A SEED.
IF WE DESTROYED THE SEED, THE TREE WOULD GO BACK TO NORMAL.
BUT IF WE CAN'T FIND THE SEED.
FINE, THEN I'LL BECOME THE PRÉTEAR OF SOUND AND GO LOOK FOR IT!
UNFORTUNATELY, WE DON'T HAVE TIME.
THIS TREE'S POLLEN IS POISONOUS. IF WE DON'T KILL IT SOON, EVERYONE WILL DIE.
BUT!
KILLING THIS ONE TREE WILL SAVE A LOT OF PEOPLE'S LIVES.
IF YOU REALLY ARE THE PRÉTEAR,
THEN YOU HAVE TO DO IT.

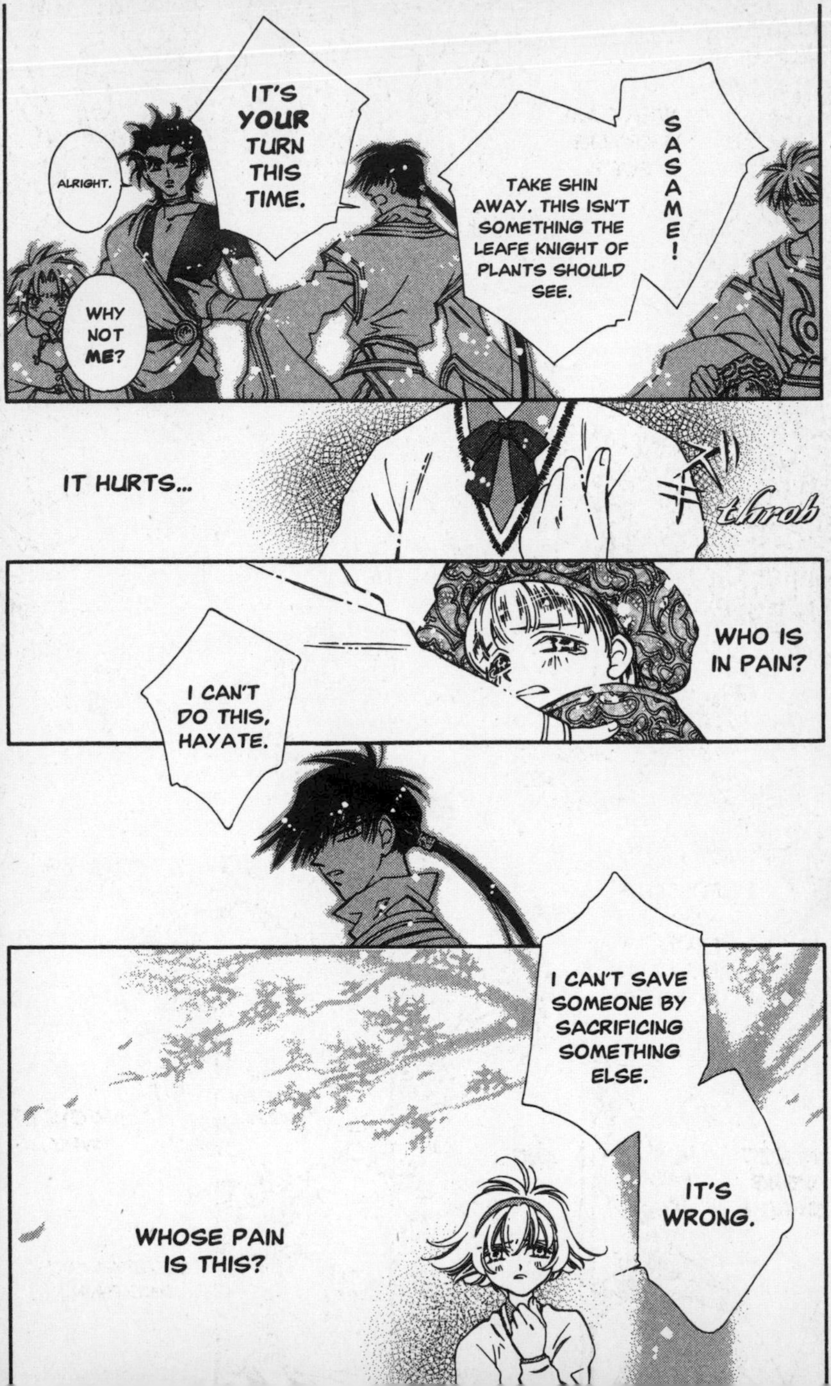
SASAME!
TAKE SHIN AWAY. THIS ISN'T SOMETHING THE LEAFE KNIGHT OF PLANTS SHOULD SEE.
IT'S YOUR TURN THIS TIME.
ALRIGHT.
WHY NOT ME?
throb
IT HURTS...
WHO IS IN PAIN?
I CAN'T DO THIS, HAYATE.
I CAN'T SAVE SOMEONE BY SACRIFICING SOMETHING ELSE.
IT'S WRONG.
WHOSE PAIN IS THIS?

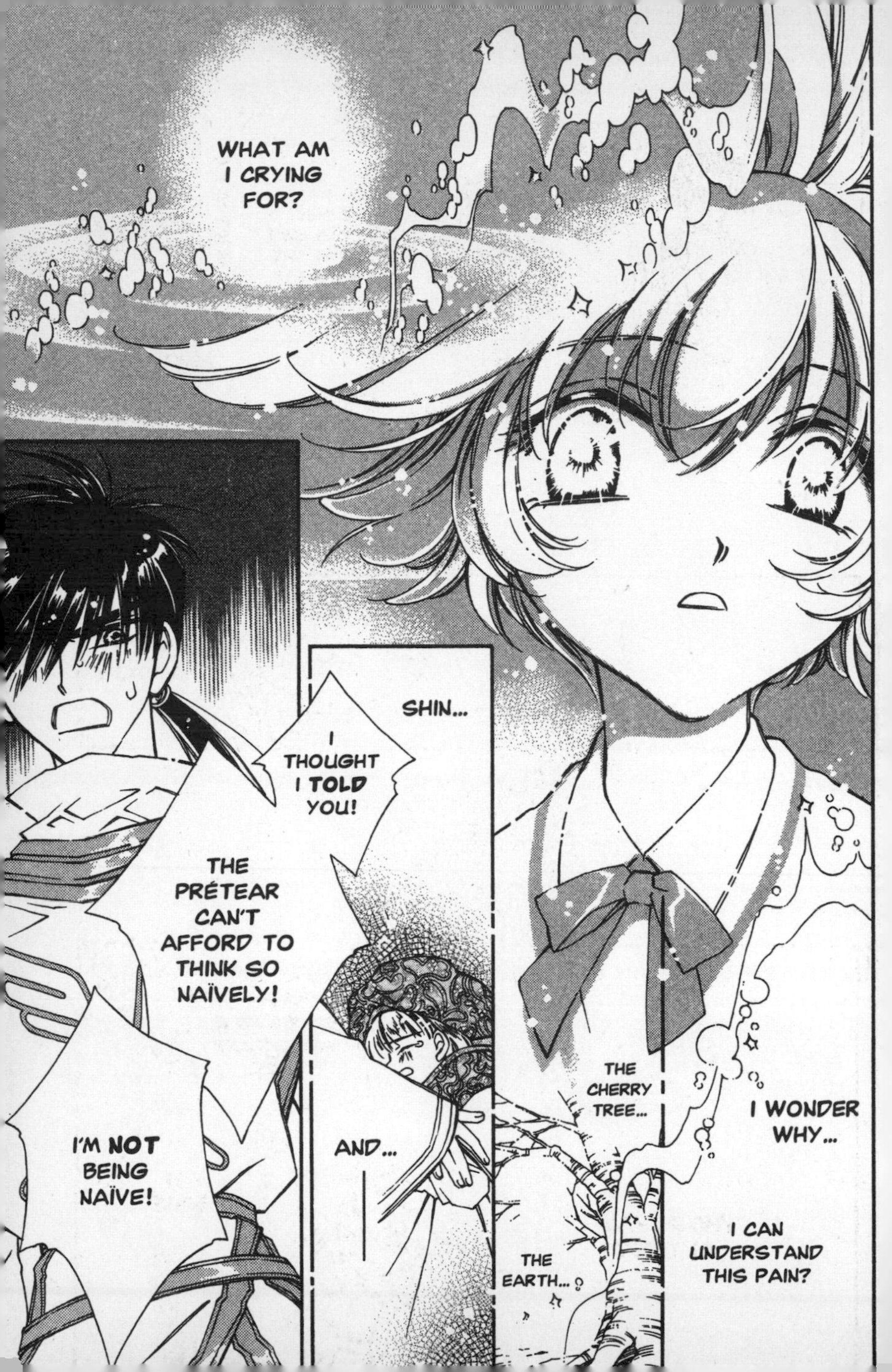
WHAT AM I CRYING FOR?
I WONDER WHY...
I CAN UNDERSTAND THIS PAIN?
THE CHERRY TREE...
THE EARTH...
SHIN...
AND...
I THOUGHT I **TOLD** YOU!
THE PRÉTEAR CAN'T AFFORD TO THINK SO NAÏVELY!
I'M **NOT** BEING NAÏVE!

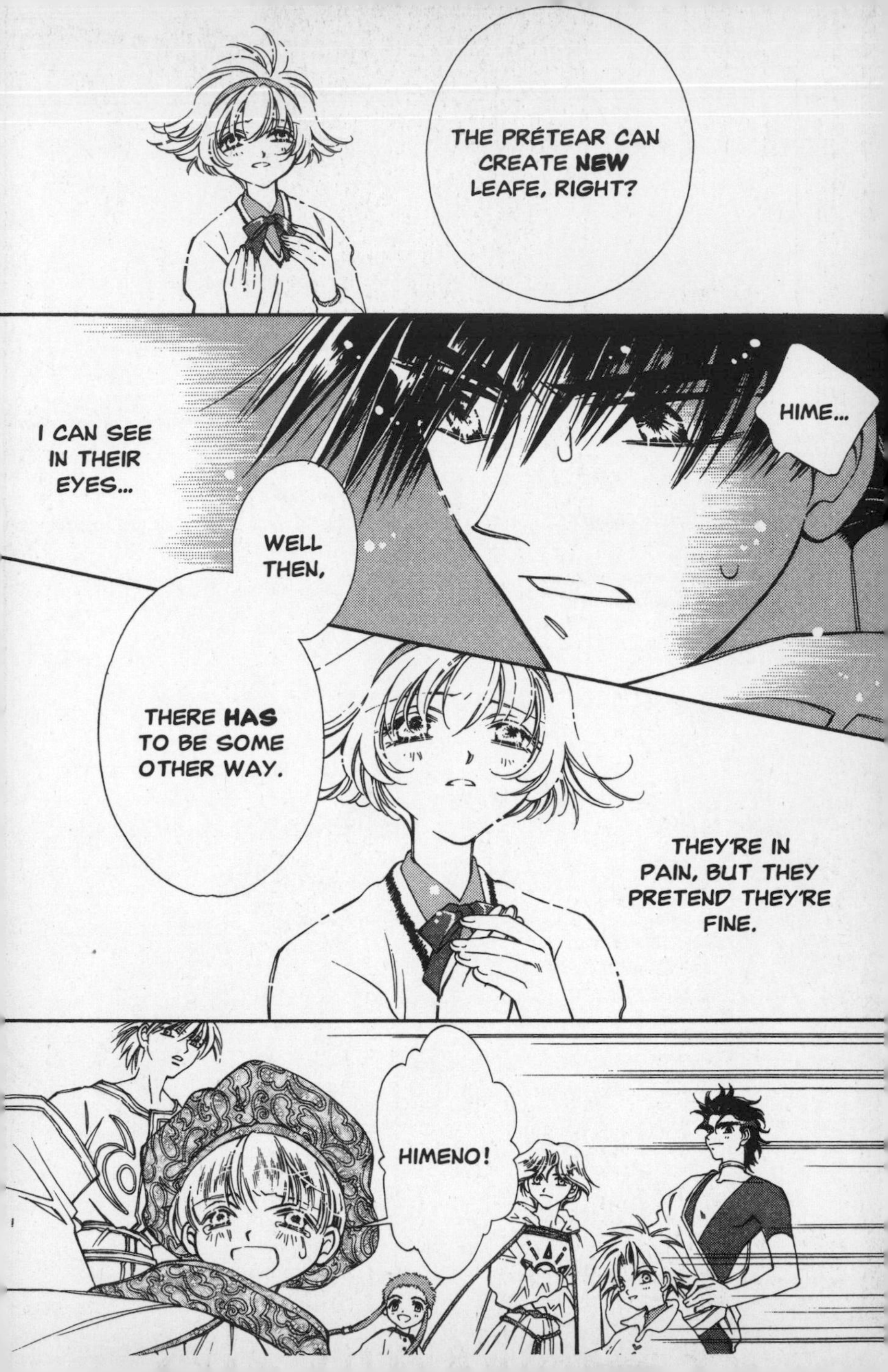
THE PRÉTEAR CAN CREATE NEW LEAFE, RIGHT?
HIME...
I CAN SEE IN THEIR EYES...
WELL THEN,
THERE HAS TO BE SOME OTHER WAY.
THEY'RE IN PAIN, BUT THEY PRETEND THEY'RE FINE.
HIMENO!

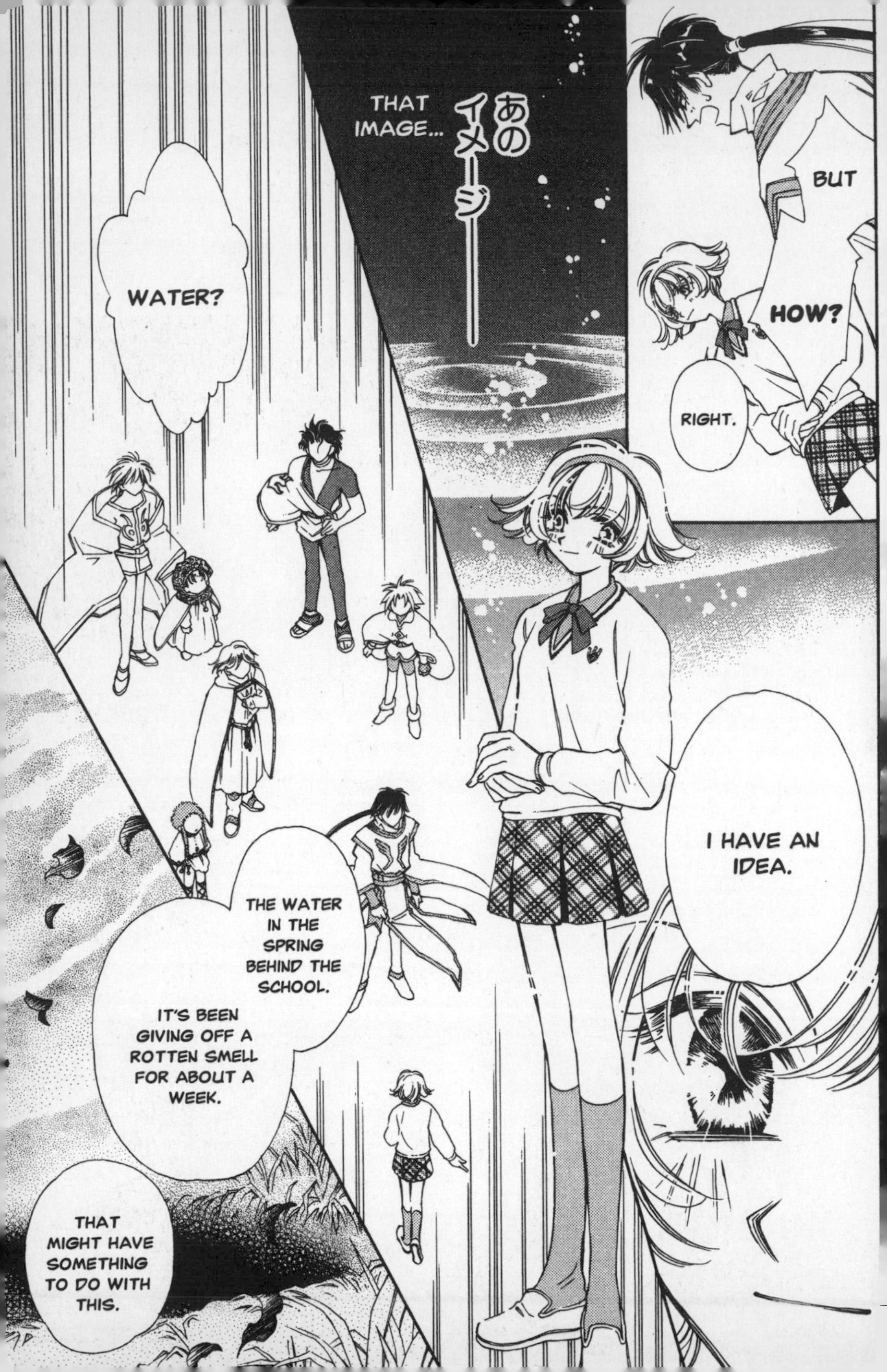
BUT
HOW?
RIGHT.
THAT IMAGE...
あのイメージ
WATER?
I HAVE AN IDEA.
THE WATER IN THE SPRING BEHIND THE SCHOOL.
IT'S BEEN GIVING OFF A ROTTEN SMELL FOR ABOUT A WEEK.
THAT MIGHT HAVE SOMETHING TO DO WITH THIS.

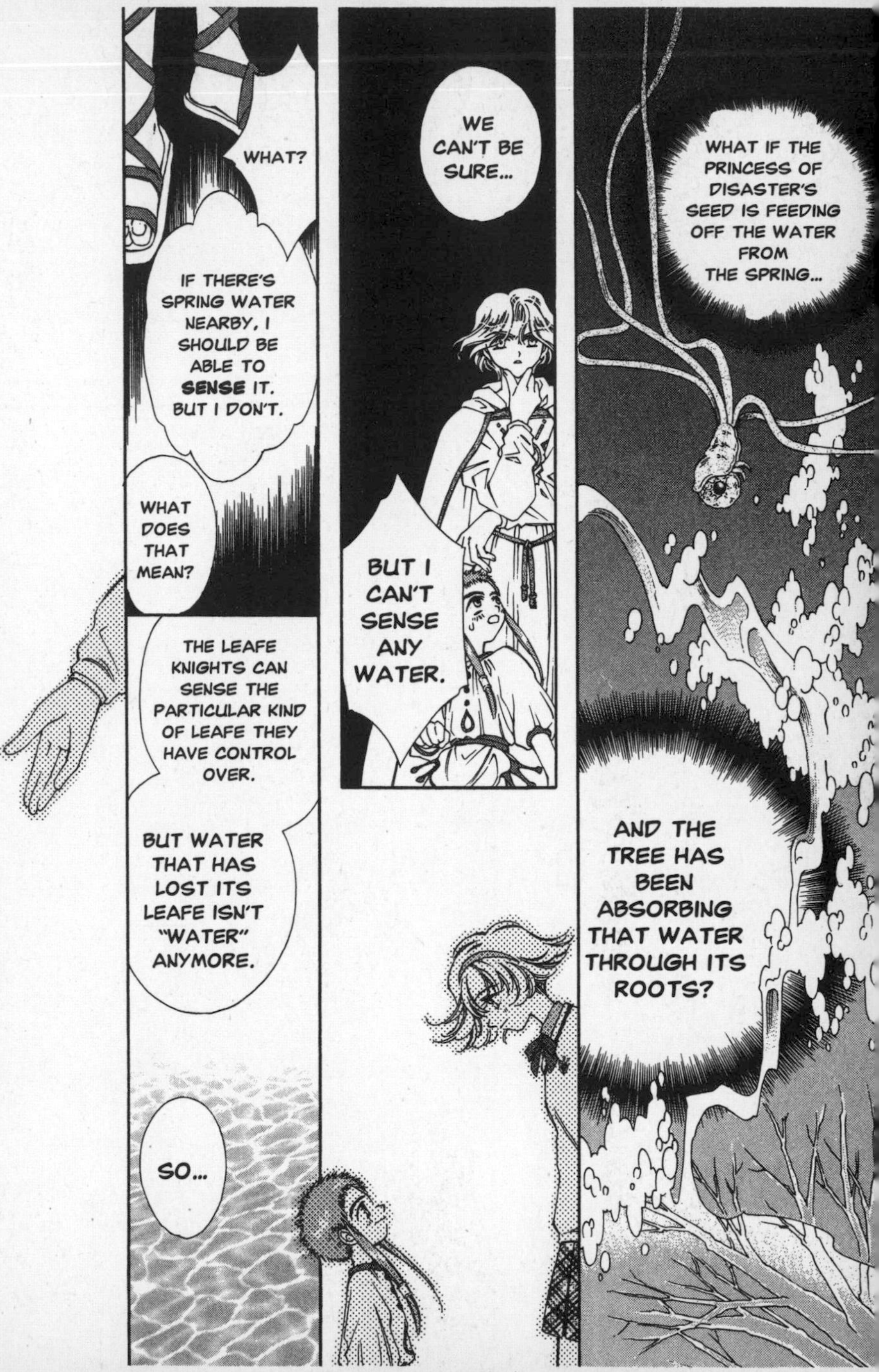
WE CAN'T BE SURE...
BUT I CAN'T SENSE ANY WATER.
WHAT?
IF THERE'S SPRING WATER NEARBY, I SHOULD BE ABLE TO **SENSE** IT. BUT I DON'T.
WHAT DOES THAT MEAN?
THE LEAFE KNIGHTS CAN SENSE THE PARTICULAR KIND OF LEAFE THEY HAVE CONTROL OVER.
BUT WATER THAT HAS LOST ITS LEAFE ISN'T "WATER" ANYMORE.
SO...
WHAT IF THE PRINCESS OF DISASTER'S SEED IS FEEDING OFF THE WATER FROM THE SPRING...
AND THE TREE HAS BEEN ABSORBING THAT WATER THROUGH ITS ROOTS?

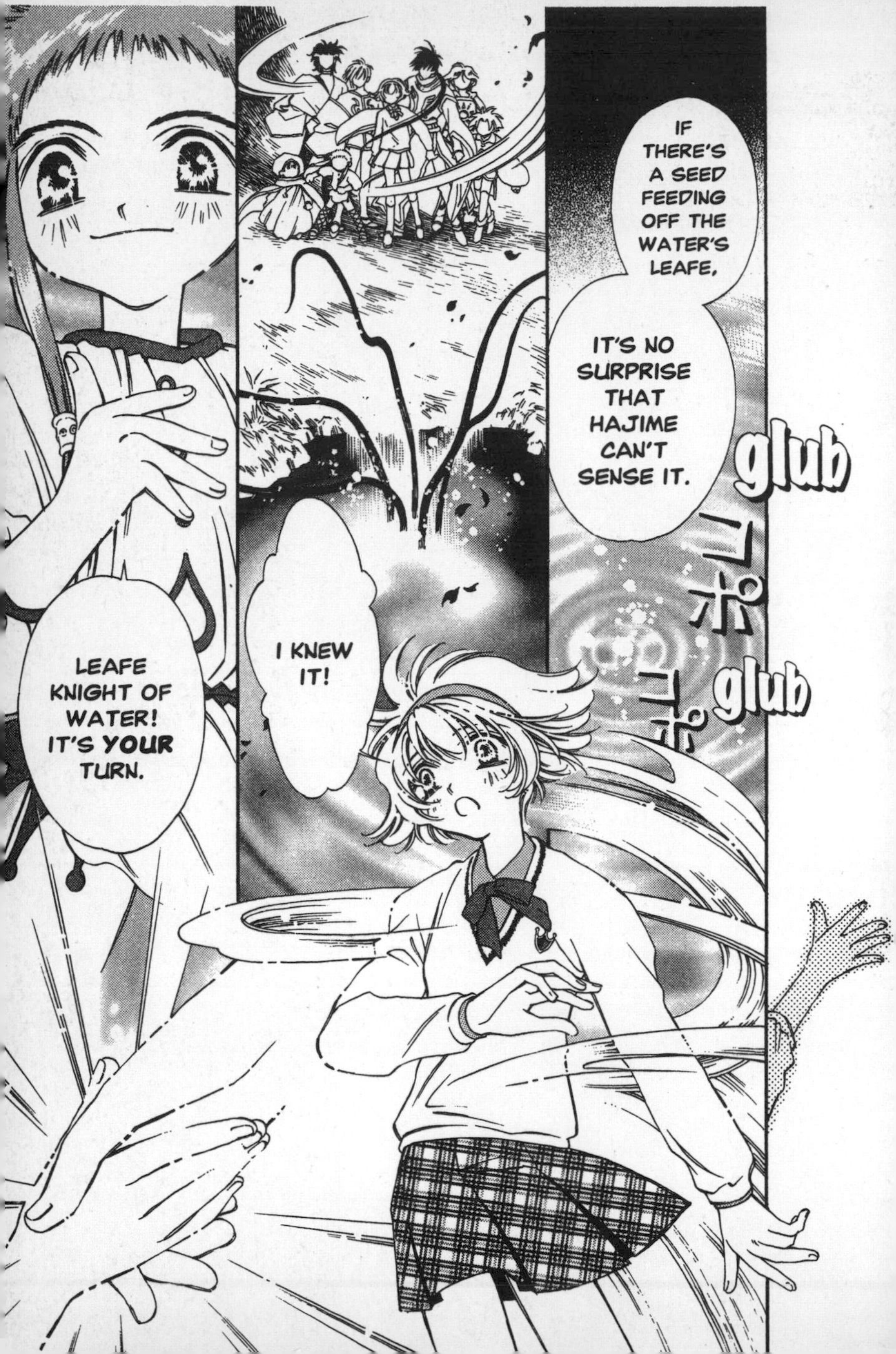
IF THERE'S A SEED FEEDING OFF THE WATER'S LEAFE,
IT'S NO SURPRISE THAT HAJIME CAN'T SENSE IT.
glub
glub
I KNEW IT!
LEAFE KNIGHT OF WATER! IT'S **YOUR** TURN.

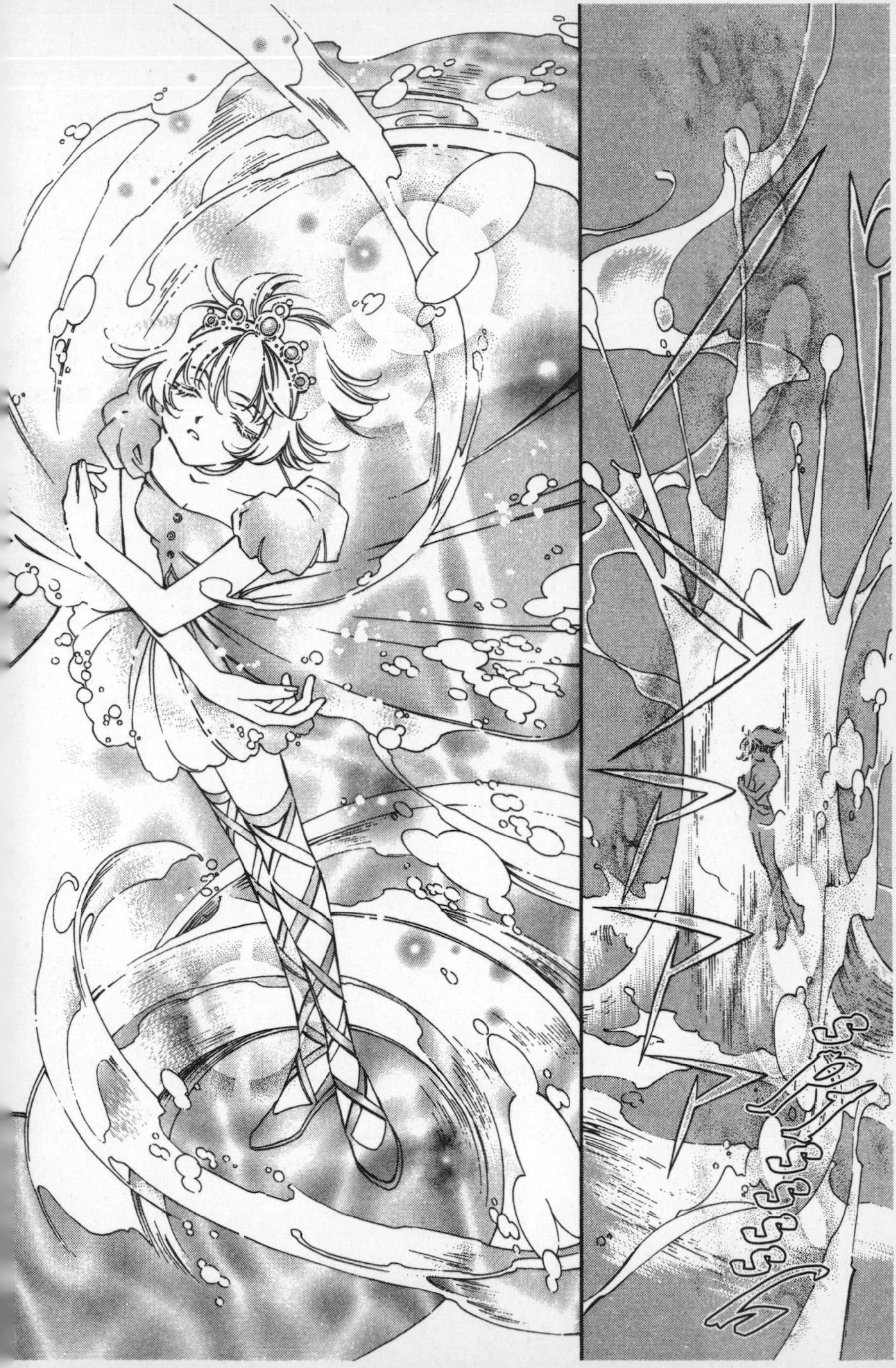

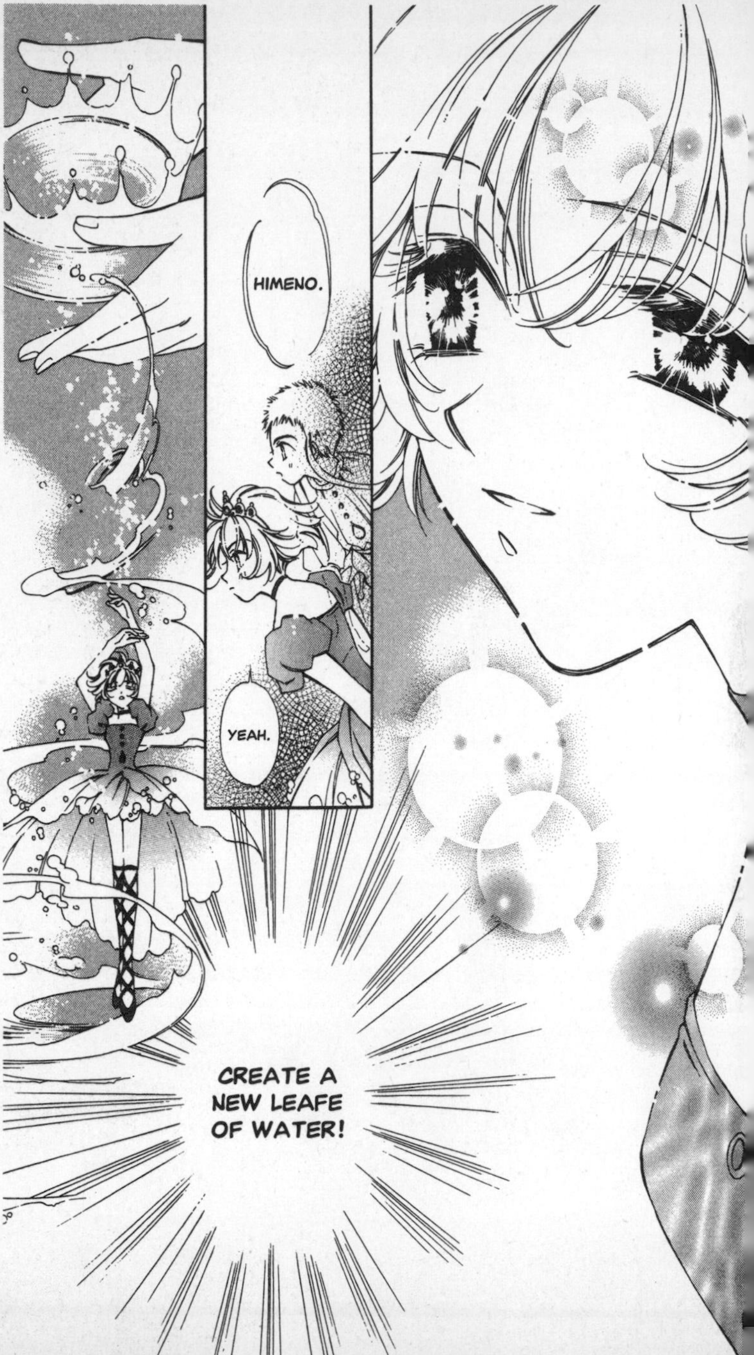
HIMENO.
YEAH.
CREATE A NEW LEAFE OF WATER!

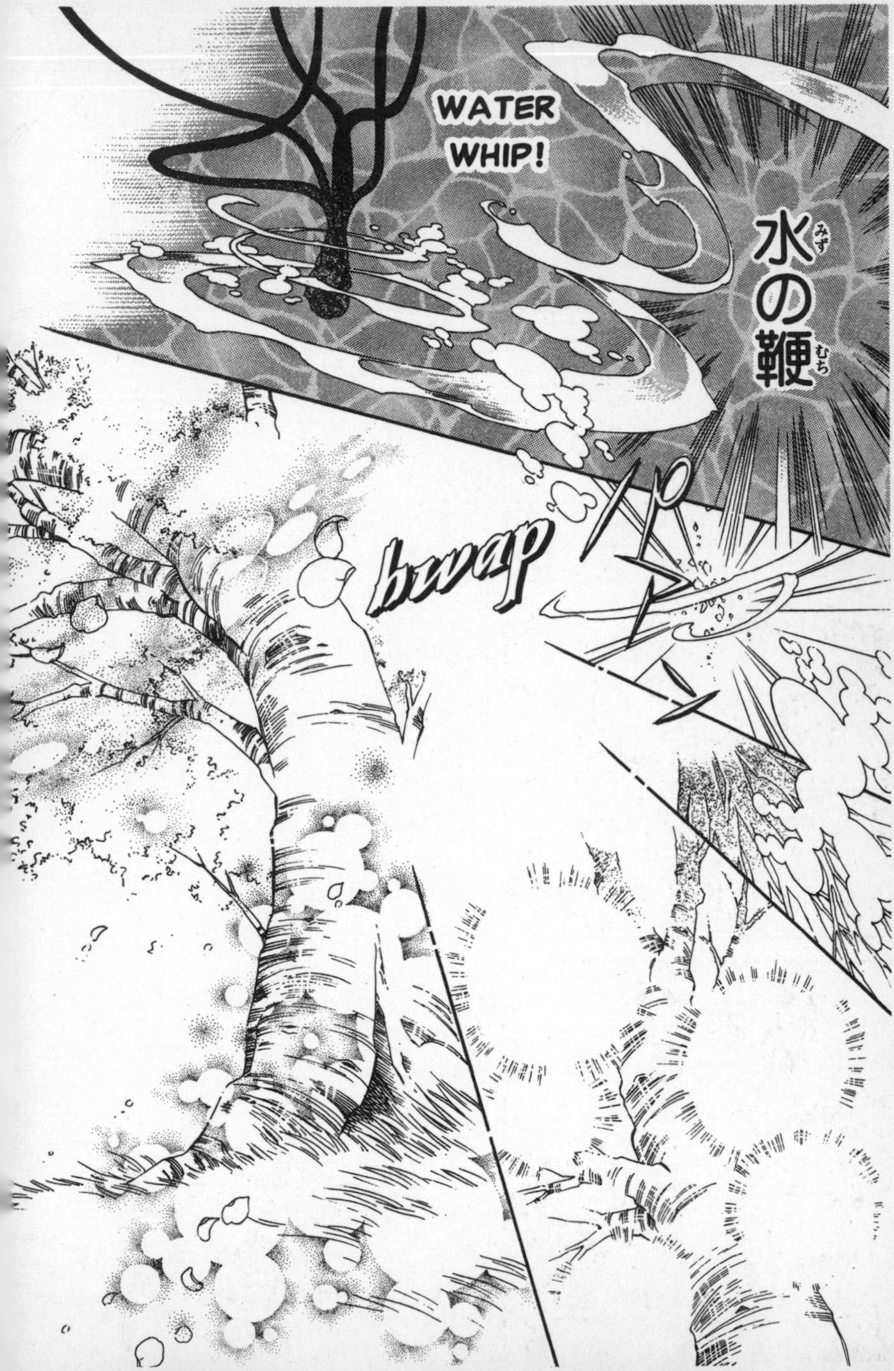
WATER WHIP!
水の鞭
bwap
パシン

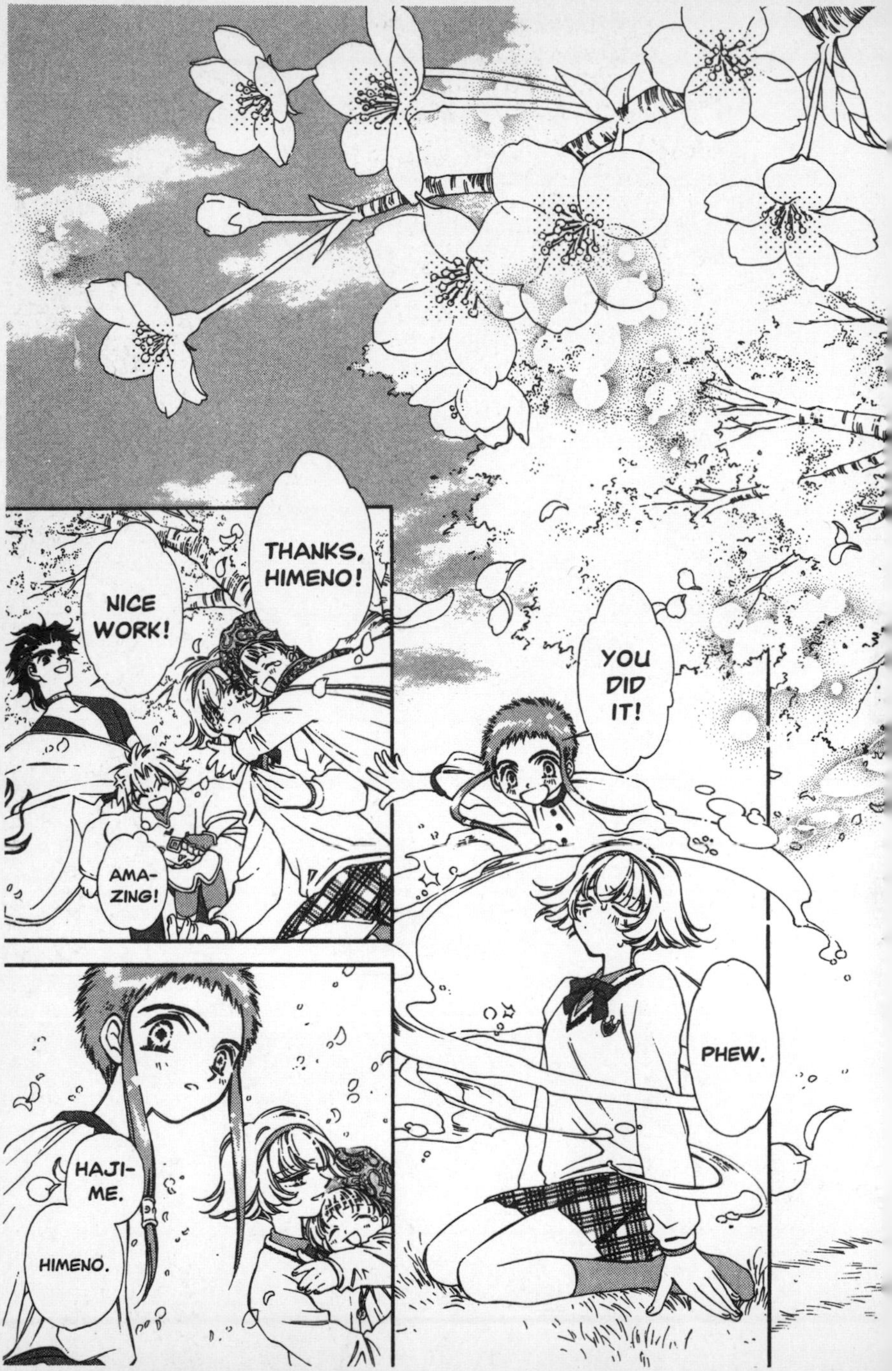
YOU DID IT!
THANKS, HIMENO!
NICE WORK!
AMA-ZING!
PHEW.
HAJI-ME.
HIMENO.

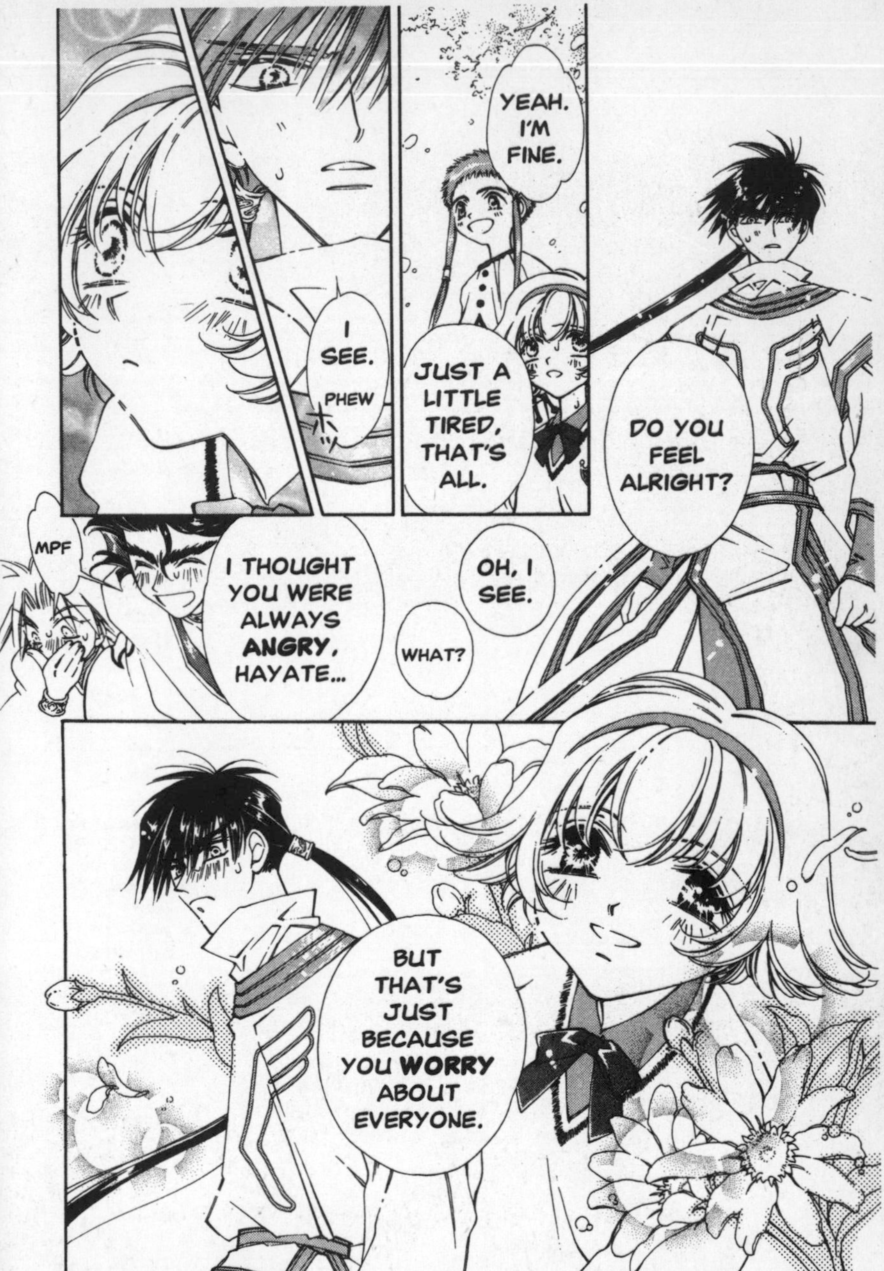
DO YOU FEEL ALRIGHT?
YEAH. I'M FINE.
JUST A LITTLE TIRED, THAT'S ALL.
I SEE.
PHEW
OH, I SEE.
WHAT?
I THOUGHT YOU WERE ALWAYS ANGRY, HAYATE...
MPF
BUT THAT'S JUST BECAUSE YOU WORRY ABOUT EVERYONE.

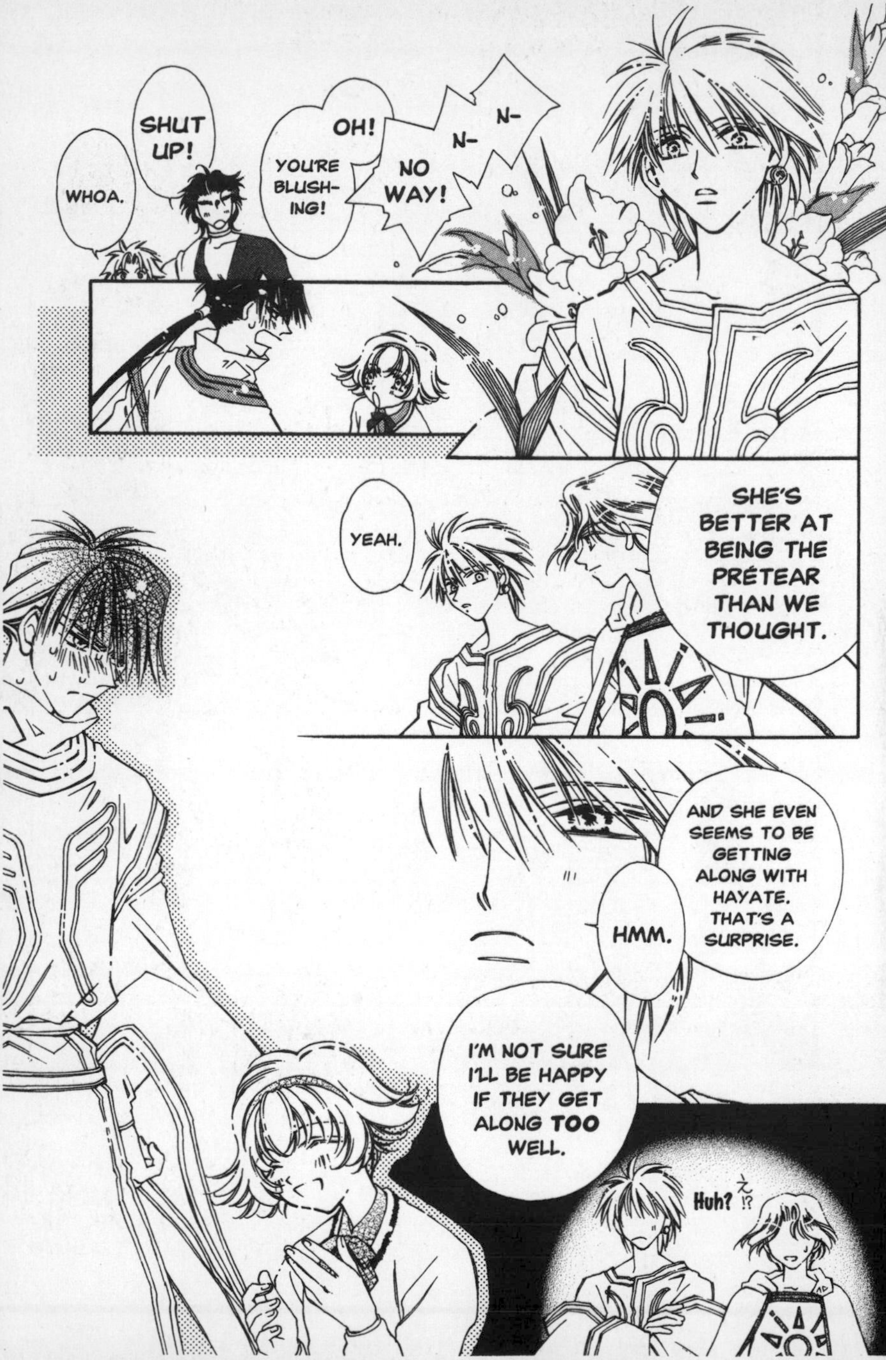
N-
N-
NO WAY!
OH!
YOU'RE BLUSH-ING!
SHUT UP!
WHOA.
SHE'S BETTER AT BEING THE PRÉTEAR THAN WE THOUGHT.
YEAH.
AND SHE EVEN SEEMS TO BE GETTING ALONG WITH HAYATE. THAT'S A SURPRISE.
HMM.
I'M NOT SURE I'LL BE HAPPY IF THEY GET ALONG TOO WELL.
Huh? え!?

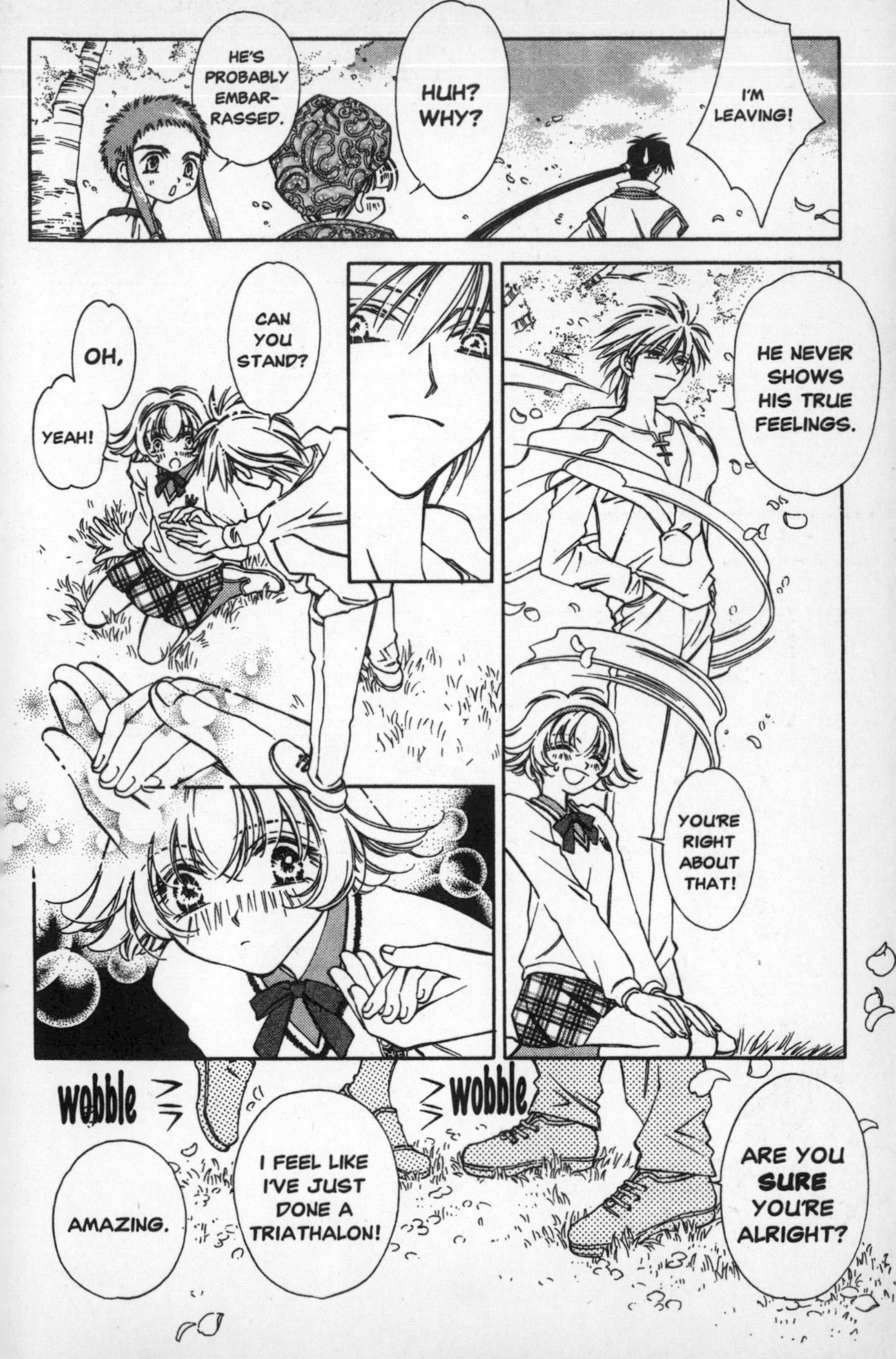
I'M LEAVING!
HUH? WHY?
HE'S PROBABLY EMBAR-RASSED.
HE NEVER SHOWS HIS TRUE FEELINGS.
YOU'RE RIGHT ABOUT THAT!
CAN YOU STAND?
OH,
YEAH!
ARE YOU SURE YOU'RE ALRIGHT?
wobble
wobble
I FEEL LIKE I'VE JUST DONE A TRIATHALON!
AMAZING.

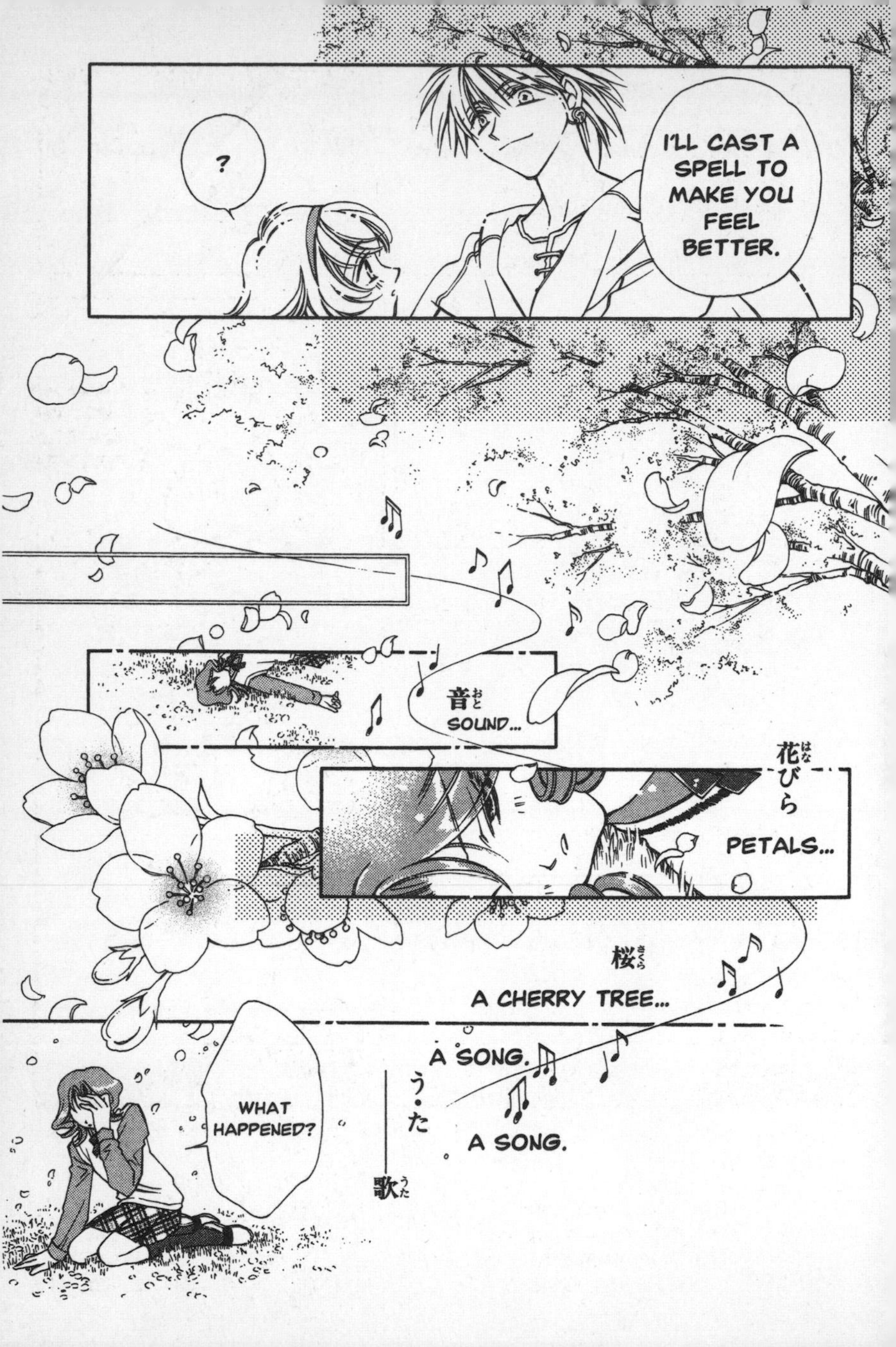
I'LL CAST A SPELL TO MAKE YOU FEEL BETTER.
?
音 おと
SOUND...
花びら はな
PETALS...
桜 さくら
A CHERRY TREE...
A SONG.
歌 うた
う・た
A SONG.
WHAT HAPPENED?

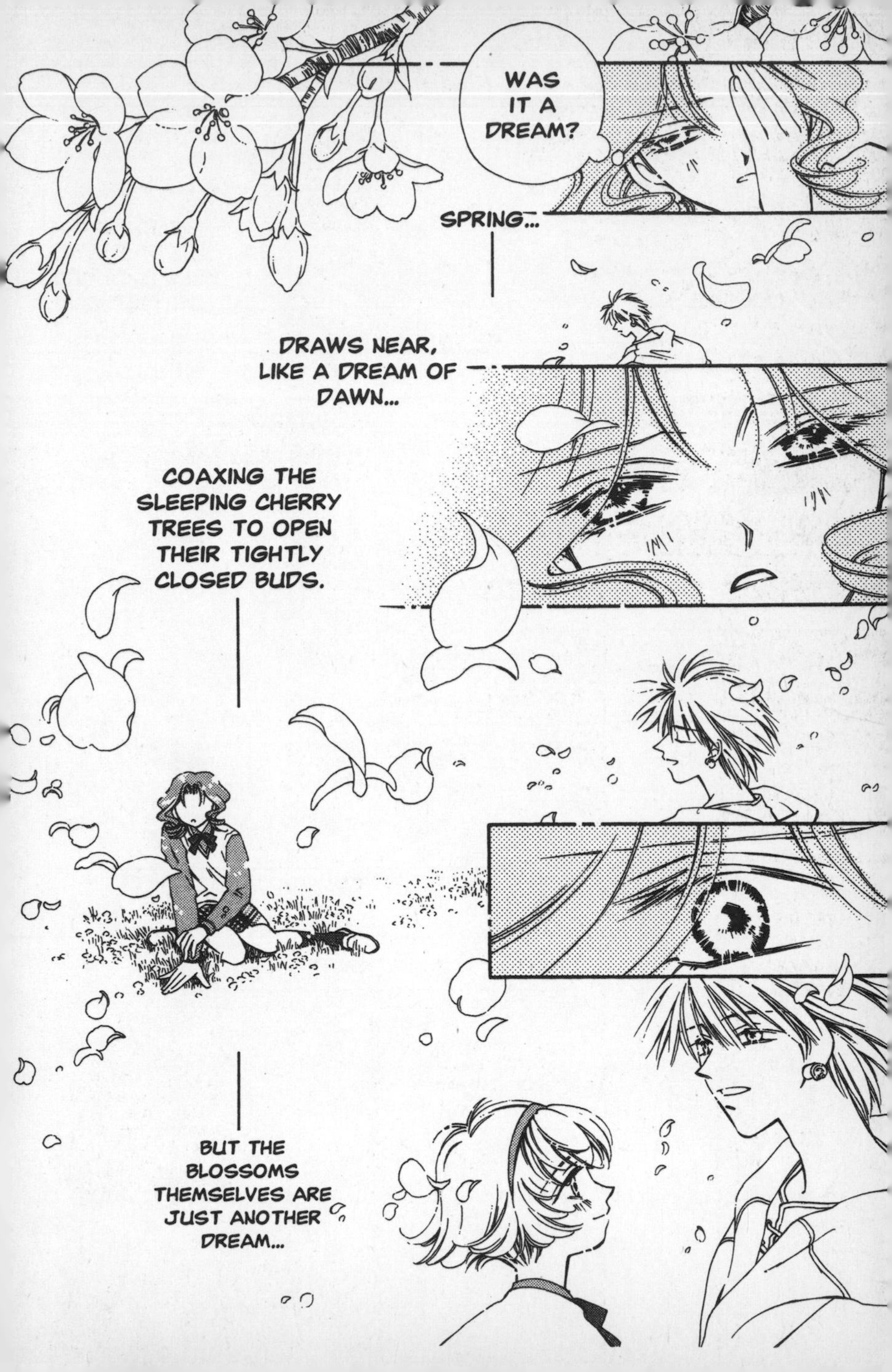
WAS IT A DREAM?
SPRING...
DRAWS NEAR, LIKE A DREAM OF DAWN...
COAXING THE SLEEPING CHERRY TREES TO OPEN THEIR TIGHTLY CLOSED BUDS.
BUT THE BLOSSOMS THEMSELVES ARE JUST ANOTHER DREAM...

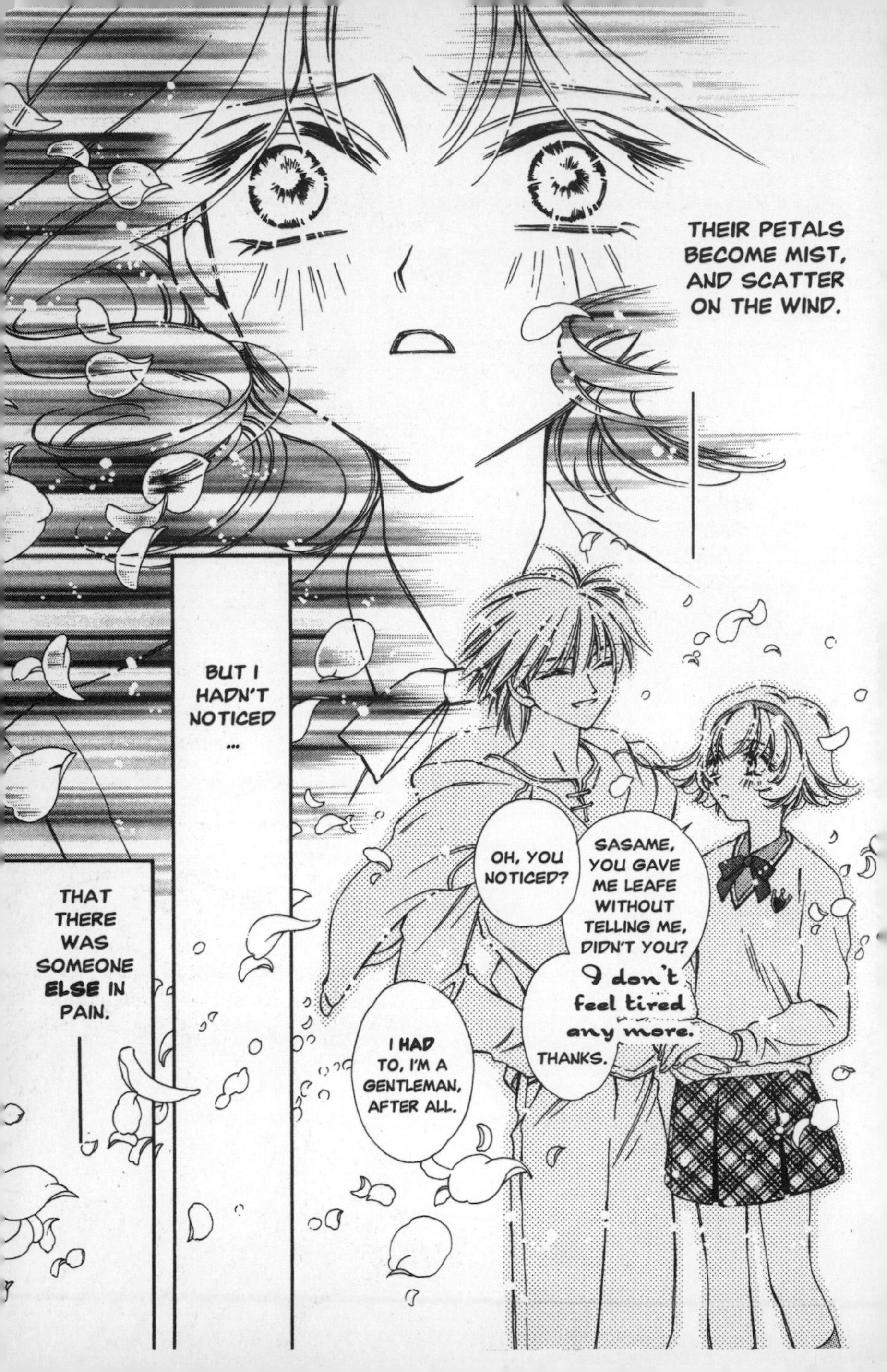
THEIR PETALS BECOME MIST, AND SCATTER ON THE WIND.
BUT I HADN'T NOTICED ...
THAT THERE WAS SOMEONE ELSE IN PAIN.
SASAME, YOU GAVE ME LEAFE WITHOUT TELLING ME, DIDN'T YOU?
OH, YOU NOTICED?
I don't feel tired any more.
THANKS.
I HAD TO, I'M A GENTLEMAN, AFTER ALL.

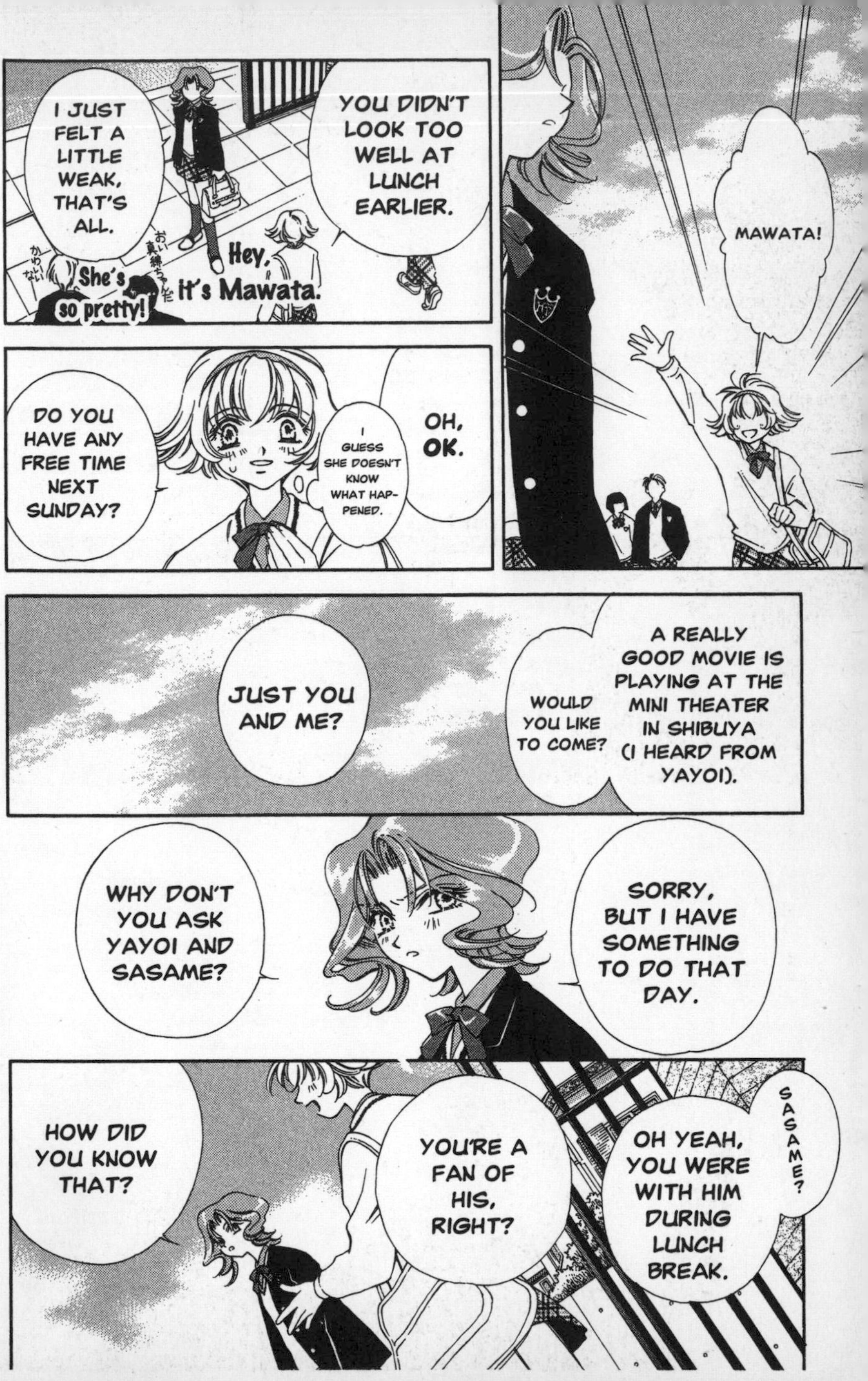
MAWATA!
YOU DIDN'T LOOK TOO WELL AT LUNCH EARLIER.
I JUST FELT A LITTLE WEAK, THAT'S ALL.
Hey, it's Mawata.
She's so pretty!
OH, OK.
I GUESS SHE DOESN'T KNOW WHAT HAPPENED.
DO YOU HAVE ANY FREE TIME NEXT SUNDAY?
A REALLY GOOD MOVIE IS PLAYING AT THE MINI THEATER IN SHIBUYA (I HEARD FROM YAYOI).
WOULD YOU LIKE TO COME?
JUST YOU AND ME?
SORRY, BUT I HAVE SOMETHING TO DO THAT DAY.
WHY DON'T YOU ASK YAYOI AND SASAME?
SASAME?
OH YEAH, YOU WERE WITH HIM DURING LUNCH BREAK.
YOU'RE A FAN OF HIS, RIGHT?
HOW DID YOU KNOW THAT?

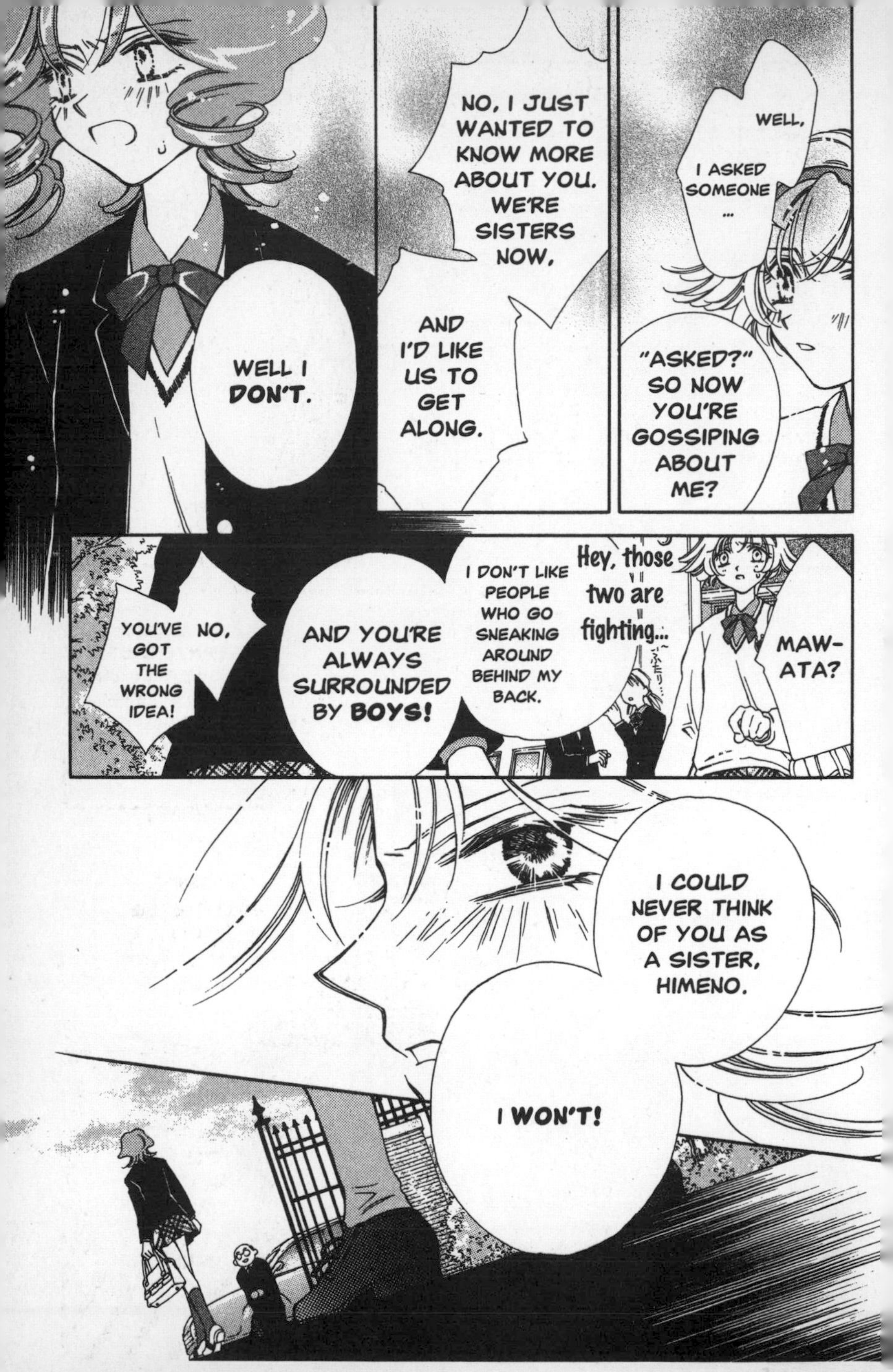
WELL, I ASKED SOMEONE ...
"ASKED?" SO NOW YOU'RE GOSSIPING ABOUT ME?
NO, I JUST WANTED TO KNOW MORE ABOUT YOU. WE'RE SISTERS NOW,
AND I'D LIKE US TO GET ALONG.
WELL I DON'T.
MAW-ATA?
Hey, those two are fighting...
I DON'T LIKE PEOPLE WHO GO SNEAKING AROUND BEHIND MY BACK.
AND YOU'RE ALWAYS SURROUNDED BY BOYS!
NO, YOU'VE GOT THE WRONG IDEA!
I COULD NEVER THINK OF YOU AS A SISTER, HIMENO.
I WON'T!

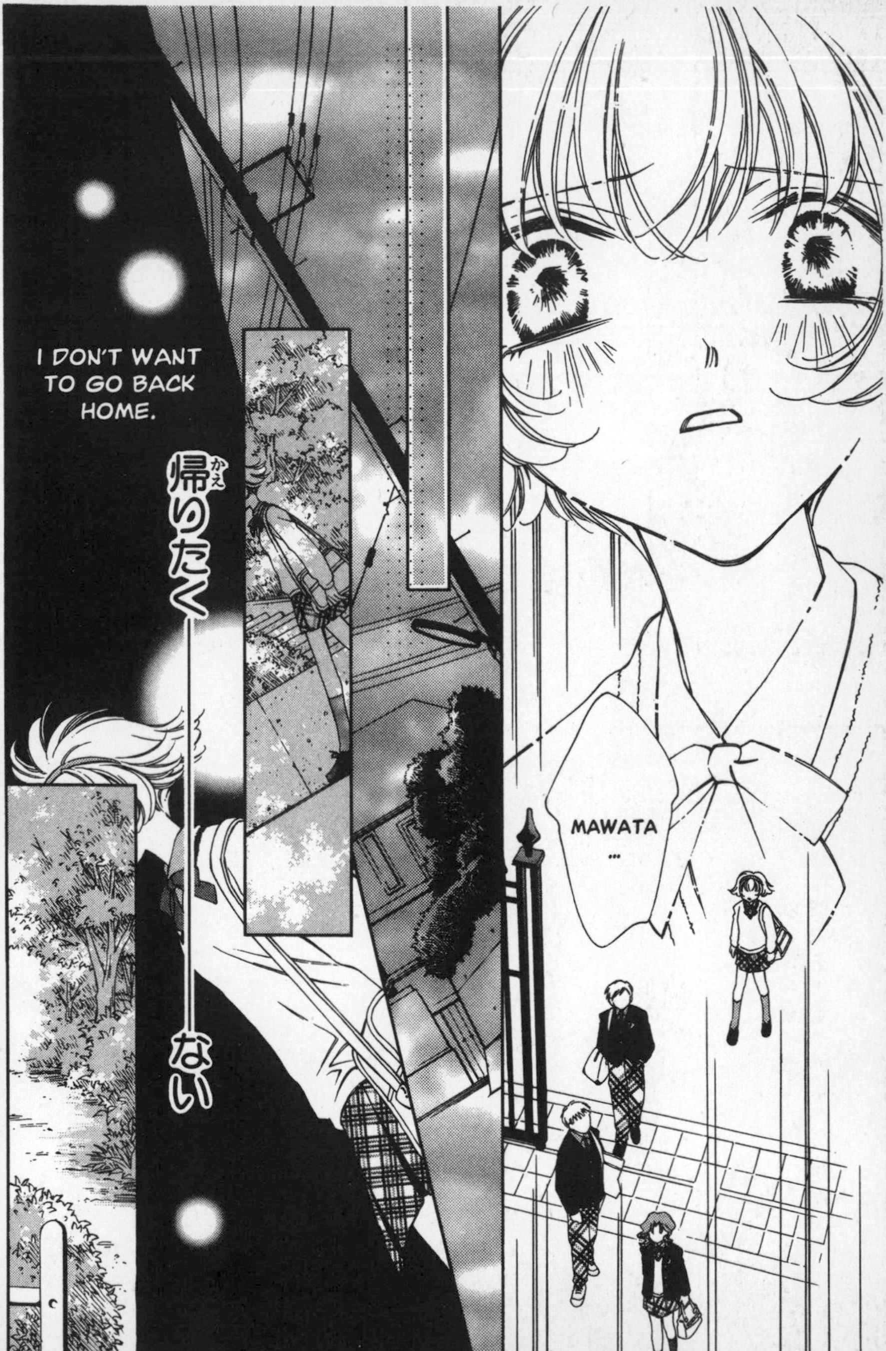
MAWATA
...
I DON'T WANT TO GO BACK HOME.
帰りたく――ない

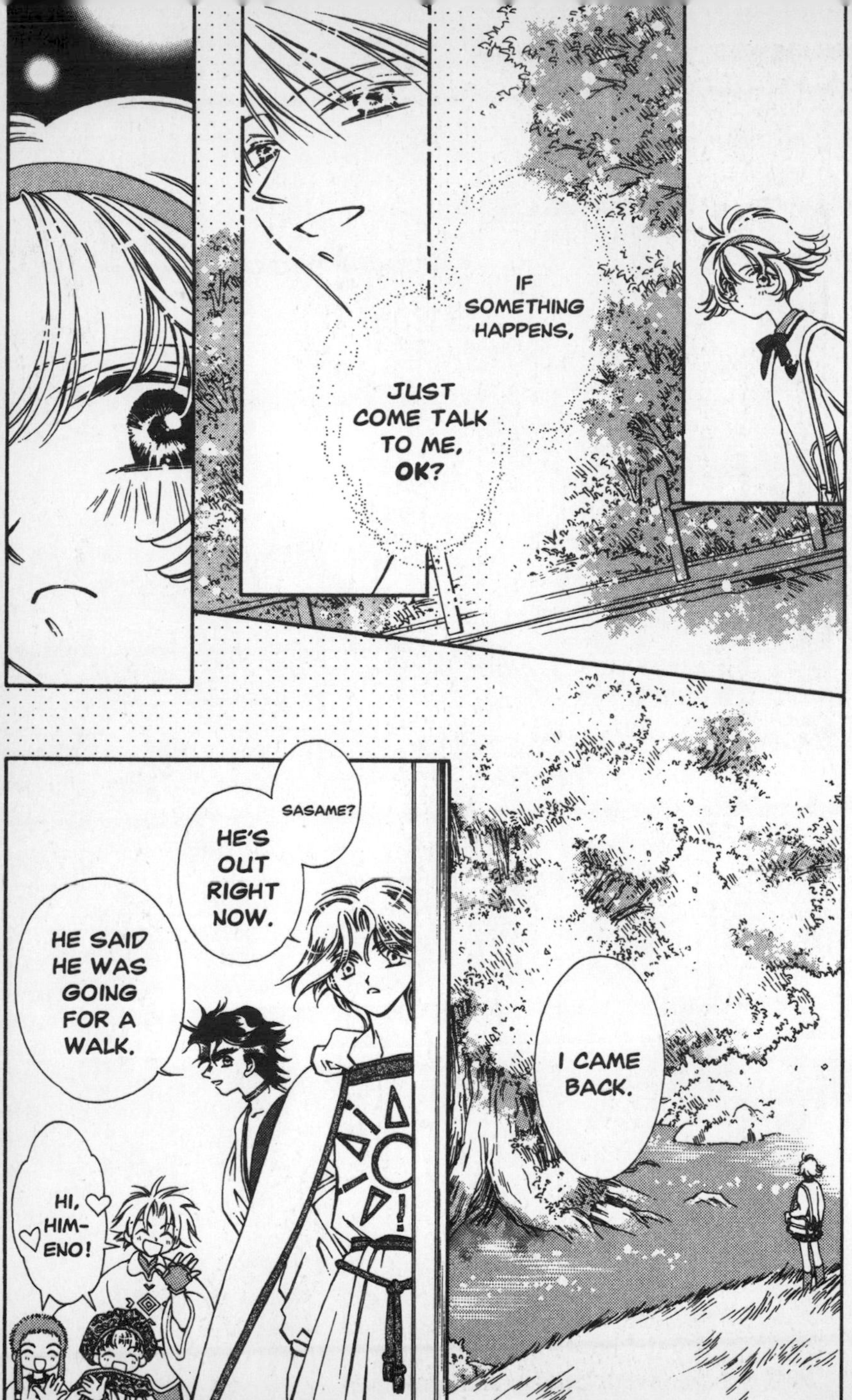
IF SOMETHING HAPPENS,
JUST COME TALK TO ME, OK?
I CAME BACK.
SASAME? HE'S OUT RIGHT NOW.
HE SAID HE WAS GOING FOR A WALK.
HI, HIM-ENO!

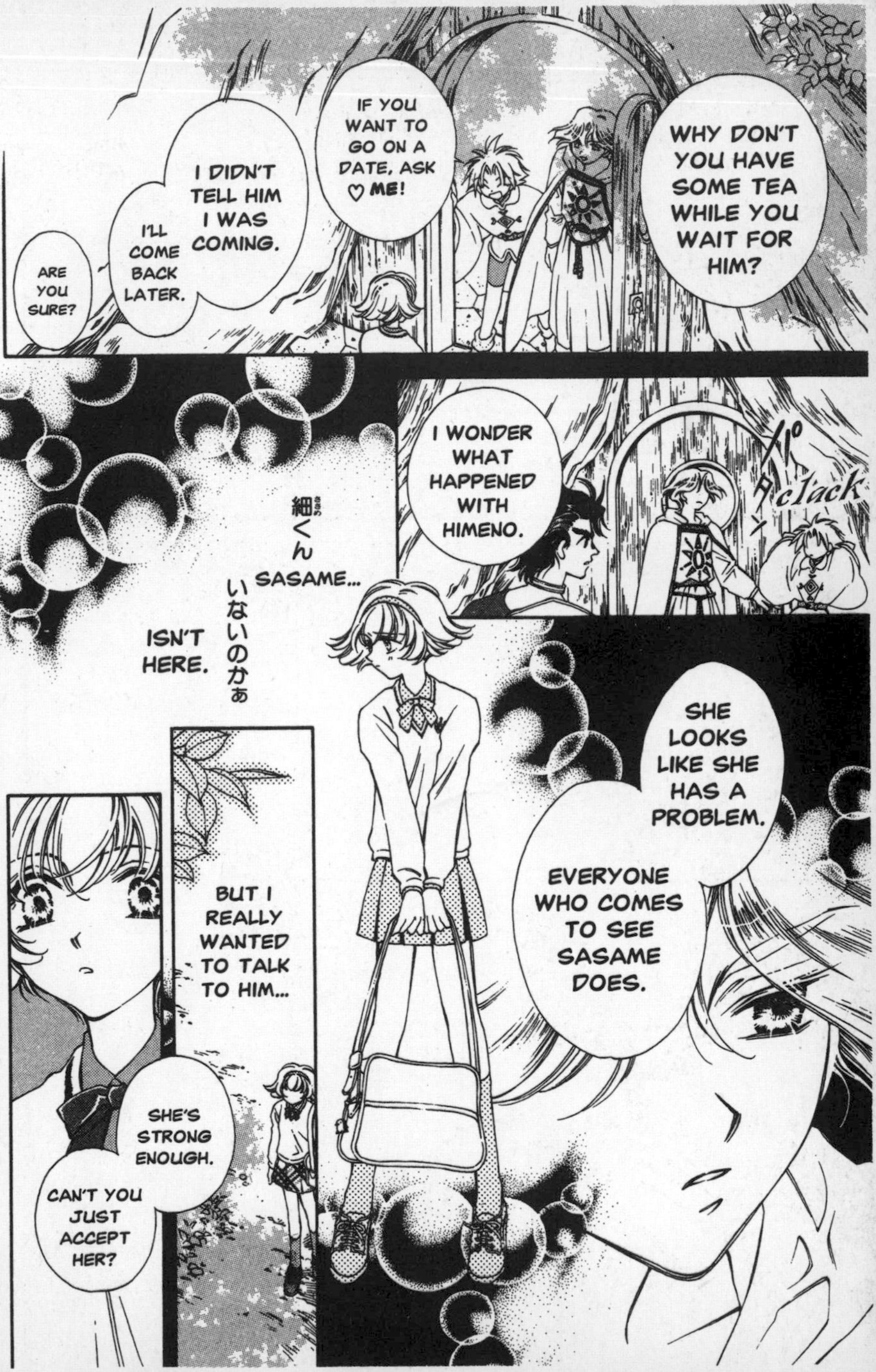
WHY DON'T YOU HAVE SOME TEA WHILE YOU WAIT FOR HIM?
IF YOU WANT TO GO ON A DATE, ASK ♡ ME!
I DIDN'T TELL HIM I WAS COMING.
I'LL COME BACK LATER.
ARE YOU SURE?
パタン
clack
I WONDER WHAT HAPPENED WITH HIMENO.
細くん
SASAME...
いないのかぁ
ISN'T HERE.
SHE LOOKS LIKE SHE HAS A PROBLEM.
EVERYONE WHO COMES TO SEE SASAME DOES.
BUT I REALLY WANTED TO TALK TO HIM...
SHE'S STRONG ENOUGH.
CAN'T YOU JUST ACCEPT HER?

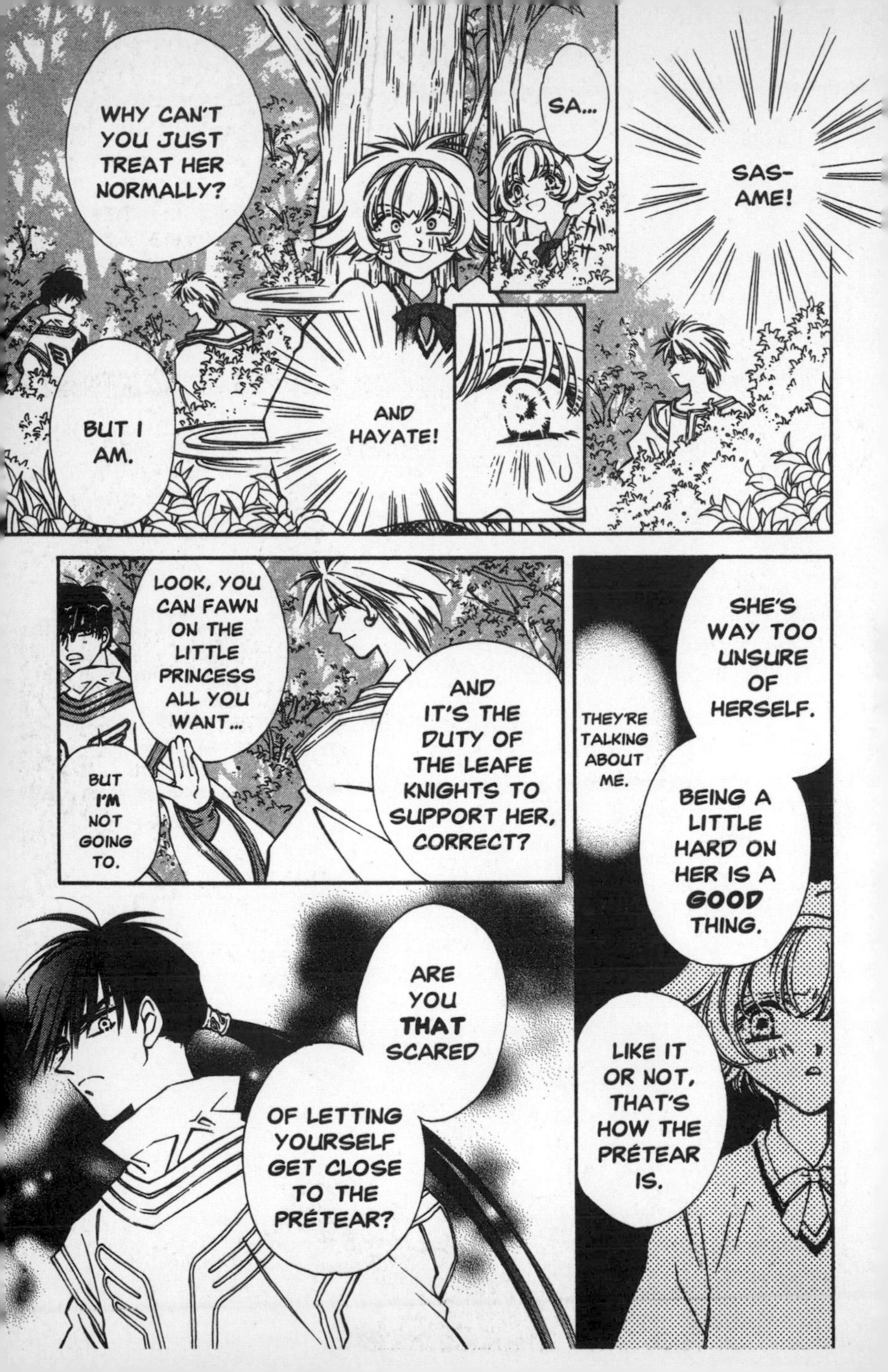

SA...
SAS-AME!
AND HAYATE!
WHY CAN'T YOU JUST TREAT HER NORMALLY?
BUT I AM.
SHE'S WAY TOO UNSURE OF HERSELF.
BEING A LITTLE HARD ON HER IS A **GOOD** THING.
THEY'RE TALKING ABOUT ME.
AND IT'S THE DUTY OF THE LEAFE KNIGHTS TO SUPPORT HER, CORRECT?
LOOK, YOU CAN FAWN ON THE LITTLE PRINCESS ALL YOU WANT...
BUT **I'M** NOT GOING TO.
LIKE IT OR NOT, THAT'S HOW THE PRÉTEAR IS.
ARE YOU **THAT** SCARED
OF LETTING YOURSELF GET CLOSE TO THE PRÉTEAR?

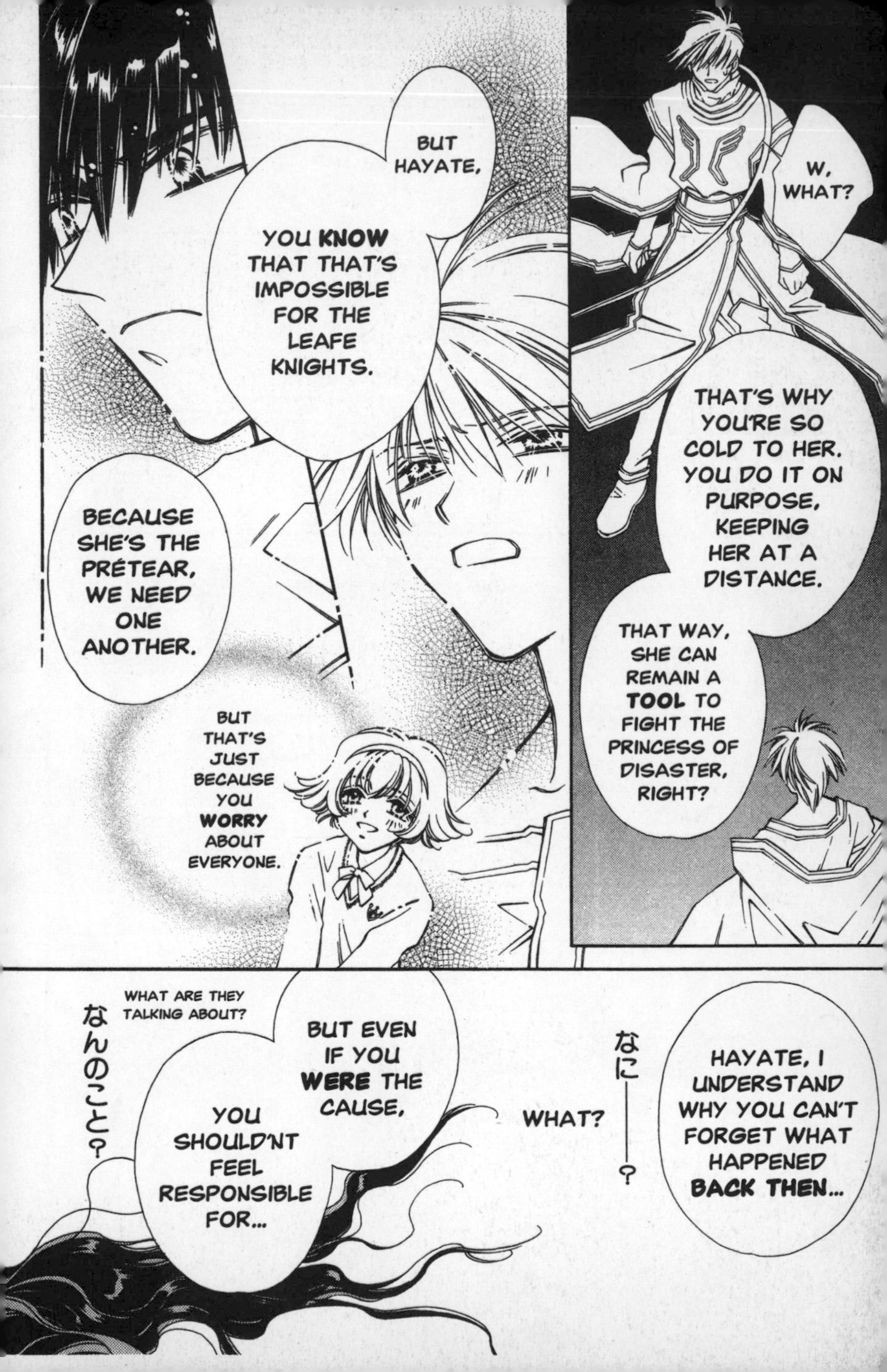
W, WHAT?
THAT'S WHY YOU'RE SO COLD TO HER. YOU DO IT ON PURPOSE, KEEPING HER AT A DISTANCE.
THAT WAY, SHE CAN REMAIN A **TOOL** TO FIGHT THE PRINCESS OF DISASTER, RIGHT?
BUT HAYATE,
YOU **KNOW** THAT THAT'S IMPOSSIBLE FOR THE LEAFE KNIGHTS.
BECAUSE SHE'S THE PRÉTEAR, WE NEED ONE ANOTHER.
BUT THAT'S JUST BECAUSE YOU **WORRY** ABOUT EVERYONE.
HAYATE, I UNDERSTAND WHY YOU CAN'T FORGET WHAT HAPPENED **BACK THEN**...
なに——？
WHAT?
BUT EVEN IF YOU **WERE** THE CAUSE,
YOU SHOULDN'T FEEL RESPONSIBLE FOR...
なんのこと？
WHAT ARE THEY TALKING ABOUT?

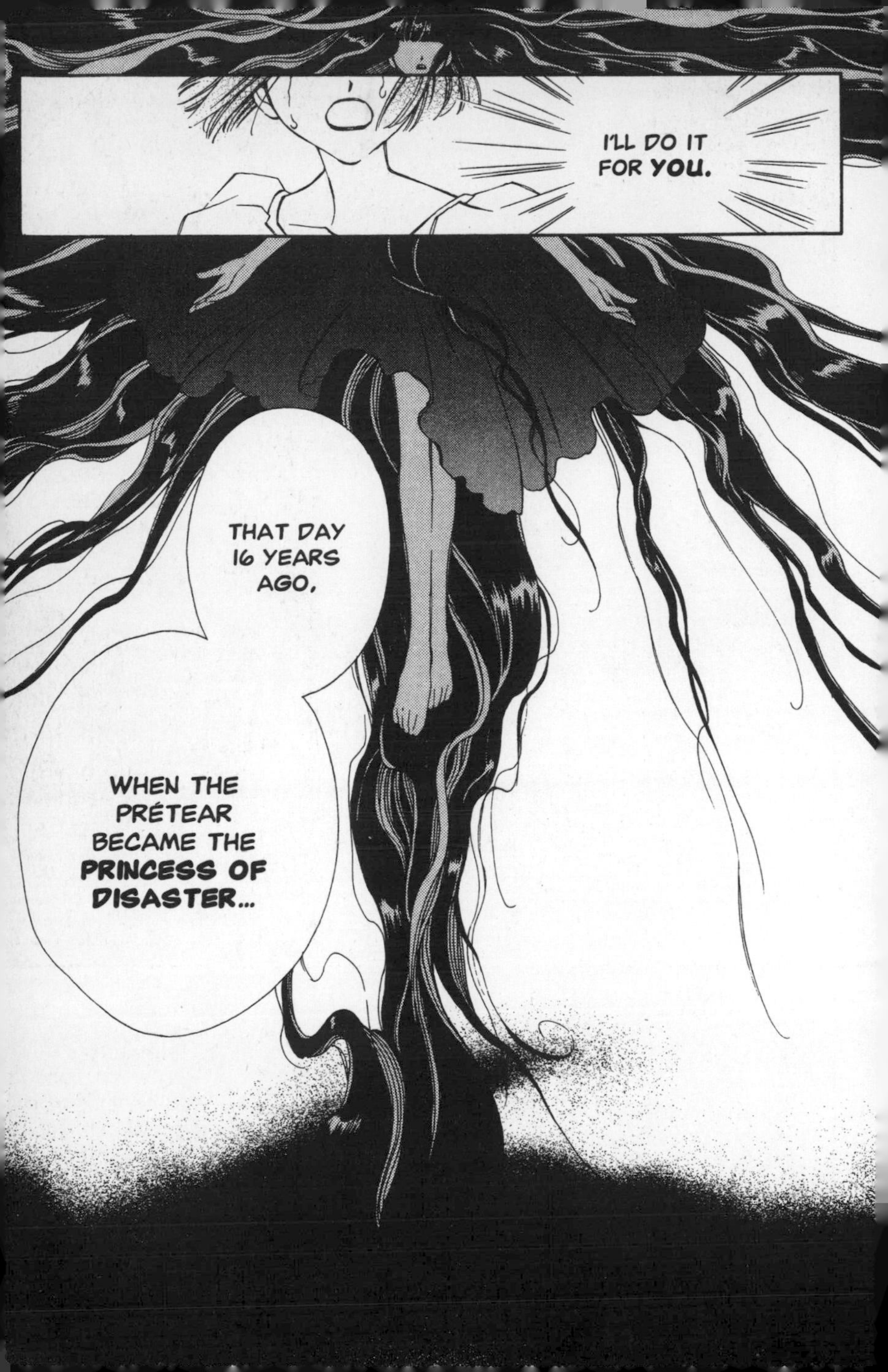

I'LL DO IT FOR **YOU.**
THAT DAY 16 YEARS AGO,
WHEN THE PRÉTEAR BECAME THE **PRINCESS OF DISASTER...**

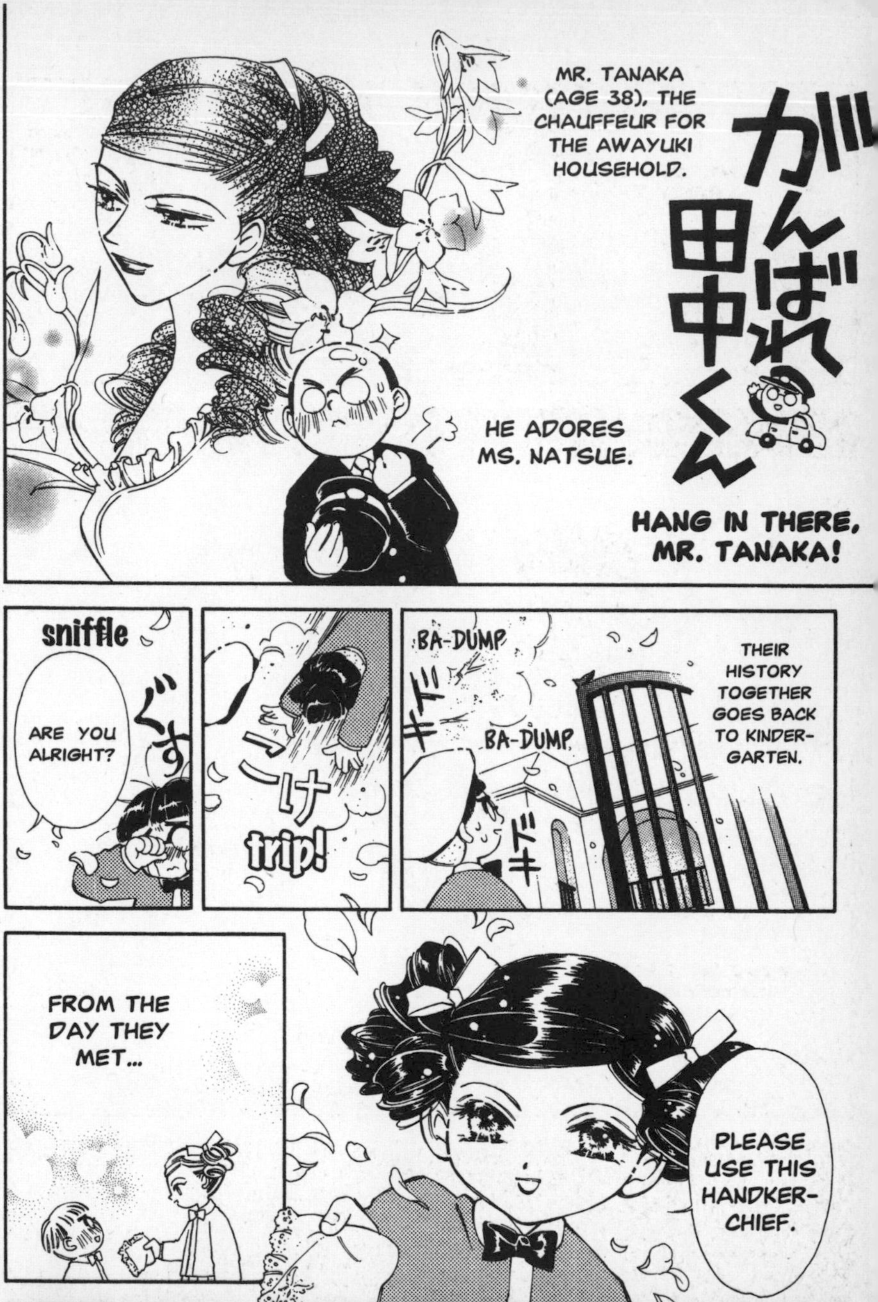
がんばれ田中くん
HANG IN THERE, MR. TANAKA!
MR. TANAKA (AGE 38), THE CHAUFFEUR FOR THE AWAYUKI HOUSEHOLD.
HE ADORES MS. NATSUE.
THEIR HISTORY TOGETHER GOES BACK TO KINDER-GARTEN.
BA-DUMP
ドキ
BA-DUMP
ドキ
こけ
trip!
sniffle
ぐす
ARE YOU ALRIGHT?
PLEASE USE THIS HANDKER-CHIEF.
FROM THE DAY THEY MET...
OF COURSE, IT DIDN'T HAPPEN LIKE THIS.

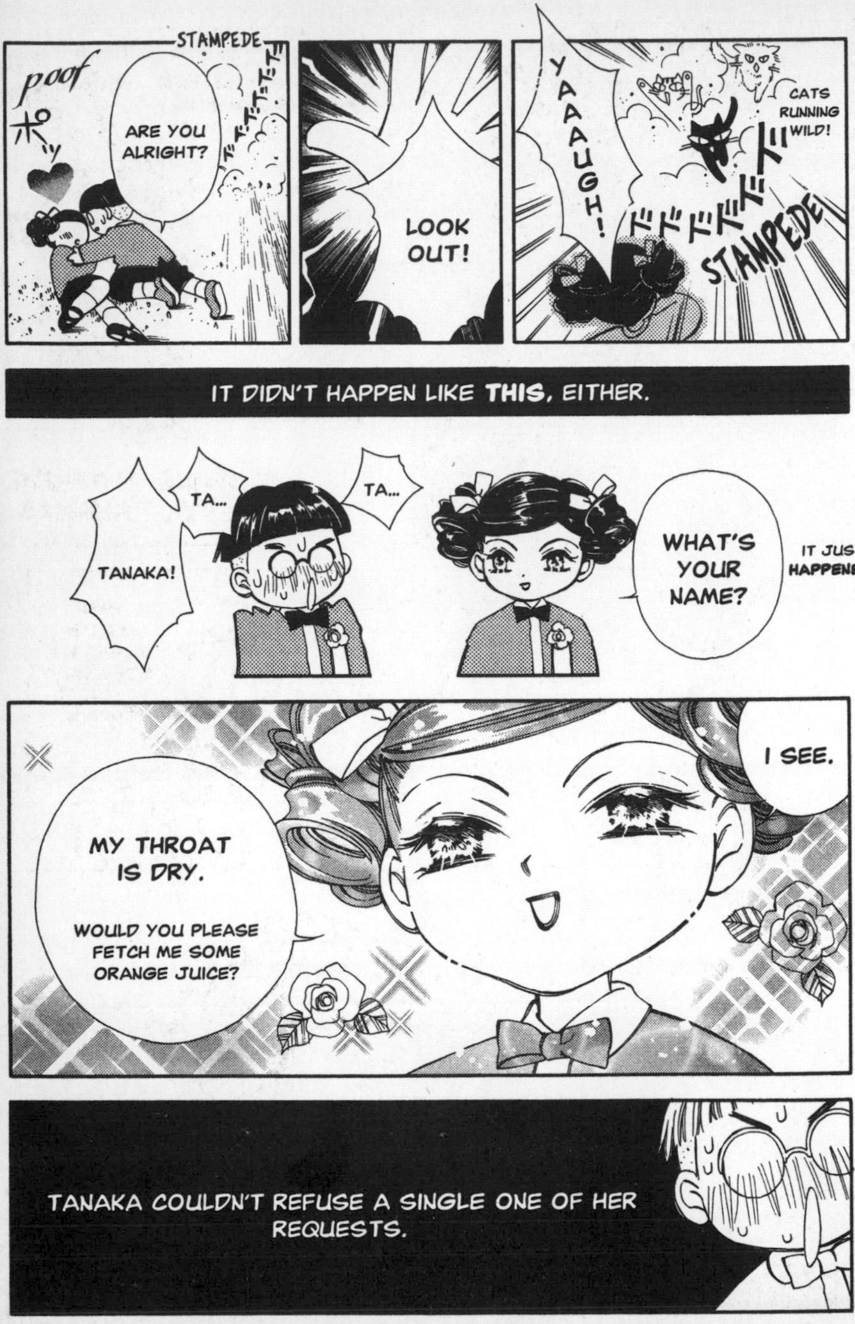
YAAAUGH!
CATS RUNNING WILD!
ドドドドド
STAMPEDE!
LOOK OUT!
STAMPEDE
ARE YOU ALRIGHT?
poof
ポッ
IT DIDN'T HAPPEN LIKE **THIS**, EITHER.
IT JUST HAPPENED.
WHAT'S YOUR NAME?
TA...
TA...
TANAKA!
I SEE.
MY THROAT IS DRY.
WOULD YOU PLEASE FETCH ME SOME ORANGE JUICE?
TANAKA COULDN'T REFUSE A SINGLE ONE OF HER REQUESTS.

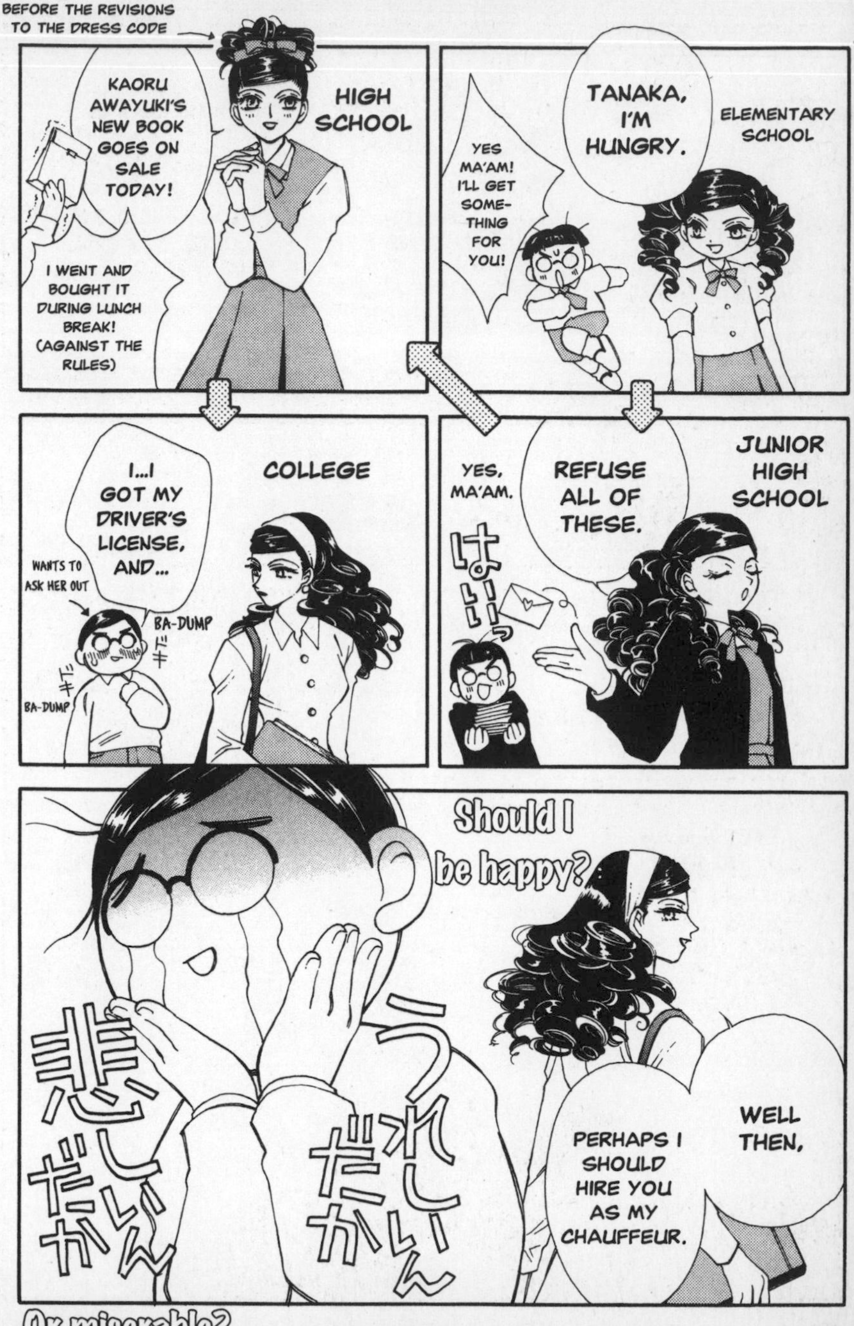
BEFORE THE REVISIONS TO THE DRESS CODE
ELEMENTARY SCHOOL
TANAKA, I'M HUNGRY.
YES MA'AM! I'LL GET SOME-THING FOR YOU!
JUNIOR HIGH SCHOOL
REFUSE ALL OF THESE.
YES, MA'AM.
はいっ
HIGH SCHOOL
KAORU AWAYUKI'S NEW BOOK GOES ON SALE TODAY!
I WENT AND BOUGHT IT DURING LUNCH BREAK! (AGAINST THE RULES)
COLLEGE
I...I GOT MY DRIVER'S LICENSE, AND...
WANTS TO ASK HER OUT
BA-DUMP
BA-DUMP
WELL THEN,
PERHAPS I SHOULD HIRE YOU AS MY CHAUFFEUR.
Should I be happy?
Or miserable?

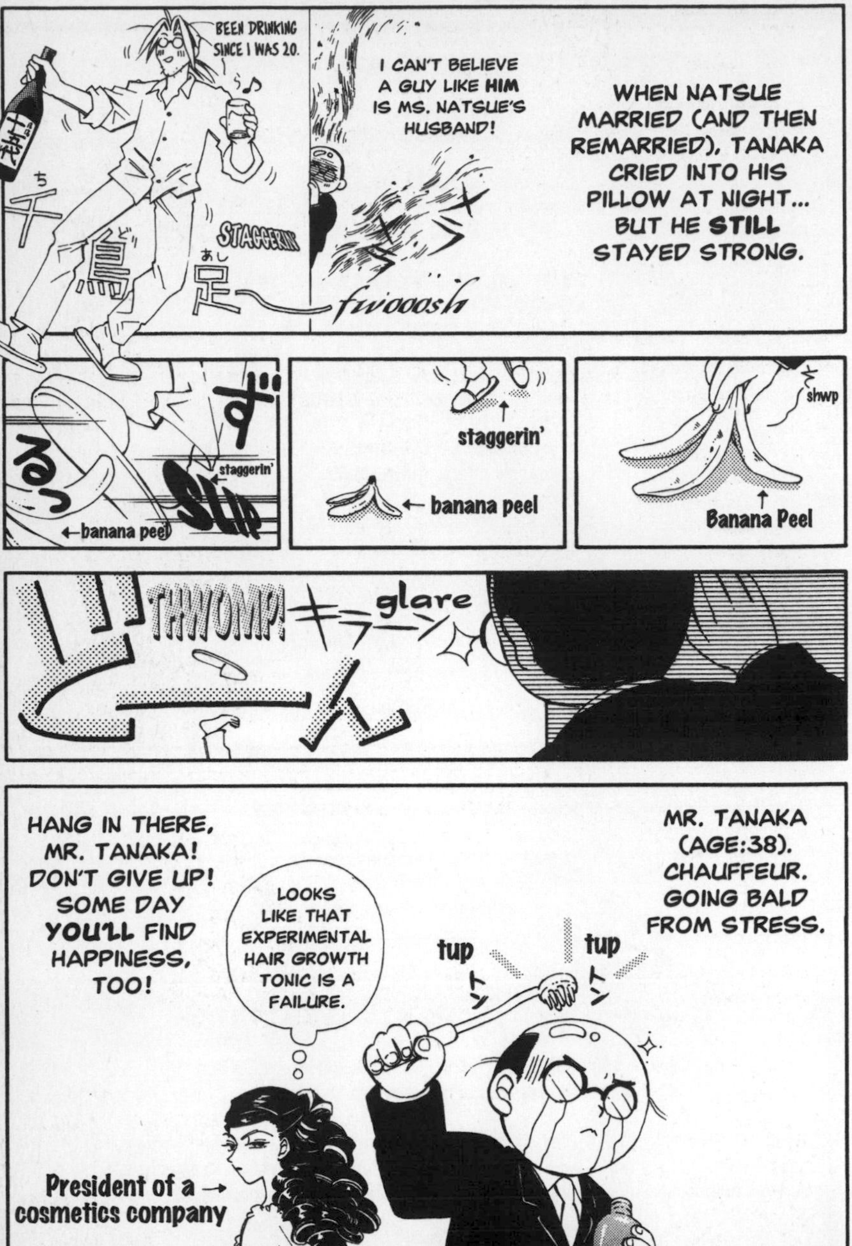

BEEN DRINKING SINCE I WAS 20.
STAGGERIN'
I CAN'T BELIEVE A GUY LIKE HIM IS MS. NATSUE'S HUSBAND!
fwooosh
WHEN NATSUE MARRIED (AND THEN REMARRIED), TANAKA CRIED INTO HIS PILLOW AT NIGHT... BUT HE STILL STAYED STRONG.
shwp
Banana Peel
staggerin'
banana peel
staggerin'
SLIP
banana peel
glare
THWOMP!
MR. TANAKA (AGE:38). CHAUFFEUR. GOING BALD FROM STRESS.
tup
tup
LOOKS LIKE THAT EXPERIMENTAL HAIR GROWTH TONIC IS A FAILURE.
HANG IN THERE, MR. TANAKA! DON'T GIVE UP! SOME DAY YOU'LL FIND HAPPINESS, TOO!
President of a cosmetics company

# PRÉTEAR
## VOLUME ONE

©Kaori NARUSE 2000
©Junichi SATOU 2000
Originally published in Japan in 2000 by KADOKAWA SHOTEN PUBLISHING CO., LTD., Tokyo.
English translation rights arranged with KADOKAWA SHOTEN PUBLISHING CO., LTD., Tokyo.

Translator **AMY FORSYTH**
Lead Translator/Translation Supervisor **JAVIER LOPEZ**
ADV Manga Translation Staff **KAY BERTRAND, BRENDAN FRAYNE** and **EIKO McGREGOR**

Print Production/ Art Studio Manager **LISA PUCKETT**
Pre-press Manager **ERNIE ZUNIGA**
Art Production Manager **RYAN MASON**
Sr. Designer/Creative Manager **JORGE ALVARADO**
Graphic Designer/Group Leader **SHANNON RASBERRY**
Graphic Designer **LANCE SWARTOUT**
Graphic Artists **KRISTINA MILESKI, NATALIA MORALES, CHRIS LAPP**
and **NANAKO TSUKIHASHI**
Graphic Intern **MARK MEZA**

International Coordinator **TORU IWAKAMI**
International Coordinator **ATSUSHI KANBAYASHI**

Publishing Editor **SUSAN ITIN**
Assistant Editor **MARGARET SCHAROLD**
Editorial Assistant **VARSHA BHUCHAR**
Proofreader **SHERIDAN JACOBS**

Research/ Traffic Coordinator **MARSHA ARNOLD**

Executive V.P., CFO, COO **KEVIN CORCORAN**

President, C.E.O & Publisher **JOHN LEDFORD**

Email: editor@adv-manga.com
www.adv-manga.com
www.advfilms.com
For sales and distribution inquiries please call 1.800.282.7202

 is a division of A.D. Vision, Inc.
10114 W. Sam Houston Parkway, Suite 200, Houston, Texas 77099

English text © 2004 published by A.D. Vision, Inc. under exclusive license.
ADV MANGA is a trademark of A.D. Vision, Inc.

ISBN: 1-4139-0144-1
First printing, May 2004
10 9 8 7 6 5 4 3 2 1
Printed in Canada

**LETTER FROM THE ADV MANGA TRANSLATION STAFF**

Dear Reader,

On behalf of the ADV Manga translation team, thank you for purchasing an ADV book. We are enthusiastic and committed to our work, and strive to carry our enthusiasm over into the book you hold in your hands.

Our goal is to retain the true spirit of the original Japanese book. While great care has been taken to render a true and accurate translation, some cultural or readability issues may require a line to be adapted for greater accessibility to our readers. At times, manga titles that include culturally-specific concepts will feature a "Translator's Notes" section, which explains noteworthy references to the original text.

We hope our commitment to a faithful translation is evident in every ADV book you purchase.

Sincerely,

**Javier Lopez**
Lead Translator

**Eiko McGregor**

**Kay Bertrand**

**Brendan Frayne**

**Amy Forsyth**

# Prêtear Volume 01

## TRANSLATOR'S NOTES

PG. 11 **Daikon leaves**
Daikon leaves are usually thrown out. They're very cheap, so it makes sense that a poor family would use them as a part of their diet.

PG. 15 **I'd sure make a lousy princess!**
In a bit of a pun, the "hime" part of Himeno's name means "princess" in Japanese.

PG. 21 The small note on the left side of the first panel gives a definition of a cult. It reads: * A religious sect. In this case, it refers to a group of people who cling obsessively to an extremely lopsided way of thinking.

PG. 22 **(1) The tulips have bloomed**
This is the beginning of a popular song that Japanese children learn in kindergarten. The full song goes like this:

| | |
|---|---|
| Saita saita tulip no hana ga | The tulips have bloomed. |
| Naranda naranda | All in a row |
| Aka shiro kiiro | They're red, white and yellow. |
| Dono hana mite mo | And all of them |
| Kireidana | Are beautiful. |

**(2) Valley girl**
In the original Japanese, the term used was kogal. This is a special brand of high school student that wears their skirts short, puts on baggy legwarmer-like things called "loose socks," and uses speech patterns that tend to get them pegged as not quite the sharpest tacks in the box (bear in mind, these are all generalizations). It's not unusual for kogals to actively acquire a tan, which is why Himeno immediately retorts that her skin isn't dark like a kogal's.

An outgrowth of the kogal was the now (thankfully dead-and-buried) ganguro trend, where the girls would bleach their hair blonde (or gray), tan themselves to the extreme, and wear outrageously gaudy outfits. The yamanba took this even one step further, outlining their mouth and eyes in white or silver liner.

PG. 120 **Kabuki**
A form of Japanese theater dating from the 1600s. Lines are spoken in monotone and accompanied by musical instruments.

PG. 125 **The flowers haven't bloomed yet.**
Cherry blossom trees usually bloom in April.

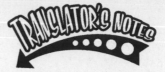

# THE ADVENTURE CONTINUES

## PRÉTEAR VOL. 2

## AVAILABLE AUGUST 2004

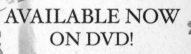

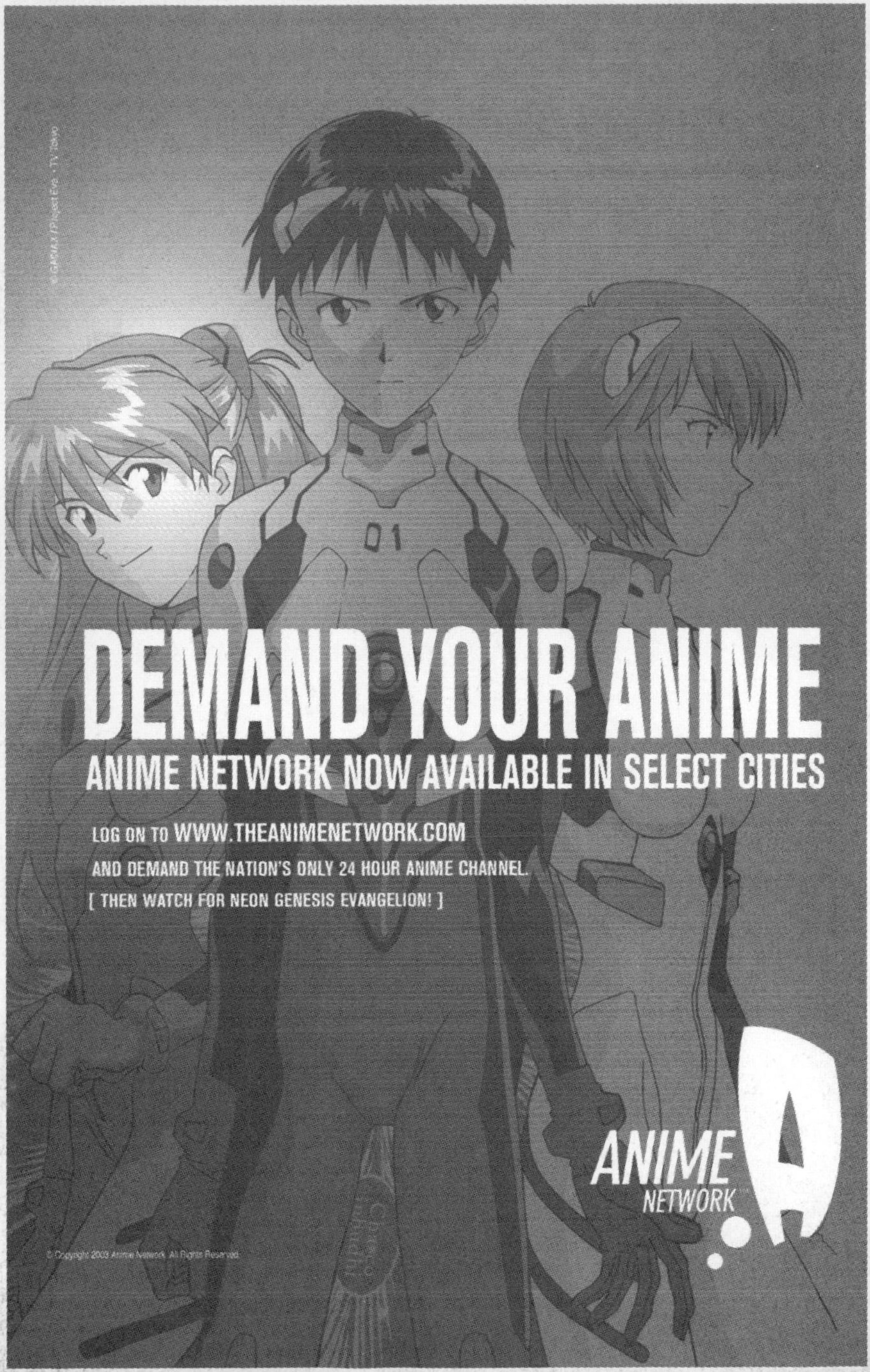
DEMAND YOUR ANIME
ANIME NETWORK NOW AVAILABLE IN SELECT CITIES
LOG ON TO WWW.THEANIMENETWORK.COM
AND DEMAND THE NATION'S ONLY 24 HOUR ANIME CHANNEL.
[ THEN WATCH FOR NEON GENESIS EVANGELION! ]
ANIME NETWORK
© Copyright 2003 Anime Network. All Rights Reserved.

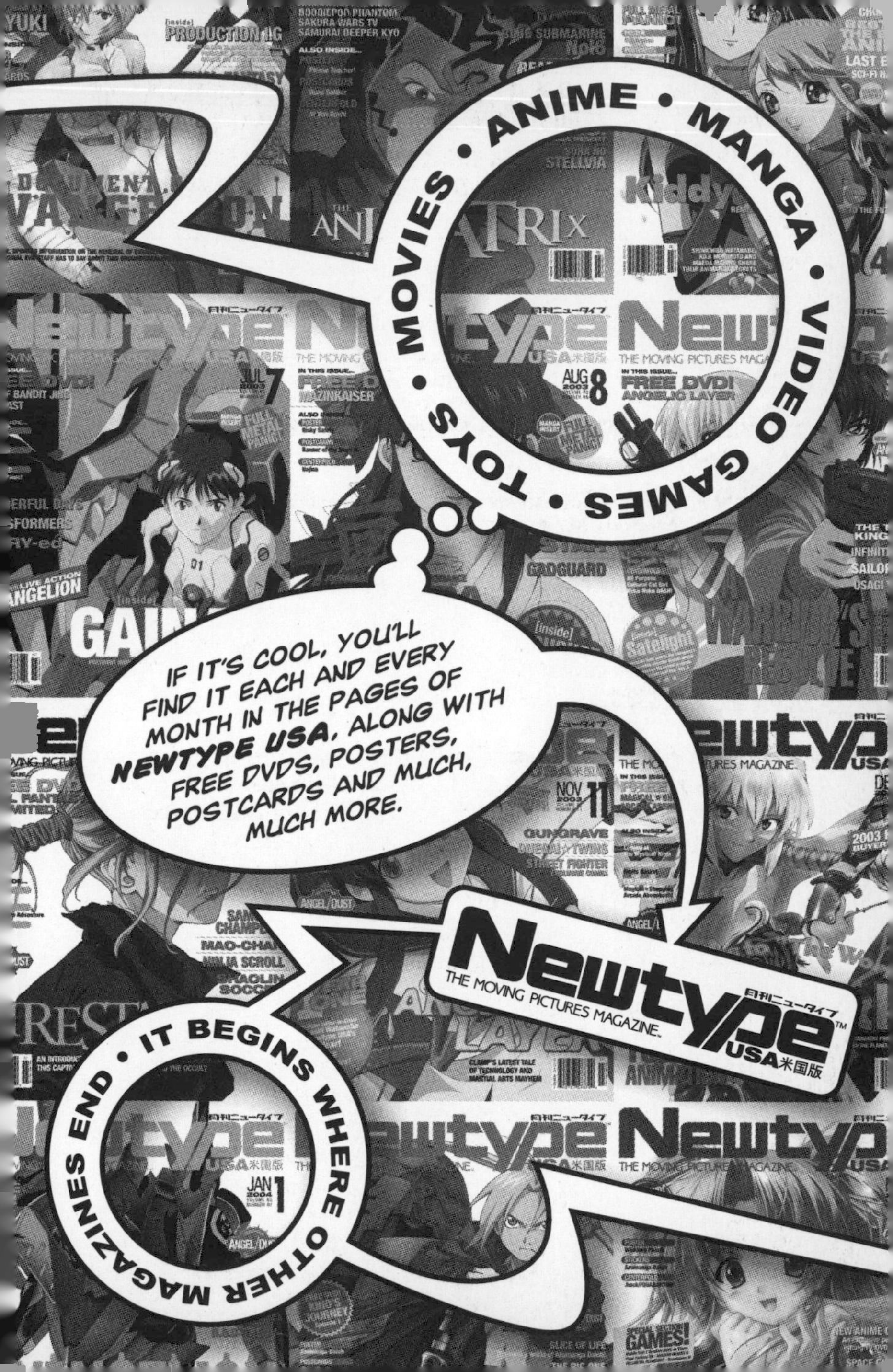
MOVIES • ANIME • MANGA • VIDEO GAMES • TOYS •
IF IT'S COOL, YOU'LL FIND IT EACH AND EVERY MONTH IN THE PAGES OF NEWTYPE USA, ALONG WITH FREE DVDS, POSTERS, POSTCARDS AND MUCH, MUCH MORE.
Newtype THE MOVING PICTURES MAGAZINE. USA
IT BEGINS WHERE OTHER MAGAZINES END •

www.adv-manga.com

# MANGA SURVEY

**PLEASE MAIL THE COMPLETED FORM TO:** EDITOR – ADV MANGA
℅ A.D. Vision, Inc. 10114 W. Sam Houston Pkwy., Suite 200 Houston, TX 77099

Name:_____

Address:_____

City, State, Zip:_____

E-Mail:_____

Male ☐    Female ☐              Age:_____

☐ **CHECK HERE IF YOU WOULD LIKE TO RECEIVE OTHER INFORMATION OR FUTURE OFFERS FROM ADV.**

*All information provided will be used for internal purposes only. We promise not to sell or otherwise divulge your information.*

**1. Annual Household Income** (*Check only one*)
- ☐ Under $25,000
- ☐ $25,000 to $50,000
- ☐ $50,000 to $75,000
- ☐ Over $75,000

**2. How do you hear about new Manga releases?** (*Check all that apply*)
- ☐ Browsing in Store
- ☐ Internet Reviews
- ☐ Anime News Websites
- ☐ Direct Email Campaigns
- ☐ Online forums (message boards and chat rooms)
- ☐ Carrier pigeon
- ☐ Other:_____

- ☐ Magazine Ad
- ☐ Online Advertising
- ☐ Conventions
- ☐ TV Advertising

**3. Which magazines do you read?** (*Check all that apply*)
- ☐ Wizard
- ☐ SPIN
- ☐ Animerica
- ☐ Rolling Stone
- ☐ Maxim
- ☐ DC Comics
- ☐ URB
- ☐ Polygon
- ☐ Original Play Station Magazine
- ☐ Entertainment Weekly

- ☐ YRB
- ☐ EGM
- ☐ Newtype USA
- ☐ SciFi
- ☐ Starlog
- ☐ Wired
- ☐ Vice
- ☐ BPM
- ☐ I hate reading
- ☐ Other:_____

**4. Have you visited the ADV Manga website?**
- ☐ Yes
- ☐ No

**5. Have you made any Manga purchases online from the ADV w**
- ☐ Yes
- ☐ No

**6. If you have visited the ADV Manga website, how would you rate your online experience?**
- ☐ Excellent
- ☐ Good
- ☐ Average
- ☐ Poor

**7. What genre of Manga do you prefer?**
*(Check all that apply)*
- ☐ adventure
- ☐ romance
- ☐ detective
- ☐ action
- ☐ horror
- ☐ sci-fi/fantasy
- ☐ sports
- ☐ comedy

**8. How many manga titles have you purchased in the last 6 months?**
- ☐ none
- ☐ 1-4
- ☐ 5-10
- ☐ 11+

**9. Where do you make your manga purchases?** *(Check all that apply)*
- ☐ comic store
- ☐ bookstore
- ☐ newsstand
- ☐ online
- ☐ other:_____
- ☐ department store
- ☐ grocery store
- ☐ video store
- ☐ video game store

**10. Which bookstores do you usually make your manga purchases at?**
- ☐ Barnes & Noble
- ☐ Walden Books
- ☐ Suncoast
- ☐ Best Buy
- ☐ Amazon.com
- ☐ Borders
- ☐ Books-A-Million
- ☐ Toys "Я" Us
- ☐ Other bookstore:
  _____

**11. What's your favorite anime/manga website?**
- ☐ adv-manga.com
- ☐ advfilms.com
- ☐ rightstuf.com
- ☐ animenewsservice.com
- ☐ animenewsnetwork.com
- ☐ Other:_____
- ☐ animeondvd.com
- ☐ anipike.com
- ☐ animeonline.net
- ☐ planetanime.com
- ☐ animenation.com